MW01121057

Yours Affectionately, Osgood

INTERPRETING THE CIVIL WAR
Texts and Contexts

EDITOR
Angela M. Zombek
University of North Carolina, Wilmington

Aaron Astor
Maryville College

Wiliam B. Kurtz
University of Virginia

Joseph M. Beilein Jr.
Pennsylvania State University

Brian Craig Miller
Mission College

Douglas R. Egerton
Le Moyne College

Jennifer M. Murray
Oklahoma State University

J. Matthew Gallman
University of Florida

Jonathan W. White
Christopher Newport University

Hilary N. Green
University of Alabama

Timothy Williams
University of Oregon

The **Interpreting the Civil War** series focuses on America's long Civil War era, from the rise of antebellum sectional tensions through Reconstruction.

These studies, which include both critical monographs and edited compilations, bring new social, political, economic, or cultural perspectives to our understanding of sectional tensions, the war years, Reconstruction, and memory. Studies reflect a broad, national perspective; the vantage point of local history; or the direct experiences of individuals through annotated primary source collections.

Yours Affectionately, Osgood

Colonel Osgood Vose Tracy's Letters Home
from the Civil War, 1862–1865

Edited by Sarah Tracy Burrows and Ryan W. Keating

The Kent State University Press

KENT, OHIO

© 2022 by The Kent State University Press, Kent, Ohio 44242

All rights reserved

Unless otherwise noted, all images are courtesy of Sarah Tracy Burrows.

ISBN 978-1-60635-440-7

Manufactured in the United States of America

Cataloging information for this title is available at the Library of Congress.

26 25 24 23 22   5 4 3 2 1

Dedicated to Osgood Vose Tracy

William Gardner Tracy

Sarah Vose Osgood Tracy

John Bayard Tracy Sr.

and

122nd New York State Volunteers

I trust you stow all my letters away in my chest

for I wish to preserve them.

—Osgood Vose Tracy to his mother,

September 30, 1863

Contents

Preface

❀ I first learned about the letters my great-great-grandfather, Osgood Vose Tracy, wrote during his service in the American Civil War from my maternal grandfather, John Bayard Tracy Sr. (1904–1988). Grandpa lived in Syracuse, New York, where he and my grandmother, Loretta Dattler Tracy (1905–1966), raised my mother, Ann Livingston (Tracy) Burrows (1932–2018), and their two sons, James Grant Tracy (1933–2015) and John Bayard Tracy Jr. (1936–1962). From the time I was born, in December 1967, through 1988, I lived just a few street blocks away. Both homes are in the Sedgwick Farm neighborhood, Syracuse's first residential historic district of twentieth-century design. In the mid-1800s, my great-great-great-grandfather Charles Baldwin Sedgwick and his second wife, Deborah "Dora" Gannett Sedgwick (1825–1901), bought the eighty acres of the land it comprises, for their homestead. On "The Hill," the couple raised their four offspring and Charles's two older children, Ellen "Nellie" Amelia Sedgwick (1841–1924), who would become Osgood Tracy's bride, and Charles Hamilton Sedgwick (1846–1924).

Osgood wrote the majority of the letters in this collection to his mother, Sarah Vose Osgood Tracy (1804–1901). A much smaller selection (thirty-eight) comprises those Osgood wrote to or received from his elder brother, James Grant Tracy (1837–1903), younger brother, Capt. William "Will" Gardner Tracy (1842–1924), Nellie, cousins, friends, and comrades.

My grandfather inherited the letter cache and other memorabilia from his parents, James Grant Tracy (1873–1943) and Florida "Flo" Seay Tracy (1880–1977). My great grandmother grew up in Rome, Georgia, and her father, Capt. John Joseph Seay (1843–1916), had volunteered at age fifteen to fight for the Confederacy in Company C, Cobb's Legion, Stevens Rifles. After their wedding in Rome, Florida and James settled in Syracuse and had four children: my grandfather and his siblings, older brother Osgood "Otz" Vose Tracy (1908–2004), and younger siblings

Ellen Sedgwick Tracy (1908–2004), and Col. Charles "Ted" Sedgwick Tracy (1911–2008).

When I visited my grandfather, he shared with me the Tracy family Civil War memorabilia, arranged by Osgood's mother and including the three scrapbooks of Osgood's wartime letters, newspaper clippings about the war, poetry and obituaries, as well as various dried flowers Osgood had picked up on the campaign trail and mailed home. My grandfather also brought out a copy of the speech Osgood gave at the twenty-fifth anniversary of the Battle of Gettysburg, numerous newspaper articles about the war pertaining to Osgood and his brother Will, an album comprising photographs Osgood had mailed home, and various military paraphernalia including rifles, bayonets, and swords.

On our walks through the neighborhood, my grandfather pointed out the house in which he grew up. Osgood and Nellie, who had married after the Civil War, built the "Tracy Home" for their children, my grandfather's parents. My grandfather explained that Charles and Dora Sedgwick were staunch abolitionists and that in 1860 Charles became the first person to give a speech on the House floor denouncing slavery. My grandfather recollected these stories from what he was told by his parents and grandparents and corroborated them with the letters, newspapers clippings, pictures, and other historical artifacts he shared with me. He brought history alive and made me believe that the Civil War hadn't taken place that long ago. That my grandfather's mother, who lived until 1977, had married Osgood's son, made a great impression on me. *I could touch and talk to Granny Tracy, who had known Osgood, and he had fought in the Civil War!*

I especially remember one moment with my grandfather, when I was about ten years old. We were standing at the end of the driveway to the Tracy Home, looking up at it on the hill. As my grandfather remincinced about the war and our family's history, I instantly comprehended the importance of his words, and believed Osgood's letters should be shared in a published book and the story be told in film. I recall thinking, too, that I wanted to be the one to make it happen.

Sometimes my grandfather would send me home with something special; a black-and-white photograph, a letter containing handwriting I thought was the most beautiful I'd ever seen, a Confederate coin or bill, or my great-great-great grandmother's scrapbook. I still recall being in my bedroom with this last in hand. My heart thumped. I took a black marker and an orange manilla folder from my desk, to create a book cover and jacket. I titled it "Sarah's Book" and wrote each letter as carefully as possible; I was proud of what was inside. Today, the cover still holds the diary. Immersing myself in this family history has been a long labor of love.

In 1992 I was twenty-five years old and had been working since college graduation at a publishing company in Boston when I decided work toward publishing Osgood's letters in earnest. I transcribed into my computer a typewritten transcription of the original letters. I then checked my typescript against Osgood's originals. Since then, I have spent countless hours researching; writing; transcribing 1800s and early 1900s news articles; visiting historical associations and societies, rare book libraries, and cemeteries; and communicating with publishers.

In 1904, George G. Walters, a veteran of the 148th Pennsylvania, eloquently pled for the importance of preserving the memory of the Civil War for future generations. "We may not," he wrote, "be able to leave to our children gold, jewels, precious stones or wealth, but there is something that money cannot buy,—honor. This is transmitted as an heirloom for which generations yet unborn will bless us and hold our memory in sacred reverence; while over the fireplace the old sword will be suspended, and many an evening whiled away in recounting the heroic deeds that reflect honor out from the dim ages of long ago. 'My father went down in the great battle of Gettysburg. My father stood on the brink of starvation in the Andersonville prison. My father helped to carry the flag above the clouds of Lookout Mountain. My father stood beneath the leaden hail at Vicksburg. My father marched with Meade through Wilderness, Spotsylvania, and heard the shouts of victory at the surrender of Appomattox in April, 1865.' These are the priceless relics transmitted to posterity that no thief in the night can steal. This is the grand heritage bought with the blood and suffering of our fathers which no engraver can counterfeit."[1]

What follows are the priceless heirlooms of Col. Osgood Vose Tracy.

---

1. Joseph Wendel, *The Story of Our Regiment: A History of the 148th Pennsylvania Vols* (Des Moines, IA: Kenyon Printing and MFG, 1904), 445.

John Tracy and Al Atterbury examine the Civil War collection of the Tracy family. Tracy holds photo of his ancestor, William G. Tracy.

Lincoln still 'lives'

John Tracy and Al Atterbury news article, *Syracuse Herald Journal*, February 12, 1980

Acknowledgments

To strive, to seek, to find, and not to yield.
—Alfred Lloyd Tennyson

❀ I first thank my grandfather John Bayard Tracy Sr. for sharing history with me. I am also grateful to his youngest sibling, US Marine colonel Charles "Ted" Sedgwick Tracy, a World War II veteran. I thank my parents, Ann and William Platner Burrows, who ensured that the Tracy letters and memorabilia were preserved and handled with care after my grandfather's passing. I commend the late Alfred C. Atterbury, who first transcribed the original letters. Finding the Tracy letters of interest, he borrowed the collection from my grandfather, transcribed each letter and created an index, which allowed our families to read the letters with ease and protect the originals from handling. My grandfather and Mr. Atterbury were featured in a newspaper article published February 12, 1980, in the *Syracuse Post Standard*.

I thank Ryan Keating for collaborating with me on this project. As a scholar of Civil War history he expertly connected the letters to the war. I thank especially Civil War historian James M. McPherson for reading the manuscript and consulting with me in later writing stages.

Many other people and organizations have supported and aided me, including the Onondaga Historical Association in Syracuse, New York, the Syracuse University Rare Books Library, the Syracuse Historical Society, the George and Rebecca Barnes Foundation (Syracuse, New York), Matilda Josyln Gage Museum (Fayetteville, New York), Jacob Leisler Institute for the Study of Early New York History, and the North Andover (Massachusetts) Historical Society. I thank historians Sue Boland and Sally Roesch Wagner at the Matilda Josyln Gage Center for Social Justice Dialogue; Patrick Schroeder, historian at Appomattox Court House; the late

Howard LaMar, former Yale University Dean and professor of history; and historian and best-selling author Eleanor Herman.

I offer tremendous gratitude also to extended family and friends who have expressed unending interest and optimism regarding my project. A special thank you to my mother's cousin Susan Hyde Scholl, with whom I share a common passion for family history. I thank my sister-in-law Meridyth Burrows for her aid in creating and expanding on family ancestry charts. Also, thank you to my friends, fellow writers, and those interested in history who have offered interest and encouragement.

Finally, I thank my husband, Peter Winch, and our three sons, Ryan, Alex, and Andrew, for their constant support. This book is a gift to my sons, nieces, and nephews—the next generation. Throughout their lives, may they learn from and honor the courage and sacrifices captured in these pages and stay curious about who lived and what occurred before them. If they do so, they will learn not only about the past but about themselves, the present, and the future.

Introduction

❀ Osgood Vose Tracy was born June 25, 1840, in Syracuse, New York, to James Grant Tracy and Sarah Vose Osgood. Osgood's mother was born in 1804 in Andover, Massachusetts, to a family with a rich legacy of military service. Her maternal grandfather was Revolutionary War hero Col. Joseph Vose, First Massachusetts Regiment, who played an important role in early action in Massachusetts at the outbreak of the Revolution and served through the surrender at Yorktown. Sarah's father, George Osgood (1758–1823), was an eminent physician in Andover (North Andover today) and a member of one of the town's founding families.[1] "The Osgood name," recalled a local historian in the 1880s, "has been remarkably influential in the town, connected both with civil and military offices. For a hundred and fifty years there was scarcely a time when there were not several military officers, captains, or colonels, in the service."[2]

In 1833, Sarah Osgood left Massachusetts for Syracuse, New York. She traveled with her older half sister, Elizabeth Osgood (1788–1848), and Elizabeth's husband, Capt. Hiram Putnam (1786–1874).[3] Stopping in Albany, Sarah met James Grant

---

1. George Osgood married Elizabeth Otis in 1782. After her death, he married Sarah Vose, of Milton, Massachusetts, sometime in 1803. Together, they had Osgood's mother, Sarah Vose Osgood (Tracy), Osgood's mother. After Elizabeth's death of consumption at age fifty, he married Mary Messer.

2. Sarah Loring Bailey, *Historical Sketches of Andover* (Boston: Houghton, Mifflin, 1880), 22.

3. Capt. Hiram Putnam was born in Danvers, Massachusetts, and died in Syracuse, New York. He went to sea in 1802 and was a ship's captain by 1812, involved with trade to European and South American ports as well as with the China trade, until 1827. This included time on the trade ships *Aurora, Rising Empire, China*, commissioned by the wealthy Boston merchant Joseph Peabody. Putnam sailed the *China* twice around the world, trading for coffee, tea, spices, and other goods. He and Elizabeth moved to Syracuse in 1829, to "get away from the sea," and there, Putnam became involved in civic matters but also with antislavery groups and the Underground Railroad. In 1828 Putnam became involved in forming the Syracuse Unitarian Society and in the founding of the Church of the Messiah, where

1852 View of Syracuse, New York (Courtesy of the Onondaga Historical Association, Syracuse, New York)

Tracy and the young couple were married in 1836. They made Albany their home until 1839, when they moved to Syracuse. There, the family flourished, and James became a well-known businessman, lawyer and an agent of the Syracuse Land Company.[4] Sarah and James had four sons: James Grant, Osgood Vose, William Gardner, and Edward Winslow Tracy (1845–1851). All were born in Syracuse.

As the nation stood on the precipice of civil war, the town of Syracuse, though physically distant from the slaveholding South, played a vibrant role in national debates over slavery. At the turn of the century, just sixty people lived in Syracuse, a small settlement of some eight houses, several log cabins, and a post office. The completion of the Erie Canal in 1826 changed everything; as historian Carol Sheriff notes, it spawned the growth of inland cities, Syracuse included, which "took on the bustle of seaports."[5] The artificial river, which connected the Hudson River

abolitionist Rev. Samuel Joseph May ministered. Elizabeth and he had three children: Mary Elizabeth (1817–1834), Lucy Blythe Putnam Phelps (1826–1907), and Edward Augustus Putnam (1832–1885). For information regarding Putnam and his family see the Hiram Putnam Papers, 1780–1885, MRBC-MS-00056, Mortimer Rare Book Library, Smith College, Northampton, MA.

4. Jared Tracy, of Norwich, Connecticut, was the son of Capt. Joseph Tracy and Ann Tracy. He married Margaret Backus, the widow of Capt. Elijah Backus. Together, they had two sons: William Gedney Tracy and James Grant Tracy.

5. Carol Sheriff, *The Artificial River: The Erie Canal and the Paradox of Progress, 1817–1862* (New York: Hill & Wang, 1996).

to Lake Erie and thus upstate New York and the Midwest to New York City and then by ship to the rest of the world, was vital to the region's trade and growth. By 1850, twenty-two thousand people called Syracuse their home.

Osgood's childhood was marked by tragedy and triumph, experiences that profoundly affected the young soldier, and apparent in the sensitivity and compassion in his wartime letters home. His father, James, died of heart trouble in 1850 at the age of sixty-nine, and his youngest brother, Edward "Eddie" Winslow Tracy, died of diphtheria four months later, in March 1851, at just six years old. As the Tracy family dealt with these losses, national tragedy unfolded around them. In 1850, the sectional compromise over slavery that underpinned national politics became urgent, as a strict Fugitive Slave Act, part of the larger Compromise of 1850, permitted slave owners to pursue escaped African Americans across state lines and return them to captivity. As Congress reckoned with the constitutionality of slavery, this act played out on the streets of Syracuse.[6] And while ten-year-old Osgood Tracy may not have understood the broader significance of these events, they likely played a role in the burgeoning abolitionist's development.

Edward Winslow Tracy, youngest Tracy brother (From the private Osgood Tracy photo album)

In 1851, William "Jerry" Henry, who had lived and worked in Syracuse for nearly two years after he escaped from slavery, was arrested under the Fugitive Slave Act.[7] The arrest outraged local abolitionists—among them Gerrit Smith, Frederick Dou-

---

6. There has been much work on the ideological and physical spread of slavery and its conseqeunces on national divisions in the years leading up to the Civil War. See Robert Pierce Forbes, *The Missouri Compromise and Its Aftermath: Slavery and the Meaning of America* (Chapel Hill: Univ. of North Carolina Press, 2009); Michael Landis, *Northern Men with Southern Loyalties: The Democratic Party and the Sectional Crisis* (Ithaca, NY: Cornell Univ. Press, 2014); Eric Foner, *Free Soil, Free Labor, Free Men: The Ideology of the Republican Party before the Civil War* (New York: Oxford Univ. Press, 1995); Manisha Singh, *The Counterrevolution of Slavery: Politics and Ideology in Antebellum South Carolina* (Chapel Hill: Univ. of North Carolina Press, 2000); Adam Rothman, *Slave Country: American Expansion and the Origins of the Deep South* (Cambridge, MA: Harvard Univ. Press, 2005); Robert E. Bonner, *Mastering America: Southern Slaveholders and the Crisis of American Nationhood* (New York: Cambridge Univ. Press, 2009); James Oakes, *Freedom National: The Destruction of Slavery in the United States, 1861–1865* (New York: W. W. Norton, 2013).

7. William "Jerry" Henry was born into slavery in North Carolina in 1811, the son of Ciel, an enslaved woman, on the property of their owner, William Henry, in Buncombe County, North Carolina. Having escaped slavery some years previously, in the winter of 1849–50 he arrived in Syracuse and then worked in a cooperage. On October 1, 1851 federal marshals arrested Jerry as a runaway. The same evening, there was a Liberty Party meeting in the Syracuse Congregationalist Church, which was attended by many prominent abolitionists, among them Gerrit Smith. Smith and other abolitionists, including Reverend Joseph May and Charles Baldwin Sedgwick, Smith's lawyer, would help plan Jerry's rescue and would use Smith's contacts as a prominent abolitionist to secure Jerry's passage out of Syracuse and into safety in Canada. With Smith's wealth, the perpetrators procured a carriage and access to multiple safe houses to transport and hide Jerry.

glass, Rev. Samuel Joseph May, Charles Sedgwick, Jermaine Loguen, and Harriet Tubman—and a local mob converged on the local jail where Jerry was being held, forced way into the jail with a battering ram, they rescued Jerry and whisked him to Canada.[8] Though he left no account of the way these events affected him, in the wake of the deaths of his father and brother Osgood matured into a serious young man, full of responsibility at a young age and his abolitionist sentiments expressed in numerous letters home suggest that this event may have resonated with the young man. Osgood's mother, determined to give her sons the best education she could, supported his ambitions. Nevertheless, financial strains weighed on the matriarch, who urged her boys to seek "honest work appropriate with their age and strength."[9] Osgood applied himself diligently to his work and at sixteen graduated with Syracuse High School's first class. In 1857, with his mother's assistance and his own earnings, he attended a one-year finishing course at the Albany Academy. Back in Syracuse, he landed his first real job in the general offices of the Binghamton Railroad Company. He held this position for a year, after which he accepted a clerkship with the H. R. Holden Coal Company where his older brother, James, worked. Osgood's younger brother, William, whose name appears often in his letters, was just beginning high school.

Osgood was nearly twenty-one years old on April 12, 1861, when Confederate forces under P. G. T. Beauregard opened fire on Fort Sumter in Charleston Harbor, South Carolina, leading the nation into a bloody civil war that would last four years and claim more than 750,000 lives. The conflict that boiled over that spring morning was the culmination of years of bitter debate over the institution of slavery and on one side, growing concern its spread west and, on the other, growing panic over abolition's threat to a way of life. Driven by a frenzy of fear, Southerners called state conventions to debate secession and only a month after the final ballots for the presidential election had been cast began to withdraw from the United States. With the explicit goal of defending the institution of slavery, Southern states joined in a loose Confederacy and awaited the Lincoln administration's response.

Throughout the North, men and women debated this unprecedented action. People were divided over the question of secession and what the federal government's proper response to it should be and attitudes reflected a radicalization along party lines. An Abolition Convention that assembled in Syracuse in early February to show support for federal intervention was broken up amid hostile cries that "Syracuse must redeem its reputation." "Syracuse," one man told reporters, "has been trampled upon for years by abolitionists." He was "happy to see the

8. Angela F. Murphy, *The Jerry Rescue: The Fugitive Slave Law, Northern Rights, and the American Sectional Crisis* (New York: Oxford Univ. Press, 2016).

9. Osgood Vose Tracy biography, Onondaga Historical Association.

people now rise in their might to crush out treason in their midst, and manifest a disposition to save the Central City from further disgrace." Further, he "trusted that the Union might yet be preserved and that his Southern brethren would receive these conservative demonstrations as the olive branches from the North."[10] This shocking sentiment in the city that was "the scene of the Jerry Rescue, and long the stronghold of anti-slavery fanaticism" nevertheless reflected larger divides that existed across the North. "The fearful consequences of abolition propagandism in breaking up the Union and inaugurating civil war are coming home to every man's business" the same editors concluded.[11]

Similar scenes played out in towns and cities across the North. Importantly, though, pro-Union sentiment in the city and elsewhere remained strong, as did support for Lincoln, whose train from Illinois to Washington, DC, was met by enthusiastic crowds at the platform in Syracuse.[12] The attack on Fort Sumter momentarily ended these debates and galvanized support for the Union. Men flocked to recruiting booths in late April and early May, volunteering to defend their flag and force their wayward Southern brothers back into the fold. Osgood left no account of his feelings during the months leading up to the war, but it is likely that he was passionate about the issues plaguing the nation, for he wrote about them often in his wartime correspondence. His family certainly was, and his brother Will, who was awarded the Medal of Honor for his heroics at the Battle of Chancellorsville, summed up the sentiment of the Tracys of Syracuse during an anniversary speech for the veterans of the 122nd New York. "Our lives," he said, recalling the years before the war, "were as sweet, our happiness as dear to us then as life and happiness are now to the men who walk our streets to-day, yet were we willing to surrender all, without hesitation and without scruple." The men who enlisted with the Tracy brothers "built better and stronger than we knew; and the work so begun also resulted in the enfranchisement of a race. We saved our Union, and at the same time created a nation of free men from a race of slaves."[13]

As Lincoln called for seventy-five thousand troops to put down rebellion in the South, observers throughout the nation rested easy in the belief that the war would be short-lived. Osgood did not enlist in the first wave of volunteers, though Will left home four days after Fort Sumter, at the age of eighteen, beginning what may well have been the most diverse service of any one soldier, North

10. "The Abolition Convention at Syracuse Broken Up by the Citizens, etc. etc." *New York Herald,* Jan. 30, 1861.

11. "The Reaction against Abolitionists—American Civilization Versus Puritan Fanaticism," *New York Herald,* Feb. 3, 1861.

12. "President Lincoln at Albany," *Albany Evening Journal,* Feb. 18, 1861.

13. William G. Tracy's 24th anniversary speech, "A Soldiers' Picnic, the 122nd Regiment Celebrates an Anniversary, Bennett's Grove, Near Fairmount; invaded by Troops last Saturday, address by W. G. Tracy," 1886, Long Branch Park, Syracuse, NY, Onondaga Historical Association.

or South, during the first year of the war. He first joined the Third New York in April and served in that unit until August, when he was granted a commission in the Twelfth New York Volunteers. He mustered out in February 1862 and then reenlisted in the Tenth Indiana Volunteers, with which he served until October 1862, when he joined the 122nd New York with his brother.[14] Osgood's decision to remain at home during the first year of the war was likely motivated by two complimenting factors: First, from his letters we can see a deep concern for his mother's well being, and it is likely that he hesitated to enlist out of fear that with two sons away at war, she might fall on hard times. Second, he held an excellent job and may have been reluctant to let that go to take a lower-paying, more dangerous position in the army. Osgood's wartime letters underscored a concern over his mother's security, so much so that he, along with Will, continually thwarted their older brother, Jim, in his attempts to enlist, so that at least one of the brothers would be home to help the widowed Sarah. His reticence to enlist during the first year of the war was, though, by no means a consequence of lack of patriotism or resolve but rather an internal struggle over loyalty to home or country, which continued throughout the conflict.

Undoubtedly, Osgood—along with most other Americans, North and South—watched anxiously as the war unfolded along a number of fronts during the first year of the war. For Osgood and his family, of course, these events were likely very personal. Having lost a father and brother, the family must have been especially concerned about Will's safety during those early months of the war, and, as correspondence illustrates, these concerns continued throughout the conflict. The Tracy family was a tight-knit bunch, and though the winds of war cast the brothers to distant fields, bonds between mother and sons appeared to have only strengthened. Soon after the defeat at Bull Run, President Lincoln called for three hundred thousand more men for three years of service in Northern armies. Still Osgood waited, watching as the war entered its second year.

Though the gray winter months of 1861–62 reflected the rather dismal outlook for the Union cause broadly, movement in the west under Gen. Ulysses S. Grant's leadership provided a glimmer of hope. The capture of Forts Henry and Donnelson and the fall of the first Confederate capital city, Nashville, Tennessee, in February 1862 gave the Union control of vital waterways into the South. The campaign culminated two months later in the major victory on the bloody fields of Shiloh. In the Gulf of Mexico, combined naval and army forces under Adm. David Porter and Gen. Benjamin Butler moved north up the Mississippi River and captured the Confederacy's largest city and key port, New Orleans. Along the Washington-Richmond Front, Gen. George McClellan had turned the disorganized forces that had retreated in chaos from Bull Run into the largest, best armed, best trained fighting

14. Tracy Family Genealogy Book, Syracuse Public Library.

force the nation had ever seen. Then he put the soldiers on boats and sailed South down the Chesapeake Bay to the Yorktown Peninsula where he planned to move rapidly on the Confederate capital from the rear. McClellan faltered at the gates of Richmond, and his grand army was pushed back by an aggressive Robert E. Lee who, after saving the Confederacy, took the offensive in a campaign that ultimately led to the fields outside of Sharpsburg, Maryland.

As McClellan's army struggled, Lincoln called for a renewed commitment to the cause, and three hundred thousand more volunteers. That June, recruiting began in Syracuse and the surrounding counties for the 122nd New York State Volunteers. Osgood Tracy finally joined the fray; he enlisted on August 9 and was appointed the unit's sergeant major. On August 25, three days before the newly formed regiment prepared to board trains and head south, the men received a send-off from the townspeople of Onondaga County. Among the speakers that late summer day in the village of Fayetteville was Matilda Josyln Gage, famed suffragist and abolitionist. Looking out over the crowd, Gage delivered a powerful speech to the new recruits and their families and friends who had gathered to send them off. "It has been said," she began

> "all that man hath will he give for his life"; but at the present time there are hundreds and thousands of men who willingly take their lives into their hands and march boldly forth into battle, for there are things dearer than life, there are things without which life would be valueless, there are things rather than lose which, we would lose life itself. And what is this for which men so willingly hazard their lives? It is not territory, nor power, nor the subjugation of a people, but it is to uphold liberty, and to maintain the government.... Let the soldiers remember what I say now. Let Liberty be your watchword and your war cry alike. Unless Liberty is attained—the broadest, the deepest, the highest liberty for all,—not for one set alone, one clique alone, but for men and women, black and white, Americans and negroes. There can be no permanent peace until the cause of the war is destroyed. And what caused the war? Slavery! And nothing else.

With these words as a send-off, the men of the 122nd New York Volunteer Infantry went south to join the Army of the Potomac. They would arrive at Sharpsburg shortly after the fighting concluded on the bloodiest single day in American history and the battle where the fate of the institution of slavery was decided.

On September 3, 1862, Osgood penned the first of many letters home to Syracuse. His correspondence continued unabated throughout the war, interrupted only twice, once during his regiment's stint on guard duty in Sandusky, Ohio, and again during his brief capture and subsequent escape from a Confederate prison in May 1864 during the Overland Campaign, an event that made headlines back home in Syracuse and was, perhaps, Osgood's most memorable escapade during his three years of service. Leaving Syracuse in late August, the unit joined the Army of the Potomac as it moved northwest, shadowing Robert E. Lee's Army of Northern Virginia, which had turned north toward Maryland after the Seven Days Battles. Theirs would be a long war. With the exception of their time at Johnson's Island between January and March 1864, the regiment was with the Army of the Potomac and was present at every major battle along the Richmond-Washington front from Antietam to Lee's surrender at Appomattox Court House.

Osgood's letters provide stark commentary on the war and the experiences of a young man far from home but deeply committed to that place and those he left behind. Dedicated to the Union cause, Osgood struggled with the realities of war, the hardships of camp, the campaign trail and battlefield, and longing for a woman who had declined the marriage proposal he made the week before he left home. A frustrating courtship with Ellen "Nellie" Amelia Sedgwick continued to play out by post after Osgood enlisted. Nellie was the daughter of New York State representative Charles Baldwin Sedgwick, an outspoken abolitionist who had posted bond and represented in court the men who broke William "Jerry" Henry out of jail. Nellie's mother was Ellen Chase Smith (1812–1846).[15] Nellie was Osgood's muse, inspiration, and reason for staying the course of the war.

Osgood's experiences also piece together a broader story of a family at war. One of his brothers and a number of his cousins served the Union war effort as well—among them Gen. Edwin Vose Sumner Jr., Gen. Samuel Storrow Sumner, and uncle, Maj. Gen. Edwin Vose Sumner—often from lofty positions in the army, awarded because of their positions in prominent families. A self-proclaimed "Black Republican," Osgood spoke frankly and often about the war, the Union's goals, and his own triumphs and struggles. His letters provide a glimpse into the war, and his experiences further illuminate the war's far-reaching consequences of those men who served in defense of their union.

The beginning of the twenty-first century has witnessed a flurry of new scholarship on the nuanced social and political impacts of the Civil War on American society. The war touched all corners of the nation and forced Northerners and Southerners, men and women, soldiers and civilians, black and white, into new, often uncomfortable circumstances. In recent years, the military history of the war has expanded beyond the traditional "bullet and battlefield" analysis to encompass the lived experiences of the men who donned blue and gray in the defense of their nations and communities. The intersection of social and military historical analysis has yielded considerable insight into the motivations behind the act of enlistment, the reasons men stayed the course in spite of the extreme violence and hardship, the affects the broader political and military moves over

---

15. Ellen Chase Smith married Charles Baldwin Sedgwick on October 17, 1837. They had five children, two of whom survived into adulthood—Ellen Amelia and Charles Hamilton Sedgwick.

four years of war had on individual soldiers, and the lingering influence of military service on veterans. Of particular interest is the ongoing debate surrounding the motivations of Union soldiers spurred on by historians such as Gary Gallagher, James Oakes, and Elizabeth Varon. Did Northerners march to war simply to bring the South back into the Union, or were their motives linked to the deeper ideological conviction of ending slavery?[16]

An avowed abolitionist, Osgood joined a regiment with other likeminded men, and his political and moral beliefs framed his war. Yet, as readers will find, Osgood's moral and political beliefs regarding slavery did not assuage his, at times, racist descriptions of African Americans he encountered which were typical of the time. As such, his letters contribute to the broader debate over soldier motivations and add to our understanding of what drove men to sacrifice themselves for their nation. These letters, like hundreds of others from officers and enlisted men who served in Union armies, complicate our understanding of the motivations that led men to serve—and thus help to expand our collective understanding of the conflict, even as the narrative becomes more complex. As the literature clearly shows, Northerners were far from united. Though Lincoln won the presidential election in 1860, his victory was by no means a mandate, for clear political divisions existed throughout the loyal North. As we see through Osgood's eyes, the war played out in personal ways. Influenced by political beliefs and driven by ideological, moral, and religious convictions, he marched to war as a crusader. Moral abolitionists composed a vocal minority of the more than 2 million men who donned blue in defense of the Union, and Osgood's letters expand our understanding of the views of this group and also help explain the reasons so many Union soldiers became practical abolitionists as the war progressed.

As the Union flag descended below the ramparts of Fort Sumter in Charleston, men across the North rushed to the flag's defense. A year later, they were joined in struggle by a new mass of volunteers who left their homes and families to put down the Southern rebellion. The war brought together men from different backgrounds, states, and ideologies and cast them into new, often uncomfortable circumstances. Historians have recently begun to analyze the relationships among men in Union armies and, in particular, the complex views that drove the officers and enlisted men to stay the course of the war, in spite of the harsh conditions of camp, the drudgery of the campaign trail, and horrors of battle. Osgood came from an upper middle-class background, and his family was well connected, both locally and nationally. Thus, his letters provide an interesting duality—readers will find intimate daily accounts of military service interspersed with a rather

16. Gary Gallgher, *The Union War* (Cambridge, MA: Harvard University Press, 2011); James Oakes, *Freedom National: The Destruction of Slavery in the United States* (New York: W. W. Norton, 2013); Elizabeth R. Varon, *Armies of Deliverance: A New History of the Civil War* (New York: Oxford University Press, 2019).

impressive "global" view of the conflict, driven both by Osgood's connections with family members who were high-ranking officers in other theaters and his intensive reading habits. His own convictions further influenced his experiences and, consequently, this collection adds considerably to the literature on the experiences of citizen soldiers in America's Civil War.[17]

The letters Osgood Vose Tracy wrote over the course of his service were varied and informative. He was well educated, and thus his language was clear, often grammatically correct, and contains few of the spelling errors common in so many letters from soldiers of this war. Thus, we have reproduced the letters as accurately as possible. We did not correct spelling errors and did not cut text from the letters included in the collection to his mother. Any included ellipses stand in for damaged pieces of letters where the words are missing or indecipherable. The editors made two changes to the letters, in order to make them more readable today. First, we added paragraph breaks where necessary to delineate Osgood's thoughts. Second, as Osgood used dashes throughout his correspondence in lieu of some punctuation, we replaced many of those with appropriate punctuation to make the letters more accessible to the average reader. The addition of these marks does not take away from the content of the letters in any way and, in fact, helps Osgood's experience stand alone on the page.

The majority of the letters in the collection were written by Osgood to his mother, but the cache also contains correspondence between Tracy and other individuals, such as his brothers, cousins, friends, and sweetheart Nellie Sedgwick. We have included some of those letters, where appropriate, to provide supplementary information and context to explain the broader perspective of Osgood's experiences and his relationships. Only in these letters did we cut any text that was repetitive. The letters that appear in this book showcase Osgood's experiences, emotions, and attitudes regarding the war and the home front and provide incredibly personal insight to the life of this young soldier. Interspersed within

---

17. In *The Gentlemen and the Roughs: Violence, Honor, and Manhood in the Union Army* (New York: New York University Press, 2010), Lorien Foote analyzes the ways officers and enlisted men's socioeconomic backgrounds affected views of manhood and honor and how these men navigated the reality of military service that was so very different from civilian life. Her work, which marks an important methodological shift in the writing about Union soldiers, has been followed by others, including Andrew Bledsoe, *Citizen Officers: The Union and Confederate Junior Volunteer Corps in the American Civil War* (Baton Rouge: Louisiana State Univ. Press, 2015); John Matsui, *The First Republican Army: The Army of Virginia and the Radicalization of the Civil War* (Charlottesville, VA: University of Virginia Press, 2016); Ricardo Herrera, *For Liberty and the Republic: The American Citizen as Soldier, 1775–1861* (New York: New York University Press, 2015); and Lesley Gordon, *A Broken Regiment: The 16th Connecticut's Civil War* (Baton Rouge: Louisiana State University Press, 2014). Such works have expanded upon this discussion, illustrating the diverse range of experiences that men had at war and the ways soldiers' backgrounds and beliefs affected their military service, interactions with their comrades, and dedication to the broader Union cause.

these letters, readers will also find Osgood's postwar recollections, especially when these accounts help to fill in gaps in his correspondence.

The letters, in general, speak for themselves. They follow, in chronological order, the experiences of the young soldier over the course of the war and are thoughtful and descriptive accounts of events: personal, political, and military. As editors, we added little in-text analysis linking individual letters choosing, rather, to have provided readers with chapter introductions that place the letters within the broader context of the war and utilizing endnotes to add necessary explanations. We identify characters who appeared often in the correspondence as well as other important figures to Osgood's wartime experience. Interspersed in these letters are references to men in his and other regiments and individuals at home in Syracuse. Where possible we identified these, if their stories contributed to the narrative. Osgood had many acquaintances and spoke of them often over the course of the war. While all were important to the young soldier, we identified only those men and women who appeared often in the correspondence. We did not identify those who seldom appeared or whom Osgood only mentioned once, for their stories rarely advanced the narrative. Osgood's close friends, some of whom he knew before the war, enlisted with, and shared, intimately, his wartime experiences, are introduced below.

After the war, Osgood spoke often of his experiences and sought to preserve the memory and legacy of his regiment, his comrades, and his service. These letters, organized, preserved, and passed through generations, are a part of his efforts. An educated man with a keen sense of his place in the world, he wrote letters that give us an intimate snapshot of his war, and we are thrilled to share them now.

FAMILY TREES AND PHOTOGRAPHS

Left: James Grant Tracy (1781–1850), image (From the private collection of great-great-great-granddaughter Susan Hyde Scholl). *Right:* Sarah Vose Osgood Tracy (From the private collection of Osgood Tracy).

Left: Ellen Amelia "Nellie" Sedgwick, age 21, 1862 (From the private photo collection of Osgood Tracy). *Right:* Ellen "Nellie" Sedgwick Tracy, wearing locket of daughter, Sarah (From the private photo collection of Osgood Tracy).

Left: Charles Baldwin Sedgwick (From the private collection of Charles Sedgwick Tracy). *Right:* Osgood Vose Tracy (From the private photograph album of Osgood Tracy).

OSGOOD'S COMRADES, "THE OLD CLIQUE," AS HE DESCRIBED THEM

These men appear throughout Osgood's letters and warrant some extended intro-duction as they were so important to the young officer's wartime experiences.

DAVIS COSSITT (1825–1909) was "a well known farmer too popular to need further mention."[18] "Cossitt's Corner" was one of Syracuse's first developed areas, before the city was named.

Capt. Davis Cossitt (From the private photograph album of Osgood Tracy)

GUY J. GOTCHES, twenty-one years of age when he enlisted, August 8, 1862, at Syracuse, to serve three years; he was mus-tered in as private, Co. H, August 12, 1862. Osgood wrote: "I have gotten to be great friends (as usual) with a very nice young fellow in the reg't by the name of Guy Gotches. He used to be a clerk in E. F. Rice's drygoods store and is the first of 'genus' I ever had any respect for"—[19] "I enclose a photo-graph of my friend Lieut. Gotches which please put in your book until the "civil war is ended."[20] Gotches worried over his ill wife and was discharged May 25, 1863, to care for her be-fore her death. He owned a dry goods store on East Genesee Street in Syracuse.

JAMES GERE (1844–1914), age thirty-seven when enlisted, August 15, 1862, at Syr-acuse, to serve three years, was mustered in as captain, Company H, on August 28, 1862. Gere, a farmer whose parents had immigrated from Ireland, recruited many farmers' sons to the 122nd New York, returned to farming, and "was a pop-ular resident of Syracuse."[21] He and his wife, Elizabeth, had twelve children, nine of whom lived to adulthood.

FRANK LESTER, thirty-one years old when he enlisted, was first lieutenant and quartermaster, was discharged November 30, 1864, and later resided in Chicago.

FRANK M. WOOSTER (1837–1864) was a lawyer Osgood Tracy described as a "persuasive, humorous, man whom no march would dampen his spirit. Frank

---

18. Tracy wrote this about Cossitt ion an undated postwar note describing his friends, inserted into the scrapbook of letters.

19. Osgood Tracy to his mother, Dec. 12, 1862.

20. Osgood Tracy to his mother, Apr. 27, 1863.

21. Kathy Crowell, "'The Onondagas': A History of the 122d Regiment, New York Volunteers," *Onon-daga County, NY, USGenweb* 1998, http://sites.rootsweb.com/~nyononda/WAR/ONONDAGA.HTM.

Lt. Frank M. Wooster (Courtesy of Kenneth Jennings Wooster)

sought popularity but was a very good friend."[22] When a regiment member was ordered executed for desertion, Wooster, in a last minute appeal, convinced President Lincoln to stay the execution. A first lieutenant of Company G, he was killed in action by a sharpshooter June 1, 1864, at Cold Harbor, Virginia. He is buried in his hometown, Tully, New York.

ANDREW J. SMITH. "Smithy," "a very kind friend, helpful, always possessing a great deal of influence."[23] "He has been a very kind friend to me."[24] At twenty-five years of age, he was mustered into service on July 26, 1862. He resided in Syracuse after the war until twenty years before his death. His obituary in the April 28, 1903, *Syracuse Evening Herald* states he was "the officer who seized and held Little Round Top at Gettysburg. Throughout his army career, and ever afterward, he was famous for his stories, jokes and songs." His funeral was held at the Tracy home and burial was in Oakwood Cemetary.

THEODORE LEWIS POOLE (1840–1900) enlisted as quartermaster sergeant in the 122nd Regiment in July 1862. He was wounded at Cold Harbor, his arm amputated. Discharged as captain and brevet major July 3, 1865, he later became county clerk of Onondaga County (1868–1870), US pension agent for the western district of New York (1879–1888), and commander of the Department of New York, Grand Army of the Republic, in 1892. Poole was elected as a Republican to the Fifty-Fourth Congress (March 4, 1895–March 3, 1897). He was appointed US marshal of New York in 1899 and served until his death, in Syracuse.[25]

CHARLES W. OSTRANDER, ALEXANDER H. HUBBS, HUBBARD MANZER, and OSCAR AUSTIN were wounded and captured during the Battle of the Wilderness in May 1864 all. Ostrander and Hubbs had amputations of the leg and foot, respectively, performed by Confederate surgeons. Ostrander and Austin were then taken to Libby Prison.

---

22. Osgood Tracy, in an undated postwar note describing his friends, inserted in one of the scrapbooks.

23. Osgood Tracy described Smith in an undated postwar note describing his friends, inserted in one of the scrapbooks.

24. Osgood Tracy to his mother, Feb. 2, 1863.

25. The *Biographical Directory of the United States Congress*, https://bioguide.congress.gov/, contains searchable biographies of every member of the United States Congress since 1774. Congress publishes it in Washington, DC, and updates it yearly.

CHAPTER ONE

❀ ❀ ❀

To War, "Baptism of Fire"

September–October 1862

I don't know where we shall go today but presume we shall be off soon for it
is against the rule for us to remain any length of time in one place. The boys
have dubbed the regiment the "flying Onondagas."
—Osgood Vose Tracy, September 21, 1863

❀ The first year of war progressed slowly for the Union and victories in the west
led by Ulysses S. Grant and Henry Halleck were only a sideshow for a nation intimately focused on events in the east, along the Potomac River.[1] To say things were
going poorly there is an understatement. Following the loss at First Bull Run in
July 1861, Lincoln promoted George McClellan to command of the forces in and
around Washington, DC—soon to become known as the Army of the Potomac.

A superb organizer, McClellan wasted little time turning the green citizen-
soldiers who enlisted during the early months of the war into a well supplied and
disciplined fighting force. He worked diligently to both restore the morale of the
men under his command and wield undisciplined and disjointed units into an orderly and well-oiled machine. As historian Stephen Sears notes, according to one
sergeant, "before he made his presence felt," the Army of the Potomac was "a great,
green, overgrown, loose concern. . . . There is great improvement," he concluded,
"since he [McClellan] took command." The commanding general was more timid,
however, when it came to engaging the enemy with his finely outfitted corps, and

---

1. On the western theater during the first year of the war, see John W. Marszalek, *Commander of
All Lincoln's Armies: A Life of General Henry W. Halleck* (Cambridge, MA: Harvard Univ. Press, 2004);
Benjamin Franklin Cooling, *Forts Henry and Donelson: The Key to the Confederate Heartland* (Knox-
ville: Univ. of Tennessee Press, 1987).

in spite of calls for action against Southern forces blocking the path to Richmond, McClellan demurred time and again in the fall of 1861 and winter of 1862. What was the rationale for this? Sears and others have suggested that it was McClellan's military orientation that was partly to blame. A student of the Swiss military theorist Baron Jomini, McClellan believed that overwhelming numbers, a single "grand army, perfectly prepared, and one grand campaign, perfectly executed with nothing left to chance" would crush the rebellion. But his hesitancy may also have been influenced by his desire to keep civilians out of the war—by focusing his efforts solely on the enemy in his front he believed he could bring the war to an end without significant impact on Southerners or their "property."[2] McClellan refused to embrace more radical ideas regarding emancipation and total war, an attitude that ultimately affected his willingness to bring the war to the Southern people, pursue Lee with abandon, and use his vastly superior forces to bring the conflict to a speedy conclusion.

That winter, though, the "Young Napoleon" devised a plan. On a map, the capitals of the two warring nations stood some ninety miles apart, with the path to Richmond blocked by a Confederate army under the command of Gen. Joseph E. Johnston entrenched at Manassas Junction, where it been since its victory there the previous July. In early March 1862, Johnston abandoned that position and moved his forces south to the Rappahannock River, where the Southerners established a new defensive position in an attempt to block the Army of the Potomac from making any movement south toward Richmond. McClellan made a surprising move, transferring his army via water down the Chesapeake Bay to Fortress Monroe at the tip of the Yorktown Peninsula, where he hoped to move on Richmond and capture the Confederate capital in a surprise assault from the rear. The symbolism here was important, for George Washington had accepted the British surrender at Yorktown, some eighty-one years earlier. For Confederates, May dawned gray. As they retreated slowly toward Richmond, by the end of the month, "100,000 Federals under McClellan had reached the outskirts of the city, more than 30,000 under Irvin McDowell stood at Fredericksburg, and thousands of others lay in the Shenandoah Valley and western Virginia.[3]

Northern papers followed events with enthusiasm, as historian Gary Gallagher has noted, and by mid-May "northerners who read such accounts and followed the advances of United States armies understandably developed positive views about how the war would end."[4] In Syracuse, among mixed reports and general

2. Stephen W. Sears, *George B. McClellan: The Young Napoleon* (New York: Ticknor & Fields, 1988), 95–98, 98–100.

3. Gary W. Gallagher, "A Civil War Watershed: The 1862 Richmond Campaign in Perspective," in *The Richmond Campaign of 1862: The Peninsula and Seven Days*, ed. Gary Gallagher (Chapel Hill: Univ. of North Carolina Press, 2000), 6–7.

4. Gallagher, "Civil War Watershed," 10.

enthusiasm, the editors of the *Daily Courier and Union* reported in early June that "The general impression is, whether Richmond has yet fallen or not, our position is strong and satisfactory, and that our flag will in a few hours wave over the doomed city."[5] Yet, at the gates of Richmond, McClellan faltered. Between late March and early June, Thomas "Stonewall" Jackson ran roughshod over Union forces in the Shenandoah Valley, winning fame for himself and momentarily securing western Virginia for the Confederacy. His victories compelled the retreat of Union armies under Generals James Shields and John C. Frémont, and allowed him to turn his forces east to unite with Confederate forces in and around Richmond, under Robert E. Lee, who had taken command of the defense of the city after Johnston was wounded at the Battle of Seven Pines.[6] Lee, who had not held a major command yet in the war—in spite of being one of the highest ranking officers in the Confederate army—concocted a daring plan to relieve Richmond and drive McClellan's forces from the outskirts of the city through a series of flanking maneuvers designed to threaten Union supply lines. During the Seven Days Battles, Lee's Army of Northern Virginia drove the mighty McClellan back from Richmond and, once the threat on the Confederate capital had been extinguished, Lee turned North in a move that would culminate on the bloody fields outside the small Maryland town of Sharpsburg.[7]

In Syracuse, men and women watched the war unfold on the pages of local papers, digesting often-conflicting accounts of the fighting. On July 2, reporting on the fight at Malvern Hill, the *Daily Courier and Union* described: "Between 12 and one they again advanced incurring and returning several heavy volleys of musketry when the rebels fixed bayonets and started at double quick toward the 1st and 11th Mass., and the 26th PA; who were ready for them. On came the rebels with a yell, but the firm front of our boys alarmed them and they broke, retreating in great disorder our troops driving them for more than half a mile at the point of bayonet. The rebels fell in heaps in this glorious charge," the story concluded, "more of the enemy falling at this charge than at that of Fair Oaks."[8] On the Fourth of July, the same outlet proclaimed: "We beat the enemy badly; the men fighting even better than before. That all the men are in good spirits, and THAT THE RE-

5. "By Telegraph: Afternoon Report," *Syracuse (NY) Daily Courier and Union*, June 3, 1862.

6. Burke Davis, *They Called Him Stonewall: A Life of Lieutenant General T. J. Jackson, CSA* (New York: Rinehart, 1954); Peter Cozzens, *Shenandoah 1862: Stonewall Jackson's Valley Campaign* (Chapel Hill: Univ. of Northern Carolina Press, 2008); Robert G. Tanner, *Stonewall in the Valley: Thomas J. "Stonewall" Jackson's Shenandoah Valley Campaign, Spring 1862* (Mechanicsburg, PA: Stackpole, 1996).

7. Kevin Dougherty and J. Michael Moore, *The Peninsula Campaign of 1862: A Military Analysis* (Jackson: Univ. Press of Mississippi, 2005); Stephen W. Sears, *To the Gates of Richmond: The Peninsula Campaign* (New York: Ticknor & Fields, 1992); Judkin Browning, *The Seven Days' Battles: The War Begins Anew* (Santa Barbara, CA: Praeger, 2012); Richard Slotkin, *The Long Road to Antietam: How the Civil War Became a Revolution* (New York: W. W. Norton, 2012).

8. "Wednesday's Battle," *Syracuse Daily Courier and Union*, July 2, 1862.

INFORCEMENTS FROM WASHINGTON HAD ARRIVED."[9] Three days later, as it became clear that Lee had driven McClellan from the gates of Richmond, partisan squabbling took over, and blame was placed and shifted. Republicans pointed at McClellan, Democrats accused abolitionists, and McClellan charged Edwin Stanton: "If I save this Army now I tell you plainly that I owe no thanks to you or any other persons in Washington," he scathed. "You have done your best to sacrifice this army."[10] The Army of the Potomac's retreat from Harrison's landing north toward Washington, DC, gave Lee an opportunity to take the offensive.

The war continued to unfold on the pages of Syracuse's newspapers and in letters home from men already at the front. In the wake of the defeats outside of Richmond, the citizens of that fine city responded to Lincoln's call for more volunteers by organizing a new regiment, and during the latter part of summer 1862, the 122nd New York began to form its ranks. Osgood joined this unit on August 9, mustering into Company I as a sergeant major, and two weeks later, he watched as Matilda Joslyn Gage presented Silas Titus, his new colonel, a flag the ladies of Fayetteville had made. Waxing poetically about the initmate links between slavery and the outbreak of the war, the outspoken abolitionist urged the new colonel to tell his men, "We are giving the flag into worthy hands, who will never disgrace it, but who will drive the enemy before them as dust flies before, and who will aid in bringing justice and liberty triumphant over the land. Tell them we shall watch the flag with pride in their success, their honor will be our honor, their success will be our joy, and when they return in peace, the Union will be restored, Slavery forever blasted, and liberty triumphant over this continent, we will welcome them home as a band of heroes; and this flag preserved here forever will be the trophy of their bravery and their victory."[11] "Thanks to the heroism of Onondaga, we have a thousand warm hearts—two thousand strong hands,—a thousand bright bayonets—that shall rally around this banner, to shield it from the blighting touch of traitors," Titus responded.

The regiment, he promised, would "bear it [the flag] bravely to the field—that will stand by it, and see it torn to a thousand shreds ere they will surrender it to rebel hands, and carry it triumphantly from rampart to rampart, until the eagle it bears shall be the beacon light proclaiming to the deluded South the return of her liberties."[12] While much of this rhetoric echoed hundreds of other farewell

---

9. "Official from General McClellan," *Syracuse Daily Courier and Union*, July 4, 1862.

10. George McClellan to Edwin Stanton, June 28, 1862, George Brinton McClellan Papers, Library of Congress.

11. Matilda Joslyn Gage, speech, Aug. 25, 1862, Fayetteville, NY, printed news article containing her words, held at Matilda Joslyn Gage Home, Fayetteville.

12. Col. Silas Titus, speech, Aug. 25, 1862, Fayetteville, NY, available in *The War Scrapbook of Matilda Joslyn Gage: Witness to Rebellion*, ed. Peter Svenson (Bethlehem, PA: Lehigh Univ. Press, 2018).

speeches given in towns and cities across the North during the first two years of the war, the emphasis placed on the eradication of slavery set a unique tone. In a war to preserve the Union, the men of the 122nd New York were decidedly in favor of a more extreme, morally righteous, goal: the destruction of the South's peculiar institution. As the green recruits boarded trains bound for Washington, DC, little did they know that they would soon face the enemy in a battle on the fields of Maryland that would ultimately determine the fate of those same men and women they had so vocally promised to free. Years later, Osgood recalled the organization of the 122nd New York and his own enlistment with great passion. "It is with a feeling of pride," he said,

> that we reflect that we enlisted at a time which was the darkest period of the war—The fond delusion entertained in 1861 that the war would be ended in ninety days had long since been abandoned and up to this time success had been upon the side of the rebels. McClellan with his splendid army had just returned baffled and defeated from his Peninsular Campaign—Lee at the head of his triumphant column having overwhelmed Pope at the second battle of Bull Run was just entering upon the invasion of Maryland—Doubt and gloom reigned throughout the South. The President called for 300000 additional troops and one thousand of our Onondaga County boys varying in age from sixteen to twenty three. . . . We men mustered into service Aug 28–1862 and on the 31st August left for Washington—upon our arrival there we were immediately sent to the front lines and became a part of General Shaler's brigade of the Sixth Army Corps of the Army of the Potomac and participated in all the memorable campaigns and battles of that gallant army from Antietam to the Appomattox, besides serving under Sheridan in the brilliant campaign of the Shenandoah Valley when he won his stars as Major General in the regular army.
>
> Going immediately into active service was I assure you a sudden change from the comforts of home but Lee was in Maryland and every man was needed—
>
> We reached Antietam the night of the battle crossed the battlefield the next morning & moved to Sharpsburg. We were under fire for the first time hearing the whistle of bullets, a sound with which too subsequently became more familiar.
>
> The battlefield of Antietam was one of the severest of the war and I can assure you that when we crossed it again two days later—the rebel dead being still unburied and in places so numerous that you could see where those lines of battle had been—we were brought to a very realizing sense of what war was.[13]

---

13. Original speech, among Tracy family memorabilia, copy available at Onondaga Historical Association, Syracuse, NY.

The letters Osgood wrote home during his first month in service provide considerable insight into day-to-day army life and, particularly, the uncertainty that men felt regarding battle and their place as part of the larger military campaigns. Held in reserve, members of the 122nd New York were spared the carnage of Antietam, though they witnessed the aftermath and spent the subsequent weeks campaigning against Confederate feints into Maryland, hoping to prove their worth in the face of the enemy.

September 3, 1862
Baltimore, Maryland

Dear Mother,

We left New York at four P.M. Monday afternoon arriving at Baltimore at eight P.M. last evening—as there were several regiments—ahead of us and not cars enough we were obliged to remain all night. The boys had to sleep on the floor of the depot and Adjt. [Andrew] Smith instead of going to a hotel "bunked" with the boys until he was aroused this morning with a kick in the ribs and an order to roll up his bed and he has just been discussing the possibility of "rolling up" a three-inch plank.

As for myself I was quite fortunate. I slept in the baggage car with the quartermasters sergeants on top of some dry good boxes and felt all right this morning except I have worn the "points" off my hip bones.

It is now about 4:00 A.M. and we have all been aroused by some fool issuing an order to be ready to move while there is still a regiment ahead of us and no prospect of going before nine or ten o'clock. We got here too late last evening to get any sights of this city in marching from our depot and the other. All the people we saw seemed to feel friendly and as we came in on the cars we were greeted with the waving of flags (not . . . ours).[14]

The Adjt. and myself were especially delighted with the funny looking little niggers. We saw one about three years old waving a handkerchief vigorously.

I did not get time to go to see Charles and William again but I saw George Bridges again for a few minutes as we were marching down Broadway.

I got myself a good rubber blanket in New York.

Good Bye. Yours affy,
Os

14. Baltimore, in which a third of Maryland's population resided, was hesitant in its loyalty to the Lincoln administration. Historian James McPherson notes, "The mayor's unionism was barely tepid, and the police chief sympathized with the South. Confederate flags appeared on many city homes and buildings during the tense days after Sumter." *Battle Cry of Freedom: The Civil War Era* (New York: Oxford Univ. Press, 1988), 285. For more on the Civil War in Baltimore and, in particular, the riot of April 19, 1861, and the attitudes of men and women in that city, see Charles W. Mitchell, *Maryland Voices of the Civil War* (Baltimore: Johns Hopkins Univ. Press, 2007). Osgood's comments, however, seem to contradict this notion of hostility.

P.S. Tell Jim not to forget to go to the coal office and get that German book and then go over gross as I directed him.

Washington, D.C., Sept. 4, 1862

Dear Mother,

We left Baltimore about 12 yesterday forenoon arriving here about 4 or 5 P.M., too late to get into camp so the regiment was sent into a log house which they just filled standing up and when they bunked for the night I can assure you it was a comical sight to see how closely they were packed. The Adjt. and myself got into another room which was not so full and enjoyed the repose which the soft side of an oak plank would naturally afford.

There are all sorts of rumors in circulation and the general opinion seemed to be that the rebels were uncomfortably near. We are going to Camp Seward[15] about a mile or two from the city, and shall probably get orders to move in a hour or so. The depot where we are is very near the capitol building and this A.M. Captain Gere and myself took an outside view, the guard informing us that we could not be admitted unless we were wounded (it is used as a hospital now I believe) but we did not think the inducement strong enough to inflict some wounds ourselves so as to qualify ourselves for admission. It is a splendid building only it is regular American (ie. unfinished). I did not get any chance to go about Baltimore.

I feel first rate since I have started. My boots hurt me a little at first but I have not had any opportunity to change them and something has given way, for they don't trouble me now but as to whether it is my boots or feet I am unable yet to ascertain.

There are a large number of paroled Union prisoners taken in the battle on Saturday[16] and released because the rebels had no rations for them. They are a rough looking set (as far as . . . goes) but are in the best of spirits and full of fight. One fellow told me this morning that he would be willing to lose four months pay if he could be exchanged and rejoin his regiment at once.

15. Camp Seward, an entry point into the Civil War for most Union soldiers, was across the Potomac River from Washington, DC. It provided defense fortifications for the city during the war. Camp Seward was named for William Seward, Lincoln's secretary of state and former rival for the presidency.

16. This likely refers to the Second Battle of Manassas, fought on August 28–30, 1862, an important Confederate victory that paved the way for Lee's invasion of Maryland. In the wake of the Confederate victory over George McClellan during the Peninsula Campaign, Lee moved the Army of Northern Virginia north, clashing with Gen. John Pope's Army of Virginia and routing them from the field. For further reading, see John J. Hennessy, *Return to Bull Run: The Campaign and Battle of Second Manassas* (Norman: Univ. of Oklahoma Press, 1993); John H. Matsui, *The First Republican Army: The Army of Virginia and the Radicalization of the Civil War* (Charlottesville: Univ. of Virginia Press, 2016); and for readings on how this fit in the larger Antietam Campaign of 1862, see Gary W. Gallagher, ed., *The Antietam Campaign* (Chapel Hill: Univ. of North Carolina Press, 1999).

Many of them talk bitterly against McDowell,[17] and one wounded soldier in Baltimore begged one of our boys to shoot him if he got a chance, but all (without a single exception so far as I have seen) almost worship McClellan. One fellow who was in the Seven Days Battle at Richmond and in their last battles saw that Popes retreat was a perfect stampede in comparison with the "charges of bass" before Richmond.

Somebody gave the Adjt a Standard of Monday which is the latest we have heard from home. Don't be worried for fear of our being ordered immediately into service for I don't think there is a possibility of transportation.

On the way down some of the cars were not very comfortable but the boys bet the field and staff (ahem!) always had a passenger car and therefore a comfortable time. Yesterday we had a luncheon of crackers and cheese to which I did much ample justice that quarter master Lester got quite frightened the job he had undertaken of providing for my wants.

Remember me to everybody and tell George I will write to him in a day or two.

Yours so,

Os

I will write again as soon as I know what my direction is.

Camp near Orfuts Cross Road

15 miles north of Washington

September 7, 1862

Dear Mother,

It is just a week ago today since we left home and I don't think it can be said we have wasted any time—I believe I wrote to you last from Baltimore on Wednesday last. We came to Washington that day and had the pleasure of trying the soft side of pine plank again.

Thursday morning we were ordered to support into Virginia but when we got to Long Bridge we were halted and after waiting all day for further order went into a vacant lot by the side of the road for the night.[18] I doubled blankets with Captain Moore and slept very comfortably. At four A.M. the next morning we started off, camping later in the day. We got our tents nicely pitched and got a good night's rest and the next day (Saturday) just as we were going to work to *arrange* our tents orders came to join Couch's Division[19] immediately and to take nothing but

17. Gen. Irvin McDowell was the Union commander at First Bull Run. For his early war goals, see Donald Stoker, *The Grand Design: Strategy and the U. S. Civil War* (New York: Oxford Univ. Press, 2010); William C. Davis, *Battle at Bull Run: A History of the First Major Campaign of the Civil War* (New York: Doubleday, 1977); Stephen W. Sears, *Lincoln's Lieutenants: The High Command of the Army of the Potomac* (New York: Houghton Mifflin Harcourt, 2017).

18. This bridge spanned the Potomac River, connecting the southern portion of Washington, DC, to Arlington, Virginia.

19. Gen. Darius N. Couch (1822–1897) was an American soldier, businessman, and naturalist. He served as a career US Army officer during the Mexican-American War and the Second Seminole War

haversacks with two days ration, leaving tents, knapsacks, and baggage. I was a little sick and the Colonel ordered me into the ambulance, but after riding two miles I felt considerably better and so I walked the rest of the way. I was with the ammunition train so we got behind the regiment and when we got to where the regiment was resting for the night, I found the Adj't who carried my blankets for me had bunked in with the Colonel so I crawled into the middle of a pile of hay and as I had my overcoat I slept like a top and awoke this A.M. feeling as well as ever. We marched this morning about two miles report to General Couch. We have been assigned to General Cochrane's Brigade, and are stationed in a very pleasant place with good water near.[20]

It is understood that our tents and baggage are to be forwarded to us and we will be kept here some time for drill. Indeed the Field & Staff officers tents are already on their way and as I tent with Adj't I am all right. We thought since we received orders to join Couch we should see service immediately, but it is said Jackson has left Maryland[21] so we are all safe for the present. I have enjoyed myself very much so far and am breaking into army fare very comfortably. I mess with the quarter masters sergeants and we have got a good fellow to cook for us and the prospects are that we shall live comfortably. When we were between Tenally town to Chain Bridge Sumner's Corps were at the former place and I sent word to Sam [Sumner] the next morning to come over and see me but they left that night and are now I hear about six miles to the right of us, so I hope to see him yet.

We have had the most delightful weather since we left home. In Albany, Philadelphia, and Baltimore we were entertained by the ladies relief association of those cities. In Albany while the ladies are giving the soldiers something to eat the gentlemen fill their canteens with ice water. We have had most delightful weather since we left home.

Since I have been here and seen the number of army wagons constantly passing . . . often wondering that this army has not lost morale. I only wonder that they do anything when it takes so much labor to keep one regiment furnished.

---

and as a general officer in the Union army during the American Civil War. He rose to command a corps in the Army of the Potomac and led divisions in both the eastern and western theaters. Ezra J. Warner, *Generals in Blue: Lives of Union Commanders* (Baton Rouge: Louisiana State Univ. Press, 2006), 95–96.

20. Brig. Gen. John Cochrane was a New York lawyer and staunch Democrat, elected to Congress in 1856. When the war broke out he raised and was appointed colonel of the Sixty-Fifth New York Volunteer Infantry. See Terry L. Jones, "Cochrane, John," *Historical Dictionary of the Civil War*: vol. 1, *A–L* (Lanham, MD: Scarecrow, 2011), 310.

21. It is uncertain what Tracy is referring to here, though he is likely commenting on part of Lee's larger 1862 campaign, which began after the Battle of Second Manassas and culminated on the fields of Antietam. See Gary Gallagher, *The Antietam Campaign* (Chapel Hill: Univ. of North Carolina Press, 1999) and Joseph L. Harsh, *Taken at the Flood: Robert E. Lee and Confederate Strategy in the Maryland Campaign of 1862* (Kent, OH: Kent State Univ. Press, 1999).

I like our officers very much. Dwight[22] (the Lt. Col) is going to make a very good officer and I am very agreeably second lieutenant. They are all very kind to me and my position is a very pleasant one and I don't regret in the least that now I am not a Lieutenant.

If you will direct to 122nd Reg't of NY. V., Cochrane Brigade, Couch Division, Army of the Potomac, I will get your letters. Love to Jim. Goodbye.

Yours affy,
Os

Cap of 122d Regt NY. V.
Near Sharpsburg Washington
Sept. 18, 1862

Dear Mother,

Yours and Jim's letters of the 10th, the first I have heard from home were received this A.M. and might welcome they were I assure you.

We have been on the move since I last wrote you on Monday we passed through and over the mountain from which General Slocum[23] drove the enemy the day before.[24] This gave us rather a realizing sense of the war for we saw a number of wounded rebels and several dead ones by the road side. Gotches who was with wagons went off into the woods where the fight was thicker and in one place he saw a rebel and Colonel Adj't and fourteen privates lying dead together.

22. Capt. Augustus Wade Dwight, Company E, was thirty-five years old when he enrolled, on July 8, 1862, at Syracuse to serve three years. He was promoted to lieutenant colonel in August 1862 and was wounded at Cedar Creek in October 1864. He was killed at Petersburg on March 25, 1865.

23. This was Maj. Gen. Henry Warner Slocum; for an excellent biography, see Brian C. Melton, *Sherman's Forgotten General: Henry W. Slocum* (Columbia: Univ. of Missouri Press, 2007). Slocum was born in Onondaga County and attended West Point, graduating in 1852 and accepting a commission in the First US Artillery. He resigned from the army in 1856 to practice law in Syracuse and serve as an instructor in the state militia. After the Confederate attack on Fort Sumter, he was commissioned as colonel of the 27th New York Volunteers and led the regiment at First Bull Run, where he was wounded. During the Peninsula Campaign, Slocum was given command of the First Brigade of the Sixth Corps. In the wake of Seven Days Battles, he was promoted to major general in July 1862. After Antietam, Slocum was given command of the Twelfth Army Corps and fought at Chancellorsville and Gettysburg before he and his Corps were transferred to the Western theater. He commanded the Twelfth Corps until August 1864, when he joined Gen. William T. Sherman on the March to the Sea, where he was given command of the Twentieth Corps following the death of General James B. McPherson. While he was commander of the Twelfth Corps, he and his men saw action at every major battle along the Richmond-Washington front. See Dwight H. Bruce, *Onondaga's Centennial: Gleanings of a Century*, 2 vols. (Boston: Boston History Company, 1896), 2:99–100; Harry Searles, "Henry Warner Slocum," *American History Central*, Aug. 13, 2020, https://www.americanhistorycentral.com/entries/henry-warner-slocum/.

24. This likely refers to the action on September 14, 1862, at Crampton's Gap, Maryland, in which Slocum's Division (First Division of the Sixth Army Corps) struck at Confederate forces holding Crampton's Gap, a pass through the South Mountain with the hopes of pushing into the rear of Confederate forces moving up Pleasant Valley toward Antietam. See Charles Elihu Slocum, *The Life and Services of Major-General Henry Warner Slocum* (Toledo, OH: Slocum Publishing, 1913), 43–46.

Our troops took it by a bayonet charge up a steep hill and the rebels having artillery too. In passing over the mountain it seemed almost impossible that we could have done it. I saw General Slocum who is looking very well and also John Dover whose regiment is attached to Slocum's division but they were not allowed to fight but kept in reserve. John gave me a soft biscuit (which is quite a luxury in these days of hardtack) and introduced me to his uncle, the Colonel.

The next day we lay quiet and yesterday we started for Harpers Ferry. 9 miles *down* the river from our position after arriving with two miles from Harpers Ferry we were ordered back and marched 8 miles *above* our position of the morning making a march of over 20 miles which would be pretty good for the senior member of the Tracy family and *considerable* for one who has never had a "weakness" for walking. I stood it first rate and after a night's rest feel first rate this morning. Our troops were very successfull in this vicinity yesterday and drove the rebels some distance. Yesterday the Adj't got tins of "hard tack" and succeeded in buying a loaf of bread and a cup of butter and I concluded that I never had known how good bread and butter is.

In crossing the mountains about here we have had some splendid views.

We have been congratulating ourselves that we were not sent to Harpers Ferry at first. There were two new regiments I believe among the paroled prisoners released by the rebels when they compelled Colonel Miller to surrender.[25] They must have felt considerably "flat."

We were near the 12th regiment this morning and several of the boys came over to see us, Ira Wood,[26] Estes[27] and Alger[28] among others. They were all looking well. They have got up only about two-hundred in their regiments. Indeed it is the general remark as we pass troops in marching that our regiment is as large as their brigade and there is the remnants of that splendid army that started for

25. As Lee moved the Army of Northern Virginia north in the fall of 1862, Col. Dixon S. Miles, who commanded at Harpers Ferry, was ordered to hold the position "to the last extremity and to shoot all dissenters"; his position could ultimately affect Lee's supply line. Miles surrendered the city on September 15, 1862, after "no more than an hour's bombardment." Harsh, *Taken at the Flood*, 99, 316–18.

26. Ira Wood was twenty-six years old when he enrolled, April 30, 1861, at Syracuse. He was mustered in as first lieutenant, Company A, on May 13, 1861, to serve two years. He was promoted to captain on September 21, 1861, and resigned, October 16, 1862.

27. Stephen A. Estes, was twenty-two years old upon enlistment, April 23, 1861, at Syracuse. He was mustered in as private, Company A, May 13, 1861, to serve two years. On June 15, 1851, he was promoted to sergeant major, was then mustered in as first lieutenant and adjutant on September 21, 1861. He transferred to Company G as first lieutenant on February 3, 1862, and was wounded on June 27, 1862, at Chickahominy, Virginia. He was mustered in as captain, September 22, 1862, and then served as acting assistant adjutant general of the Third Brigade, First Division, Fifth V Corps, from December 1862 until he mustered out of service in May 1863.

28. Porter R. Alger was twenty-eight when he enlisted in the Twelfth Regiment, on April 23, 1861, at Syracuse. He was mustered in as first sergeant, Company A, on May 13, 1861, to serve two years. He was mustered in as first lieutenant on September 21, 1861, and made quartermaster on February 3, 1862. He was mustered out with his regiment, May 17, 1863, at Elmira, New York.

the peninsula and yet after all their suffering I have not seen a soldier that says a word against McClellan or blame him for taking them there. By the way, what has become of General Pope since the battle of Bulle Run?

Frank Lester says he is going so I must close this letter.

Good Bye—Love to all

Yours affy

Osgood

Sept. 1862 122 Reg't N.Y.V.

On the road from Harpers Ferry

Dear Mother,

We have moved every day more or less, I believe since I last wrote to you. I have been very well and stand the marching splendidly. The other night we were out in the rain but the Adjt. & myself slept very comfortably under a brush hut. Yesterday we were in a very pleasant place near Nolan's Ford.

The Col. Adj't and four or five of their officers invited me to take supper with them at a house near the camp and we had a splendid supper. You should have seen your boy sail into the fried chicken, hot biscuits and coffee with milk in it. The people seemed quite intelligent but still had a little of the negro twang to their conversation. She told us that she had some Confederate officers to dinner a few days before and they asked grace, rather a reflection upon us who did not.

From Washington to Poolsville the country is very poor and hilly but from Poolsville to our present situation we have been passing through a most delightful looking country. The farms are finely cultivated and really exhibit some signs of Northern thrift.

For the last two days we have heard firing in the distance which we presume is at Harpers Ferry.

Last night I slept in the company's wagon and we had so many extra blankets to lay upon that I must have imagined myself in a feather bed for I dreamt of being at Syracuse and of cautioning Joe Seymour not to get any good clothes.

We were discussing this morning what the Syracuse people would say if they could see us and see (we) look clean and respectable in comparison of that we meet here.

I believe I wrote you that I sent some of my things home in Andrew's valise and wish you would go to Mrs. Smiths[29] (54 Onondaga St.) and get my things. I repeat this as I thought you might not get my former letter.

We have got the nicest fellow for our Drill Officer, Major Hamblin[30] of the

---

29. This was likely Adj. Andrew Smith's mother.

30. Joseph Eldridge Hamblin appears throughout these letters. Born in Boston, the officer lived in Massachusetts, New York, and Missouri before the start of the war, in 1861 returning east, where he was mustered into service as lieutenant of the Fifth New York (Duryea's Zouaves). He was later trans-

Cochrane Regiment. He was formerly Adj't of Duryea's Zouaves. He is 6 ft. 4 in. in height and well proportioned. He is the most soldierly looking man I ever saw and as full of fun as he can stick.[31] He and Col. Dwight together can tell about as many stories as Jim alone. When we had supper last night we had the luxury of a looking glass and you should have seen how I dove for it. Will you be kind enough to tell George that my beard has attained a "tremjous" length.

Dr. (Tefft)[32] is very kind to me and keeps a watchful eye over me—comes over every day or two and congratulates me on looking so well—but since I got a sight of myself in that looking glass I have not been inclined to be vain.

We have been on the go so much that we had had but one or two opportunities for regimental drills but we hope after Jackson[33] is caught or got off we shall go into order we have is that we shall only take the top rail of fences for our fires but as each new . . . comes later the top rail it doesn't take a great while to get to the bottom of the fence.

I have been told by the "veterans" that the two great interests of a soldier are to sleep all he can and secondly to eat all he can and I assure you I am nearly perfect in both.

I have not heard anything from home since I left except two or three Standards that I have seen. There is such a scarcity of transportation and such an immense amount of provisions to be moved that our mails are slow in coming up.

For two days our brigade did not have a ration served, and even the old soldiers grumbled but our boys managed through as they have all got more or less money. I mean by this that they had two days ration served to them and it was four days before they got anything from the Government in that as far as the Government was concerned we had nothing to eat. I don't think it was Frank Lesters' fault for now the brigade company has their charge of the rations.

---

ferred to the Sixty-Fifth New York Volunteer Infantry, with which he fought in every major engagement in the eastern theater. He was wounded at Cedar Creek and promoted to brigadier general for "gallant and meritorious service." Ezra J. Warner, *Generals in Blue: Lives of Union Commanders* (Baton Rouge: Louisiana State Univ. Press, 2006), 197.

31. This seems a reference to the Sixty-Fifth New York Volunteer Infantry, the US Chasseurs, organized at Camp Thompson on Willett's Point, Long Island, in July and August 1861. See Frederick Phisterer, *New York in the War of the Rebellion*, 3rd ed. (Albany: J. B. Lyon, 1912).

32. Nathan R. Tefft served as the surgeon of the 122nd New York Volunteers. Tefft was "one of the best known physicians in Onondaga county. . . . [T]hough unassuming and characteristically modest, he was endowed with rare tact and perseverance, and invariably succeeded in whatever he attempted. . . . In 1862 he was commissioned surgeon of the 122nd Regiment . . . and remained in active service in the War of the Rebellion for two years, when ill-health forced him to resign." Bruce, *Onondaga's Centennial*, 98.

Nathan R. Tefft, at fifty-four, enrolled July 21, 1862, at Syracuse, to serve three years. He was mustered in as surgeon, on July 26, 1862; discharged, April 8, 1864. He was commissioned surgeon on September 10, 1862, with rank from July 24, 1862.

33. Truman A. Jackson enlisted at Syracuse, to serve three years, and was mustered in as private, Company E, August 18, 1863, He was captured in action on May 6, 1861, at the Wilderness, Virginia, and, a prisoner of war, he died of disease on November 18, 1864, at Andersonville, Georgia.

Company sergeant Gotches of our regiment is a very nice fellow and has given me a standing invitation to sleep in the regimental wagon.

At the camp we were at day before yesterday I had the luxury of a bath and washed my shirt wrung it out and put it on and instead of catching cold as I should at home it did not hurt me at all.

It is just two weeks this morning since we left home and with the exception of some singing of methodist hymns by the boys at a rest this morning it has seemed very little like Sunday.

Do you hear anything from Willie lately and how was it that he was thrown out again on the fourth?

I see by a paper received this morning that Buell's forces are moving up to protect Cincinnati.[34] I do hope we shall be able to catch Jackson. I don't think the United States would be large enough to hold the 122nd if they should have a hand in it. Please send some postage stamps as I can't get chance to get any. I repeat my direction in case former letters have not arrived.

Sg't Major O.V.T.
Cochrane Brigade
Couch Division
Washington.

P.S. Is Flo married yet and if so have George[35] ask Bella Fenton to write me a description of it.

Camp 122nd Reg't N. Y. V.
near Williamsport, Washington, Co Md.
Sept 21, 1862

Dear Mother,

Another march and another "skedaddle." Soon after my last letter of day before yesterday we were ordered to march and passed over a portion of the battlefield and through Sharpsburg and encamped just beyond the town but the enemy got

---

34. Ohio native and career army officer Gen. Don Carlos Buell graduated from West Point in 1841 and served in posts across the nation before the Civil War. When war broke out, he was appointed brigadier general of volunteers. He served most of the war in the west, notably at Forts Henry and Donelson, Shiloh, Corinth, and Perryville. Warner, *Generals in Blue*, 51–52. See Stephen D. Engle's excellent biography: *Don Carlos Buell: The Most Promising of All* (Chapel Hill: Univ. of North Carolina Press, 1999).

Osgood's letter refers to the fall 1862 Confederate offensive into Kentucky led by Gen. Braxton Bragg and culminating in the Battle of Perryville on October 8, 1862. See Earl J. Hess, *Braxton Bragg: The Most Hated Man of the Confederacy* (Chapel Hill: Univ. of North Carolina Press, 2016); Kenneth W. Noe, *Perryville: This Grand Havoc of Battle* (Lexington: Univ. Press of Kentucky, 2001); Thomas Lawrence Connelly, *Autumn of Glory: The Army of Tennessee, 1862–1865* (Baton Rouge: Louisiana State Univ. Press, 1971); Larry J. Daniel, *Conquered: Why the Army of the Tennessee Failed* (Chapel Hill: Univ. of North Carolina Press, 2019).

35. George Hunt (1833–1902), sometimes referred to as "Hunty," was Osgood's close friend.

all across the river safely about three the next morning (yesterday). News came that the rebs were in force at Williamsport and off we started.[36] We marched about ten miles, were drawn up in line of battle, advanced to within a short distance of the rebels pickets, so near in fact that our skirmishers saw them and a battery of artillery they were fixing for us. Some few bullets fell near us. On the left wing where I was a piece of a shell fell very near us. On the right one man in Co. A got hit in the leg, a slight wound which will lay him up for a day. We have "been under fire." (That sounds kind of grand). This morning we expected a battle here, but this morning they were all "over the river and far away."

I don't know where we shall go today but presume we shall be off soon for it is against the rule for us to remain any length of time in one place. The boys have dubbed the regiment the "flying Onondagas."

In our last two marchs' we have had a chance to see a larger portion of the battlefield and my ideas are considerably changed. In the first place I had no idea of the extent of it. I was told yesterday that the line of battle was nearly eleven miles long. Only think of it.

The wounded had all been removed but many dead bodies remained and I think without the least exaggeration I must have seen over one-hundred as we passed along the road. These were mostly rebels, and in some places five or six laid together. It was rather a sickening sight for our green and inexperienced regiment and gave them a realizing view of what they had undertaken. There were any quantities of balls-shells, muskets etc. lying about but I wanted to get some memento of the field to send home and finally picked up a secesh letter. There is nothing particularly interesting in it except the fact that it was picked up on one of the bloodiest battlefields of the war.

In the woods where we encamped night before last this rebel force was not fairly out. We picked up a number of rebel letters the style of which was just as bad as those we frequently see published. Some of the boys found some rebel note paper and envelopes and I hoped to have one to write home to you on.

On our march day before yesterday I was agreeably surprised to meet Sam

36. After the fight at Antietam, Lee's army retreated across the Potomac River at the Shepherdstown Ford, but, as historians Ezra Carman and Thomas Clemens note, "Lee intended to continue his ambitious plan. He led his Army of Northern Virginia back to the Virginia side of the Potomac River while planning to move upstream and re-center Maryland at Williamsport." "In order to threaten McClellan's right and rear, and make him apprehensive for his communications and thus prevent pursuit," they further explain, Lee "sent Wade Hampton's cavalry brigade up the Virginia to cross over at Williamsport, and put his army in motion for the same point, with the intention of re-crossing the river and moving upon Hagerstown." On August 19, Hampton joined with J. E. B. Stuart at Williamsport, where the Confederate cavalry and a battalion of infantry skirmished with Union forces on September 20 before crossing back to Virginia. Osgood's letter here is likely a reference to this action. See Ezra Carman and Thomas Clemens, *The Maryland Campaign of September 1862*: vol. 3 of 3, *Shepherdstown Ford and the End of the Campaign* (El Dorado Hills, CA: Savas Beatie, 2017), vii, 15–16.

Sumner. I saw him but for a few minutes as we were bound in different directions. He was looking very well and had passed through the battle all safely. He said he rode across a field over which the bullets flew unpleasantly thick. The Col. had a liver purchased for him last evening and we had a most elegant breakfast this morning and moreover supplied General Cochrane, who slept under a tree near us. By the way, anybody who has been in the habit of associating Generals and handsome uniforms would be slightly surprised at the appearance of General Cochrane. He wears a felt hat that I will wager went through the peninsular campaign and an old suit of blue clothes with nothing to distinguish him but a very moderate pair of shoulder straps.

We have been fortunate in regard to water so far. Only today we are obliged to send about a mile. I never realized before how indispensable an article water is. This morning my canteen is full of good cold water and I feel quite rich.

Just two weeks ago today we left home and in spite of the little rough life I have run I feel as well as I ever did in my life and if my clothes are a little dirty, my beard a little long (ahem) and my hair a little short still I am a pretty good looking fellow after all.

Has the 149th[37] left yet? We have been hoping to see them down here and make fun of them at going to war with good clothes.

I have not worn my boots yet but am saving them for wet weather as my leather shoes are much more comfortable and I have a pair of canvas leggings.

You sent me more penny stamps than three-cent ones so please send me some more. Tell Hunty that if he wishes to hear from me to come up and see you as I intended to devote most of my letters to you. Remember me to Nell and Marie when you see them and tell them the Adj't and myself will have a vesper service this evening.

Ask Jim to call at Mrs. Titus'[38] and say that he is well as usual.

Good Bye

Os

Camp 112 Reg't NYSV near
Williamsport, Md. Sept. 24

Dear Mother,

Yesterday we received a regimental mail, the second since we left home, and

---

37. The 149th Regiment New York State Volunteer (NYSV) Infantry was mustered on September 18, 1862, and was mustered out June 12, 1865. Col. Henry A. Barnum raised its forces principally in Syracuse, Pompey, Onondaga and Geddes. "149th Infantry Regiment," *New York Military Museum and Veterans Research Center*, https://museum.dmna.ny.gov/unit-history/infantry-2/149th-infantry-regiment.

38. Eliza McCarthy Titus (1837–1882) was the wife of 122nd New York State Volunteer colonel Silas Titus. Her parents were Thomas McCarthy, War of 1812 veteran, and Percy Soule. Their marriage certificate was the first Catholic record in Onondaga County.

you should have seen the rush. The Adj't, Lt. Colonel and myself assorted it and I can assure you it was quite trying to keep on assorting and leave our letters unread until we had finished but we are growing "heroic."

On Saturday we thought we were in for a fight sure, just this side of Williamsport. We advanced "in line of battle" and while our regiment was standing in a piece of woods, a volley of musketry was heard on our right and I thought we were in for it but with the exception of one man slightly wounded no one was hurt. We fell back some distance but the next morning instead of having a fight we found that the enemy was not in as large a force at Williamsport as was supposed and that we might have captured them without difficulty but alas by morning they had "skedaddled."

We moved from our last camping place about two miles yesterday afternoon. The last place was in the woods and quite pleasant, and for a wonder they left us in peace three days. We had our tent and I not being a 2nd Lieutenant but only a Sergeant Major was compelled to sleep there instead of out-of-doors. We started to have a big mess, the field and staff and myself. I was to turn in my rations and the others paid, but it was too big to work so the Adj't seceded and he and I mess alone. His servant cooks for us and we get along very nicely. This morning his servant was not on hand so I got breakfast and I don't doubt you would have been amused if you could have seen me, the relish with which I devoured my salt pork, coffee and hard crackers. The best way to eat those hard crackers is to fry them in with pork, although I can live very comfortably on them dry. I have not been troubled much with bowel complaint and my cholera medicine I got in New York has checked it immediately but it has been very prevalent in the regiment and I have helped several fellows who were in a bad way (the Colonel and several of the officers).

The "Chasseurs"[39] which is in our brigade and to which Major Hamblin (our "instructor") belongs contains some jolly fellows. Last evening an officer of the Chasseurs came to Colonel Titus' quarters and had another officer with him who was dressed in the uniform of a secession Captain and reported that he had captured him out on picket. Most of us knew that he was a brother officer in the Chasseurs but Dr. Knapp[40] got beautifully sold.

Just returned from guard mounting and dress parade and received the welcome intelligence that a mail had come and the still better news that there were two letters for me.

---

39. *Chasseur* is a French term for *hunter.* During the Civil War, the US Federal Army adopted Chasseurs as a scouting and skirmishing force for use against the Confederate army. Their uniform was in the French style, with a short, vented coat, though the Chasseurs were issued grey kepis. The Sixty-Fifth New York Volunteer Infantry, a notable Chasseur unit, also known as the First US Chasseurs, chose M1858 uniform hats (popularly known as Hardee hats) rather than the kepis.

40. Edwin Abbott Knapp, age thirty-nine, enrolled at Syracuse to serve three years, mustered in as assistant surgeon on August 19, 1862. He became surgeon May 27, 1864, when N. R. Tefft resigned.

I am sorry to hear Willie is short of rations but we have not been much better off than he in the way of tents until tonight when some tents for the men have come. You must not feel worried about his starving for soldiers, I find, they are the handiest fellows in the world to pick up a living—our boys managed to get along two days without anything to eat.

Tell Jim I sent home my revolver because first, it is of no great use to me, and secondly it is something to carry and every little counts, and thirdly I was in such a hurry that I did not stop to argue the question.

Adj't and I were very much amused at your question—if "officers dressed like privates"—and after mature deliberation (conclude) that the only difference is that the officers are a little the dirtiest and don't carry muskets.

"Our" mess (Adj't and myself) succeeded in getting a coffee pot tonight so hereafter we shall have better coffee. I was very much shocked to see by the papers that Mr. Wilkinson[41] was dead. Please say to Mrs. Wilkinson[42] how much I sympathize with her and how thankful I feel for all Mr. Wilkinson has done for you and us.

I suppose you have been to Mrs. Smith's and got my things. I told Adj't when you wrote me that he has sent two suits home that he must have been trying to appropriate my fatigue suit. Tell Jim not to feel hurt if I don't write to him personally for my letters home are of course as much to him as to you. I wish I could kiss you good night but as I can't in reality I do in imagination.

Your boy,
Os

P.S. *Send me some stamps.* We are not attached to any corps I believe—Couch's Division was formerly attached to Kryer's Corps but that has broken up and now it is independent.

Tell George I will write in a day or two.

I am glad to see that Joe is better. I feared our hydrant cone was going to be "broken."

---

41. John Wilkinson Jr. (1798–1862) was born in Syracuse, New York, to parents John Wilkinson Sr. (1758–1802) and Elizabeth "Betsey" Tower (1764–?). John Wilkinson Jr. was a lawyer and the first postmaster of a Central New York community known as Bogardus Corners, Cossitt's Corner, and Salina. As a young man, he took inspiration from a poem about an ancient city and named the new village Syracuse, in time for the opening of the Erie Canal. Wilkinson was an original town planner and helped lay out and name village streets. He also served as an assemblyman and founded the Syracuse Bank in 1838. He and wife Henrietta Wilhelmina Swartz had eight children, two of whom were Joshua Forman Wilkinson (1829–1889) and Alfred Wilkinson (1832–1886). The latter's son of same name (1858–1918), became engaged to Confederate president Jefferson Davis's daughter, "Winnie." Winnie later called off the marriage at her parents' request due to Wilkinson's ties with abolitionism. Charles Elliott Fitch, *Encyclopedia of Biography of New York, . . .* 3 vols. (Boston: American Historical Society, 1916), 1:123; *Syracuse Post-Standard,* Aug. 27, 2002; *Syracuse Herald,* May 28, 1918.

42. Henrietta Wilhelmina Swartz (1802–1873) married John Wilkinson. She was one of the managers of the Orphan Asylum and a generous Home Association donor. She taught piano lessons; among her students was Anna Sedgwick, Charles and Dora Sedgwick's daughter.

Osgood wrote the following letter to Nellie Sedgwick's friend Marie Saul.[43]

Camp 122nd Reg't N.Y.S.V.
near Williamsport, Md. Sept. 24–1862

Dear Marie:

If you could have seen the rush yesterday when it was announced that the regimental mail had arrived—Adj't Lt. Col. and myself had to assort it and I can assure it was rather trying to keep at work leaving our letters unread until we were through. But we are growing "heroic."

You must not feel alarmed that I shall feel provoked at your giving me advice, and Marie, I will try to follow it, and in making the last allusion to the subject, I wish you would tell Nellie that I destroyed the note she wrote me in Syracuse on Saturday last when we expected to get into a fight, our pickets having already commenced firing. At the camp we were the evening before we amused ourselves by reading rebel letters and I had no idea of their amusing themselves over my letters. By the way, the "style" of the letters we saw was just as bad as those we see in the papers. But to return, tell Nellie that I will write to her as a *friend* and try hereafter to *think* of her only as such, but today as I have got to write home, she will have to take part of this letter to herself.

We have had several "scares" and the boys have been very anxious to get into a fight but as yet have born disappointment remarkably well. We have several times been just one day behind. The only difficulty being that Stonewall Jackson was a little smarter than we were. We arrived at that contested battlefield near Sharpsburg—the next day after the fight and the sight of the field gave our green regiment rather a realizing view of the war. We can hardly say that we have been under fire but we have had one man slightly wounded and had several shells burst near us, with no more result than to scare a few timid ones (I will not specify what class I belong to). Jackson is said to have gone to Richmond if so our "active services" (ie. marching—we went 22 miles one day) will be over and we will probably go into camp for the instruction which we so much need.

I think it would amuse you very much and shock your ideas of housekeeping if you could have seen me getting breakfast this morning (the Adjt's man who cooks for us usually, being busy). I will not say the coffee was as good as you would have made but considering that it was boiled in an open cup, it tasted very fair. Of course a "new broom sweeps clean" but I do really like the life very much so far and roll up in my blankets and sleep as comfortably on the ground as I would

43. Marie Regula Saul Jenney (1842–1922) became a suffragist pioneer and intellectual mentor of women for generations. She was first vice president of the State Federations of Women's clubs, president of the Political Equality Club, president of the Women's Union, cofounder of the Syracuse Council of Women's Clubs, and cofounder, with Colonel Jenney (whom she married in 1863 at age eighteen) of the Charity Ball. *Syracuse Herald*, July 14, 1922.

at home. Since we started we have been without tents (with the exception of four or five days) and as the only baggage we are allowed is what we carry ourselves, officers and all, I am afraid our friends to profit by your advice.

I remain,

Yours affectionately (in a brotherly way)

Os

My regards to your father and tell him he must remember the arrangement we made, that we are "paired off" for the congressional election this fall. Mr. Martin sends his regards. There is quite a curious circumstance in connection with him. He found among some soldiers lying dead on the battle-fields of to Creek an old townsman of his. He was able to prove the identity by letters from Hamburg [New York] which he found in his pocket. My "rebel" envelope will not stick so I will substitute a "Union" one. My regards to Mary Titus[44] and say the Colonel is well.

Camp 122d Reg't N.Y.S.V.

Near Downsville, Md. Sept 30–1862

Dear Mother,

On Sunday we moved our camp into the next field beyond where we had been for a day or two—and now we have got a regularly organized camp—laid out in streets—and it looks quite military. The men have got the shelter tents as they are called. Every private carries one piece and when they halt they put two together and make a tent. We have three large tents. The Col., Lt. Col. and Major occupy one, the surgeons and Chaplain another and the Adj't Maj. Hamblin and myself the third. We have also got an Adj'ts desk and other comforts are accumulating. Maj. Hamblin, who by the way, is one of the handiest men at "fixing" things said he was going to have some bedsteads made. I was very amused at the conversation I overheard between a couple of boys who were putting up the tents under his direction on Sunday. No. 1 remarked "well ain't that Maj. a handy fellow putting up tents." "Well, I should think he ought to be," replied No 2, "he used to travel with a "show." He was the clown."

There is a report that he was at one time an actor although I don't believe it and this was probably their idea of acting. I hear nothing more in regard to future movements but General Cochrane has gone to Washington so that would indicate that we were not to move immediately. Yesterday three companies from our right was doing picket in towards the rear and they arrested one fellow who claimed to be a deserter from the rebel army and that he had swum the river but as he had on underneath his "secesh" clothes that were wet a nice dry suit of black broadcloth his story was hardly credited. He was taken to General Couch and I have not heard what became of him.

44. Mary was the daughter of Silas and Eliza Titus.

The Adj't has not been very well for a day or two but is better this morning. Yesterday Gotches sent him some hasty pudding and we had some of it fried this morning for breakfast at home.

Our reg't has improved so much in drill that I understand Maj. Hamblin has invited some friends from old regiments over this afternoon to see our regiments parade and I can tell you it would astonish you to see the "flourish" with which the Adjt's and Sergeant Major perform their duties.

On Sunday evening the Adj't and myself were lying in our tent and were entertained by the two Majors—Hamblin and Davis—singing hymns. Maj. Hamblin I regret to say is something of an infidel and atheist. I was very sorry to hear it as I like him very much in every other respect and I should judge from what I have seen and heard him say about the army and the duties of officers that he was one of the most honorable of men but he quite shocked us the other evening by his conversation in regard to a future status. He said that he thought it was the same when he dies as was when a dog dies, but I don't believe that he is as bad as he talks.

Gotches has just invited me to go and take a ride this afternoon and if possible I shall avail myself of the invitation.

Good Bye
Yours affy,
Os

Oct. 4, 1862
Camp 122 Reg't N.Y.S.V.
near Downsville, Md.

Dear Mother,

I should have written you before but Adj't Smith was busy with the "matinals"[45] day before yesterday and yesterday we had a Division Review.

On the day on which I last wrote to you I did not take the ride I anticipated as I was unable to get away, but Gotches and Poole went over to the 12th and brought Steve Estes[46] back with them. He spent the night and part of the next day with us. We had a nice visit from him and it gave me an opportunity to send a note to Lt. Auer[47] in reference to poor Louis Amms and Steve said he would interest himself in the matter. The next day we had two more visitors in the persons of General Slocum

---

45. Osgood is likely noting here that the officer's morning work in preparation for division review kept him from writing.

46. Stephen A. Estes served as adjutant of the Twelfth New York. The regiment was organized in Elmira, New York, in 1861 and mustered into service as a ninety-day regiment in May. It was later reorganized as a three-year regiment under command of Col. Henry A. Weeks. See Phisterer, *New York in the War of the Rebellion*.

47. The twenty-two-year-old Swiss-born Lt. Michael Auer, Company I, Twelfth New York, worked as a cigar maker in Syracuse before enlisting in May 1861. He was mustered out of service two years later and joined the Fifteenth New York Cavalry as a first lieutenant in July 1863.

and Ed Thurber. Col. Titus had the reg't drawn into line and he and General Slocum each made a little speech. General Slocum is looking very well. Ed Thurber spent that night and the next day with us and left this morning. He expects to be at home in about ten days. I told him I would not trouble him to call but if you will call at the store you can learn all about how we are getting along.

Yesterday we had a Division Review. We marched about 3 miles, laid around in the sun for about 3 hours and then we were reviewed by the President. The "review" consisted of Lincoln moving past our lines rapidly accompanied by about 20 mounted men, including Generals Franklin and Couch. There was no cheering and Lincoln looked tired and worn out. Taken altogether it struck me as a big "sell."[48]

The "old soldiers" about us are a little inclined to play tricks on our boys and the other day they sent one of them up to General Cochranes Headquarters to purchase pies telling him that it was a sutler's shop. It is enough to say that he did not succeed in getting any.

A very strict order has been issued today in reference to officers or soldiers leaving camp without passes and every time I have attempted to go to work today I have been interrupted every two minutes to sign passes.

It is rather a difficult matter to make a very interesting letter out of the daily routine of camp life. In the A.M. we have guard mounting at 7½ and Battalion Drill take up my mornings. In the afternoon I have no duties except office work until Dress Parade at 5 o'clock—this time I use for reading and writing and after supper generally crop into Capt. Moore's quarters and play a few games of euchre.

Good Bye

Yours affy

Osgood

Camp 122d N.Y.S.V.

On the road to Richmond

about twenty-five miles from Berlin

Oct. 5, 1862

Dear Mother,

We are still acting as wagon guard and have been marching for two days in the valley between the Blue Ridge and the Bull Run ridge. It is a most beautiful country and with the exception of an absence of rail fences does not appear to have suffered any from the war.

---

48. This refers to Abraham Lincoln's visit to the Antietam Battlefield in the wake of the Union victory there to congratulate the Army of the Potomac troops and encourage McClellan to pursue Lee's Army of Northern Virginia. See Slotkin, *Long Road to Antietam,* 381–87; Joan C. Waugh, *Lincoln and McClellan: The Troubled Partnership between a President and His General* (New York: Palgrave MacMillan, 2010); Stephen W. Sears, *George B. McClellan: The Young Napoleon* (New York: Ticknor & Fields, 1988), 330–36.

I received your letter of the 31st this am. Tell Willie not to be impatient. There are going to be some more vacancies in the regiment and I think I can get him in yet. I shall try hard for the first vacancy. The reason I did not say anything about my intended promotion as I did not know but that something might happen and then you would feel doubly worse and I have not been acting in that position, still having the status of Sergeant Major as Martin who is to take my place is still sick. We are laying still to-day but I suppose will go forward to-morrow but Church[49] has just come in and says this mail is going so

Good-Bye

Yours

Os

Oct. 6, 1862

Camp 122d N.Y.S.Vols.

near Chim Run or Indian Spring, Md

Dear Mother,

I received your letter of the 15th last night. I noticed you did not say anything about that muster-in-roll of the Field & Staff Officers of this regiment dated August 28 and signed by Captain Edgerton. It is a very important document and I shall be in a terrible "mess" if it is lost. I have written home several times about it and I still feel very confident that it is in one of the pockets of my fatigue coat that I sent home and if not then look in the top bureau drawer in my room and if not there have Jim go to Mrs. Smith's and see that if it is not among Andrew's things or in some of his pockets. If it can't be found let me know immediately and I will see that . . . can be done without it.

As an offset to this worry I have some pleasant news to communicate and I know it will be more welcome to you even than it would be to myself even. There is a vacancy in the regiment caused by Captain Jilson's death[50] and the papers have gone to Albany recommending Adj't Smith's promotion to Captain in place of Jilson deceased. "Mot" Church is to be Adj't. This leaves a vacancy in Co. I (Capt Dwight) and 2d Lieutenant Dillingham[51] is recommended for 1st Lieutenant and

---

49. Morris H. "Mot" Church enlisted in the Twelfth New York in May 1861, before being discharged for disability that September. On August 16 of the following year, he was commissioned, at Syracuse, as first lieutenant of Company I, to serve three years. He was mustered in at that rank on August 28 and as adjutant on October 8, following Jilson's death.

50. Capt. Harrison H. Jilson lived in Elbridge, New York, and worked as a pail maker before being commissioned as captain of Company G on September 10, 1862. He died on October 8, 1862, of typhoid fever at Relay House, Maryland. American Civil War Research Database; Eighth Census of the United States; "Rosters of the New York Infantry Regiments," *Unit History Project,* New York State Military Museum and Veterans Research Center, Saratoga Springs, https://dmna.ny.gov/historic/reghist/civil/rosters/rostersinfantry.htm.

51. Lt. Lucius A. Dillingham, of Syracuse, twenty-five upon his enlistment, August 16, 1862, at

Sergeant Major Tracy for a 2d Lieutenant to take Dillingham's place. And now has extended upon his duties and Church is acting Adj't. I have not taken my position yet as Martin who is to be the new Sergeant is back sick at our last camp and I am still Serg't Major and to-day the position is full as pleasant as we are having a cold rain and HeadQuarters tents are very comfortable, except it is rather cold work writing and a bad day for this display of one's penmanship. This change is certain only lacking the Government's approval which will probably be given but if Mr. Davis[52] or Mr. Monroe[53] should happen to be in Albany it might do no harm for them to hurry up matters for I should feel better to have my commission. Don't have them trouble themselves to write about it. I should have tried to have got Willie into this vacancy but that young man wrote me very positively that he would not accept a commission here until I had got one and knowing that when he once made up his mind it was very much like the laws of the "Moors and Persians." I did not push the matter. I would not say anything about my promotion until the thing is fairly fixed and please don't direct my letters to Serg't Major still and by the way I would suggest that Willie should put on the number of this regiment which he did not on the last but as one of our boys is brigade postmaster I got it all right.

You very kindly ask if there is anything you can do for my comfort but I believe until we get into Winter Quarters my wants are limited to the knit night cap I wrote you about but when we do I want Willie and a box of dried fruit and jelly & c as I shall hereafter specify and I will try and entertain the young man for a couple of weeks or as much longer as he will be content to stay.

Does Jim still continue in the canal office and how does he like it?

I drew on my bank act for ten dollars the other day and tell Dudley[54] I shall draw for $20 or $40 more as soon as I assume my position as I shall need to get some more things and for myself and we probably shall not get our pay for two months more.

Mot Church and I are at present messing with Captain Brower[55] and as he is an

---

Syracuse, to serve three years, was mustered in as second lieutenant. Company 1, August 18, 1862, as first lt. October 8, 1862 and as captain, Company A., March 1, 1864. He was discharged September 3, 1864. Muster and descriptive data for the 122nd New York State Volunteers, available online at the Division of Military and Naval Affairs, New York State, website, https://dmna.ny.gov/historic/reghist/civil/rosters/Infantry/122nd_Infantry_CW_Roster.pdf.

52. Thomas Treadwell Davis (1810–1872) was born in Middlebury, Vermont and graduated from Hamilton College in Clinton, New York. He became a lawyer and practiced law in Syracuse and was elected to serve in the Thirty-Eighth and Thirty-Ninth Congresses. (1863–67). Thomas Treadwell Davis. See Charles Lanman, "*Davis, Thomas Tredwell,*" *Biographical Annals of the Civil Government of the United States from Original and Official Sources* (New York: J. M. Morrison, 1887), 504.

53. Perhaps this refers to James Munroe (1815–1869). His brother George Clinton Munroe (1814–1883), of Hillsdale County, Michigan, was an abolitionist. George's house was an Underground Railroad stop.

54. This is a reference to Dudley Post Phelps, the husband of Osgood's cousin, Lucy Putnam.

55. Capt. Jabez Brower, Company A was promoted to major in January 1864 and died in action at

old campaigner we live nicely but as our kitchens are out of doors he sent word that the chances for dinner were rather slim but fortunately the HeadQuarter dinner was served up and Colonel Dwight and Major Hamblin were visiting and Colonel Titus being in Washington Major Davis was going to eat dinner alone but we suggested the propriety of taking dinner with him. We had a very nice dinner winding up with some splendid apple dumplings which were decidedly suggestive of home.

We got to our present encampment on Wednesday, worked hard, got our tents pitched and things fixed comfortably, went to bed at 12 o'clock. Orders came to march at Day Break. Up at four, tents all down, everything packed. Regiment drawn in line, arms stacked and we waited and waited for orders to move until about 3 o'clock in the afternoon when orders came to pitch tents again. Fortunately it is not much work as the men had left their tent stakes standing and it takes but very little time to up shelter tents. We soon had the Head Quarters tents up again and we have got ours arranged very nicely. Major Hamblin is a genius, They have left us in peace ever since and we have got a very comfortable situation unless this steady rain should raise a brook that runs by the side of our tents and drown us out but we have hope.

How natural it must seem to have Sam and Will together once more. I hope you will not forget to "poke up" General Sumner in Willie's behalf. Is it true that Bill Teall[56] is Lt. Colonel and on General Sumner's staff as I saw it stated in the paper?[57]

We received a Standard of the 20th by this last mail containing an account of Kirby Smith's[58] funeral. Poor fellow this was the first I had heard of it. How I pity his mother. Tell Nelly Sedgwick I have written to her.

Don't forget about that muster-in-roll for it is very important to me. I am going to begin numbering my letters to you so you will have the satisfaction of knowing that you receive them all.

> Love to all—Good-Bye
> Your boy
> Os

Cedar Creek in October of that year. *Muster and descriptive data for the 122 New York State Volunteers;* American Civil War Research Database.

56. William Walter Teall (1818–1899) was a lawyer, banker, and postmaster of Syracuse. President Lincoln appointed him commissioner of the Army of the Potomac, and he served 1862–64. He married Sarah Vose Sumner.

57. Sarah Vose Sumner Teall (1838–1928), daughter of Brig. Gen. Edwin Vose Sumner, was Osgood's cousin. She is considered Syracuse's first historian. She published *Onondaga's Part in the Civil War* (Syracuse, NY: Dehler Press, 1915). As a young woman, Sarah attended President Lincoln's first inauguration ceremony dinner, where the president promoted her father to brigadier general. See William M. Beauchamp, *Past and Present of Syracuse and Onondaga County New York* (New York: S. J. Clarke, 1908), 781–89.

58. This likely refers to Col. Joseph Lee Kirby Smith of Syracuse. Smith, with the Forty-Third Ohio, was wounded at Corinth, Mississippi, in early October 1862, and died shortly thereafter.

P.S. Send me some stamps. I have used up all you sent me for change. Tell Dudley that Mr. Austin who will present that check for ten dollars can give him some late information about me as he was here two days ago. I am perfectly well and Andrew insists getting fat. I guess my little bit of sickness was what I needed to get me up.

Near Downsville, Md.
October 10, 1862

Dear Mother,

I received a letter from Marie yesterday but none from you. Almost the first mail I think we have received since we left home which has not brought one from you. Marie wrote me that she and Nell called on you the Monday before she wrote. I received those letters from Willie a few days before. What a splendid letter he wrote me although I am rather sorry you should have "exaggerated" about my doings for fear the young man would not take a commission if I could get him one.

Don't forget to remind Jim about that "muster-in roll." I wrote him about this the other day and in case he did not receive the letter will you say to him that quite an important document—the muster-in roll of Field & Staff—signed by Capt. Edgerton as mustering officer cannot be found. We think you may have sent it home with our things, so if he will look in the pockets of my fatigue coat I think he will find it. If it is not there he had some of Andrew's clothes or somewhere in the valise he sent home. If he does find it have him mail it insured to Adj't Andrew J. Smith 122 Reg't NYSV, John Cochrane Brigade, Couch's Division and also write to me when you send it or if on the contrary you can't find it please notify me at once.

I have been a little unwell for the last few days and yesterday Dr. Tefft who has fitted up with a pleasant little school house as a hospital insisted upon leaving the Adj'ts tent which is rather a busy place and came over here where it is quiet. I shall probably go back in a day or two and meanwhile am most comfortably situated and receive the best of care. I should not have said anything about it but feared you might hear of it through some other source and would be most worried unnecessarily. Dr. Tefft says he will be adding a "medical certificate" as to my health.

John Webb,[59] Lieut. in Co. B shot himself through the calf of the leg yesterday while cleaning his revolver so I have some company. I never regretted that I sent home my revolver. It is only an extra weight to carry and an "extra danger" to have about you. I will write you again tomorrow or next day and send a "bulletin" of the state of my health.

With love
Your aff boy
Os

---

59. William Judson Webb, twenty years of age, enrolled on August 14, 1862, at Syracuse, to serve three years. He was mustered in as second lieutenant, Company B, on August 28, 1862. He died of typhoid fever on February 28, 1863, at camp near Falmouth, Virginia.

I can't find that other letter of Willie's that you sent me and fear I must have lost it. Hereafter I will try to be more careful.

Near Downsville, Md.
October 12, 1862

Dear Mother,

I am improving rapidly and have entirely recovered from the little feverish attack I had but the Dr. thinks I had better remain here a day or two longer before returning to my duties at the camp. They are all very kind here and as we are near the camp I have plenty of visitors. Captain Walpole is here sick, nothing very serious. He has got some fever and has kept at his duties longer than he should have done.

Day before yesterday I received your letter announcing Willie's arrival. Before I opened the letter I thought the direction looked very much like his writing but I could not reconcile that and the post mark Syracuse. How delighted you must be and I trust if the young man is determined to go to the war that he will succeed in getting an appointment and indeed amongst all these new regiments there must be plenty of vacancies. I wish you could keep him home. I think he has done his share of the work.

We have learned by a telegram in one of the New York papers that Mr. Davis has received the nomination for Congress. How do the opposing candidates feel? I suppose there is no danger of any of them running "independent" is there?

We had a visit from some ladies yesterday. Three of Captain Walpole's[60] men are guarding their house and they brought him some milk and cookies. It is quite refreshing to see friendly faces down here and you know I always had a "weakness" in that direction, even at home. I think I have received all your letters and must beg pardon for not acknowledging the receipt of them, the last was the one announcing Willie's arrival. Yesterday I received Wills letter of October 5th and one from George of the same date containing some shoe strings for which please thank him and tell him I will write in a day or two.

Last night the regiment received marching orders and we felt rather dismal at the idea of being left behind but before they had got half a mile the orders were countermanded and to-day they are all in camp again. We have heard that the rebel cavalry have made a "foray" into Chambersburg and done considerable damage but we did not get any papers yesterday and accordingly have not learned any particulars.[61]

60. Capt. Horace H. Walpole, twenty-five years of age, enrolled at Syracuse to serve three years and was mustered in as captain of Company E, August 15, 1862. He was captured in action on May 11, 1864, at Spotsvlania, Virginia, and escaped on November 1, 1864. He was mustered in as lieutenant colonel on March 26, 1863, and mustered out with regiment June 23, 1865 at Washington, DC.

61. This refers to J. E. B. Stuart's Chambersburg Raid, October 9–12, 1862, designed to disrupt Union transportation in Pennsylvania. See Robert W. Black, *Cavalry Raids of the Civil War* (Mechanicsburg, PA: Stackpole, 2004), 20–25.

I received a note from Belle Fenton enclosing a very pretty little note from Flo, written on her wedding day, thanking me for those sleeve buttons. Belle had neglected to send it to me before.

Major Hamblin has had some bedsteads built for our tent, a nice double one for Andrew and myself where we sleep very comfortably. I tried them a couple of nights before I came here. It is much more healthy. I presume as it keeps us off the ground we make a good bed of straw and it seems quite luxurious.

Well the life here is not remarkably exciting so you must accept this dull letter in lack of a better one.

Now don't feel the least bit worried about me for I am doing very nicely and expect to go back to camp to-morrow. I shall take good care of myself and not undertake too much at first.

Yours affy
Os

Camp 122d Reg't N.Y.S.V.
near Downsville, Md.
October 14, 1862

Dear Mother,

I am back at camp again feeling much better and with a little care I shall get along very well. I shall not attempt "drill" at present but I can attend to my office duties. Dr. Tefft was very kind to me and made me comfortable. We had two quite severe rain storms while I was in the hospital which I passed through more comfortably perhaps than I should of if I had been in a tent. Captain Walpole is better but the doctor thinks it better for him to remain at hospital for the present.

I doubt if there is any prospect of our going into Virginia this fall but I think we may go into Winter Quarters and as soon as we do get settled down, and if Willie has not meanwhile received an appointment I shall expect to have a visit from him.

Do all parties become reconciled to Mr. Davis' nomination yet? We have not received the papers containing the particulars yet only a telegram in the Herald but I have heard the Sedgwicks friends have turned over to Davis. I sent a congratulatory message to Saul[62] on the result and can almost imagine how mad the old gentlemen must be at the defeat of Mr. "Leavenworth."

Good Bye
With much love
Yours affy
Os

---

62. He likely means George Saul (1812–1886), father of Marie Saul Jenney.

Camp 122d Reg't N.Y.V.
Downsville, MD
October 15, 1862

Dear Mother,

I am much better and shall resume my duties to-day. The Adj't has got a new cook and we live nicely. This morning he gave me some nice beef-steak and pan cakes. Our Maj. Hamblin is a "brick" as yesterday he said to me that he thought he had something that would do me good, viz; a bottle of currant wine that his mother put up, nothing intoxicating about it. I told him I was much obliged but perhaps I had better not take it. "Well" says he "it is under the bed here and remember it is yours, all of it."

And so Stuart has got away again safely after doing so much damage. Major Hamblin this morning says he does not believe there will be any Virginia campaign this winter. Our General Sumner has gone to Syracuse. How pleasant it will be for Will and Sam. Will it not be a good opportunity to make a strike for Will? A General of his position can do almost anything he wants to so don't give him any excuses.

Good Bye
Yours affy
Os

Camp 122d Reg't N.Y.S.Vols
near Downsville, Md.
October 16, 1862

Dear Nell,

Your letter of September 29th just reached me to-day. It is a rainy night in camp. The Adj't has a very good tent which I share with him. Major Hamblin our regimental instructor also occupies it with us. He is about six feet four in tall and as full of fun as he is tall. As he has been in the service since the war broke out he is posted on all the little "comforts" so that our tent abounds in "luxuries." We have a floor of red cedar boughs, a "rack" to hang our swords etc. on—bedsteads, a table etc. They have been allowing us to remain in quiet for the last few weeks with the exception of a few false alarms and we spend a lot of our time discussing the problems of a Winter Campaign into Virginia and it is astonishing how "interested" we get in it.

We are flattering ourselves at present that the indications are that we shall go into Winter Quarters somewhere about here so good bye to all plans for meeting you in Washington next Winter. At all events every days delay renders the Winter campaign more improbable. I almost wish we were settled for the Winter and then we could send home for some things and begin to live in a more "ship shape" manner. My valise, or rather my "half" of it, made its appearance a few days ago after not having seen it for over a month and you may be sure its contents were welcome and nothing more so than your needle book.

And so Will is at home and since you have got that light on your sidewalk I feel safer about him. Poor boy, he seems destined not to be in any battles. He left just too early this time. I hope he will be contented with mother this Winter. Sam too is at Syracuse and quite a hero I suppose and I am sure anyone who faces through the battle of Antietam was to be from what I saw of the battlefield. Hoping to have more than a "sick" day at the "island" after the war is over, I remain in regards to your mother and family,

aff,

Your brother

Os

P.S. Your photograph is a little worse for wear and I should like a new one very much.

Camp 122d N.Y.S.V.

near Downsville, Md

October 16, 1862

Dear Mother,

I received a "Vanity Fair" by the mail today but nary a letter but upon examining the dates of the papers I found I was not entitled to one. I haven't begun to drill yet but am taking the world kind of easy doing my office work and "flourishing" out on Guard Mounting and Dress Parade. I have put on the boots that George gave me which I have been saving for Fall and Winter and with a pair of gauntlets which I have purchased I am quite a fancy looking fellow. We have had quite a sharp rain storm this evening and it is just beginning again but our tent does not leak a drop but is just as dry as though we had a shingled roof and it is quite pleasant to sit here comfortably and listen to it. It is the "soft rain on the roof" only more so. Our cook has been giving us some plum puddings lately for dinner. He has succeeded in getting some flour and raisins and although they are not very ripe yet I can assure they are considered quite marvelous in camp.

Andrew has been so kind to me I wish that you would go and see his mother sometime. I think it would gratify him and I should like to do something to repay him.

We have nothing new about moving. Stuart appears to be the only General on the move nowadays. Wasn't that disgraceful? I don't know what people will think of us if he makes the circuit of our army a few times more.

We have been flooring our tent with cedar boughs which makes it both warm and fragrant and if we can get some boards we talk of having a regular floor built. If it was only certain how long we were going to remain here we could "fix up" comfortably. By the way, Major Hamblin has something that I have envied for a long time viz. a knit skating cap to sleep in and if you hear of anyone who wants to make me a present I would suggest that. It could be sent best by mail and would not cost much to get it here. Don't have it made "fancy" but good to wear. Perhaps you could buy one. Among some things which Major Hamblin had sent to him the other day was an air pillow and as it was too small to suit him he has given over the use of it. It is very comfortable.

You, who always made fun of my beard would be astonished at the great length it has attained. Indeed, I have nothing to compare it to but Spencer Ruets . . . except mine is black instead of red.

My regards to General S,[63] and love to you all at home.

> I remain,
> Your boy
> Os

> Near Downsville, Maryland
> October 16, 1862

Dear Mother,

Nothing remarkable has occurred since my last. I have resumed all my duties and feel better than I did before my little fit of sickness and as well as I have at anytime since I have been out. I see New York Central is getting up above "fair." Have you been tempted to sell or haven't you succeeded in investing the money you already have on hand?[64]

I suppose General Sumner is considerable of a "lion" in Syracuse and would it be respectable to call Sam a young "cub?" That is what they call "little" lions do they not?

The cold nights we have had lately are suggestive of Winter. The Adj't raised an extra blanket yesterday so that we were very comfortable last night. We succeeded in purchasing three chickens for our mess. Our cook proposed to "fat" them but we have concluded we can't wait but have given him orders to serve up one each day as long as they last. We are afraid marching orders might come and then we should be apt to lose our chickens.

We received a couple of flags yesterday and last evening the Adj't fastened them up across one end of the tent so that our tent forms quite a fanciful appearance. Will you have Will go to Coswells and get U. S. Infantry tactics, bound in one volume and send it to me by mail? I did not have any opportunity to get me one in

63. Here, he refers to his uncle Gen. Edwin Vose Sumner.

64. He is writing about shares in the New York Central Railroad Company, one of the major American railroads that connected the East Coast with the interior. Founded in 1853, it was a consolidation of ten small railroads that ran parallel to the Erie Canal between Albany and Buffalo; the earliest was the Mohawk and Hudson, New York State's first railroad, which opened in 1831. See, John E. Clark Jr. *Railroads in the Civil War: The Impact of Management on Victory and Defeat* (Baton Rouge: Louisiana State Univ. Press, 2004) for a discussion of the growth of railroads in the antebellum period and their contribution to the war effort.

Left: General Edwin Vose Sumner (From the private photo album of Osgood Tracy). *Right*: General Samuel Storrow Sumner (From the private photograph album of Osgood Tracy).

New York or Washington and I have had to depend on others for a chance to study. Please have him attend to it right off. You can pay for it or have it charged to me just as you please. I think it does not cost much to send a book by mail—prepay it.

I see that our troops have taken possession of Charlestown, Va. This looks a little like an advance but we see no signs yet of our moving.

Major Hamblin has received some books and among others "Edwin Brothertoft" by Winthrop which I have been reading. I don't like it near as well as "John Brent."[65] We get New York and Philadelphia papers the next day after they are printed so that we keep fairly well posted on the news of the outside world. Have you found that "Muster-in-roll" yet? It will cause us a great deal of trouble if it can't be found but somehow I feel very confident that it is in one of the pockets of my fatigue coat.

Good Bye, with love to all

Yours

Os

65. Tracy is referring to the works of author Theodore Winthrop, *Edwin Brothertoft* (Boston: Ticknor & Fields, 1862), a volume about the American Revolution, and *John Brent* (New York: Dodd, Mead, 1861), a biography of the first Union officer to be killed in battle.

October 22, 1862
Near Hancock, Maryland

Dear Mother,

On the march again and so we have to dispense with the luxury of pen and ink but will try and write plainly. We left our camp Saturday about five o'clock P.M. and marched about ten miles to Clear Spring, [Maryland]. I stood the march first rate, the Adj't insisting upon my riding several times. We spent the night in a field which was comfortable enough only a little cool. The next day they marched us to our present position about fifteen miles. We are about a mile and a half from Hancock, a little town at the narrowest portion of Maryland and near where Stuart crossed when he made his raid into Pennsylvania. Yesterday we rested all day on a very pleasant location and from the top of a hill by which we are "bivouacked." There is a very pretty view nearly all the way from Clear Spring. We marched along the bank of the Potomac and it was at almost any point it would take a large army to "picket" if it is the same as this all the way down. This morning we were ordered to hold ourselves in readiness to march immediately after breakfast so we flew around and got ready and orders came countermanding the previous orders and just now orders came to go and find a place to camp as there is not room enough here to pitch all the tents of the Brigade. This looks as if we were to remain here a few days.

Yesterday Captain Moses[66] and myself obtained a pass and we went over to Hancock [Maryland]. The town was full of soldiers and the stores were full. In one store I saw a couple of rough looking soldiers who had just purchased some "stand-up" linen collars which they had fastened on to their flannel shirts and they certainly were a comical looking sight. Every store was about bought out of the necessary articles such as sugar & c as their means of receiving goods had been shut off. The railroad by which they receive their goods running on the other side of the river where the rebels have an unpleasant way of stopping trains. The town does not amount to much. It is all built on one street which makes it a very "strung out" sort of affair.

Yesterday we had a large hut built of bough and we slept very comfortably notwithstanding there was quite a heavy frost and I fear the men must have suffered considerably as they have but one blanket and I just managed to keep warm under three blankets.

The Colonel's mess did not bring anything with them by mistake and our cook came away provided so that we supplied them for a couple of days. This morning their cooks came up with a nice lot of provisions and partaking of a nice breakfast they got up this morning and saw the result of casting our "bread upon the waters."

---

66. Lucius Moses was twenty-four years old when he enlisted. He enrolled at Syracuse, to serve three years, and was mustered in as captain, Company F, August 28, 1862, and commissioned captain September 10, 1862. He was discharged on February 24, 1863.

Our tents have come up so we shall be all right for to-night and I am glad the men have got their tents too. Our march from our camp near Downsville to our present position twenty-five miles in twenty-four hours was rather tough on our boys and we lost about sixty men, dropped out and used up but all but about ten got in yesterday. It does not seem very fast travelling, a mile an hour but that includes the time we had for resting and it is very different walking for pleasure and marching with a gun, equipments, an overcoat and a blanket. I have dropped my shoes and put on my heavy boots and tell George I bless him fifty times a day (would Jim think that strictly or slightly exaggerated?) They are splendid and are the envy of lots of poor fellows. We received a mail last night (i.e. the regiment did but I did not with Syracuse papers as late as the 13th by which I saw that General Sumner was to have a grand reception and supper).

I suppose the "Cap't"[67] flourishes on the occasion and so Bill Gifford[68] has got the nomination of District Attorney. I am mighty glad of it as I think he is a very nice fellow. I rather guess that Bill Wallace's[69] change of mind in regard to going to the war may have had something to do with his chances of getting the District Attorney's position, that probably was the "business" he couldn't leave.

I am perfectly well after my marching and think our "exercise" was what I wanted to "develop" my strength. General Newton[70] now commands our Division but you can direct the same as usual for the present.

Love to Lucy, Dudley, uncle and the children[71] with "heaps" for yourself and the boys.

Yours

Osgood

October 23, 1862

Indian Spring, Maryland

Dear Mother,

Alas the uncertainty of human events and marching orders. We were just getting ourselves in comfortable shape in our quarters near Hancock from where I

---

67. He is perhaps referring to cousin Sam Sumner.

68. William H. "Bill" Gifford (1839–1871) was a lawyer and member of the law firm of Hiscock, Gifford & Doheny in Syracuse and a district attorney for Onondaga County.

69. This is possibly William "Bill" Wallace (1808–1876), a partner with John Dean Hawley in the jewelry and silverware business. "Willard & Hawley's Store" was established in the 1840s.

70. Virginia native Gen. John Newton (1822–1895) attended West Point and graduated in 1838. He commanded a brigade of Slocum's division of the Sixth Corps for the Battles of Sharpsburg and Fredericksburg. He stormed Marye's Heights at Fredericksburg during the campaign of Chancellorsville and directed the First Corps at Gettysburg. Brendan Wolfe, "John Newton, 1822–1895," *Encyclopedia Virginia*, encyclopediavirginia.org/entries/newton-john-1822-1895/.

71. Osgood is mentioning specifically his cousin Lucy Putnam; her husband, Dudley Post Phelps; Lucy's father, Capt. Hiram Putnam, and Lucy and Dudley's two living children at the time, Lucy Putnam (1850–1926) and Anna Redfield Phelps (1852–1938).

wrote you yesterday had got one tent up and were about to put up the others when orders came for us to march and it was just about the darkest night one could often see, raining part of the time. Our men struggled badly. We marched back about seven miles on the road to Williamsport and stopped near a little tavern called Indian Spring. We fortunately got near a straw stack and I slept very comfortably. Gotches, the Adj't and myself "clubbing" blankets. We have now moved down into a field and the men are at work pitching their shelter tents which they carry with them. Our tents are also here and we have got them up so I shall be very comfortable. We are situated in a field surrounded by hills so that it is quite a sheltered situation and a nice brook runs within three feet of our tent but there is no certainty of our remaining here but probably if our rebel cavalrymen should make his appearance on the opposite side of the river within ten miles of us we shall probably be marched off to prevent a "crossing."

Another mail today and "nary" a letter for Osgood. I suppose however that Uncle Sam is at fault and not you folks at home but consoling myself with the saying "No news is good news." I trust you are not sick.

Yours & c
Os

P.S. I send this by a Mr. Austin who is going home.

October 28, 1862
near Williamsport, Maryland.

Dear Willie,

Yours and *six* other letters were received last evening. I was very much troubled for fear that my name having been forwarded for promotion might induce you to withdraw but I tell you not to and if the Governor gives you a commission in this regiment you take it, for there will be more vacancies in the regiment so that my chances will still be good. The head officers may object some so you had better make your arrangements for a staff appointment in case they make your place unpleasant.

We marched to our present position about thirteen miles from our last camp yesterday. Captain Smith stood his first march splendidly. We are now in a piece of woods about one mile from Williamsport and on the very spot where we tried to have a fight with the rebels on September 20th only one was afraid and the other dared not. It is rather cold nights but we build a big fire between our Head Quarter tents and we keep very comfortable and to-day we get a lot of straw and to-night we have got a bed about two feet thick.

I am very sorry that you could not find that muster-in-roll. I felt very certain that it was in one of the pockets on the inside of the flaps of my fatigue coat. However there is no use of worrying about it as I presume something can be done to replace it. We are going to see the Adj't General to-morrow and see what can be done. I presume that among so many volunteer regiments it is not the first instance that has occured.

Tell Nell and Marie that I received a letter from each last night and will write as soon as possible.

Nothing more in reference to Winter Quarters except that a very thorough inspection has been ordered throughout McClellan's army whether to ascertain its effectiveness for a Fall or Winter campaign or whether to learn what force goes into Winter Quarters I know not. One rumor the other day said that barracks were being built for us at Hagerstown but rumors are as numerous as they are various.

Please say to mother that all signs of fever have left me and that I never felt better and if she could have seen me down hasty pudding and syrup this noon she would have thought I was surely well. Tell mother that Frank is getting acquainted with his duties and we have no complaints to make as we see the 149th do about moves. We were very much amused at their complaints which we saw in a "Courier." One fellow complains that they have had nothing but bacon, hard bread, sugar and coffee and molasses. You have "sogered" enough to know that a person ought not to complain of such things.

Now don't think of giving up that place on my account for I tell you there will be more vacancies and besides Heaven knows I would be willing to remain Sergeant Major three years if I could have you with me as Lieutenant but if the Head Quarters Officers should make it unpleasant for you why then you can fall back on your staff appointment so don't make a "lunatic" of yourself on my account but let things take their natural course trusting in the maxim that it is all for the best.

A Lieutenant has just brought the acting Adj't and myself about a quart of pudding and milk. Isn't that a luxury "for camp fare."

Good-Bye

Yours affy

Osgood V. Tracy

CHAPTER TWO

The Grand Advance

November–December 1862

Marching orders have come at last. We have been notified
to hold ourselves in readiness to move at daybreak.
—Osgood Tracy, December 3, 1862

❀ After a hard day of fighting, the Army of Northern Virginia and the Army of
the Potomac stood face to face across the bloodied fields outside of Sharpsburg,
Maryland. Despite urging from Lincoln to "destroy the rebel army," McClellan
hesitated, as he had many times before, and allowed Lee to escape south across
the Potomac with his army intact.[1] In October, frustrated with McClellan's continued hesitance (first shown in the winter and spring of 1862 when the newly
minted commander of the Army of the Potomac failed time and again to press
the Confederates with superior numbers and firepower), Lincoln visited his army
at Antietam, where he "urged McClellan to get moving before the Confederates
could be reinforced and refitted" and while the roads were still intact ahead of
the coming winter storms.[2] McClellan demurred, and in early November Lincoln
promoted Ambrose Burnside who, despite the encroaching winter, decided to
pursue Lee. The new commander "did not dare consider the alternative," historian

---

1. For accounts of the Battle of Antietam and Lee's campaign during the summer and fall of 1862
see Benjamin Franklin Cooling, *Counter-Thrust: From the Peninsula to the Antietam* (Lincoln: Univ.
of Nebraska Press, 2007); James M. McPherson, *Crossroads of Freedom: Antietam* (New York: Oxford
Univ. Press, 2002); Gary W. Gallagher, *The Antietam Campaign* (Chapel Hill: Univ. of North Carolina
Press, 1999). The dispute between Lincoln and McClellan has been widely written about but for the
sake of this book please find the concise citation in McPherson, *Battle Cry of Freedom* (New York:
Oxford Univ. Press, 1988), 545.

2. McPherson, *Battle Cry of Freedom*, 568.

George Rable notes, understanding, of course, that McClellan's removal was motivated by Abraham Lincoln's anger at the lack of movement of his army against the Confederates that fall.[3]

The 122nd New York spent the weeks after Antietam in pursuit of Confederate feints along the Potomac River and adjusting to military life, which, from Osgood's letters, was constantly interrupted by forced marches. For Osgood, though, the November dawned bright, and the young officer joked that he would soon be entertaining his Syracuse friends at the regiment's "winter quarters in Richmond." The regiment found itself in the vicinity of Harpers Ferry, and Osgood and his comrades eagerly anticipated a renewed campaign against the Confederate forces in Virginia. The orders to move south reached the "Flying Onondagas" on November 2. "We are to cross [the Potomac] at 8 to-morrow morning," Osgood wrote to his mother that evening. "This will be my first appearance on the 'sacred soil.' Well I hope we shall not stop till we get to Richmond." While rumors of command change and debates over whether a Democrat could still be loyal occupied the minds of the men from Syracuse, their focus remained on the enemy in front of them. As they moved further into Virginia, Osgood reflected on his comrades' attitudes. "I myself think it is the general feeling that we are doing something more than when we were "skedaddling" about Maryland," he wrote, clearly satisfied that the army was finally moving in the right direction; toward Richmond. As November unfolded, it became clear that General Burnside intended to bring the fight to Lee, encamped in and around Fredericksburg.

Fredericksburg stood astride the Rappahannock River and was a hub on the Richmond, Fredericksburg, and Potomac Railroad. It stood directly in the path of the primary overland route south from Washington, DC, to the Confederate capital at Richmond and in the waning days of 1862 was witness to a terrible clash of armies as the men from the Army of the Potomac threw themselves against a well-entrenched Confederate foe. The Battle of Fredericksburg was an unmitigated disaster for the Army of the Potomac, as more than twelve thousand men fell on the cold fields of Virginia.[4] The men from Onondaga County again missed out on the action, playing the supporting role in defense of an artillery battery— a frustrating fate, it seems, for men who wanted more than anything to prove

3. George C. Rable, *Fredericksburg! Fredericksburg!* (Chapel Hill: Univ. of North Carolina Press, 2009), 57.

4. Scholars have written at length about the Battle of Fredericksburg. See Rable, *Fredericksburg! Fredericksburg!* Gary Gallagher, *The Fredericksburg Campaign: Decision on the Rappahannock* (Chapel Hill: Univ. of North Carolina Press, 1995); Daniel E. Sutherland, *Fredericksburg and Chancellorsville: The Dare Mark Campaign* (Lincoln: Univ. of Nebraska Press, 1998); John Matteson, *A Worse Place Than Hell: How the Civil War Battle of Fredericksburg Changed a Nation* (New York: W. W. Norton, 2021); Francis Augustin O'Reilly, *The Fredericksburg Campaign: Winter War on the Rappahannock* (Baton Rouge: Louisiana State Univ. Press, 2006).

their worth in the face of the enemy. As the Army of the Potomac retreated back across the Rappahannock River, Osgood's optimism and hope for a Christmas in Richmond faded. "I feel a little disheartened," he wrote in his last letter before the holiday, "that we should have been compelled to fall back across the river but with my happy faculty of believing that all is for the best I shall wait patiently for the result." He would have some time to wait.

> Camp 122d Regt N.Y.S.V.
> near Berlin about 8 miles
> below Harpers Ferry
> November 2, 1862

Dear Mother,

Since I last wrote to you we have been on the march again. Orders came for us to move at four o'clock the next morning and to act as escort to the Division wagon train. We had to be up about 2½ and marched as far as Rohrersville [Maryland] arriving about noon. We remained there until about five when we were moved two miles farther on where we remained all night. We were mustered for pay and did not get through until about eleven and were under orders to march again at three which we did and arrived at this place about 9½ A.M. and spent the afternoon and night and didn't I sleep. Our rear guard consisting of three companies Captain Smith among their number under the command of Lt. Colonel Dwight[5] got behind the train and losing their way got about three miles into Virginia crossing the pontoon bridge here. As soon as we found they had gone a mounted orderly was sent after them and they got back about four o'clock tired and dirty. We made lots of fun of them about their masterly advance and as we heard quite heavy firing in that direction we told them that we thought they went on until there was some chance of getting into a fight and then they concluded to turn back.

Yesterday and day before was beautiful for marching. We are in the midst of Indian Summer and yesterday we came through a beautiful country and if it had not been for the beautiful color of the leaves of the trees one would have thought it a Spring morning.

After resting all the afternoon we wound up with a large mail and I received a letter from Willie saying he was going to Albany to prevent the commission being made in his name. I wish he had left it alone for there is going to be another vacancy soon and we might have been together. If it is not too late now I wish he would have the commission made in his name. Colonel Titus will not object to it. I also received a "round robin" from Marie, Nell & Co. congratulating me on my appointment which I see has got into the Syracuse papers but they are in a little

---

5. Augustus Wade Dwight (1827–1865) was a lawyer and served in twenty-one battles. He was wounded three times, the last being fatal. He took over for Colonel Titus while Titus was sick.

haste for I am still Sergeant Major and if Willie will only have that commission made in his name I'll be the happiest fellow alive.

The night we left our camp at Downsville [Maryland] I received my knit cap which came just in the "nick of time" as we occasionally have to sleep out of doors although we generally get our tents up but don't worry for instead of snow as we hear you are having in Syracuse we are having very mild weather and I have slept out once or twice very comfortably.

I also received my tactics, much obliged.

There has been heavy and constant firing across the river to-day and every-thing indicates a "Virginia Campaign."[6] We are all the time expecting orders to move across. If we continue to act as guard to the wagon train we shall probably bring up the rear.

I have not felt in better health at any time since I have been out than I do now and am ready for Virginia or anywhere else and I shall be happy to entertain any of my Syracuse friends at our Winter Quarters in Richmond. We are lying alongside of a railroad (the B&O)[7] and it is the most homelike sound I have heard in along time, to hear the cars passing. It is said a large number of troops have crossed here and things look as though the "Army of the Potomac" was on the move.

I received a letter from Mr. Holden in which he complained of "inactivity" but you people at home have no more idea what an undertaking the movement of an army is but when we get started we shall go.

I sometimes think what a large amount of learning we used to do at the coal office but since I have seen the number of army wagons I have concluded to get Midler down here and get the contract. Captain Walpole we left sick at Williams-port with our chaplain.[8] He said he had found a very comfortable place to stay and had about recovered from the fever but was still very weak. It has got to be after 4 p.m. and no marching orders yet so we may remain here all night. I have been very busy to-day getting off last month's reports. But of all things that has caused me to be happy was my finding in a package of papers which came from our old camp

6. Tracy is referring to an overland route from Washington, DC, to Richmond, which would take the Army of the Potomac through Northern Virginia. Ultimately, Ambrose Burnside's decision to pursue this advance in the late fall of 1862 led to the Battle of Fredericksburg and, the following spring, Joseph Hooker's continuation of the campaign that led to the fight at Chancellorsville.

7. The Baltimore & Ohio Railroad was the first common carrier railroad and the oldest (1830) in the United States. It proved crucial to Union success during the American Civil War, as it was a vital artery of supply, linking Washington, DC, and the eastern theater to the Midwest. For excellent read-ings on the role of railroads in the Civil War, see William G. Thomas, *The Iron Way: Railroads, the Civil War, and the Making of Modern America* (New Haven: Yale Univ. Press, 2011); John E. Clark Jr., *Railroads in the Civil War: The Impact of Management on Victory and Defeat* (Baton Rouge: Louisiana State Univ. Press, 2004); Thomas Weber, *The Northern Railroads in the Civil War, 1861–1865* (Bloom-ington: Indiana Univ. Press, 1999).

8. Linus M. Nickerson enrolled at Syracuse to serve three years, and he was mustered in as chap-lain on August 28, 1862. Nickerson, a Methodist, would become a member of the Freedmen's Bureau.

near Chain Bridge that identical muster-in-roll of Field and Staff that I have been troubling you so much about and wasn't Osgood a happy boy "guess not."

Well Good-Bye

Your boy

Osgood

P.S. The orders have come. We are to cross at 8 to-morrow morning. This will be my first appearance on the "sacred soil." Well I hope we shall not stop till we get to Richmond.

Love to all

Good night

Os

Camp 122d N.Y.S.V.

near Thoroughfare Gap

November 7, 1862

Dear Mother,

We arrived here last evening after rather a tedious march in as much as we were behind the wagon train and you have to jerk along instead of marching steadily. Yesterday we got hold of a Herald of the day before which claimed Seymour's election.[9] I could scarcely credit it. Can New York have changed so much?

This morning we are having quite a little snow storm but we have got a "rousing" big fire directly in front of our tent and throwing it open the tent it heats up the inside nicely. The indications are that we shall remain here to-day which will not be objectionable provided it does not interfere with the "grand advance." There seems to be a large number of troops about here and I understand that we are to push through Thoroughfare Gap and "forward to Richmond." But on mature deliberation, although I have decided to eat my Christmas dinner in Richmond yet I think you need not begin packing up the things yet. Yesterday I think some twenty or thirty sheep must have been killed by our drivers and our boys seem to learn readily of the old soldiers for fresh mutton seems to be quite plentiful in camp this A.M.

Well I don't approve of stealing as a general thing but we are now getting into a country where the people refuse to sell anything and in some cases where they have anything to sell refusing to take our money for it and I don't think a little foraging will do any hurt. Our mess (Captain Brower,[10] Church and myself) have

9. This refers to the 1863 election of Democrat Horatio Seymour as New York governor. Seymour was an outspoken opponent of Lincoln and proponent of loyal opposition. See William C. Johnson, *Two against Lincoln: Reverdy Johnson and Horatio Seymour, Champions of the Loyal Opposition* (Lawrence: Univ. Press of Kansas, 2017). Much has been written about patriotism and loyalty in both North and South during the war, but for a concise account see Robert Sandow, ed., *Contested Loyalty: Debates over Patriotism in the Civil War North* (New York: Fordham Univ. Press, 2018).

10. At thirty-nine, Jabez M. Brower enrolled at Syracuse, to serve three years, and he was mustered in as captain, Company A, on August 6, 1862. He was promoted to major on March 1, 1864, then killed in action on October 19, 1864, at Cedar Creek, Virginia.

been living quite sumptuously as we raised two geese and two ducks the other day and Brower understands how to cook them nicely. I drew for ten dollars more perhaps you may think I am living extravagantly for a Sergeant Major but you must remember I expect to be a Lieutenant soon and I tell you a little money occasionally improves our mess table wonderfully. Our sutler made his appearance yesterday with a four horse team and large wagon load of provisions. He had some soft bread and some remarkably good cider, both of which were very acceptable.

Tell Will that a Lieutenant has resigned here and as soon as his resignation is accepted I will try and get him recommended for the place. I have also heard of several vacancies in the 149. Tell him to be patient and all will come right.

Well I have got some work to do so Good Bye, Love to all.

Your boy
Os

The trees and ground are beginning to get white and we shall see that we are getting to be veterans. Please sometime in your next letter send a fine tooth comb. I prefer an India rubber one.

Camp 122d Reg't N.Y.S.V.
near New Baltimore, Va
November 10, 1862

Dear Mother,

Today Theodore Poole, our Quartermaster Sergeant, returned from Harper's Ferry and informed us that he saw a fellow riding downhill while there who he noticed was not the most expert of horsemen and upon nearer approach said solitary horseman bore a striking resemblance to Will Tracy and it proved to be him for sure. He said Will was looking very nicely and had got a government horse. This was the first news I had of his appointment and you can imagine how delighted I was. To think after all our worrying that we should finally get him into the very place of all others we desired for him. As to riding, people tell me that he will soon learn.

Colonel Dwight said although of all outsiders Willie would have been his choice yet he objected to the precedent of appointing outsiders but it does not make much difference if they so object. Will has got his appointment in the regiment and upon the staff and he is all right and as for myself there will be one vacancy very soon and I know of probably several more so I am all right. I was in hopes Will would have been obliged to report to his regiment so as to have given me a chance to see him.

We are in the midst of conflicting rumors about Burnside & McClellan until we are so "mixed" that we have some doubts whether we have got any commander-in-Chief. And another rumor says that the "Grand Advance" is halted and there is some prospect of our going into Winter Quarters in the neighborhood of Warrenton

[Virginia] but this is one of a hundred rumors in circulation however I guess I will take back, for the present, what I said about that Christmas dinner in Richmond.

To-day McClellan & Burnside passed here. We had no regular review but the Division was drawn up alongside of the road. I got a very good view of them. McClellan looks very much like the pictures I have seen but Burnside not so much so, as most pictures of him I have seen have been without his hat which with a bald headed man makes a vast deal of difference.

Theodore Poole told me that Willie has written me giving the particulars of his appointment which I have not received yet, in fact we have not had a mail for some time but if we remain here a day or two longer I think we shall get one. Well tattoo is beating and I am sleepy and so with three cheers for the new "aid"

I remain
Your boy
Os

Camp 122d Reg't N.Y.S.Vols
near New Baltimore,Va
November 15, 1862

Dear Mother,

Your letter of the 3d arrived together with one from Geo [Hunt] and Marie last evening. I am sorry the conflicting claims of your sons' should have caused you so much anxiety but cannot feel thankful enough that you succeeded in convincing the young man for it. He had received the appointment when somebody else in the regiment had been recommended for it as now I am the principal person interested and of course willingly resigned my claims. Marie wrote me that Willie had some vignettes taken. I wish you would send me one I am anxious to see how the boy looks after his Western campaign and as General Slocum is to be left at Harpers Ferry, I believe, I fear I shall not get a chance to see him very soon although I have written to him that I consider it his duty to report to the regiment. As to acting as Lieutenant, I prefer my present position most decidely until I receive an appointment which will be very soon probably and besides I promised to stay with the new Adj't until they found another Sergeant Major. He is tip-top on the military part of the business but not much posted on the office part.

Day before yesterday Captain Brower gave us a dish of baked beans that seemed more like home than any dish we have had. It only lacked the "crispy" ones on top which I suppose are not to be had with out-of-doors cooking. Frank Lester invited me down to dinner the other day to partake of boiled turkey. It was very nice although we "omitted" the oyster sauce. Perhaps I dwell rather too much on our "bill of fare" but I trust Jim will not be disgusted. And so Syracuse went 200 for Seymour and Leavenworth is defeated. Well I am so disgusted and ashamed that I have some thoughts of selecting some other place to reside.

Major Hamblin, who is quite a warm Republican, said he had made up his mind that a modern Democrat could not be a "patriot." Major Hamblin was ordered back to his regiment yesterday. Onondaga Co. ought to feel grateful to him for the good he has done this regiment whose condition will bear a most favorable companion with the 149th if the rumors we hear about them be true. I am mighty sorry to have him go but perhaps it is better for our officers to learn to depend upon themselves. On our account his leaving is rather a benefit to us as he has occupied a tent with us and now the Adj't and myself have a wall tent to ourselves.

I was very much . . . at hearing a Captain in the Chasseurs relate a dream he had the night before. He said he thought he was in New York and yet seemed still to be in the army and passing along he came to a woman selling eggs. Inquiring the price and finding it to be but 12 cents a dozen he immediately purchased all he could carry in his handkerchief (they are only 40 cents a dozen hereabouts) and pretty soon he saw a couple of old tin cans lying in the street which he immediately seized upon as such "handy" things to cook coffee in (to appreciate this last you should see the various "machines" they have to cook in. Canteens split into two parts make good frying pans and an old preserve can makes the handiest kind of a cooking kettle.

We are expecting orders to move as it was rumored yesterday that the "grand advance" will begin to-day, and some heavy firing towards the front would seem to indicate. The weather has been most favorable and I trust we have not waited too long but a fairer day could not have been selected that this to "start" for Richmond. I trust we shall keep on. I have great "faith" in rumors. Our Division is in the rear being the very last of the advancing army so that our chances of seeing any battle will be exceedingly small but you may rest assured that if we ever succeed in getting to Richmond that we shall talk as "large" as any of them.

I have seen nothing of Sam yet and presume he has been too busy to come over but I shall probably get a sight of him here long.

In Harper's Weekly of November 15th on one of the inside pages you will find a tip-top map of this part of Virginia. You will be able to trace our course from Berlin when we crossed the river through Lovetsville, Union, and New Baltimore about five miles from Warrenton and thence to Richmond. It is almost noon and no marching orders yet so there is some chance of our remaining here to-day.

So Good-Bye and with much love for you all I remain,

Your aff' son

Osgood

Camp 122d Reg't N.Y.S.Vols
near Stafford Court-House Va
November 19, 1862

Dear Mother,

We left New Baltimore, where I last wrote to you on the 16th[11] and marched to Weaverville about three miles beyond Catlett's Station[, Virginia,] which you will find upon the map. Just as we were crossing the rail-road a passenger train came past and it was decidedly suggestive of home.

That day we happened to be the advance regiment of the Division and accordingly the first to encamp at night as we were first into the woods and next to a rail fence. It would have done you good to see how quickly our boys appropriated that fence before any of the other regiments could get ready. The next day we marched about ten miles encamping for the night in one of the prettiest spots we have been in. We marched into a narrow meadow with pine groves on each side, the trees quite small and thick stacked arms on the edge and the boys put up their little tents and built their fires just in the wood on that side. Our Hd Qrs were in the woods on the other side of the meadow and as you looked across the effect was very pretty and we all wished that we might have had a photograph to send home. The next day we marched to our present location (about two miles from Stafford Court House) arriving here about noon.

William Gardner Tracy, CDV (From the private Osgood Tracy collection)

We have been here to-day in quiet and the rumor is that we remain to-morrow. To-night we received the order announcing that the Army of the Potomac was divided into three grand Divisions. The left (in which we are) commanded by Franklin, the center by Hooker and the right by Sumner. In the assignment of the different Corps no mention is made of Slocum so I presume he is to be left at Harpers Ferry. If so I shall stand more chance of seeing Richmond than he. Wouldn't I "crow" over him if that should happen. I believe it will for with three such columns moving upon it you may rest assured that Richmond's days are numbered. I myself think it is the general feeling that we are doing something more than when we were "skedaddling" about Maryland.

I repeat our official title now. We are in the 1st Brigade, 3rd Division, 6th Corps in the left "column" of the Grand Army of the Potomac, that you may be able to keep track of our whereabouts.

I wish you would send in your letters soda or saleratus for we can occasionally get flour (as we did today for instance) and Captain Brower manufactures some

11. The previous letter in the scrapbook is November 15, so either Osgood was incorrect in his date here or the letter is lost.

remarkably fine puddings. You must not send a very large amount at a time but a little in each letter which would not amount to much in weight but a great deal in the way of pudding.

I enclose a little white flower which I got in Weaverville and you may keep it with the recollection that it was picked on the road to Richmond. We have got into the country for persimmons but I must say I don't think much of them. Rabbits are plentiful (quite plentiful) about here and several were caught by the boys yesterday afternoon. I tasted of a piece of one broiled and it was exceedingly good. Our sutler started from Alexandria [Virginia] on Sunday with two wagon loads of provisions but he has not made his appearance yet. If we don't move to-morrow I am in hopes he will overtake us as a few little "extras" help wonderfully. It has been a little rainy for the past few days but I think the road cannot be damaged any yet. Oh if "we" can only have two or three weeks good weather "we" will show you what can be done.

But tattoo is beating and I am sleepy.

Your boy

Os

P.S. I have not read "Ravenshoe"[12] yet and should be pleased to have you send it on. Tell Geo. I received his letter and will write to him soon and also I am much obliged for the "Vanity Fair" which I receive regularly. Tell Jim that he must write to me (that my letters home are for you both and let me know how he gets along).

That letter in the Standard in which was mentioned "Adj't losing the bread" was from Colonel Dwight's. It was unfortunately too true for it was when Andy and myself were together and I remember distinctly that there was a scarcity of bread that morning for breakfast.

One more good night

Os

Camp 122d Reg't N.Y.S.V.

near Stafford Court-House, Va.

November 25, 1862

Dear Mother,

Here I sit this evening as comfortable as one could wish, for we have got our Headquarters tents fixed up in fine style thus with a rousing fire (such as a Vermont man would delight in), which warms up the tents finely and makes it perfectly comfortable for writing. We have got an evergreen fence about three feet high built around the opening which keeps the wind off and makes it very comfortable sitting about the fire. I received a letter from Will besides the one you sent me. He writes me that he is perfectly delighted with his situation and I am sure he is not more so than I am and now I have some more good news to communicate which

---

12. This is likely a reference to Henry Kingsley's novel *Ravenshoe* (London: Ward, Lock, 1860).

I wish you to keep very secret and indeed I don't think I should have told even you if I had not thought you might hear of it some other way and speak of it. It is this—I had a visit from Sam and Lt. Colonel Teall yesterday afternoon.[13] Sam told me that he came over on business, principally, to viz: to inform me that his father desired him to say that as soon as I received a commission he would appoint me additional aid-de-camp on his staff. Hurrah for the Tracy family. Who says they are not ahead. Now the reason I want this kept quiet is this—Colonel Titus is very much "prejudiced" against staff appointments inasmuch as it takes an officer away without creating a vacancy and I fear that if he knew of anything of this kind being in contemplation he might not exert himself to procure a commission so keep the secret and you must not for the "present" direct my letters as "Aide-de-camp."

Sam and Colonel Teall were both looking very well and Sam was looking particularly gay in his fancy staff jacket. He told me that the rebels were in strong force at Fredericksburg and that there would probably be a hard fight before our forces could get across in which we shall probably not participate as we are in the left and now the rear grand division, Hooker and Sumner both being in front of us.

Yesterday was a beautiful day and as we went out for dress parade I noticed that it was literally true that not a cloud was to be seen. To-day it is somewhat cloudy but I think that it is not going to storm. The last two nights have been pretty cold and I fear the boys must have suffered in their little shelt tents with but one blanket apiece although three or four generally sleep together and club blankets. Our mess are going to endeavor to secure a turkey for our Thanksgiving dinner but I regret to say in ease of a failure I shall try to sponge an invitation out of the quartermaster who I understand has got a good sized turkey fattening for the occasion.

When I get in my "new" position I shall be sending home for slippers and that other "aid." At present my highest idea of luxury is having somebody to warm a fellows boots before he puts them on these cold mornings.

Well hoping that I may eat my Thanksgiving dinner next year at home and that we may all be united to finish up with opening that long kept bottle of wine.

Love to all
Your boy
Os

Camp 122d Reg't N.Y.S.V.
near Stafford Court House, Va.
November 25, 1862

Dear Will,

Your letter of November 13th was received yesterday and you can be sure I was

---

13. Osgood is writing about his cousin Sam Sumner, uncle Edwin Vose Sumner and Colonel Teall, who married Edwin's daughter, Sarah Sumner, a local Syracuse historian and woman suffragist.

very glad to hear how pleasantly you were situated. Well you had had rather a tough time of it so far in this war and I think you deserve to enjoy yourself. My compliments to Moreley and Rodgers and tell Moreley that when we used to have such violent discussions in the bank in regard to the "conduct" of the war that I hardly realized that we should assist in "conducting" it.

I had a short and quite unexpected visit from Sam and Colonel Teall yesterday. Sam is about ten miles from here and expecting there would be a big fight. He came over principally to tell me that as soon as I received a commission his father desired him to say that he would appoint me additional Aid-de-camp on his staff. So hurrah for the Tracy family for I am sure of the commission but don't mention it to anyone for if Colonel Titus should hear of it he would never give me a commission as he is "prejudiced" in regard to staff appointments. Sam will teach me how to ride and taking it altogether I think it will be a very "big" thing. I shall write to mother about it for fear that hearing of it through the Sumners she might speak of it when it would get to the ears of the powers to be. I saw your letter to Colonel Titus and will take care of the commission when it comes. We have not received any official notification of your appointment yet but I presume you have one and that the commission will arrive in due time.

We have been having some pretty cold nights lately but Church, Brower and myself sleep in the Adj't's tent and by "clubbing" blankets manage to keep very comfortable. We are in the left Grand Division and in the present position of affairs in the rear and about ten miles from Fredericksburg where I imagine we shall remain here until Sumner gets across the river. Well take good care of yourself and don't let that spirited Government horse throw you.

Camp 122d N.Y.S.V.
near Stafford Court House, Va
December 3, 1862

Dear Mother,

Marching orders have come at last. We have been notified to hold ourselves in readiness to move at daybreak. It is rumored that our destination is Belle Plains at the mouth of Potomac Creek. Everybody is pleased at the prospect of moving and if it is time that we are going to Belle Plains it rather confirms the idea that we are going by the way transports but I suppose you will have learned from the papers before this reaches you. Remember we are in Newton's Division, Smith's Corps, Franklin Division.

Yours affy
Os

Near Fredericksburg, Va.
Sunday, December 4, 1862
10:00 A.M.

Dear Mother,

We crossed the river day before yesterday but did not actually participate in the engagement yesterday but while supporting a battery experienced quite a lively shelling but only two men in the regiment were wounded.

I am acting Lieutenant in Andy's Company and only wait for an opportunity to send the appointment off to Albany and when my appointment is confirmed as of course it will be I shall be all right but until that time please don't say anything about the "staff" appointment until all is fixed. Will you have time to go to Mrs. Smith's and assure her that up to this time Andy is safe and well.

Last night Wells[14] and myself slept under one blanket very comfortably as the night was very mild. My "darky" I left in the rear in the A.M. and he did not get up with my blankets waiting for orders. Andy told him if it occurred a second time there would be a "shooting match" with him for a "taret."

I received a host of letters night before last of all dates from yours of the 20th to George's of December 7. George said if he was given to drinking that he would get drunk immediately if he heard of my promotion so tell him to begin immediately.

I think I shall like my new place very much. The Colonel is very well disciplined and everything works harmoniously. From the coolness with which our boys stood the severe shelling yesterday, I do not fear but that our regiment will behave well when we actually get into the fight.

A person can form no idea of the number of troops here without seeing them and I can advise that I took all the "airs" off that I might be disposed to assume on taking my new position when I discovered that a 2nd Lieutenant wasn't of so much account after all. Frank Lester has been made a Captain and Guy Gotches a Lieutenant. Captain Walpole returned yesterday A.M. He is looking quite well again although not very strong yet but you never saw a fellow so delighted to get back and his "Co." seemed equally pleased to get him back. There is a rumor that Slocum's Corps crossed last night and confirmation of the fact that they were coming Willie sent word to me by one of our boys who has been in hospital at Harper's Ferry that he should be here soon. I shall keep a bright lookout for him.

I am writing this A.M. under the disadvantages of Marie's lover. Don't forget to have Jim go and see Mrs. Smith.

Good Bye
your boy
Os

14. Herbert S. Wells enrolled at twenty-four years of age on August 6, 1862, at Baldwinsville, to serve three years. He was mustered in as second lieutenant, Company A, on August 28, 1862, then as first lieutenant, Company G, December 3, 1862.

P.S. If there should be an engagement today don't worry about me for we are in the reserve and probably shall not participate. I enclose a letter received in reference to Louis Ennis.

Camp 122d Reg't N.Y.V.S.

December 7, 1862

Dear Mother,

I cannot give our exact location but we are between the Rappahannock and Potomac Rivers about ten miles east of the railroad from Acquia Creek to Fredericsburg. How long we are to remain here is a little uncertain but the Adjutant General of the Brigade told Church that we might remain here a week. We arrived here day before yesterday about noon just about the time that a rain and snow storm arrived. I must admit that it looked a little dubious as three or four of us stood under a piece of shelter tent around the fire waiting for our tents up with a good fire in front and our "darkey" made us a bed about two feet from the ground and as Brower Church and myself sleep together it gives us plenty of blankets. Last night was very cold and although I slept as warm as the "toast" I am so fond of yet I could not help thinking how some of the poor boys must have suffered.

The five resignations have been accepted and but one of the vacancies has been filled as yet. The orderly sergeant of Co H has been made 2nd Lieutenant. This is not a desirable position and the Colonel told Church that he was going to give me a commission and don't get the military committed to doing anything for since Willie's appointment they are terribly down on "home" interference in the matter of appointments but leave the matter in my hands and it will come out all right. The appointments will be decided on in a day or two and I will let you know the result immediately.

I received that package of stockings last evening and am very much obliged to you. They are just what I wanted and fit me nicely. Church is quite envious and if you see his wife next Sunday I wish you would tell her where you got them and say that he would like a couple of pairs sent by mail.

Will you also say to my friends Nell and Marie that the promised description of the grand "entertainment" has not yet reached me and I hope they are not going to forget me.[15]

We heard rather directly last night that our forces were crossing the Rappahannock seven miles below Fredericsburg. If this be true our present position would indicate that we are about to follow suit and on to Richmond.

The roads in some places are getting very bad and the poor mules suffer in the absolute necessity of getting provisions to the army for soldiers must eat if all the mules and horses get killed in supplying them.

---

15. This line suggests that Osgood was wary his friends would be moving on without him, a prevailing concern among soldiers.

We ie. our "mess" has got so fond of "hardtack" in the various ways in which we cook it that we think of giving "hardtack" parties after the war is over inviting only "veterans."

And the 51st are going to do guard duty again are they? Well tell Jim I trust that he will be as well "rationed" as I was while on duty at Camp Monroe.

Do you remember the day you and Lucy[16] arrived with that supply of provisions. We thought that was something like real soldiering but I wish that the Corps boys could have awoke down here this morning. Day before yesterday we ran across John Dow on the march. He at present has charge of the ammunition train of Brook's Division which is in their Corps. He thought it was a little the roughest teaming he had seen.

We heard yesterday of Dr. Didama's[17] being in Washington but unable to get down here as the orders in regard to passes are very severe.

I told all the resigned officers that they must stop into the canal office and see Jim and I trust one out of the number will remember their promise.

If I don't get an opportunity to send this today I will "enlarge" it to-morrow.

Love to All
Yours Lovingly
Osgood

Camp 122d Reg't N.Y.S.V.
near Belle Plain Landing, Va.
December 9, 1862

Dear Mother,

Your letter of the third was received this A.M. and I hasten to assure you that my cheerfulness is not assumed but that on the contrary I have been in the best of spirits ever since I left home and though I should not object at any time to "drop in" for an evening yet I never have been the least bit sick of my bargain.

We have just received the orders to hold ourselves in readiness to march in the morning with three days cooked rations in the mens' haversacks twenty extra rounds of cartridges to be distributed to the men bringing their supply to sixty rounds (the fighting standard). I should not write you such startling intelligence if I were not aware that ere this reaches you, you will know through the papers what the result of this "scare" is and furthermore that we have had so many "scares" I have no faith in them, but I think myself that it may be that we are to cross the river below

---

16. Lucy Putnam Phelps was Osgood's cousin.

17. Henry Darwin Didama (1823–1905) was a doctor and prominent citizen in Syracuse. He relocated to that city in 1851, five years after his graduation from the Albany Medical School. During his life, he served as dean and professor of the Medical College in Syracuse, and in 1894 he was elected trustee at large of Syracuse University, and he held the post until his death. "Henry Darwin Didama MD Collection," *New York Heritage Digital Collections,* https://nyheritage.org/collections/henry-darwin-didama-md-collection.

Fredericsburg and "flank" the confounded rebels, and providing we shall not get "flanked" ourselves we may date my next from considerably nearer Richmond.

I lay our movement entirely to Captain Brower. He finished his log house to-day and it is always a sure sign of marching orders when he gets fixed. We have got our Head Quarters tents fixed up in nice style and Andy Smith's street looks like a larger garden. I would not believe it possible that a person could live so comfortably out of doors in such cold weather but we have had an evergreen fence about the tents which kept off the wind and roaring good fire in front of the tent and I bid defiance to wind and weather.

There has been nothing more about the appointment yet and I do not think there will be until we make a little longer stop but my chances are first rate I think. Love to all and tell the children I am going to write them a good long letter "one of these days" and with much love for yourself

I remain,
Your Dutiful Son
Osgood

December 16, 1862
Near Fredericksburg
North side of Rappahannock

Dear Mother,

Perhaps my letter had better have been more appropriately dated "Hammons Landing" for we have made another change of "base." Of course, I feel a little disheartened that we should have been compelled to fall back across the river but with my happy faculty of believing that all is for the best I shall wait patiently for the result but as I shall probably have time to-day to give you a full account of the last few days proceedings. Last Thursday morning we marched from our camp near Belle Plain Landing[18] arriving on the bank of the Rappahannock about noon. All that afternoon we lay in field, witnessed the bombardment of Fredericsburg and the rebel batteries on that side of the river. The heaviest of our batteries were on a high bluff just behind us and all the shells they fired passed overhead, perfectly harmless of course but it served to get us used to the "whirr" of them.

Our forces commenced crossing about 4 p.m. and we got started just at sunset but after getting down to the bridge were ordered back and slept in a cornfield that night slightly muddy. The next morning the appointments of which I wrote you on Sunday were announced and we crossed the river early taking a position

---

18. Belle Plains Landing, Virginia, was a steamboat landing and unincorporated settlement on the south bank of the Potomac Creek off of the Potomac River, in Stafford County, Virginia. In the early nineteenth century, Belle Plains served as landing for steamboats to Washington, DC. See "The Army of the Potomac: The Flying Column. Potomac Creek and Its Landings," *New York Times*, Feb. 22, 1863.

but a little distance from the bank where we remained very quietly all day (but one or two shells bursting near us). The next morning (Saturday) we were ordered forward and placed as a support to a battery. There was considerable fighting going on all day to the left and right of us but very little in front until just before sunset when the rebel batteries opened up on the one we were supporting and didn't the shells come, whew! It is needless to say how readily we obeyed the orders to lay down. I received a position next to Major Davis who being quite a fleshy man I was satisfied would form a good "earthwork."

The "old soldiers" said that for the time it lasted (about three quarters of an hour) it was as severe as any they ever heard but "old soldiers" are not always reliable especially when talking to "recruits." It was severe enough to suit me at all events but fortunately but one man was wounded and the piece of shell that entered his thigh tore off part of the collar of the overcoat of a man next to him without injuring him in the slightest. This I know to be true. I could relate any number of marvelous escapes that I heard of. We had lots of fun joking each other about the alacrity with which we assumed our positions. Andy and Captain Walpole were standing up talking when the first shell burst near us and you should have seen them drop. Andy says a person could not have inserted a piece of paper between himself and the ground and insists that Captain Walpole got his hands well down into the ground and then drew himself in. Captain Walpole returned from his sick leave that morning and it was rather doubtful which was more pleased—he to get back or the company to have him back. He is quite well again and has stood the fatigue of the last few days remarkably well.

But to return to my history, Sunday passed very quietly. Monday we were "supporting" a battery but if it is no harder work supporting a family I shall get married immediately upon my return. I like our officers very much. The lt. colonel is going to make a very good officer and I am very agreeably impressed. They are all very kind to me and my tent, or post, is a very pleasant one and I don't regret in the least that I now I am not a Lieut. If you will direct to 122d reg't N. Y. Vols. Cochrane's Division Army of the Potomac, I will get your letters. Love to Jim.

Good bye
Yours affect.
Os

P.S. Send me some postage stamps. I have had no opportunity to get any. Today is the first quiet day we have had since we left home and the men are getting the rest which they really need. P.S.P.S. Excuse erasures and blunders as I have written this while the Adj't and Major have been discussing some question in a very animated manner and there are four others talking.

Camp near Fredericksburg, VA
Dec. 17, 1862 p.m.

Dear Mother,

Yesterday afternoon Frank, Andrew and myself were startled by the cry "get out of that tent," which we did as quick as possible and not any too soon for a tree which somebody had carelessly felled took down the back part of our tent and barely escaped "squashing us." You may imagine there was some lively scrambling and Andy who was in the back part of the tent was out first as he went over me I thought I was hit sure. There is a rumor this p.m.. that we are about to move again but where I know not. This last move is said to be a "feint." I only wish I could see it in that light.

I wish Jim would see Allen Monroe and tell him that having been recommended by Col. Titus for a 2d lieutenancy in this regiment he would use his influence and have the appointment confirmed and my commission forwarded to me. Good-Bye and may God bless you.

Your boy
Os

General Sumner's Head Qrs
December 19, 1862

Dear Mother,

Yesterday while we were changing camp Col. Teall came up with us he having been quite anxious to know whether or not we participated in the fight and was determined to find us. He invited me to come over to see them at the earliest opportunity and accordingly this morning I obtained leave borrowed Frank Lester's horse, a decent looking coat (straps and all) and came over, and he and I discussed the question last night whether it would not be more "stylish" to mount Meosco (our darkey) upon our pack horses and bring him along as groom—to fully appreciate it you should see both horse and servant—but I finally concluded not to. General Slocum, Sam and I found, had gone to General Burnside's Hd Qrs but I found Col. Teall who was very polite and having supplied me with the late papers I learned the first news about the great battle. Col. Teall says that a consultation is going on this morning as to whether or not the army shall go into Winter Quarters and that it is rumored that the General and his staff will go to St. Louis, that the General will have command of the West but he will probably write more fully to-night.

The General's Head Qrs are in a fine brick house just opposite Fredericsburg and the room in which I am sitting is as pleasant as one can imagine especially after camp "life" experience—a pleasant fire in the grate, marble mantels and wash stand, comfortable arm chairs and in fact all the luxuries of life.

Slocum's command has not arrived yet, Co. Teall tells me. I thought he could not be here or I should have seen Willie before this. I presume now that it will be a little doubtful whether he comes.

I see that the "World" has a terribly severe article against Lincoln in connection with this recent battle. I heard all of the firing and could see some of the guns on Saturday but did not have the faintest idea that such a terrible engagement was going on.

I will write again in a day or two and let you know what further transpired during my visit, and while waiting for Sam to return will write myself once more to the papers.

Good-Bye Love to all

Yours affc

Os

P.S. If you want to hear of the doings of our brigade I think you had better get a Herald occasionally as one of their correspondents stays at General Cochrane's Hd Qrs.

CHAPTER THREE

Long Winter, Short Furlough

December 21, 1862–March 6, 1863

It is very funny how we get this life and our "home life" mixed up in our dreams.
—Osgood Vose Tracy, January 1, 1863

⚜ More than twelve thousand Union soldiers lay dead or wounded on the field at Fredericksburg as the winter snows finally arrived, turning roadways to mud and grinding Ambrose Burnside's subsequent attempt to flank Lee's army to a halt in what newspapers throughout the north termed the "Mud March." Two weeks later, Abraham Lincoln took pen to paper to address the men of the Army of the Potomac. "Although you were not successful," he wrote, "the attempt was not an error, nor the failure other than an accident. The courage with which you, in an open field, maintained the contest against an entrenched foe, and the consummate skill and success with which you crossed and re-crossed the river, in face of the enemy, show that you possess all the qualities of a great army, which will yet give victory to the cause of the country and of popular government."[1] The optimism with which the commander in chief wrote belied what could only have been a looming sense of defeat. Failures by the army to capitalize on the victory at Antietam and outspoken contempt for the Emancipation Proclamation in towns and cities across the North were cause for concern. One Irish soldier in the Eighty-Eighth New York noted in poignant terms that might well have summed up the broader spirit of the army in the wake of Burnside's unmitigated disaster: "We are slaughtered like sheep, and no result by defeat."[2] Republican losses in the

1. Abraham Lincoln to the Army of the Potomac, Dec. 22, 1862.
2. Capt. William J. Nagel, Eighty-Eighth New York in Susannah Ural Bruce, *The Harp and the Eagle: Irish-American Volunteers and the Union Army, 1861–1865* (New York: New York Univ. Press, 2005), 134.

1862 elections saw Democrats gain thirty-two seats in Congress and seven in the Senate. These results suggested a growing frustration with both the war effort and the president's political decisions.[3]

Despite this, as the armies settled into their winter camps, with the end seeming far away, Osgood and his comrades were rather optimistic. The 122nd New York avoided the slaughter on the fields of Fredericksburg that December, playing a supporting role in yet another bloody engagement. The soldiers were also fortunate to miss out on Burnside's failed "Mud March" in the wake of Fredericksburg, sitting snuggly in newly constructed cabins while their comrades struggled through the quagmire that were the early winter dirt roads in Virginia. As the men settled in for the winter, Osgood diligently recorded his experiences. His correspondence illuminates a number of themes, from the perspective of both a soldier and an observer of the larger war. His letters show the rigors and routines of camp life interspersed with news from home and abroad—though most allude to a continued sense of enthusiasm for army life. Because of family connections, Osgood was keenly aware of the broader scope of the war, which he often discussed in his letters, providing important commentary on the issues plaguing the nation that cold winter. Yet, while the larger confluence of events swirled around him, Osgood remained intimately connected to his home and, especially, Nell, whom he saw in Washington while on brief leave from his regiment and continued to court, in spite of growing anxiety that she would choose another suitor.

> Camp 122d Reg't N.Y.V.
> near Fredericsburg, Va
> December 21, 1862

Dear Mother,

To take up the account of my visit to Gen'l Sumner where I dropped it. Sam and his father returned about 4 o'clock. I had the pleasure of dining with them and General Prince[4] whom perhaps you remember as having been taken pris-

3. James Oakes, *Freedom National: The Destruction of Slavery in the United States, 1861–1865* (New York: W. W. Norton, 2013), 533–34; T. Stephen Whitman, *Antietam 1862: Gateway to Emancipation* (Santa Barbara, CA: Praeger, 2012), 118–19.

4. Brig. Gen. Henry Prince (1811–1892) served with the Fourth US Infantry during the Seminole and Mexican Wars, during which he was seriously wounded, and was then commissioned brigadier general of Volunteers August 28, 1862. He assumed command of the Second Brigade, Second Division, Second Corps, Army of Virginia on July 16, then took command of the Second Division on August 9, for the Battle of Cedar Mountain. He was captured and held until December. Following the Battle of Gettysburg, he led the Second Division, Third Corps, Army of the Potomac. He was mustered out of volunteer service April 30, 1866. He was promoted to lieutenant colonel of regulars in the paymaster's department March 3, 1877, and retired on December 31, 1879. Depressed over his ill health and pain from Civil War wounds, he died by suicide, in London, England, on August 19, 1892. "Henry Prince," American Civil War History Research Database, http://civilwardata.com/active/hdsquery.dll?SoldierHistory?U&144.

oner in Popes campaign.[5] When we were about through dinner, the congressional committee on the conduct of the war who had been holding an investigation in regard to this last battle came in upon us.[6] They having quartered themselves on the Gen'l for the night but they kindly brought their "rations" and cooks. Senator Wade[7] was the chairman and Senator Chandler,[8] Mr. Odell[9] and several other members of Congress made up the balance. Senator Wilson[10] was also there but not as a member of the committee.

Three or four of them occupied the floor of the General's room and Sam and I slept on the floor of the bathroom adjoining. It was quite rich to hear the Hon. Com. talk about "roughing" it—sleeping on the floor of a comfortable house with a fire burning in the grate. I wish I could have put them into a shelter tent for one night.

Some of the Generals aids were slightly "wrathy" at giving up their rooms and one of them who supposed he had given up his room to a lady who was there taking care of a wounded brother and had accordingly got out some clean towels, when he found the M C's were going to occupy it, vowed he would send his serv't after them and all his bedding.

The next morning the Com. were to have another session and I had the opportunity of seeing General Hooker.[11] He is a very fine looking man. About ten Sam and I rode over to see Win. at Stoneman's[12] head qrs.

We found him living very comfortably in a tent and after spending an hour or

5. This is likely a reference to Prince's capture at the Battle of Cedar Mountain in August 1862. See Robert R. Krick, *Stonewall Jackson at Cedar Mountain* (Chapel Hill: Univ. of North Carolina Press, 1990), 286–88.

6. Congress organized the Joint Committee on the Conduct of the War in December 1861 to oversee all aspects of the Union war effort. Osgood is referring to this committee's investigation into the Union defeat at Fredericksburg and, in particular, fears among some Republicans, that civil and military support of the ousted George McClellan had intervened in the campaign to undermine Ambrose Burnside's efforts. For a concise overview of this committee, see Bruce Tap, "The Joint Committee on the Conduct of the War," *Essential Civil War Curriculum,* accessed Oct. 27, 2021, https://www.essential-civilwarcurriculum.com/the-joint-committee-on-the-conduct-of-the-war.html. For further reading, see Brian Holden Reid, "Historians and the Joint Committee on the Conduct of the War, 1861–1865," *Civil War History* 38 (Sept. 1992): 319–41, and Bruce Tap, *Over Lincoln's Shoulder: The Committee on the Conduct of the War* (Lawrence: Univ. Press of Kansas, 1998).

7. Osgood is referring to Radical Republican senator Benjamin Franklin Wade of Ohio.

8. This is Republican senator Zachariah Chandler of Michigan.

9. This is New York representative Moses Odell.

10. This is Senator Henry Wilson of Massachusetts.

11. Gen. Joseph Hooker was given command of the Army of the Potomac after Burnside was relieved following Fredericksburg. For information regarding Hooker and his role in the 1862–63 campaigns in Northern Virginia see Edward G. Longacre, *Commanders of Chancellorsville* (Nashville: Rutledge Hill Press, 2005); Stephen W. Sears, *Chancellorsville* (New York: Houghton Mifflin, 1996); Gary W. Gallagher, *Chancellorsville: The Battle and Its Aftermath* (Chapel Hill: Univ. of North Carolina Press, 1996).

12. Gen. George Stoneman was a Union cavalryman. See Ezra J. Warner, *Generals in Blue: Lives of Union Commanders* (Baton Rouge: Louisiana State Univ. Press, 2006).

two very pleasantly partaking of a very nice lunch we started to come back when Gen'l Stoneman called out to Sam to hold on as he was going over so I had to ride back rather faster than was gratified to my inexperience for I felt delicate about suggesting to Gen'l S, as I had to ride "slower." After remaining a little while I started for home having had a very pleasant visit. The last thing Gen'l S said was to let him know just as soon as my commission comes so if you have not will you be kind enough to ask Mr. Monroe to get it confirmed and forwarded if possible before Gov. Monroe retires. From their Hd Qrs you can see the rebel camps and fortifications very easily and the rebel pickets are on the opposite side of the river.

From what I can learn nothing is decided as yet in regard to the winter campaign.

Cap't Kent[13] arrived to-day and brought me a very nice pair of stockings and I am now very well provided for in that respect. Slocums Corps had not arrived Gen'l S. told me.

Good-Bye

Yours affy Os

Camp 122d Reg't New York Vols.

near Fredericsburg,Va.

December 24/62

Dear Mother,

Yours of the 19th was received today. I don't think I could have telegraphed to you and even if I could I perhaps should not have thought the occasion warranted it as I did not realize until a day or two afterwards what a severe battle it has been although the heaviest fighting could not have been more than three miles from us.

You ask if our soldiers are poorly clad. The government provides the best of everything but sometimes there is a little delay in getting things and if you were to see the number of soldiers you wonder not that a few were occasionally neglected but that the Gov't was able to supply half. To-day we received the knapsacks belonging to the reg't which the men were obliged to leave behind when they left Washington. as a natural consequence, some of the articles left in them were missing and we had a great time distributing them. Quite a large number of bed ticks[14] came up in our company box and we secured two for our tent which I had filled with boughs, and they are fully equal to spring mattresses and I have no doubt but that I shall be able to spend Christmas with you in my dreams to-night

---

13. Noah B. Kent, age thirty, enrolled in the 122nd New York State Volunteers on August 19, 1862, at Syracuse to serve three years. He was mustered in as captain, Company K on August 28, 1862, commissioned with that rank on September 10, with the rank made effective from August 19 the same year. He was discharged October 2, 1863.

14. *Bed ticks* was a Civil War–period term for a mattress, likely of cotton ticking straw. Ticking was a tightly woven, heavy, cotton fabric, usually blue, grey or brown striped.

which will be the next best thing reality, but never mind mother, I shall only enjoy it all the more next year for being deprived of it this year. I wish I could enclose something for a present for you but there is a scarcity of stores hereabouts. If there was a jewelers near here I don't know but that I might be tempted to sacrifice my whiskers and have them manufactured into a hair breast pin for you. Wouldn't that be "touching."

We have been intending to build for several days but Col. Titus does not like to have the trees about us cut down as we may be here for some time and they will serve as shelter but we have got the promise of a wagon for day after to-morrow and we are going to get enough logs to build a respectable house. We purchased some buckwheat flour the other day I regret to say our cooks have not succeeded in making them taste exactly like "home" yet.

We expect Steve Estes[15] over to spend the day to-morrow and news has just come that 200 men from our reg't will have to go out on picket to-morrow and I should laugh if our company should be detailed after Andy had made all his arrangements. I was at Cap't Walpole's quarter the other evening to hear some singing and I can tell you it was quite a picture to see the group about the camp fire. He has several very good singers and they sang some very beautiful negro melodies.

I have gotten to be great friends (as usual) with a very nice young fellow in the reg't by the name of Guy Gotches. He came out as commissary Sergeant and did his duty so well that the Col. nominated him as Lieutenant at the same time that he did me (this last time). He is now acting as 2d Lieut. in Co. F and when I wrote W. Lansing the other day in reference to getting my appointment confirmed I asked him to speak a good word for Guy. He used to be a clerk in E. F. Rice's Dry goods store and is the first of "genus" I ever had any respect for.

The boys have been sure considerate about my being "run out" again by my brother on the strength of that rumor published in the Journal that Wm. G. Tracy had been appointed 1st Lieut. Co.

By the way, I have seen or heard nothing from Will although I have written him several times and sent him his commission. If you have any "correspondence" with him will you be kind enough to present my compliments to him and say that I should be pleased to hear from him.

I have purchased a cavalry overcoat. They are longer and have a much larger cape than the infantry overcoat. I shall have it lined at the first opportunity and it will make a very comfortable garment.

In regard to that shelling to which we were exposed on that Saturday I am probably not as good a judge as Col T, and perhaps my modesty subdued my description.

15. Stephen A. Estes, twenty-two years of age, enlisted on April 23, 1861, at Syracuse. He was mustered in as private, Company A, on May 13, 1861, to serve two years, then promoted sergeant-major, June 15, 1861.

Regretting, once more, my dear mother that my only present this year can be only the renewed assurances of my dearest love and respect for you who have been both father and mother to us boys and praying that your life may be spared for many years to come. I once more wish you a Merry Christmas and remain

Your dutiful son

Os

Love to Jim and tell him he owes this letter now. P.S. Please have Jim send me a N. Y. draft for enclosed and have concluded to make myself a Christmas present.

Camp 122d Reg't New York Vols

near Fredericksburg, Va.

Dec 27/62

Dear Mother,

We have got a house with a "fireplace" in it and I think if you could drop in and see how comfortable Wells[16] and myself look as we sit writing at our table you would feel perfectly easy about me. We got moved in yesterday and I think it must have had a sort of "house" influence about for I spent last night at home in my dreams at least and if I was inclined to believe in "spiritualism" I should say that the "spirit" left the "form" for the night and went home on a visit.

We had quite a pleasant time on Christmas. Maj. Root[17] and Capts' Randall,[18] Behan[19] and Estes from the 12th[20] were here and took dinner with us. Andy got a couple of ducks and persuaded a "secesh" female nearby to roast them for us. We had some new white bed ticks come to us the day before and accordingly indulged in the luxury of a table cloth and Frank Lester had about half a dozen fancy glace covered dishes which he found somewhere which we filled with various articles and which helped to "set off" the table wonderfully.

Cap't Lester rec'd a letter from Mrs. May last evening announcing the shipment of three boxes containing mittens to him.[21] I trust they will soon arrive for

16. Lt. Herbert S. Wells was a member of Company G.

17. George H. Root, age twenty-two, enlisted May 13, 1861, at Syracuse. He was mustered in as sergeant major, field and staff, the same date, to serve three months but was discharged for disability, June 18, 1861, at Washington, DC. New York State Military Museum and Veterans Research Center, Division of Military and Naval Affairs, State of New York, website, https://museum.dmna.ny.gov/.

18. Charles B. Randall was a member of Companies K and G, field and staff. New York State Military Museum and Veterans Research Center, Division of Military and Naval Affairs, State of New York, website, https://museum.dmna.ny.gov/.

19. Thomas J. Behan, twenty-four years of age, enlisted April 30, 1861, at Syracuse. He was mustered in as second lieutenant on August 3, 1861, then as first lieutenant on September 21, the same year. He was transferred to Co. A on February 3, 1862, and mustered out with company May 17, 1863, at Elmira, New York.

20. Osgood is referring to the Twelfth New York Infantry, mustered on May 13, 1861, mustered out May 17, 1863.

21. The Reverend Joseph May coordinated soldier relief efforts such as the distribution of mittens knit by local Syracuse women.

although the weather for the last week has been remarkably mild and pleasant yet we are liable at anytime to have cold, disagreeable weather when men would suffer sadly for many of them have nothing to wear on their hands.

It is astonishing how our teams have to eat any and everything. Yesterday Wells got some onions and we had them boiled for supper and I who never would have thought of touching them at home made quite a supper of them. If Willie's experience is the same, we shall not be troubled with as great a variety of tastes at our family table hereafter as formerly.

Rumors of moving are again current but whether it is to be merely a change of camp to enable us to get more wood or whether to fall back nearer supplies is not fully decided. The "latest" is that we are going back to Washington to do "provost & garrison" duty but "I don't see it." I must say however if Winter Quarters has been decided upon I should have no decided objection to Washington.

From reading the testimony taken before the war committee I am induced to believe that the non-arrival of those pontoons was owing to neglect of duty by the authorities at Washington.[22] I think the country ought to thank General Sumner for persuading General Burnside not to renew the attack on Sunday for I believe that it would have been but the repetition of Saturday's fight with perhaps more fatal results and we the left wing would have been engaged and perhaps the 122d might have suffered as badly as some of the other reg'ts who were in Saturday's fight.

Yours of the 22d was rec'd yesterday morning and although one day too late it served very nicely for a Christmas "present." In regard to my changeableness about asking the influence of the war committee I would say in explanation that I did not wish them to do anything until the Colonel had decided where to put me and that having been done I wrote you to get their influence to have his appointment confirmed. I also wrote to Lansing and I have no doubt it will be all right. Willie wrote me that he rec'd a note from Lansing asking if Gov. Morgan[23] could do anything more for him before he went out. He seems disposed to go more for us than any of our couriers. I am glad Marie called and now that the engagement is "out" I wish you would call there and see how nicely she keeps house.

I was very much surprised when Geo. wrote me that Northrup and Eliza Fitch[24] . . . for although but a little acquainted with him yet I should not have

22. As George C. Rable notes in *Fredericksburg! Fredericksburg!* (Chapel Hill: Univ. of North Carolina Press, 2002), part of Gen. Ambrose Burnside's plan at Fredericksburg relied on the pontoon bridges with which to cross the Rappahannock River. These were delayed, and Burnside, who "presumed the pontoons would arrive shortly," delayed crossing the Rappahannock, allowing Lee to consolidate his forces in and around the city (81).

23. Edwin D. Morgan, Chair of Republican National Committee (1856–64), twenty-third governor of New York (1858—62) and US Senator (1863–69). See "Gov. Edwin Denison Morgan," *National Governors Association,* https://www.nga.org/governor/edwin-denison-morgan.

24. Eliza Fitch (1842–1914) married prominent Syracuse lawyer Ansel Judd Northrup in 1863. "Northrup, Ansel Judd," Charles Elliott Fitch, *Encyclopedia of Biography of New York,* 5 vols. (New York: American Historical Society, 1916), 4:180.

thought him suited to Eliza's "taste." His brother Jud, I got quite well acquainted with while the reg't was organizing and I liked him very much. He, by the way, is quite devoted, Col. Dwight tells me, to Mattie Gifford—and she you know was my "first love" which, of course, adds an additional interest.

I am in a bad "fix" about Johnny Wilkinson.[25] I had neglected writing to him for some time and after his father's death I strangely forgot to write and now that I have neglected it so long I hardly know what to do. I am ashamed to write now but yet I can't see how I shall benefit the matter by waiting.

I wish I could make New Year's calls in Syracuse and I think they might be few and not very fashionable.

Part of our regiment are on "picket" on the banks of the river and I understand they carry on considerable conversations with the rebel pickets and I heard they sent some whiskey over on a plank.[26]

Wishing you a "happy New Years" though I presume you would hardly thank me if I added Widow McGinnis' wish "May you see a thousand."

Yours lovingly,
Os

Near Fredericksburg, Virginia
January 1, 1863

Dear Mother,

A happy New Year to you and I wish some good spirit could make my wish audible in your ear as you lay asleep perchance dreaming of me for the New Year has hardly begun (it is but a little after one). I am on as officer of the guard to-night. We have no guard house here but fortunately our tent is but a few feet from the guard station and I accordingly made my "house" headquarters and with a fire in the fireplace. Lieut. Wells sweetly sleeping I sit as comfortable as you please.

I rec'd your letter of the 20th to-night. I was very much amused at the account of the exploits of Cochrane's Brigade as given by the Tribune only regretting to spoil so fine an account by saying that we did not cross the river that night but

---

25. Joshua Forman Wilkinson (1840–1889) was the son of John Wilkinson (1798–1862), who gave Syracuse its name, was the city's first postmaster. The elder Wilkinson gave railroad passes to fugitive slaves wishing to flee the area. Reverend May, an abolitionist, led his funeral service, and Wilkinson was buried in Oakwood Cemetery. John Forman enrolled September 3, 1862, at Syracuse to serve three years. He was mustered in as captain Company D, September 17, 1862. "Forman," was named for Joshua Forman, founder of Syracuse. Forman's father was John Wilkinson, Syracuse's first postmaster. Forman served as captain in the 149th New York Regiment. *Syracuse Daily Standard,* Sept. 20, 1862; "Wilkinson, John," *Encyclopedia of Biography of New York,* 115.

26. Soldier fraternization, which occurred throughout the war, has been the topic of recent historical inquiry. See, for example, Lauren K. Thompson, "Escaping the Mechanism: Soldier Fraternization during the Siege of Petersburg," *Civil War History* 63 (Dec. 2017): 349–76, and Lauren K. Thompson, *Friendly Enemies: Soldier Fraternization throughout the American Civil War* (Lincoln: Univ. of Nebraska Press, 2020).

slept in a wet cornfield and crossed the next morning in a very practical manner inasmuch as other troops had crossed the night before and cleared the way for us. If I had only known of this article I might have told a much larger story myself.

We have been expecting that we should move to-day but last night marching orders came for the whole reg't to go off on fatigue duty at 8 in the am at which time I am relieved but having been on duty for twenty-four hours I shall be excused from duty the rest of the day and accordingly shall have a nice quiet time all alone, for it is has not arrived yet but I presume it will come through alright as I have been very fortunate in regard to my mail matter, not having lost a single letter that I am aware of.

Frank Lester and myself have rec'd several letters from Mr. May[27] announcing the shipment of boxes to us. To-day Frank wrote fully to him in reference to them there is considerable difficulty in getting the boxes from Washington.

Last night I received a letter from a young lady in Fayetteville announcing the shipment of a box of articles for Co. C to my care by the advice of Rev. Mr. May, as none of the present officers of Co. C are from Fayetteville, but as Frank Lester now commands this company I shall hand this box over to him when I get it. I also received a very pleasant letter from Willie dated at Fairfax on the 25th. He was still a little anxious to make a journey home but I have not much hopes of his doing it, however if some of the rumors we hear be true we may fall back to his neighborhood. Public opinion is divided as to whether the coming movement is to be an advance or retreat. I think we shall fall back for I don't see how an advance could take place now.

Col. Teall made us a short call the other day. I sent word to Sam to come over and spend New Year's with me.

And so Jim is working for Alf. Wilkinson.[28] Well of all funny ideas this struck me as the funniest that could be thought of. I trust Alf will act decent enough for Jim to remain with him for it will give him a chance to learn something about the banking business.

I see railroad stocks are very high now. Does not engineering ... frighten for they certainly will begin building so as to bring them back to their old place below par.

I could have partaken of your oyster soup and chicken salad and I am sure I should have found no fault with the cooks although I sometimes think I shall be very particular about eating when I get back to civilization once more.

It is very funny how we get this life and our "home life" mixed up in our dreams. The other night Frank said he dreamed that he was standing on Coggswells steps

---

27. Prominent abolitionist and Syracuse resident Reverend Samuel Joseph May (1797–1871). May was born in Boston and the brother of Abigail May Alcott.

28. Alfred Wilkinson was a banker in Syracuse. See Peter Morris et al., *Base Ball Pioneers, 1850–1870: The Clubs and Players Who Spread the Sport Nationwide* (Jefferson, NC: McFarland, 2012), 76.

and seeing a woman pass with furs, he immediately wished to secure one as one does here.

It is quite a wonder to me, who am always so ready to go to sleep that I manage to worry through the night but the Sergeant and myself have been making candy and with reading and writing I shall manage to use up the night.

I have just finished Jean Valjean being obliged to skip the intermediate two between Cosette[29] and this did not make it quite so interesting. However anything would be interesting here [where] our literature consists of newspapers, tactics and army regulations. Have you been able to find that novel you liked so much in pamphlet form yet? When you do please send it to me.

I shall feel a strong desire to get to Washington after the Sedgwick's arrive but I fear it will not be gratified.

Among other rumors in circulation is one that we are to do provost and garrison duty at Washington but as Moore Summer's in writing to the Standard mentions the same rumor in connection with the 149th I presume it is a prevailing epidemic throughout the army.

Tell Jim that I rec'd his letter also to-night and am much obliged to him. It was just the kind of a letter a fellow wants from home full of news. I will write to him next time.

Well good night or good morning rather & believe me

Yours affy—

Os

Camp 122d Reg't New York Vols
near Brandy Station, Va.
Jan. 3d, 1863

Dear Mother,

Yesterday I received your letter written on the 29th and one from Willie written on Christmas day. you two are the only regular correspondence I have now. George seems to have dropped me entirely.

What can induce people to having morning weddings by gas light? I always remember what a disagreeable feeling it used to be when I attended panoramas in the daytime and came out in the daylight again and I think a wedding of this kind would affect me somewhat in the same way.

New Years passed off very quietly, Lester invited Wooster and myself to dine with him but Connie and myself had accepted an invitation from Col. Dwight. The Col. gave us a very nice dinner winding up with a plum pudding which would have disgraced your table (Can I give it any higher praise?).

---

29. This is a reference to Victor Hugo's *Les Miserables* (New York: Carleton Publishing Company, 1862), which Tracy read while in the service.

I was very much pained to hear of Aunts sickness and Uncles continued illness. I do hope that I shall find them both better when I come home. By the way, I cannot learn anything definite as to when leaves of absence are again to be granted but apply to Smithy for information every time he makes his appearance.

I shall have about 6 hours in Washington and if you will send me Nell's address I will try and call, for your sake.

I am almost tempted to swear, when I think how all my old friends have deserted me—everyone either married or gone away. Well, I shall have to cultivate some new acquaintances.

Wooster just came and said that Lester and Mr. Hayes, the Tribune correspondent, were coming to dine with and proposed inasmuch as the tent is rather small that we should join with him and we furnish the dining room and he would furnish the turkey. I shall be inclined to think that young man Wooster is seeking for popularity. This entertaining correspondents in the army is decidedly suggestive.

Lt. Armstrong of Gen'l Shalers' staff died last evening after a very short illness "malignant encipela." He was a very fine fellow indeed and very popular in the Brigade.

The night before New Year's we had quite a scare, receiving an order late in the evening to be in "readiness to move, by rail, at a moment's notice." The 3rd Brigade of our Division did pack up in a rainstorm about midnight and march to Brandy Station where they took cars for Washington. I understand that they have gone to Harpers Ferry, the rebels being reported in force at Winchester. We have received no further orders and I understand that there is now no probability of our going.

We have had very cold weather for the last day or two. Yesterday morning after our fire had been going sometime the thermometer (you see we are not entirely deprived of the "luxuries" of life) stood a few degrees below the freezing point— But we soon got warmed up and were very comfortable for the rest of the day. One of our men had his feet freeze quite badly while sleeping in his tent, but as it was New Year's night I fear the poor fellow must have been drinking enough to make him stupid. To-day is much warmer.

What a jolly time Willy must have had Christmas eve at the dance at Decherd but the young rascal took away half the champaining by mentioning that they found a few "snuff sticks" on the floor after the fair ones had departed. He also writes me that his arm is steadily Improving. Sunday is always a quiet day in camp and I think I miss home more then, than at any other time. I always look back with pleasure to the hour just between daylight and darkness when we used to sit without candles and attempt to sing and only wish to-night that Willie and I could draw up our chairs on each side of you

Camp near Falmouth, Va.
January 6th, 1863

Dear Mother

I have rather neglected you for the last few days but I have been quite busy with our muster rolls and besides have those of our own company to make out I have been assisting Church to examine all for the regiment. I went out on Fatigue Duty on Friday, cutting poles to repair roads. We had but a short job to do and soon finished it.

I rec'd your letter of the 30th enclosing stamps and also one from Jim enclosing Draft for $20. We are in hopes of getting paid this month which will relieve me of the necessity of sending home for more. I have purchased a jacket for myself. It is much more comfortable than a coat and my dress coat, which I brought away from home was beginning to look a little "seedy." If I thought there was any chance of getting it I would send home for a coat, but as 9 out of 30 boxes coming to the reg't were lost or stolen between here and Aquia Landing, the other day, I have not cared about risking it. Frank Lester sent to Washington, by our sutler for the boxes Mr. May sent and I trust that he will bring them up.

I have not rec'd my commission yet nor any notification of it but having rec'd assurances from Lansing that it was all right and as I am "acting" and would not leave Andy until we can't get the company clothing acc's straightened.

There have been any quantities of rumors in circulation in regard to our movements but as yet they have proved to be but rumors. I saw the other day that Slocum's Corps was to be disbanded. I trust that would not affect Willie.

This afternoon we are having the commencement of what looks to be a steady rain storm but we have got a log house fireplace and plenty of wood who cares. George Williams (C. B's son) was over here yesterday looking well and hearty. It is said that we are to be reviewed to-morrow or next day by General Burnside but I imagine it will depend very much on the state of the weather.

Tell George I have just succeeded in getting those boots he gave me, tapped and am ready now for Virginia or any other mud. Excuse this dull letter but I thought that even a dull letter might be acceptable from

Your aff son
Osgood

Camp 122d Reg't New York Vols.
Near Falmouth, Va. Jany 10/63

Dear Mother,

It is emphatically a rainy day in camp. I have just got in having been out since seven this morning with a party building "corduroy" road but as it began raining about noon we stopped work and I can tell my log house and fireplace seemed very much like "home" coming in out of the rain.

I rec'd a letter from Willie last night dated the 5th. He hoped that I should be able to get up to Washington and kindly offered to loan me some money to purchase my outfit when I went onto Gen'l Sumners staff.

Yesterday I was over to the commissary's and weighed myself, and, you will hardly believe it, weighed 147 lbs. If the scales were correct it is a gain of over 20 lbs since I left home. I am beginning to believe, what everyone tells me that I am really gaining flesh and I know that I never felt in better health. Andy says I always have my appetite with me.

What terrible fighting there has been in the West. it seems as though Willie was destined to escape all the severe fighting.[30]

Mot Church has gone to Washington on business and is to bring up all the express packages that are there. He is somewhat expected back to-night and I expect will bring those boxes Mr. May has sent us. Steve Estes has received those Mr. May sent for the twelfth.

I have just finished reading "Orley Farm."[31] it came out in Harper's. It is not remarkably good but down here where reading matter is so scarce it seemed quite interesting. Frank Lester got the December No. of the Atlantic the other day. There is a very good article on Henry Ward Beecher in the review of his new book.

I rec'd your letter written New Year's and think you will have to move onto a more fashionable street. I wish that you might have "counted one" as I used to when I first commenced calling.

Wells had a very good ambrotype taken yesterday about a mile and a half from here and I shall try to have one taken but you must excuse (remember) that "whiskers" don't look as long in a picture as they really are.

Love to all loving ones

Yours affy

Osgood Tracy

I am getting a little short of stationary now I have left the Adj'ts office and I guess you had better send me a little of this thinnest note paper and envelopes—such as is used for foreign correspondence.

---

30. Major campaigns occurred in the western theater, especially along the Mississippi River and in Tennessee and Kentucky, during the late fall and winter of 1862–63. Osgood is likely referring here to the Battle of Stones River, where Confederate forces under Braxton Bragg clashed with Union forces commanded by William S. Rosecrans. For further reading on this and the winter campaigns in the west, see Larry J. Daniel, *Battle of Stones River: The Forgotten Conflict between the Confederate Army of Tennessee and the Union Army of the Cumberland* (Baton Rouge: Louisiana State Univ. Press, 2012); Earl J. Hess, *Braxton Bragg: The Most Hated Man in the Confederacy* (Chapel Hill: Univ. of North Carolina Press, 2016).

31. Anthony Trollope, *Orley Farm* (London: Chapman, Hall, & Piccadilly, 1861–62).

Camp 122d Reg't N. Y. Vols
near Falmouth, Va—
Jany 15, 1863

Dear Mother,

I returned last night from 3 days absence on Fatigue Duty. Last Sunday there was a detail made for "picket" and I was crowing over Lieut. Wooster (our next-door neighbor) who was detailed but alas I had hardly got to sleep when the Adj't woke me up to inform me that I must report at 3½ the next morning for fatigue duty. We went a little beyond Belle Plain Landing and had 3 days experience in building corduroy roads so that I consider myself quite expert in the art. Capt. Kent,[32] Lieuts Cossitt (a cousin of Jim Lawrence's, very nice fellow by the way) Clapp,[33] Hall,[34] and myself were the officers with the party. We did not have any tents with us but we had a brush house built and managed to live very comfortably. It was quite a busy scene at the landing as a large portion of the army about here obtains their supplies from there. And as many of the troops are being paid off there is consequently a great rush of sutlers store. It was rather a hard march back yesterday afternoon inasmuch as the roads are somewhat muddy and when I got back last night tired and hungry and found that the boys had been improving the log house in my absence and when I sat down to a nice hot supper by my own fireplace I felt that this army life was not very uncomfortable after all.

I was sorry to learn that Charley Fitch[35] and Col. Barnum[36] had been here during my absence for I should liked to have seen them and I wished to have Charley's evidence as to my increased proportions.

The boxes Mr. May sent were rec'd on Sunday and all the privates packages distributed as soon as the rest of the reg't return from picket which will probably be this afternoon. From what Nell and Marie wrote I supposed that there would be a package and directed to me especially for my company but there was nothing in the boxes directed to me. Our orderly sergeant gave me some "home-made" nut cakes as an addition to my supper last evening and I can assure they did taste nice.

I have heard nothing further in reference to my commission and just to satisfy

32. Capt. Noah B. Kent was a member of Company K.

33. Lt. Alonzo H. Clapp of Company A. was later promoted to captain of Company K and, again in 1864 to major.

34. This was likely Sgt. James B. Hall of Company C, later promoted through the ranks to captain.

35. This was likely Charles "Charley" Elliot Fitch (1835–1918), who, after the war, became a lawyer and editor in chief of the *Syracuse Daily Standard* and *Rochester Democrat and Chronicle*. He later went into government service as collector for the US Internal Revenue Service, lecturer for the New York Department of Public Instruction, and 1880 US Census supervisor. He married Louise Lawrence Smith at Syracuse on July 21, 1870. See "Fitch, Charles E.," *Encyclopedia of Biography of New York*, 339–43.

36. Henry A. Barnum, formerly major, Twelfth Infantry, was mustered in as colonel on September 17, 1862. He was commissioned colonel on October 4, 1862, and then discharged, to date March 31, 1865, to accept a brigadier general commission with the US Volunteers.

myself I wish you would get somebody who happens to be going to Albany to make further inquiries at the Adj't Gen'ls' office and see what the matter is.

A pontoon train went past us this morning and it of course gave rise to all sorts of rumors about crossing the river again but I don't think an advance from here is possible. There has been a very heavy warm wind and I expect that by about to-morrow or next day we shall catch it. Love to all

Yours aff

Osgood

Camp 122d Reg't N. Y. Vols

near Falmouth, Va-

Jan. 15, 1863

Dear Nell,

I am much obliged for the photograph, which I think is excellent. But, the expression reminded me instantly and only too forcibly of you as I remember you looked the last Sunday morning before I left home, but I forbear. That is a subject not to be talked of.

Mr. Mays boxes have arrived and the mittens were distributed this afternoon fully supplying all those in the reg't who needed them and there are still some twenty or thirty pair left which are to be kept for those who are now absent sick but who may rejoin the reg't at any time.

I returned last evening from Belle Plain Landing on the Potomac where we were engaged in building "corduroy" roads. I consider myself quite experienced in that line of business now and if when I return to Syracuse *that* sidewalk is not fixed I shall endeavor to make a contract with your father to "corduroy" it. During my absence, Charley Fitch & Col. Barnum were here. I was very sorry to miss seeing them, as the sight of a Syracuse face is a real blessing. We are fixing up for Winter quarters, and most of us have log huts. Frank and Andy have a very nice one and boast of a stove but I try and think a fireplace is better and we all know it is much more cheerful and I can assure you that when I got back to camp last night rather tired after a six mile march in the mud, my log house and fireplace did look very comfortable. Frank, Andy, Wells (the 1st Lieut. Of our Co.) and myself mess to-gether. I like Frank [Wooster] better and better as I get more acquainted with him. He makes a first rate Captain, is learning the tactics very fast and seems to be popular with his company. Johnny Butler called on us the other day and took dinner with us. He is Lt. Col. Of the 147th N. Y. Reg't.

There is said to be an ambrotype here about and if I get an opportunity I will try and have taken in return for the photograph you so kindly sent and to show you how well this army life agrees with your friend.

Os

Camp 122d Reg't N. Y. Vols
near Falmouth, Va.
Jan'y 16—1863

Dear Mother

I wrote you yesterday but the rumor of a move to-morrow has assumed so definite a shape that I thought it best to drop you a line although at the risk of being tedious. Last evening I rec'd three letters one from you, George and Marie all written on Sunday.

I was not so very sick last fall Poole to the contrary notwithstanding and when I asked Frank and Andy if they thought I was in good health now they remind me to tell you that I was the "saving" one of our mess. I never let anything go to waste. But joking aside I assure you my Dear Mother that you may place the utmost confidence in me when I say that I never was in better health than I am now and am ready for a march anywhere.

A few moments ago I was in Capt. Dwight's tent and he asked me how much I have gained since I left home. I replied, about 20 lbs whereat he expressed surprise saying that to judge from my looks one would think I had gained much more but my face shows it more than anywhere else.

Our "log palace" leaked a little last night. We slept dry and comfortable notwithstanding the heavy rain. This morning it has cleared off nicely and the prospects for a nice day tomorrow are good.

One of our boys died this morning in the hospital and several more are sick there and it is terrible for them to lay there and have a man beside them. I have fully made up my mind that when I get so sick that I cannot march with the reg't I shall "point" for home without waiting for a furlough. They may call it desertion or anything else they please but this is no place for a sick man and I shall not stay.[37] But I trust that my health may yet be spared as it has been so far.

Geo. Wrote me that the directors had raised his salary $100, without any solicitation on his part. Quite a gratifying compliment.

It is about time for the mail to leave so Good-Bye. I will endeavor to keep up my good reputation in regard to writing home and can not imagine how I came to neglect you as I did.

Yours lovingly
Os

---

37. On Civil War desertion, see Kenneth Noe, *Reluctant Rebels: The Confederates Who Joined the Army after 1861* (Chapel Hill: Univ. of North Carolina Press, 2010); Bob Sandow, *Deserter Country: Civil War Opposition in the Pennsylvania Appalachians* (New York: Fordham Univ. Press, 2009); Mark H. Dunkleman, *Brothers One and All: Esprit de Corps in a Civil War Regiment* (Baton Rouge: Louisiana State Univ. Press, 2004); Lorien Foote, *The Gentlemen and the Roughs: Violence, Honor, and Manhood in the Union Army* (New York: New York Univ. Press, 2010); Ricardo Herrera, "Self-Governance and the American Citizen as Soldier, 1775–1861," *Journal of Military History* 65, no. 1 (2014): 21–52; Ella Lonn, *Desertion during the Civil War* (Gloucester, MA: Peter Smith, 1966).

HeadQuarters Right Grand Division
Army of the Potomac
January 17, 1863

Dear Mother

Our marching orders were so far modified yesterday afternoon as to read Monday morning, instead of this morning as the time designated for the movement of our troops and it was such a beautiful morning just cold enough for walking that I took the opportunity to make a call on Sam [Sumner]. I found him confined to the house with a sore throat. He is about cured but is keeping in-doors at present. He invited me to stay to dinner and urged me so strongly to spend the night that I have consented and now while he is "dozing" after dinner I take the opportunity of dropping a line to you trusting you will not feel offended at my writing you daily.

I am still in the dark as to our destination but even if there should be an engagement feel as easy as you can about my welfare. I have just made Sam promise that he would hunt me up immediately after any fight that may take place that we may be mutually assured of each others' welfare. Col. Teall has I trust, corroborated my evidence in regard to my good health and I trust that by this time you have regained your confidence in your son.

As there is some talk of consolidation of the right (reg'ts) in the field, I think it would be a very good idea for me to be sure of my lieutenancy to avoid being consolidated into the ranks, but I presume my commission will soon be here as Col. Titus has written Adjutant Gen'l Sprague[38] in reference to them. You need have no fears of my following the patriotic course of my brother, in the event of a consolidation as I do not see the chance of a private's life. Gen'l Sumner told me this afternoon that Slocum's Corps had left Fairfax so I may see Will ere long but don't mention this as it may not be generally known. Gen'l S is very kind and inquired if my commission had come yet. Wondering at its delay. I think I shall go onto the staff as soon as I get it, of course the Gen'l is ready for me.

Love to all the loving ones and
believe me
Your aff son
Osgood

Washington—Jany 21/63

Dear Mother

You will probably be as much surprised to learn that I am here as I was to get here but on Sunday night about 12 men from our reg't deserted and Monday morning the Col. Decided to send an officer after them and offered me the chance which of course I accepted as anyone in camp always jumps at a change even for the worse.

---

38. John Titcomb Sprague (1810–1878) was the adjutant general of the State of New York.

At first a pass came for me to go off on patrol and return at tattoo that night but afterwards another came and not specifying any time for return and giving me a pass anywhere within the lines of the army. I went to Aquia Creek Landing on Monday afternoon, spent that night there and not learning anything in reference to my deserters and learning that my pass would take me to Washington I concluded that it was my duty to come here. The boat was delayed and we finally anchored off Alexandria for the night and instead of spending a pleasant evening at the Sedgwick's as I anticipated, I had a very dull time on the boat. However we got here this morning. I went to the Provost Marshall and "posted" my deserters and then with a Lieut. With whom I "scaped" acquaintance as usual, I went to the Capitol Patent office & c I called the Sedgwick's but they had gone to a hospital at Georgetown, D.C. To be back this evening, which I propose to spend with them.[39]

As my pass is so "liberal" I should think it my "duty" to follow those deserters to Syracuse were it not for the fact that I have left five men at Aquia Landing who might be tempted to follow their example if left too long alone and since I have been here I have heard that Franklin's Division moved at 12 o'clock yesterday so I am anxious to get back although the severe storm of last night and to-day and (it is still raining) must stop them, I fear.

I saw Mr. Davis at the National to-day. He saw Willie when he was here. What a pity that I should have missed the "infant."

If nothing prevents I shall leave at 12 o'clock to-morrow.

Slocum is at Dumfries [Virginia] I hear.

I consider myself very lucky in escaping this storm if I have not lost any chance for distinguishing myself. I refer you to Mr. Davis as to the state of my health

Good-Bye

Love to all

Os

Camp 122d Reg't N. Y. Vols

near Falmouth, Va.

January 24/63

Dear Mother

I left Washington yesterday morning having remained over one night longer than I expected to. I spent both evenings in Washington at Sedgwick's. The first

---

39. Per a letter Charles Sedgwick letter wrote to his wife, Dora, on January 21, 1863, Osgood visited that evening. Charles described Osgood as having "grown large and stout and quite manly albeit his whiskers and mustache are rather faint." Nellie and her friend Emma Saul had been visiting Louisa May Alcott, who was hospitalized, gravely ill, diagnosed with typhoid pneumonia. "Miss Louisa Alcott is very ill at the Union hospital at Georgetown. Her father is here and intends taking her home tomorrow night much to her disgust as she insists she shall soon be well enough to return to her duties at the hospital." Prior to her illness, Louisa had been nursing soldiers in the same hospital.

evening in Washington . . . in the hall at Williams I have grown so fleshy . . . whiskers a la Burnside that they hardly. . . . But the most aggravating about my visit was . . . that Wilber had to serve through last Friday before . . . that . . . through last Friday fore instance . . . that . . . got his . . . while there—If I had not met him I fear it would have been expansion . . . for himself . . . I saw Mr. Davis, Cap't Myers, Jim Belden,[40] Mr. Hiscock[41] there—Mr. Davis will be able to give a good an account of both of your boys as he also saw Willie. Mr. D, told me that it was all right about my commission but since I have been away the Colonel has rec'd official notice from Albany that but one of our vacancies (that in Co. C) has been filled. There seems to be some mistake about it. Perhaps our friends who had inquired about it have asked if there was a commission made out for Tracy, and no affirmative reply getting Willie mixed up with me.

If Jim could get away for a day I think it would pay for him to go to Albany and ascertain which of those appointments recommended by Colonel Titus under date of Dec. 4th (but more especially mine) have been confirmed, and if none of the vacancies have been filled, can't you not get William Tracy[42] to write a letter to Gov. Seymour asking him to confirm the Colonel's appointment. As I should not object to get on the staff before any more active movements take place in the mud, I leave this for you to attend to knowing that you will do all that can be done to arrange.

I got to Falmouth yesterday afternoon and as my foot was a little sore I went up to General Sumner's and Sam told me that he would lend me his horse to go home that evening—but he thought it much more advisable for me to spend the night with him and he would send me over this morning which I fully agreed to. There were three "Sanitary females" there from Philadelphia,[43]—very pleasant ladies indeed. After dinner, we had quite a religious discussion. They were strong

40. James Jerome Belden (1825–1904) was an American politician and US Representative from New York. He served as mayor of Syracuse in 1877–78.

41. This was likely New York attorney, judge, and legislator Luther Harris Hiscock (1824–1867), who used his middle name. In 1855, with his brother Frank, Harris founded the law firm known today as Hiscock & Barclay. Prominent in Democratic politics, Harris served as Onondaga County surrogate judge from 1852 to 1856. In 1865, now a Republican, he was elected to the New York State Assembly, and he served until he was murdered, on June 7, 1867.

42. This was not Osgood's brother but a William Tracy, a lawyer, of New York City. He was Osgood's first cousin and grandson of Capt. Jared Tracy (1741–1790).

43. This is a reference to the US Sanitary Commission, organized to support soldiers by supplying them with such necessities as clothing, medical supplies, and foodstuffs and ensuring that the armies followed certain standards of cleanliness and that nurses were available to support the army medical staff. On the US Sanitary Commission, see Judith Ann Giesberg, *Army at Home: Women and the Civil War on the Northern Home Front* (Chapel Hill: Univ. of North Carolina Press, 2009); Judith Ann Giesberg, *Civil War Sisterhood: The U.S. Sanitary Commission and Women's Politics in Transition* (Boston: Northeastern Univ. Press, 2000); Nina Silber, *Daughters of the Union: Northern Women Fight in the Civil War* (Cambridge, MA: Harvard Univ. Press, 2005), 175–200; Patricia L. Richard, *Busy Hands: Images of the Family in the Northern Civil War Effort* (New York: Fordham Univ. Press, 2003).

presbyterians, and we discussed the doctrine of original m&c. The General is very kind whenever we go there and I think my position will be very pleasant.

I suppose you have heard before of the grand movement of this army. The boys had a terrible rough time and now we are back to our old camp. I crow over the boys continually to think I escaped it, so nicely. As long as nothing was accomplished and I was off on duty, I quite congratulate myself upon my escape from 3 days experience in the mud. I suppose nothing will be done at present.[44]

I had about half an hours lively conversation with Mrs. Spencer at Williams the other morning. She has rooms at the same place that the Sedgwick's have. It was the first opportunity I had for visiting the Capitol. The painting, Westward the Star of Empire takes its war[45] is splendid. The inside is nearly completed the stairs are all marble and the floor those colored tiles and when the outside hall be finished we can well be proud of it. I also spent about an hour in the patent office. I did not succeed in finding any deserters but I had a very nice time and got rid of our move in the mud.

It is said that the rebel pickets read Burnsides advances to our pickets and offer to come over and help move our artillery and pontoon trains. Capt. Garland told us of a funny instance—A little drummer boy in one of the reg'ts as they started back for camp drew himself up, struck an attitude and sung out—"Comrades, the auspicious moment has arrived—forward."

Love to all, Good Bye

Yours

Os

Camp 122d Reg't N. Y. Vols

near Falmouth, Va

Jany 25/63

Dear Mother,

Perhaps you may object to a daily mail but I have got a "fit" of letter writing this afternoon have already written five letters yet don't feel willing to stop—I wrote Cousin William this afternoon asking him to use his influence with Governor Seymour to get my appointment confirmed so I think it will be all right.

Our reg't got quite used up on their tramp and I cannot feel thankful enough

---

44. This is a reference to the Mud March, Ambrose Burnside's attempt to continue the offensive against Lee in the wake of the Fredericksburg disaster. Though the flanking maneuver was in theory a good one, a winter storm turned the roads to mud and the army faltered in its move and was ridiculed by the Northern press.

45. This was an Emanuel Leutze mural, representing American manifest destiny. Leutze painted it in the US Capitol between July 1861 and November 1862. *Westward the Course of the Empire Takes Its War* can be viewed online at *Architect of the Capitol*, accessed Oct. 4, 2021, https://www.aoc.gov/art/other-paintings-and-murals/westward-course-empire-takes-its-way.

that I escaped it. Yesterday afternoon I had quite a severe headache and you should have seen the almost motherly care with which Andy got me some tea and toast there happened to be some soft bread in camp. I suppose it is unnecessary to say that the "toast" cured me immediately.

Last night the mail did not get in until after ten but I having a presentment that there would be something for me sat up until that very late hour for camp and was amply rewarded by receiving your letter of the 20th which someone had opened but as you did not speak of any enclosure and presuming that the person was not familiar with your writing. He could not have been much benefited. That diary you spoke of sending me has never been rec'd and I have about given it up.

It has cleared off nicely to-day and if the good weather should hold for two weeks perhaps the auspicious moment in this reg't will be when the paymaster arrives.

I think I shall write to Lanning again in reference to my appointment, the only way that he could have been mistaken in reference to it must have been that they got Willie's and myself "mixed up" at the Adj't Genls.

I have made a trade of the balance of this fine paper you sent me for some heavier paper the colonel has, which I like better for writing upon than this. I wrote to the Phelp's[46] this afternoon I am (ashamed) that I have neglected them so long.

Cap't Chamberlain[47] resigned on account of ill-health I believe. He was very ill at the time he was obliged to leave the reg't in Maryland.

Wishing that I could go to church with you this evening I remain.

Your aff son
Os

Camp 122d Reg't N. Y. Vols
near Falmouth, Va.
Jany 25/63

Dear Nellie,

When I arrived at Aquia Landing I found that my "guard" had got tired of waiting for me and had gone to rejoin the reg't and that the army of the Potomac were returning to their old camps and that I might just as well have made a visit home and to "cap the climax" when I reported to the colonel and informed him that I had thought of going home from Washington he "regretted" that I had not done so, ("consoling wasn't it"). However I am a great believer in the doctrine "all is for the best" and never waste any regrets on what has passed.

When I got back to camp next morning I found the muddiest, crossest, set of fellows that I have ever met and one exclaimed, "you lucky fellow" greeted me on

46. This is a reference to the Phelps family; Osgood's cousin Lucy Putnam married Dudley Post Phelps, a Syracuse lawyer. The Putnam, Phelps, and Tracy families remained very close and are buried in the same plot in Oakwood Cemetery, Syracuse, New York.

47. Capt. Webster R. Chamberlain was with Company B.

all sides. They left camp on Tuesday but caught in the rain that night, marched through the mud and rain on Wednesday and back to camp over the worst possible roads on Thursday.

Frank did not get in until yesterday noon as his company with several others were detailed to help a wagon train along through the mud. It is said that the rebel pickets read Burnsides advances to our pickets on Wednesday and kindly offered to come over and help our artillery and pontoon trains out of the mud. So that you see besides having a very pleasant time in Washington I escaped a very disagreeable profitless march. Frank was very grateful for his boots. Since I have been away Col. Titus rec'd official notice from Albany that my appointment has not been confirmed but this time up to the 1st of Jan'y so that appointment now rests with Gov. Seymour and although most of my friends at Albany are Republicans yet fortunately cousin William Tracy of New York is an old resident of Utica and well acquainted with Governor S[eymore] and I have written to-day asking for his influence in my behalf and as Col. Titus has recommended me for the position I think that I will be all right. But it could be a rather sour joke, I should have to go back to my position of Serg't Major after having assumed the duties and "airs" of a Lieut. I found a letter from Willie awaiting my return. He hoped I would be able to get a ten days leave and meet him in Washington. However I hear Slocum's Corps are at Dumfries and I hope soon to see him.

I fear Nellie, you must have thought me very stupid during my visit in Washington but seeing you again brought the last week I spent at Syracuse[48] so forcibly to my mind that it was no wonder I did not feel talkative. My regards to Miss Murray.

Truly yours

Os

It has just occurred to me that I don't owe you a letter. I trust you will pardon my mistake.

Camp 122d Reg't N. Y. Vols

near Falmouth, Va.

January 27/63

Dear Mother

It is a rainy day in "camp." I am writing in Frank [Lester]'s house. Since I got back from Washington, Frank and Andy [Smith] have insisted upon my sleeping in their log house which is "water tight" while mine will leak just a little. Andy and I have just been "cleaning up" which has only served to disgust Andy with my laziness, which trait of character he insists I possess to an alarming degree. I received your letter of the 17th on Sunday night. From your allusion to my drawing upon my fund, I fear you think I am getting "extravagant" and perhaps I am a little but

---

48. This is likely a reference to Osgood's marriage proposal to Nellie, and her decline.

I beg to assure you that I don't waste it on mess. But joking aside if our mess is a little expensive. I think it is not money ill spent when the changes of diet we are enable to have, enable me to preserve such good health and actually to grow fleshy and if Gov. Seymour will only see fit to send me a commission I shall be all right.

We heard startling rumors yesterday which having been confirmed to-day, I suppose must be true—viz: That Burnside, Sumner and Franklin had been relieved of their commands and Hooker had been assigned to the command of the army. Sumner and Burnside the rumors said were relieved at their own request. You may imagine I was very sorry to hear this for although presuming that Sumner will be given another command it may not affect my appointment upon his staff. Still until that does [take] place it was a very pleasant place for me to visit. Sam and his father have been very kind indeed to me and I have had several pleasant visits. But, Dear Mother, if anything should prevent my appointment on his staff don't let it worry you for fear that it will be a disappointment to me yet I am very well contented here. My position is very pleasant indeed and I think I ought to be thankful for that I have been promoted so soon.

I don't like the idea of changing commanders so often. I know nothing of Hooker further than his title "Fighting Joe Hooker" would imply that he was an active energetic sort of a Gen'l. but this I do know and although I don't agree with the feeling myself yet I cannot help seeing it, is that McClellan is the favorite of the army yet and I do believe in the remark that I heard made the other day, that nothing would please the army more than to see him restored to his command.

We are beginning to get an idea of Virginia mud. Our camp fortunately is upon a hill and the soil is quite gravelly so that we are not troubled much here "at home" but the roads, about here are in a terrible condition. When our troops returned from their late "excursion" up the river Frank Lester's company and two others out of the reg't were detailed to help the wagons and artillery along.

If our troops had got across the river just before this storm—how terrible would have been the result.

I brought several books from Washington so we are quite well supplied with reading matter for this rainy day. Among others I brought Mrs. Fremont's book just out. Have you seen it? It is composed of letters from the General and his staff during the Missouri campaign. Ross of course "shines" but his letters are really very lively and well written.[49]

Sam & I had quite a discussion about him the last time I was there, Sam insisting that he was not smart, only "showy." But we both agreed to one thing that he was disagreeable.

Our latest Syracuse papers spoke of a projected carnival at the skating park. We tried to imagine ourselves there but did not quite succeed.

49. Jessie Benton Frémont, *The Story of the Guard: A Chronicle of the War* (Boston: Ticknor & Fields, 1863).

I regretted that I did not have my photograph taken in Washington but I trust to my numerous friends who have seen me lately.

Andy & Frank are playing euchre and I having finished by "daily epistle return to my book."

Good Bye

Yours lovingly

Os

Camp 122d Reg't N. Y. Vols.

Near Falmouth, Va.

Feby 2/63

Dear Mother,

I returned from Gen'l Slocum's this morning after a very pleasant visit indeed. Will took compassion on my appearance and fitted me out with new shirts (and) cap shoulder straps and insisted on lending me $50—the dear old boy—wanted to give it to me as a slight compensation for the fancied injury he thought he had done me, but I am not going to sell my birthright for a mess of . . . "green backs" so I only accepted of it as a loan. Will is very pleasantly situated indeed. Those members of the staff that I saw I like very much. They are all gentlemen. Dr. McNulty was away whereat I was quite sorry as I was very anxious to see him.

Yesterday Willie & I rode over to see the 149th. We found them all well and the "Joes" very much astonished to see how fleshy I had grown. Col. Barnum was looking much better than I expected to see him. He stood the fatigues of the late march very well indeed. I got back to camp this afternoon slightly "sore" after my experience in riding for the last few days and found that Cap't Smith had gone home on furlough. I wish you would send my inking case and (please see that it is filled) and my silk sash back with him. My fatigue suit I do not want at present, but I should like a couple of pair of dark-colored knit drawers.

I found a nice long letter from Marie awaiting me upon my arrival. What a "fashionable" party the Whites[50] must have had. Marie wrote that she didn't go until half past ten and then was among the first. George wrote Willie that he did not attend. What is the matter? Is he retiring from society? Marie was polite enough to say that she wished she could have transformed my brother Jim into "Os." tell Jim not to feel hurt.

I found that I had got into a nest of the worse kind of Democrats when I went over to see Will. Mostly who used to be one of the "rabid" Republicans carried a torch in their wide-awake procession and all that sort of thing is now as bad as any.

---

50. The White family left many marks on the Syracuse community, including the White Memorial Building (1876), the Hamilton White house (1842), the White monument in the park, and other landmarks. See Dick Case, "White Family Left Legacy in Syracuse," *Post Standard,* Mar. 2, 2006.

I rec'd a very kind note from Mr. Murray to whom I had written to ascertain if my appointment had been confirmed. He (expressed) a great deal of interest in the welfare of Will and myself.

To-day our reg't has been paid off up to the 31st of Oct. this gives me two months pay as Serg't Major. As I have my overcoat and several other things to pay for I guess I will keep this and the $50 Will lent me for the present.

I hope you will be very polite to Andrew for he has been a very kind friend to me. Has done everything in his power to help me along and I cannot feel sufficiently grateful to him.

But supper is ready so Good Bye

Yours lovingly

Os

Camp 122d Reg't N. Y. Vols.

Near Falmouth, Va.

Feby 6th/63

Dear Mother,

Rain, rain, rain. It commenced yesterday in the afternoon and has been raining pretty steady ever since. Yesterday I was sent out with a fatigue party to cut poles to floor the mule stables. the work you can get out of soldiers is very light. We went out twice, once in the morning and once in the afternoon getting four loads each time.

I rec'd your letter night before last, in which you speak of my prospects on the staff which I judge are very slim but as I before wrote you I feel that I have no reason to complain of my situation but on the contrary to be very grateful. In regard to my being engaged I thought you were aware that Joe Davis generally knows of an event in advance of the parties interested and as to his information in regard to this case I regret to say that he is entirely mistaken and you may rest assured my dear mother, that when any such event in my life shall occur, you shall be the first one informed.

Frank and myself have got along very nicely in our housekeeping—During Andy's absence except Frank has some trouble in calculating his habits of ordered into my mode of life.

Three men from Co. H deserted last night.

If all the regiments in the service are as unfortunate in this respect as ourselves I must acknowledge that the prospect looks rather gloomy for the spring campaign, but, I am hopeful naturally and I trust that will come out right yet.

I had a call from Col. Teall yesterday who brought me the tea and candy and what was still better the assurance that you were looking well this winter. The tea we have not tried yet, but as soon as we can get hold of some soft bread Frank and I propose to luxuriate on "tea and toast" evenings and to be extremely "fashionable" shall make it ourselves. Andy I suppose you have seen ere this and I trust that he has given good account of

Your loving boy

Os

Camp 122d Reg't N. Y. Vols.

Near Falmouth, Va.

Feby 8/63

Dear Mother

I am sorry that I cannot go to church with you on this beautiful Sunday morning. It is a most delightful day, the only drawback being that this Virginia soil is very "sticky."

Yesterday it was reported through camp that the Brigade Commissary had soft bread for sale. As we have not been able to get any for quite a long time you should see the "stir" the announcement created and soon you could see officers and privates tramping back through the mud (the commissary quarters are about three-quarters of a mile distant) with four to ten loaves in their arms.

We, who have been lately promoted, went over to get mustered into the U.S. Service and after our return I made a cup of tea and with some buttered toast you, who know my weakness for the latter article, can imagine what a sumptuous supper I had. In accordance with the recent orders in regard to furlough, Co. Titus' Adj't Church and ten privates left this morning on a ten day leave. I am filling Mot's place during his absence and it seems very natural to be back in the Adjt's office again. Frank Lester has been rather unwell for the last few days but this morning he feels better. Now that I am a "full-fledged" Lieutenant, I enclose my Sergeant Majors warrant which I wish you to preserve carefully as after the war is over I am going to have that Lieutenant's commission framed.

There is not much prospect of my getting home as there are many in the regiment who besides having left a family at home, left their business unsettled in the hurried departure of the regiment and who have much greater claim to go home then I have but if I cannot visit you in body you may be sure I do in spirit and that often. Don't ask Church to bring anything for me as he is not very accommodating and I don't wish to be under any favors from him.

It is rather dull to-day so please accept this in fault of a more interesting letter and believe me

Yours affy

Os

Camp 122d Reg't N. Y. Vols.
Near Falmouth, Va.
Feby 10/63

Dear Mother,

Yesterday we had so many visitors from home that it seemed almost as good as a three days furlough. About noon, Lt. Col. Richardson (I believe he has resigned now) Cap't Randall, Mr. McKinstry of Syracuse and last but not least by any means, Jim Johnson (the ex-candidate for Mayor and your old yankers grocer looking as I "swoonish" as ever if not more so—He said he could tell "mother" that he had seen both her "soldier boys"—Lt. Covell of the 149th who was formerly a clerk in his store came over also.

Just as we were forming the line for dress parade somebody rode across the parade ground that looked very natural and upon a closer inspection it proved to be Tom Wilkinson.[51] He was accompanied by Maj. Root and Bill Covell (formerly a jeweller in Syracuse) and you may imagine I was a little "flustered" at having so many spectators to witness my second attempt to act as Adjutant. However I managed to get through without any mistakes. Forman, Maj. Root and Covell spent the night, but the rest went back. Forman has not changed any except that his experience in the army has given him a new topic upon which to "eulogize." I sent by him a pipe made out of laurel root by an Indian in the reg't, for Jim. Knowing that young man's taste for "outlandish" looking pipes I think he will like this. There is a small hole he will perceive which will need stopping up and then I think the thing will smoke

Lt. Burton[52] of Frank Lesters' Co., who has been quite unwell for the last two weeks, was ordered to Washington for medical treatment last night. He expects to go home however instead of remaining in Washington. He is a brother-in-law of Dean Hawley's a very clever fellow indeed. Lt. Nye[53] of Co. B. who resigned a little while ago on account of family sickness at home rec'd his discharge last night. Our company is next to his in line and consequently we have got very well acquainted. He is a very nice fellow and I am very sorry to lose him from the reg't as he is also a very good officer. He leaves to-day. As he lives at 63 James St., next to Mrs. Savage's it will be but a little trouble for you to call and he could give you all the information you desire as he has been with us ever since we left home.

Dr. Slocum went over to visit his brother this morning and promised to do his best to bring Willie back with him. Now that I am acting Adj't (ahem) I have more room and can accommodate him better.

Our pleasant weather continues and the mud is beginning to dry up so that

51. This was likely a nephew of John Wilkinson, of Syracuse.
52. Lt. James Burton was with Company F.
53. His full name was Charles G. Nye.

we can resume our drills. Tom (Forman) told me that Wills and Moreley's nominations as Captains on the staff had been sent to the Senate for confirmation. I wonder if the boy will be very airy if that august body should approve it. Hugh Middleton has got to be a captain the 3d N.Y. By the way that regiment's time is up sometime in April. I wish Willie could be in Syracuse when Johnny Butlers' Co. comes home.

Love to all and goodbye
Your boy
Os

Camp 122d Reg't N. Y. Vols.
Near Falmouth, Va.
Feby 14, 1863

Dear Mother,

Although the custom of sending valentines is getting out of date, still I will keep it up and not let the day pass without sending you one.

Dr. Slocum brought Willie back with him as he promised and the young man spent the night with me. The next day before he went back he rode down to Falmouth and looked at the place where we crossed the river and where the battle of Fredericksburg was fought. I could not very well go but Davis Cossitt offered to act as "courier" and showed him all the points of interest. Willie, is a queer fellow, as far as regards his ideas of what the Tracy family can do. I couldn't help laughing at his remark after witnessing Guard Mounting (in which the Adj't takes a prominent part) the morning he was here. Well Os, "you did not do that very stylish, did you?" Encouraging to a beginner isn't it? But in spite of his self depreciation he is never at all afraid to undertake anything and do his best. Now don't think from the foregoing that I am getting vain of my accomplishments or that I feel hurt that he did not flatter it. I only mention it as an instance of the "ruling passion." How pleasant it is to have Willie so near to me as not only that I can see him so often but I feel easy in case I should be sick I could send him word and be taken over to his Head qrts. Not that I anticipate anything of the kind but it is pleasant to feel secure.

To-day has been a beautiful day just cool enough to make it pleasant walking and about noon Frank Lester came in and said he and Woosterwere going over to have their picture taken and invited me to go with them. I rushed down to my palace, got on a paper collar and after considerable inquiry found the place and enclosed you have the result which please accept as my "valentine." I think it is quite good although perhaps it flatters me a "little." You must bear in mind that whiskers don't "take" well, *always* appearing *less* in the picture than they really are. Tell Sam that just as we came out of the gallery we saw that the Phillips House (their old Hd qrts) was on fire. It was about a quarter of a mile distant so we did not go over. Capt. Brower and Lt. Cossitt who happened to be near them helped get the things out and said that they saw Wins' trunk among the things saved. the building was destroyed.

I had another picture taken with my cap on, and will send it to you in my next. You can take your choice between the two and keep which you like but give the other to Marie.

To-night some boxes arrived and among others a larger one for Frank sent by his mother from Chicago. as it has been sometime on the way some of the things are a little "moldy" but fortunately the mince pies, of which there are a number, are in a fine state of preservation so that our "mess" will live luxuriously. Frank was the more delighted to get it as he had about given it up for lost. I trust yours will come before long so we can decide whose mother makes the best mince pies.

I am going to write George [Hunt] to-night suggesting the idea of his coming down here to make me a visit and I wish you to urge it upon the young man. 1st it will be a good opportunity to visit Washington before Congress adjourns and while he can have two such agreeable "cicerones" as Nell and Emma. 2d He never will have a better opportunity to visit the army inasmuch as the 149th, 12th and 122nd are close together, and I will agree that he shall see more in the two weeks he shall be gone from home than he can in the same period for the rest of his life, and as he has not been away from the bank for a long time I think he must feel no hesitation in asking for a short "furlough." I wish Jim could come with him. Charles B. could get them a pass. Several persons who have wished to obtain passes and c from the Departments say that he has as much if not more than any member of Congress. I hope you will make the boys come.

How I wish I could have attended Capt. Sumner's birth-day party. I can imagine the boy in his glory. George wrote me that it was a very pleasant party.

Trusting that the enclosed will corroborate the statements in regard to my good health with much love to yourself and Jim, I remain

Yours affectionately,

Os.

Camp 122d Reg't N. Y. Vols.

near Falmouth, Va.

Feby 19/63

Dear Mother,

Your box of hard gingerbread sent by Dr. Pease arrived this morning just as we were at breakfast. It was a little broken up but I can assure you that Frank and myself thought it very eatable. I have not tasted anything since I left that reminded me so strongly of home and I could almost see Jim sitting by the parlor table with a book in one hand reaching after gingerbread. I told Frank that he would think nothing of devouring such a box-full as you sent me in the course of an evening. but perhaps I "exaggerated" a little.

We have had a lady in camp during the last week. Dr. and Mrs. Wiggins from Cicero who have a boy[54] sick in the hospital. As the Colonel was absent we fixed up his tent for her as comfortably as possible. the first day or two they were here, the weather was very pleasant and the Dr. was quite charmed with the delightful weather of Virginia and was accordingly patriotic but the next day a severe snow storm set and the Dr.'s patriotism and his admiration for Virginia weather disappeared to-gether. They left for home yesterday morning. We are having a very severe storm. It commenced day before yesterday morning, snowing and it has been raining since. to-day it is sort of half mist and half rain.

The Colonel returned last evening. He did not go beyond Washington. We expect Mot. Church and Andy to-night or to-morrow night, when my duties as "acting Adj't" will be at an end and I shall subside back into an ordinary 2d Lieut once more.

Have you seen ex-Lieut. Nye yet, that I wrote about? He lives next to Mr. Savage and knew him quite well.

I enclose the other picture of which I spoke and wish you to take your choice between the two keeping which you consider the best and giving the other to Marie. Did George show you the "group?" I sent it to him to keep until I shall return when I wish to have it as a reminisce of a pleasant day's excursion as we had quite a jolly time. That face that you do not know is Frank Wooster, a young fellow from Tully who was clerk in Hiscock's law office at Syracuse. I never knew him then, except by sight, but since I have become acquainted with him I like him very much. Frank was laughing at me this morning because I complained at not having heard from home for four or five days. He said he considered himself fortunate if he heard from home once in two weeks. I suppose added to my natural desire to hear from home was a little anxiety in regard to my box of mince pies. Frank and myself are flattering ourselves that Andy will bring them when he comes.

I rec'd a letter from Marie last evening. From her accounts I should think it was quite gay in Syracuse. She wrote of attending a very pleasant party at Outwaters and said Jim was very devoted to Eva Sabine.[55] She said that Lucy told her that you hoped to have me home soon on a furlough. You must not look forward to my coming home this winter as I wrote you that my chances for a furlough are exceedingly slim. Marie wrote that Jim had been quite sick with the Diphtheria. You said nothing about it. Is he better?

I think the little picture has the pleasanter expression, don't you?

Yours affectionately,

Os

---

54. Eugene Wiggins, age twenty-eight, enlisted, on August 11, 1862, at Syracuse, to serve three years. He was mustered in as private, Company B of the 122nd New York State Volunteers, on August 14, 1862.

55. Eva Sabine (1844–1877) was the daughter of abolitionist William Sabine. William's twin brother was Syracuse's Commissioner Joseph Sabine, who oversaw the trial of Jerry McHenry following his capture. Eva was the first wife of Gen. C. D. McDougal, of Auburn, New York.

Camp 122d Reg't N. Y. Vols.
near Falmouth, Va.
Feby 23, 1863

Dear Mother,

What a storm we have had. It commenced snowing night before last and snowed all day yesterday but as good luck would have it. We got our new house and splendid one it is I can assure you finished the night before and how we did enjoy it yesterday.

Andy returned on the 20th bringing my dressing case, sash and the two pr of drawers which were just what I wanted. It seemed very good to see someone who had seen you, talked with you and dined with you. By the way Andy says you gave him the very best cup of coffee he ever had.[56] We had two visitors during the storm viz: a Mr. Baird from Fayetteville and a Mr. Jaques from New York. Fortunately our new house is much larger so that we accommodated them very comfortably but they got an insight into the rough side of campaigning. There was a detail from the reg't out on picket and had a tough time of it, but fortunately I was not on the detail. Frank thought it was quite a joke upon me the other day. The Col. brought word Dr. Fazer had something for me in his trunk in addition to the gingerbread—visions of mine-pie &c floated before me and I fussed around, got a couple of horses for two of our boys and sent them over after my packages. When they returned I rushed out to meet them and rec'd a pkg of books from Mr. May. Now don't understand me that I was not glad to get them, only that they arrived just when I expected something from home. These are a very nice service book and I shall distribute them among those of my friends who I think will appreciate them.

Our house is so large now that we have both a fire-place and a stove so we shall keep comfortable. this afternoon Andy and myself put down a floor in our parlor and as Frank had a carpet we are going to put that down. Frank has got a furlough and will leave to-morrow or next day. He will probably mail this in Washington but he will be in Syracuse soon and of course see you. as he won three mince pies of me which I beg of you to make him eat while there so that he cannot claim them out of my box. In sending my dressing case you forgot to put in my razor which is such a necessary article order with me now. Please have Jim get a good one and have it put in good order and send it with a razor strop and my little "shut-up" looking glass by Frank. Don't burden him with anything else as he will have considerable to bring for himself, unless he should insist.

Just got back from fatigue duty, Tuesday evening, having been over with a detail cutting wood for the brigade bakeries. brought back a loaf of warm bread. had a good supper and now sit down to finish my letter. By the way, I got a compliment. When I was starting for home Capt. Ellmaker (the Brigade Commissary)

---

56. Osgood's mother was often complimented on her coffee, and it was something she enjoyed making for others.

sent for me and wished to know if I could not come again to-morrow, saying I had accomplished so much to-day, but having some work to-do I respectfully declined. Excuse my vanity in telling you of this and don't mention it. I only told it to you thinking you would like to hear any flattery of your boy.

Andy brought us several books and among others a West Point love story "Cupid in Shoulder Straps"[57] that Joe May[58] sent Frank—it having been written by a young lady who used to visit in Syracuse—Jeannie Cray—I was disappointed in the book as I was rather taken by the title (Don't you think it descriptive of me?)

I haven't had a letter from you for over a week but have trusted you were well and perhaps thinking that having seen so many from home I did not need any letters, but I do. however I won't complain as you are very kind in writing so often. Andy told me that Willie was at home and I have since seen it noticed in the Syracuse papers (what a distinguished family we are getting to be—ahem!) I am looking forward to his return for of course he will ride over and bring me all the good news from home. I should have liked it to have been at home with him and opened that bottle of wine but never mind we shall still have a chance and what a happy reunion it will be.

I rec'd a nice letter from Johnny Wilkinson the other day.

Andy sends his regards to you.

Yours affy
Os

Tell that long legged brother of mine that he owed me a letter this time—I trust you have got those pictures I sent you ere this.

Camp 122d Reg't N. Y. Vols.
near Falmouth, Va.
Feby 27, 1863

Dear Mother

Your letter of the 22d was rec'd last evening. I am very glad you had such a pleasant visit from Willie, but you must not build your hopes too high in regard to seeing me—In regard to that box of "perishables." I wish Willie could have brought it to Stafford Court House as the great delay in our express goods occurs between Washington and here, but if you will see Frank Lester and tell him the box is in Washington, and contains articles for the benefit of the mess he will bring it along. It rained hard nearly all day yesterday, wind-up the snow and has given us the finest mixture of Virginia mud we have seen. As Andy remarked when we heard the rain yesterday morning, "Good for one more month of quiet."

---

57. Jeannie H. Grey, *Tactics; Or, Cupid in Shoulder-Straps: A West Point Love Story* (New York: Clareton, 1863).

58. Joe was a son of abolitionist Reverend Samuel Joseph May. He was named Joseph after the Mays' first son, also Joseph, died young.

Three Captains have resigned Moses, Crysler[59] & Chamberlain.[60] Moses is a very nice fellow and I am very sorry to have him go. He is well acquainted in Cortland and we used to have very pleasant times talking over our mutual friends. Crysler is also a very clean kind of a fellow but was not a very energetic officer. Chamberlain has [not] been with the regiment [long enough] for us to know what he amounts to—Lt. Platt[61] will have Mose's Co. and a very fine fellow he is. This arrangement will leave the Adjutant's position vacant and last night the Colonel offered it to Lt. Wooster (to whom he belongs by all rights of the case) but he generously told the Col. that he thought I was aspiring to it and did not wish to interfere with me. The Col. then left it for Wooster and myself to talk over. Wooster says if he can get the 1st Lieutenancy of Co. F. he shall insist upon my taking the Adjutantancy, and thus the matter stands at present. Andy however has a great deal of influence with the colonel and Lt. Platt of Co. F. is also interested in the plan so the arrangement may yet work. As for myself I am not so particularly anxious as my present position is such a pleasant one—although I of course should not object to a "bar" and I rather like the Adjutant's duties, but please don't say anything about the matter at present and I will write you as soon as the programme is decided upon.

Dr. Tefft who has been absent over a month has returned. He has had charge of the Division Hospital at Aquia Creek. I had a long talk with him yesterday. There were hospitals for every division in the army and altogether they had accommodations for over four thousand patients. His health is much better and he says he is so well that he should be ashamed to go home now to remain that he is [in] such good health.

Jud Webb,[62] a Lieut. of Co. B has a very severe attack of Typhoid Fever. Dr. T. told me yesterday that it was the worst case they had had at the outset. He is comfortably situated in the hospital and will receive the best of care. He is a very pleasant fellow, a son of ex-Sheriff Webb—and has just been promoted to a 1st Lieut. in his company. Dr. T. wrote to his father yesterday.

59. Cornell Crysler, thirty-two, enrolled at Syracuse, to serve three years, and was mustered in as captain of Company D, on August 28, 1862, commissioned at this rank on September 10, 1852, with the promotion dated August 11. He was discharged on February 24, 1863.

60. Webster R. Chamberlain, twenty-nine, enrolled at Syracuse, to serve three years, and was mustered in as captain of Company B on August 28, 1862, commissioned at this rank September 10, 1862, with the promotion date August 11, 1862. He was discharged on February 21, 1863.

61. George W. Platt, twenty-four, enrolled, August 15, 1862, at Syracuse, to serve three years, and was mustered in as first lieutenant of Company F on August 28, 1862, commissioned at this rank on September 10, 1862.

62. William Judson Webb, "Jud," twenty when he enlisted, August 14, 1862, at Syracuse, to serve three years, was mustered in as second lieutenant at camp near Falmouth, Virginia, commissioned at this rank on, September 10, 1862. He was promoted to first lieutenant, not mustered, on February 25, 1863, dated February 9.

My health is still excellent and the dr. did not know me when he first returned remarking that he must come to camp oftener if it would keep track of me.

Andy brought me an excellent photograph of Orrie which that clever "fat" man sent me.

I see the corps were to have made a parade on the 22d. I wish we could have had them march a little here that day—they would have a realizing idea of "sogering."

Capt. Gere, who went home on a furlough at the time an Frank did, promised to call on Dudley and give him a good account of the "subscriber." You have seen so many who have seen me lately that it is almost as good as my coming home.

I think that picture was such a flattering likeness that I should not have to go home for fear of disappointing you. I suppose you have by this time rec'd my other picture and transferred same to Marie.

Just now Walpole, Andy and Platt have come in and are now amusing themselves singing & c. Andy who as "Officer of the Day" has his sash and sword on is spouting Shakespeare so excuse any confusion in my letter. We have such pleasant quarters now that we have plenty of visitors. We have got a floor extending over about half of it and not another box is to be had for lover or money to finish it. We are very anxious to finish it before Frank returns as he is always abusing Andy and myself for being so lazy. Don't forget to send the razor and looking glass by Frank and tell him that my box is in Washington. I am sorry George and Jim could not come down. Frank promised to do his utmost to bring George back with him, and I hope he may yet be successful.

Please remind Lulu and Anna[63] that I am entitled to a letter from them. I hope there is a specimen of Lulu's cooking in my box.

Yours affy

Os

Once more I beg of you not to say a word about the promotions.

Camp 122d Reg't N. Y. Vols.

near Falmouth, Va.

Feby 28, 1863

Dear Mother

I am on "duty" as officer of the guard to-night, and must therefore keep awake I know of no better way to do so than to talk with you, or rather to come as near to talking as one can when the conversation is all on one side. I somewhat expect to go out on picket to-morrow and if I do it will be three days before I shall have another opportunity to write you.

Lt Webb died this evening. He was a very pleasant fellow and a good officer. It will be a terrible blow to his poor parents for he was the oldest if not the only

---

63. Anna Redfield Phelps (1852–1938) was a daughter of Lucy Blythe Putnam and Dudley Post Phelps.

son and was a brother-in-law of Jepson conductor on the Brigham tow road. Col. Titus has applied for leave of absence for two officers to take the remains home, Lieuts Gotches and Dillingham. We are going to have the body embalmed and defray the expense of sending it home. If Lieut. Gotches goes I shall have him call to see you.

In regard to the adjutantancy of which I wrote about in my last the programme is still undecided but I don't think that I shall get it and indeed I would not take it unless Frank Wooster gets a 1st lieutenancy somewhere. Gen'l Cochrane has resigned and goes home to-morrow. Col. Shaler of the Chasseurs commands the brigade temporarily and I wish that he might permanently have the command as he is *every inch* a soldier and he is six feet tall so you will perceive there must be considerable soldier about him.

We were mustered for pay to-day and I can assure you I looked very gay in my new coat (Andy's old one) no sash and white cotton gloves. There is a rumor that we are able to be paid early in March, in full up to the first of that month which I hope is true and I will then be able to "repair" my reduced account at the savings Bank. By the way, will you please ask Dudley how much stands to my credit at present at that institution.

Yesterday was quite warm and spring like and to-night we are having a warm rain which will make the picketing pleasant to-mmorow.

> Camp 122d Reg't N. Y. Vols.
> near Falmouth, Va.
> March 6th 1863

Dear Mother

Your letter enclosing Will's picture was rec'd the other day, and this is the only sight I have had of the young man since he got back from his visit home. We have had several beautiful days which I confidently expected that the young man would avail himself of, but he has not as yet. I suppose you have before this rec'd my letter which I sent by Major Davis announcing my appointment as Adjutant. I have commenced acting in my new capacity. We shall have a jolly mess now. Wooster, who is Andy's first lieutenant, Frank, Andy and myself. That Wooster is a perfect brick. He would have preferred the adjutancy but if he took it I should not have had any promotion but he kindly took a position he did not like so well to give me a chance, wasn't that clever.

This new "conscript bill"[64] provides that when a regiment is reduced below

---

64. Osgood refers to the Enrollment Act of March 1863, in which each congressional district was assigned a quota of volunteers to be drafted if a district was unable to meet its quota of recruits. See, for example, Eugene Converse Murdock, *One Million Men: The Civil War Draft in the North* (Westport, CT: Greenwood, 1980) and James W. Geary, *We Need Men: The Union Draft in the Civil War* (DeKalb: Northern Illinois Univ. Press, 1991).

the minimum of numbers only such appointments shall be made as are actually necessary to command the reduced numbers. Our reg't now numbers but 761 so they may cut short some appointments. I should not care so much about my own for I am a 2d Lieut. anyway but it would be very hard on our reg't (Serg't Major) Wright[65] who would have to carry a musket again.

I have been interrupted in writing this by the arrival of Jack Hawkins, looking as homely and honest as ever, accompanied by Judge Holmes of Syracuse and Maj. Root of the 12th—Jack gave me the gratifying information that he sealed up a box of mince pies for me shortly before he left home. They took dinner with us and Andy went back to the 12th with them.

Our new 2d Lt (Mot Wright) goes home on a furlough as Serg't to-night and will call and see Jim—He lives in Jordan. In regard to my coming you may rest assured that I shall come if possible but the chances are very doubtful. Having just entered upon the duties of my new position I feel some hesitation in asking for a leave, but as soon as I see a good chance I shall do so.

I enclose my pen which I wish Jim would have repaired, send back by the first one of our officers who is coming back. It makes such a coarse mark that I cannot use it and either needs a new point or to be sharpened up.

I send this letter by Silas,[66] the Colonel's son, who has promised to deliver it and call on you. I am glad you are beginning to find out that Flo is not a flirt and would suggest that the next time she is in Syracuse that you should call and see for yourself. I have just rec'd this evening your letter of March 1st.

I have got some papers to make out this evening to try and get a discharge for a poor sick boy in our Co. Randall Carson[67] (The son of Carson the temperance man) so good-night. Believe me dear mother that it is not for want of inclination that I do not visit home. My box has not arrived yet but I presume Frank or Guy will fetch it. Tell Jim to send my pen in such a case as jewelers use to keep expensive rings in.

Good night and believe your loving boy—Os

---

65. Morris E. Wright, twenty-nine, enrolled on August 8, 1862, at Jordan, to serve three years, and was mustered in as first sergeant, Company G on August 15, 1862. He was mustered in as second lieutenant on March 1, 1863.

66. Silas Wright Titus (1849–1922), was a bugler, at age twelve, in the Twelfth New York Regiment. Silas was named for a friend of his father's, Silas Wright, a US senator, governor of New York, and member of President Andrew Jackson's cabinet. In late nineteenth century, Silas developed and patented deep water pumping technology and early water supplies. He was known as "The Water Wizard." Silas Wright Titus obituary, *New York Times*, Jan. 10, 1922.

67. Randall Carson, twenty-five, enlisted on August 6, 1862, at Elbridge, to serve three years. He was mustered in as corporal of Company G on August 15, 1862.

CHAPTER FOUR

"Waiting for the Fight"

March 21–June 1863

Trusting, my dear mother, that I shall be spared to return
to your "apronstrings" once more—but remembering that
whatever may happen "God doeth all things well."
—Osgood Tracy, April 27, 1863

❀ Having secured a furlough after all, Tracy rejoined his regiment in time for the
spring campaign and witnessed institutional changes as Joseph Hooker attempted
to reorganize the Army of the Potomac and boost morale among the men. Each of
Hooker's men was ordered to sew a cross on his cap. "Aside from its convenience
in recognizing at a glance where a soldier belongs," Tracy wrote his mother, "it
will help to establish our 'Esprit De Corps' and a soldier will soon learn to take
a pride in his belonging to his Corps." As the spring campaign loomed heavy on
the horizon, with drills and parades, the newly minted second lieutenant's letters
speak to the excitement and anticipation of future battle as well as the more subtle
frustration with the regiment's place in the Army. "The 'latest,'" he wrote glumly,
"is that the 6th Corps are to be the "Army of Occupation." As March turned to
April, Osgood's letters reflected both the mundane—drill and picket duty—and
the more exceptional, including encounters with enemy pickets, newly liberated
slaves, and the destruction of once grand Southern plantations. Subtle references
to his political leanings shine through much of his correspondence and provide
some insight to the war as one soldier saw it. "Cap't Dwight informed me that
yesterday there were several darkies on duty as pickets upon the 'rebel' side [of the
river]," he reported. "If this be true I don't think that the North ought to hesitate
about using them."

Following the path of Burnside's failed Mud March, the new commander of the Army of the Potomac "Fighting" Joe Hooker moved on Robert E. Lee's depleted Army of Northern Virginia, still entrenched along the heights of Fredericksburg. Short on rations for his troops and fodder for his horses, and with Union forces holding Virginia's southeastern coast posing a threat to Richmond, Lee dispatched some twenty thousand men from divisions commanded by John Bell Hood and George Pickett to block any Federal advances toward the Confederate Capital in the winter of 1862.[1] As winter turned to spring, Lee's greatly depleted army now stood astride the path to Richmond with a force of less than sixty thousand men. At the end of April, Hooker divided his army, leaving John Sedgwick's corps, about forty thousand men strong, at Fredericksburg to hold the Confederates in check, while skillfully moving the rest of his army, almost sixty thousand men, west and south, crossing the Rappahannock and Rapidan Rivers, flanking the Army of Northern Virginia, and placing Lee's force in a precarious position.

On May 1, Lee responded to this Federal threat to the rear of his position. Leaving a force under Gen. Jubal Early to defend Fredericksburg, the remainder of the Army of Northern Virginia turned toward Hooker's army and advanced, despite being outnumbered nearly two to one. Hooker balked, drawing his army into a defensive line around the village of Chancellorsville. Dividing his army yet again, Lee sent Gen. Thomas Jackson's command of nearly thirty thousand men around Hooker's right. On the afternoon of May 2, Jackson's forces crashed into the Union Eleventh Corps, driving them back and forcing Hooker's to give up the campaign. That evening, Hooker's grand offensive against the Army of Northern Virginia crumbled as the union flank folded to the Confederate onslaught. Riding high in the wake of a string of stunning victories, Lee turned his army north and moved into Pennsylvania. As at Antietam and Fredericksburg, the men of the 122nd New York missed out on the fighting at Chancellorsville, holding the Union line opposite Fredericksburg as Hooker and his main force moved on Lee's flank. The Army of Northern Virginia turned north that summer, intent on taking the war out of Northern Virginia and resupplying the Southern forces. As Lee's army slipped away, Hooker was replaced by Gen. George Meade, in a campaign that ultimately ended at the small town of Gettysburg where, over the course of three days, two massive armies clashed in a battle that ultimately determined the fate of the nation.

Camp 122d Reg't N.Y. Vols.
March 21, 1863

Dear Mother

I arrived this afternoon in a rainstorm and on my way over from the station

---

1. Stephen Sears, *Chancellorsville* (Boston: Houghton Mifflin, 1996), 32, 36.

met Capt. Garland[2] who was formerly on Gen'l Sumners' staff, I stopped to speak to him and he told me the sad news of Gen'l Sumners' death,[3] which he had learned by telegraph about an hour before. I was very much shocked as I had not considered him as very sick, and the day I left Sam said that he was better. What a terrible blow it will be to Mrs. Sumner and the boys . . .

We had a very pleasant time in New York, called at Fannys and Charles. At Fannys we saw all but Kitty Parker and Mr. Wells. Fanny was very anxious for Jim to come and stay there but he declined. At Charles we found nobody at home but Kitty Parker who happened to be there. I was sorry at missing Clara. Ex-Cap't Moore took dinner with us at the International and after dinner we called upon Clara Dickson and Louise Pomeroy, had a very pleasant time. From there we went to Wallacks [Theater], The play was the "School for Scandal." The scenery is new and handsome, the dresses very fine, and the acting good. I enjoyed it very much. As the Baltimore train left at 11½ I concluded that I ought to leave the theatre at 10½ but when that hour arrived, it was just in the middle of an interesting scene and late or not. Court Martial or not, I was bound to see it through and waited about ten minutes longer and then I can assure you there was some lively "skedad-dling" but I got there in time.

I called upon Henry Stoddard at Washington. Endeavored to find my box but could not, and did not find it upon my return to camp, however I have faith that it will yet make its appearance and if the cake should be a little stale I think we shall be able to eat it. I found one letter from you but it did not contain any stamps. The letter was dated March 8th but perhaps Jim forgot to put them in or perhaps there is another letter containing them, on the road. I did not take cold in my face, thanks to your forecast in sending me back for a muffler. I found a long letter from Willie. He said he could not come over at present but wished us to come over and see him. He said he sent my box to the Provost Marshall of the Corps. If so it will come eventually. Please ask Jim about those stamps.

I did enjoy myself much during my visit home and can almost enjoy it over again in thinking of it.

We have nothing definite about moving. The roads are somewhat froze now but a few days of warm weather will bring forth the mud again in all its glory. Mot is building to-day and will leave me in undisputed possession the Adjutants'

2. Edward Goiland, thirty-one years of age, enlisted in the First New York Infantry on April 22, 1861, at New York City. He was mustered in as private, Company B, on April 23, 1861, to serve two years, and transferred to Company K, Fourth US Artillery, on December 10, 1862. He is also listed as Garvey and Garland in the military records.

3. Gen. Edwin Vose Sumner, Osgood's uncle, asked to be relieved of command after Gen. Joseph Hooker was given command of the Army of the Potomac. Sumner was subsequently assigned to the Department of Missouri but died in Syracuse, New York, before reaching that theater. Ezra J. Warner, *Generals in Blue: Lives of Union Commanders* (Baton Rouge: Louisiana State Univ. Press, 2006), 490.

tent. I have about decided to buy his house but shall not pay him until pay-day. I did not get my pay in Washington but the paymaster will be down soon to pay us up to March 1st. I got me a very nice rubber blanket in New York but although George Pridger got it for me at wholesale price yet I found that prices had increased considerably over last year. I got "Ravenhoe" in Washington and am very much interested in it. I see it is written by Henry not Charles Kingsley. Stoddard and I went to the theatre in Washington. The acting was rather "terrific" but a young fellow in front of us enjoyed it exceedingly and whispered to his companion, "Why this is just like the New York "Ledger."

I must write to Sam and so Good Bye

Yours affy
Os

Camp 122d Reg't N.Y. Vols
near Falmouth, Va.
March 25/63

Dear Mother,

We have instituted a very pleasant arrangement. Two or three times a week, Cap't Roome,[4] the Ass't Adj't Gn'l of the Brigade comes over and we have readings, principally by Andy and Roome and Lester. It is quite refreshing to have anything of this kind in camp, where there are so few refining influences. We have also another institution, viz: Brigade Drills. This is very useful as it accustoms the Brigade to maneuvering to-gether. I like them very much. It gives us pretty good exercise as they last about three hours. Every thing seems to trend to an active campaign. about every day orders come, for us to do something new in the way of preparation. Yesterday we rec'd an order that badges should be worn by the officers and soldiers of each Corps to distinguish them so that it would be known what Corps "straggled" &c.

The badge of our Corps will be a "cross." The badge to be worn upon the cap. Aside from its being a convenience in recognizing at a glance where a soldier belongs it will help to establish our "Esprit De Corps" and a soldier will soon learn to take a pride in his belonging to his Corps.[5]

My box does not yet make its appearance and I am beginning to be discouraged.

I wrote to Will the other day asking him again to try and come over but especially if there were any immediate signs of a move to be sure to come.

I saw by the Journal the first detailed account of Gen'l Sumners death. How sudden it was.

---

4. W. P. Roome was colonel of the Twenty-Third Regiment Pennsylvania.

5. This was a part of Hooker's general reorganization of the Army of the Potomac, demoralized after the string of defeats in 1861. See John David Billings, *Hardtack and Coffee: Or, the Unwritten Story of Army Life* (Boston: George M. Smith & Co., 1889), 256–58; Sears, *Chancellorsville*, 67.

We have several visitors from the 149th to-night among others Cap't Seymour[6] (not Joe, I regret to say)

Now Brigade Drills are instituted. tactics have to be studied. Good night

Yours lovingly

Osgood

P.S. Don't forget to send me a copy of the photograph of George and myself.

Camp 122d Reg't N.Y. Vols

near Falmouth, Va.

March 30, 1863

Dear Mother,

On Saturday morning the reg't went out on picket, but as the Adjutant does not have to go and Cap't Smith was not among the "fortunates" we thought it would be a capital time for an excursion. So yesterday morning Andy and myself having obtained permission from our soft-hearted major. The Col. is out with the pickets. Started for Stafford Court House about ten, intending to reach the 12th at dinner time, but as soon as we arrived there Steve Estes thinking undoubtedly that we looked rather hungry said that he was going over to the 149th and suggested that we should go with him. So off we three started arriving at the 149th just in time for a fine dinner with Col. Barnum. Just as we finished dinner Col. Root of the 12th and Lt. Clay of the 14th regulars. Jim knows him the younger brother. He has now charge of the ambulance train of Sykes' Division. He is a very pleasant fellow and tell Jim he inquires after him. After spending an hour or two at the camp of the 149th we started for Stafford Court House, our party having considerably increased consisting now of Andy, Estes, Randall, Clay, Seymour, Covell and myself. After traveling three miles over a little the roughest road conceivable we got to Stafford Court House and found that Willie had got a five days leave. Lt. Conley had gone Acquia Creek, but Dr. McNulty did the honors in the absence.

Willie's absence rather disarranged our plans as Andy and myself were going to spend the night with him, so Andy went back with Estes and I accompanied the 149th boys home. We got back in time for Dress Parade which gave me an opportunity to see Joe S[7] perform as he is acting as Adjutant in Dallmans absence. I had a very pleasant time with the two Joes. Col. Barnum looks very badly. He started

---

6. Ira B. Seymour, twenty-nine years of age, enrolled at Syracuse, to serve three years was and mustered in as captain of Company E on September 3, 1862. He was commissioned captain on October 4, 1862, with rank from September 5, 1862. He mustered out with the company on June 12, 1865, near Bladensburg, Maryland.

7. Joseph Seymour Jr., twenty-two years of age, enrolled on August 29, 1862, at Syracuse, to serve three years. He was mustered in as private, Company D, September 2, 1862, and promoted to sergeant major on, September 18, 1862. He was mustered in as second lieutenant, Company A, March 12, 1863, and commissioned at that rank on March 3, 1863, with the rank dated February 8, 1863.

for home this morning and is going to put himself under Dr. March at Albany. Tell the children that I saw Maurice who is looking very well and seems to enjoy "sojering."

I left the 149th this morning stopping at the twelfth for Andy. While waiting there Mosley[8] made his appearance. He was on his way to our camp so we all three came over together and he remained and took dinner with us. So you perceive that we had a very jolly time. The only drawback being that I missed seeing Willie, but as you were enjoying his society I suppose I ought not to complain. And I have fully impressed upon Mosley's mind that it is the 'infants' duty to come over to me immediately upon his return.

It has been beautiful weather yesterday and to-day and with the exception of the road from Brooke's Station and Stafford Court house we found the travelling very fair. There are of course any quantity of rumors about a movement and you can have your choice of half a dozen different routes to Richmond. At the 149th we learned that the 12th Corps was going to remain here.

I should have liked very much to have been home at Gen'l Sumners' funeral and am very glad that Willie was permitted to be, I thought that he would get upon somebody's staff.

I am going over to Stonemans[9] Hd Qrs to-morrow or next day as I presume Win. has returned by this time.

I have not heard from home since my return and am longing for my correspondence to get back into its old "channel" again. But I am somewhat tired and slightly "sore" from two days riding. an exercise to which I am not much accustomed yet and this afternoon have been wishing myself at home where I could have a pillow to sit on.

But Good night
Yours sleepily
Osgood

Camp 122d Reg't N.Y. Vols
April 3, 1863

Dear Mother,

We were reviewed to-day by Gen'l Hooker. Gen'l Slocum was here and Mosely startled me by saying that they had received a telegraph from Willie saying you were sick and asking for an extension. It has made me feel very anxious but I trust

---

8. William W. Mosley, twenty-five years of age, enrolled on September 3, 1862, at Syracuse, to serve three years. He was mustered in as second lieutenant, Company D, on September 17 and as first lieutenant on December 7 the same year.

9. Gen. George Stoneman (1822–1894) was a prominent cavalry commander during the war and later served as governor of California from 1883 through 1887. See Ben Fuller Fordney, *George Stoneman: A Biography of the Union General* (Jefferson, NC: McFarland, 2007).

that it cannot be anything very serious or you would have telegraphed me. I shall anxiously await intelligence from home-

We abound in reviews. had one yesterday when the Division was reviewed by Gen'l Sedgwick and again to-day when we were reviewed by Hooker. To-day I made my first appearance mounted. After the division was reviewed, Col. Shaler[10] invited all the mounted officers of this Brigade to accompany him to the review of the other two divisions of the Corps. At Brooks' Division I found Mosely and filled Willie's place on the staffs for a little while. By the time we got to Howe's Division, the cavalcade amounted to about 200 officers of all grades from Gen'l Hooker to a 2d Lieut. I saw many of the generals of the army of the Potomac, Sickles, Wadsworth, Butterfield, Meade, Sedgwick &c. Two ladies on horseback were present and of course received plenty of attention from the crowd of officers.

It has been a most beautiful day for the review and decidedly suggestive of marching orders, but I understand that they have received furloughs in several corps when they had stopped granting them, which would seem to be an indication to the contrary.

I have received but one letter from Syracuse since my return and that from Marie, but what with Willie's visit and your sickness I suppose you have been unable to write. I told Mosely to send Willie over immediately upon his return. Trusting that you will soon recover your good health, I remain

Your affectionate son
Osgood

Camp 122d Reg't N.Y. Vols
April 10, 1863

Dear Mother,

I have neglected writing you for the last day or two as I have been waiting for a letter from you. My last news was Willie's letter of the 2d stating that you were better and if you continued improving that he should leave on Sunday night. If he had done so I should have thought he would have been over here before this. I hope to-night to get a letter in your familiar handwriting which although it might not be considered by some as remarkable is to me the handsomest of all.

We had a grand review by President day before yesterday.

We left camp about 8 o'clock A.M. and marched over beyond Falmouth where our Corps was assembled. The President looked about as handsome as usual. Among others accompanying him was his little boy about 10 years old mounted on a little pony. He seemed to enjoy it very much riding along side of Gen'l Sedgwick.

---

10. Alexander Shaler, of Hamden, Connecticut, was given command of the First Brigade, Third Division, of the Sixth Corps after Fredericksburg. See Warner, *Generals in Blue*, 435. The 122nd New York was a part of this brigade between October 1862 and January 1864.

I looked anxiously for Slocum and his staff among the cavalcade hoping to hear something of Will, but they were not present. After our Corps was reviewed quartermaster Connie and myself rode over to the review the 2d, 3d and 5th Corps—making in all about 60,000 troops which is considerable of a sight for one day. At the 5th Corps Connie and I "mixed in" with Hookers staff and rode down the line as grand as possible. To-day we have been mustered in accordance with orders from Washington to enable Provost Marshall Gen'l to arrange the troops and expect to be filled up with conscripts.

The weather is beautiful but the "latest" is that the 6th Corps are to be the "Army of Occupation." Iin contradiction to this rumor however are the orders to turn in all extra tents and they have reduced allowances of the "Field & Staff" to three tents so the Col. and myself have been obliged to tent together. I still "mess" with Frank, Andy and Wooster. We have got a very comfortable place, our bunks in our corner steamboat fashion, one above the other.

I am reading "No Name" by Wilkie Collins[11] which is very interesting. Captain Wragge one of the characters, is very similar to Connie Fosco, except in personal appearance and habits but he has the same cool "tricky" ways.

Steve Estes is over here to-day, Only twenty days more for the "old 12th" I tell Steve that he will never be contented at home and I expect to see him back in about two months.

Love to all and a double quantity for you if you are well enough to stand the dose.

Yours lovingly,

Os

Camp 122d Reg't N.Y. Vols
April 11, 1863

Dear Mother,

Willie made his appearance in camp to-day and I obtained permission to ride back with him and spend the night. I have had a very pleasant time talking over home if my letter is disconnected please remember that Willie is lying upon the bed supplying me with "items" as I write. I am very sorry to hear you have been so sick but hope soon that you will be able to be about again. We have just been talking about it and decided that we ought to write often while you are sick so you may expect to be "bothered" often.

I believe I wrote you in reference to those stamps. I found but one letter from you upon my return and that contained no stamps. There may have been another letter which was lost or you may have forgotten to put the stamps into that letter.

We are going over to call upon Maria Holyoke's lover to-morrow morning and I shall make a short visit to the 149th.

---

11. Wilkie Collins, *No Name* (London: Sampson Low, Son & Co., 1862).

The weather is beautiful and very warm. Willie sends love to which I add my "quota"

Yours

Os

Camp 122d Reg't N.Y. Vols

April 11, 1863

Dear Mother,

This morning Dr. [Jonathan] Kneeland of Onondaga made his appearance in camp and I rode down to the river with him, with my usual faculty I soon got acquainted with him. He knew Dudley very well and promised to call and see him upon his return and upon my informing him that my name was Tracy he went off into ecstasies about a letter that Dudley read him once. I of course had to acknowledge that I was only brother to the "here."

This is the first time I have been down to the river since we crossed and I enjoyed it very much. It seems very strange for foes to be within a stone's throw, literally speaking, of each other and on the best of terms. As I was riding along the back this morning I passed a rebel picket post upon the opposite bank where two "rebs" were sitting and one of them jumped up and "presented arms" I of course returned the salute. I took the Colonel's field glass down with me and amused myself for an hour or two "staring" at the "reb" pickets, several of them were fishing. Cap't Dwight informed me that yesterday there were several darkies on duty as pickets upon the "rebel" side. If this be true I don't think that the North ought to hesitate about using them. There was no talking this morning as the orders were very strict in regard to it.[12]

On our side where our regiment are on picket are two fireplaces known as "Morrisons and Pollocks." They are surrounded by negro huts and outbuildings and must in their day have been very fine places. At Morrison's there is the remnants of a flower garden and as I passed to-day I noticed some in bloom and I am very sorry I did not stop for a specimen.

I found Andy cheerful notwithstanding yesterday's rain. Cap't Platt told me that he made the rounds twice three times getting wet through each time.

Since I have been writing the mail has arrived and imagine my surprise and delight at beholding your "pot hooker" as you are pleased to call them. Yes, my

---

12. This observation has likely contributed to the longstanding myth of Black Confederates, which supporters of the Lost Cause have used in an attempt to dispel the idea that the Civil War was over the institution of slavery. The most recent and conclusive study to contextualize and dispel this is Kevin M. Levine, *Searching for Black Confederates: The Civil War's Most Persistent Myth* (Chapel Hill: University of North Carolina Press, 2019). Adam Domby's *The False Cause: Fraud, Fabrication, and White Supremacy in Confederate Memory* (Charlottesville: University of Virginia Press, 2020) provides an excellent overview of the creation of the Lost Cause, including the role of Black Confederates in this mis-memory of the war.

box is a gone case. Willie says he sent it to Falmouth. On my way home which was soon after the time he sent it I saw Col. Todd the Prov. Marshall and he had then seen nothing of it. I asked him to keep a look-out for it and take care of it which he promised to do and on Tuesday I sent to him again but he had never seen anything of it. It is too bad after you took so much trouble but we must submit to the fate of war.

It is a city I had not received that information this morning in regard to that wonderful Spring near Fredericksburg as I should have been tempted transgress the rules and asked the "rebs" about it.

Charley Bell[13] got back last night and brought my bridle. It is a very nice one and tell him it suits me exactly.

I enclose my commission as 2d Lieut. having received mine as Adjutant. Please preserve it and my Serg't Majors warrant for if the 122d should distinguish themselves I shall feel very proud of them in after years.

The paymaster of one of the other brigades in our division is here and I trust that ours will make his appearance next. Fortunately Frank has got some money left so he supports the mess and as long as you get enough to eat there is not much more use for money here.

I am very sorry to hear Uncle Hiram does not improve. Give my regards to him and the Phelps family. Tell Anna I wish I could drop in this evening and take a music lesson and help Lulu and himself sing.

Well, good night and may God bless you and keep you safe until the return of your loving boy.

Os

P.S. I send this by Cap't Dwight who goes home on a furlough tomorrow morning.

Camp 122d Reg't N.Y. Vols
April 12, 1863

Dear Mother,

I got back this afternoon just before Dress Parade but I kept out of sight until Wooster, who was performing my duties during my absence, had got started and I had the pleasure of looking on. Our regiment is looking finely now. We are reduced in number but what we have are very efficient and will be able to stand another campaign without suffering much. How soon that campaign is to begin no one seems to know. Dr. McNulty got back from Washington just before I left to-day and says the prevailing opinion is that our movements will depend entirely upon the success of our army at Charlestown. If we succeed there he thought that

---

13. Charles S. H. Bell, twenty-three years of age, enlisted on August 13, 1862, at Jordan, to serve three years. He was mustered in as private, Company G, on August 15, 1862, and deserted, July 1, 1863, on the march to Gettysburg, Pennsylvania.

we should advance upon the enemy here. He did not enlighten us as to what the prospect would be if we were not successful at Charlestown.

I was very much pleased with Capt. Moore of the 2d reg't who is acting Provost Marshall upon the staff. He is a very gentlemanly fellow, very quiet.

But you should see how Capt. Best enjoys Willie and Mosely's discussions. They never agree and one never makes an assertion without the other disputing it and yet they are the best of friends and willing to do anything for each other. I like Capt. Best very much except he is so bitter against abolitionists and republicans. Willie is quite improving. they call him an abolitionist over there now. I think he is seeing the error of his ways.

This morning we rode over to the camp of the 3d Wisconsin and made a short call upon Dr. Bartlett. I was quite pleased with his appearance. Willie rode back as far the 149th with me. We saw the two Joes and took dinner with Capt. Randall.[14] Joe Seymour seems to be in better spirits. When I have seen him before I have thought that he was not very well pleased with army life. He seems very well contented now.

Wooster and Andy are both writing and we are all talking so don't say anything if my letter is disconnected. Andy sends his regards to you and kind wishes for your recovery. I am very anxious to have you able to write again for your letter are so full of news that Frank and I depend upon them. Will posted me up on all the news. What a brick he is. I love him more and more as I learn him better. Cap't Morse asked which one was the oldest wasn't that rather severe on Osgood.

I think I must be improving in riding inasmuch as I do not feel the need of a pillow to-night.

Willie had one of my photographs. I think (they are not flattering) that I must be getting handsomer. You ought to send Aunt Holyoke one in return for her defence of me when you used to say so much about my homeliness.

I see that the theatricals have taken place. How I should liked to have been there. Did Marie look lovely as ever? Did I tell you about her last trial? I think not, but don't mention my having spoken of it. She wrote me in her last letter that her father has lost money and would be obliged to sell his house and was talking of moving up into the 2d Ward (Germany) to live over a drug store. She wrote that it would probably affect her position in society but that she would have an opportunity to test her friends, but she knows it is her duty and she submits with a resignation that cannot be too highly praised. I think she is just a little the finest girl I ever met and I will not except even Flo.

14. This is likely Capt. Charles Bertrand Randall. Randall enlisted in the Twelfth New York in April 1861 in Syracuse and was discharged for promotion on June 8, 1863, commissioned into the field and staff of the 149th New York Infantry. He was wounded at Gettysburg on July 3, 1863, and was killed in July 1864 at Peachtree Creek, Georgia.

The weather for the last two days has been very warm and this evening after supper we sat out-of-doors singing and talking. You should hear Andy sing to really appreciate it most.

Mr. May has sent me two or three anti-slavery standards so I must write to-night acknowledging them. I will try and write every day until you get well again, although I fear the frequency of my letters may make them dull.

> Good Night-
> Your Boy
> Os

I have written several times for a copy of that photograph of George and myself taken when I was at home and if I don't receive one soon I shall make it a ground for an application for another leave of absence.

> Camp 122d Reg't N.Y. Vols
> April 14, 1863

Dear Mother,

To-day is very busy with us. We rec'd orders this morning to have everything in readiness to move to-night. We shall not probably move before to-morrow or next day but still everything must be ready to-day. So many things accumulate during three or four months sojourn in camp that the first breaking up is rather hard and especially when the transportation allowed is of such a limited quantity. However as I am now "mounted" I can get along much more comfortably.

The cavalry corps moved yesterday. Dr. Pease made us a short visit the evening before. I had been intending to go to see Willie but had neglected it and now shall have to wait until we revert South of the Rappahannock. I hear nothing in regard to the 12th Corps as yet, but shall keep a lookout for a small red-headed staff officer. I rec'd Jim's letter last evening containing the photographs of George and myself. I think it is very good of George, one of the best I have ever seen of him, Altogether it is a very gay picture. One rarely sees two such handsome fellows (ahem).

You will probably know our destination before we do, but the supposition now is that we are to cross the river below here. It is rumored in camp to-day that Stuart is up into Maryland again, and this movement may be to head him off. If we don't move tonight and I can think of any news I shall write tomorrow.

> Yours Truly
> O. V. Tracy

> Camp 122d Reg't N.Y. Vols
> April 15, 1863

Dear Mother

If you hear the rain pouring down you would probably be as well satisfied as I am at remaining in camp. I don't know whether this storm will be severe enough to delay the movement or not, but as yet we have received no further orders. We are all packed ready for a start. This morning nearly all the reg't were sent out on picket. Andy had to go off in the rain but the rest of the "mess" are fortunate enough to be left in camp. If it clears up to-morrow we are going down to visit him. I have not been down to the river since we crossed after the battle of Fredericksburg and I have almost forgotten how a rebel looks.

Who should make his appearance in camp last evening but Bigelow,[15] Jim's friend from Baldwinsville. He came over from Pettits Battery[16] and only spent an hour or two. He has promised to come over again before he rides. Frank got part of the Programme of the 1st Entertainment last night from Emma Waring.

Now that you are sick I fear I shall not get any description of the affair unless you can impose upon George that is his duty to write me upon the subject.

My regards to Ann and tell her she must get you well as soon as possible for I miss your letters very much.

Good Bye
Your Boy
Os

Camp 122d Reg't N.Y. Vols
April 23, 1863

Dear Mother,

Your letter of the 19th was received to-day, you cannot think how delighted I am that you are getting able to write once more. If you could see with what pleasure I receive your letters you would be fully repaid for the trouble of writing, And so I have got two rivals and both widowers, as to Frank I can keep watch of him especially as I have the assorting of the mail to attend to generally and might "suppress" the letters from Nellie but of Ware[17] I feel rather afraid. Perhaps I might get George to take care of my interests in that quarter. I fear however that in spite of all my efforts success in that quarter is hopeless and by the time the war is over Nellie will be settled down the wife of some good fellow and I beginning to wonder how an old bachelor feels. I also rec'd a letter from Johnny W. to-night informing me that he was to be married on Thursday, that is to-day, and by this time he is a married man. I thought your remarks about the Wilkinson boys was rather severe. Perhaps you intended an insinuation for myself for you know I have always had rather a weakness in regard to your apron strings but who wouldn't with such a mother.

---

15. Pvt. George F. Barlow was with Company B of the First New York Light Artillery.

16. This is a reference to Company B, 1st New York Light Artillery, raised in the summer of 1861 in Onondaga County, New York.

17. This is in reference to another of Nellie's suitors, whom Osgood feared would steal his love interest. "George" was George Hunt of Syracuse.

This must be a great country for peaches. Every house, no matter how small has a few peach trees about it and now that the land is cleared off and the peach trees in bloom you can tell whenever there is a house within some distance of us by the pinkish hue.

I expected last night when I went to bed that we should receive marching orders during the night and be off to-day sometime, but just after I got to bed it commenced raining and has continued during the day which will probably put a stop to all movement for a day or two. An officer who is connected with the pontoon train says that they had orders to lay the pontoons last night but were prevented by the storm. I don't hardly believe it however.

After many false alarms the paymaster has at last arrived and will pay us to-morrow afternoon. You can imagine what a happy set of fellows we are to-night, as the available means of our mess are reduced to about $4.

I wish I could be at home and enjoy the large family. Give my love to the Holyokes. Andy who is living at Division Hd qrs, now is just going over and it is my last chance for the mail so I must bid you goodnight. If I have enough money left after paying for my horse I will send home some.

Good night once more
Your loving boy
Os

Camp 122d Reg't N.Y. Vols
Sunday, April 26/63

Dear Mother

I have just returned from a visit to Col. Titus who is on picket duty. Andy, Capt. Roome and Lieut. Johnson of the Brigade Staff, the quartermaster and myself rode down together. It is a beautiful day and we had a very pleasant time. At Morrisons Andy and Roome got one of the old darkies to pick them each a "bouquet" and an "octoroon" to arrange them. There are quite a number of negros left at Morrisons and if you could see how neat and comfortable their houses looked, you would think that Virginia family servants did not have a very hard time. Now don't be shocked, fearing I am liking slavery, for I am a good deal "blacker" a republican to-day than when I left home.

We then rode down the river about a mile to the Fitzhugh place. The house itself is not particularly handsome but the situation is beautiful. Knowing your admiration for scenery, I wish you could have been there with me to-day. The view is splendid and to add interest to what nature has done. you can see the Rebel camps on the hills across the river with the "pickets" down near the bunker. Mr. Fitzhugh, one of the darkies told us, is quartermaster in the Rebel Army, although Mrs. F. whom the colonel knows says he only South to look after some unsettled business. Mrs. F. still lives there and has one or two pretty daughters. Our party having rec'd the addition of Col. Titus and Maj. Healy of the Chasseurs, dashed up in front of the house in grand style hoping that, the fair creatures might be prompted enough by curiosity so that we could catch sight of them, but in passing the first time we were rewarded only with the sight of a falling curtain, but as we returned we caught a glimpse of a very pretty girl (and you should be out of sight of all beautiful womenkind for some time to really appreciate the blessing). I am almost afraid that were there any pleasant secesh young ladies in waiting distance I should be tempted to take the chances of having any secrets wormed out of me.

We have still 8 days rations on hand, and are expecting to move at anytime. Maj. Healy told me this morning that the pontoons were down near where our pickets are stationed and that an engineer party was at work down at the river near them last night.

I am sorry that you should feel hurt that I did not tell you that we were ordered to Fortress Monroe, but although I thought I had heard all the camp rumors I must confess not to have heard that. I have about concluded from what I can hear, that if we do move we shall cross the river not over 20 miles below here and push forward as rapidly as possible so that by the time our 8 days rations that the men and 5 days extra which are to be carried in the wagons, are consumed we shall be able to get our supplies "via" York River. My health has been excellent since my return. A party of us went over to serenade Co. Hamblin, our old instructor last evening, (now don't make any disparaging remarks about my singing for you don't know how much I improved) and he commenced at me by remarking, "who would believe that big fat fellow is the same one who came out of the hospital at Downsville looking so "peaked."

Our regiment was paid off yesterday up to the first of the month. I have paid for my horse and paid some debts, had here and will try to send $50 home by the next officer going on furlough.

I hope that Marie's lover will succeed in getting a furlough. Can Willie help him obtain it? I think if the circumstances were stated to Gen'l Slocum that he would take pity.

I am so sorry that the Holyoke's did not arrive before I left but I hope to see them all next fall. You will be able to keep track of me as soon as we get started by the papers and you know I will write at every opportunity.
Love to all, and believe me

Your affectionate boy
Os

Camp 122d Reg't N.Y. Vols
April 27/63

Dear Mother,

I hope the good people of Syracuse will not be so enthusiastic over the return of the twelfth that they will not save some for the time, two years and four months from now when the 122d shall return and God grant that we may come back with full numbers and an honorable record. We have received orders to move early to-morrow morning and everyone is busy packing, casting sad glances at all the little comforts and "contrivances" which serve to make camp life so pleasant and which are not "possibilities" on the march.

We have taken Davis Cossitt, Jim Lawrence's[18] cousin and a very nice fellow into our mess to supply Andy's place and if we succeed in getting a horse, to-night as we expect shall be all right. The boys all appear to feel in good spirits and ready for a start notwithstanding the general impression is that we are to cross the river near our former place of crossing. I enclose photograph of my friend Lieut. Gotches which please put in your book unto the "civil war is ended."

Trusting, my dear mother, that I shall be spared to return to your "apron-strings" once more, but remembering that whatever may happen "God doeth all things well."

I remain your loving boy
Os

The next two letters are dated May 1 and May 3, 1863. When Osgood wrote them, he had no idea that on May 2, his brother Will, who was then a twenty-year-old lieutenant in the 122nd US Infantry and aide-de-camp on the staff of Maj. Gen. Henry W. Slocum would be seriously wounded at the Battle of Chancellorsville. Will wrote their mother, "This was a magnificent army in high spirits and with great hopes. It was a finely planned campaign, promptly executed by the Corps Commanders who advanced under fire as they waded the Rapidan in water up to their armpits." Hooker had ordered an advance, then, surprisingly, a return to the original line. Will continued: "The reason he vouchsafed to the astonished Corp Commanders was that he had information Lee was coming to attack and he would await him there. His information was true. Lee was coming, and did so with a vengeance."

On May 2, Will's general sent him to deliver a message to Gen. Alpheus Wil-liams,[19] to bring back the troop lines. After giving Williams the order, Will soon found he had ridden within enemy lines. Gen. A. P. Hill witnessed the event and ordered, "Shoot him! Kill him!" What happened next became a turning point in the war for the Tracy brothers and family.

18. James S. R. Lawrence, twenty-one years of age, enlisted at Marcellus to serve three years and was mustered in as corporal, Company F, on August 5, 1862.

19. On May 2, 1863, during the Battle of Chancellorsville, Alpheus S. Williams (1810–1878), a Union brevet major general, and the Seventh Corps "was able to entrench hastily and able to stop the Confederate advance before it overran the entire army, but it suffered 1,500 casualties in the process." Before the war Williams had been a lawyer, judge, and journalist, and after the war he was a US congressman.

Camp 122d Reg't N.Y. Vols
May 1, 1863
1 P.M.

Dear Mother,

We have not moved since yesterday but there has been some fighting on the right and Hooker appears to be working down in the rear of the Rebels. Newton[20] is now commanding our Corps and Wheaton[21] our Division. Gen'l Sedgwick having the command of this movement on the left, consisting of our corps and the 1st commanded by Gen'l Reynolds. To-day has been very pleasant, aside from the good news from the right we hear that Heintzleman[22] is at Front Royal with a good chance of cutting off the Railroad communication with Richmond and our forces are said to hold Gordonville on the right thus cutting off their communication with the West. Cap't Wheeler of the 149th was here last night on the way to his reg't. I sent word to Willie that I was all safe. I wish I could hear from the boy for I fear from the firing the 12th Corps, may have been engaged to-day, but if anything should happen, you would hear of it immediately. I still think we shall not make any attack here, but merely threaten their centre to keep them from throwing their whole force on either flank.

Everything looks bright and we are all in the best of spirits. Good bye for the present

May 3, 1863

Dear Mother,

Just after supper last evening we rec'd orders to fall in and having an opportunity to send my letter I sealed it without having a chance to finish which will account for the abruptness of the close. We marched about a mile down the river making as large a display as possible with the hope, I suppose, of deceiving the "Rebs." We got back to our camp about eleven. This morning we marched down the river about two miles. when Reynolds Corps was withdrawn and the bridge taken up and moved up to the right, it is supposed to reinforce Hooker, and we

---

20. Gen. John Newton, commissioned brigadier general of volunteers in September 1861, led troops during the Peninsula Campaign, Antietam, Fredericksburg, Chancellorsville, and Gettysburg before being promoted to lead the First Corps after the death of Gen. John Reynolds on the first day of Gettysburg. Warner, *Generals in Blue,* 345.

21. Gen. Frank Wheaton's father-in-law, Gen. Samuel Cooper, was the ranking general in the Confederacy. Wheaton joined the Second Rhode Island when the war broke out and was promoted to brigadier general on November 29, 1862. Warner, *Generals in Blue,* 553.

22. Gen. Samuel Heintzelman, a Pennsylvania native, graduated from West Point in 1826 and served in posts throughout the west before the Civil War. In early May 1861, he was appointed colonel of the Seventeenth Infantry and later was promoted to brigadier general of volunteers. Wounded at Bull Run, he was given to a number of different posts as the war progressed. Warner, *Generals in Blue,* 227–28.

have just moved back to our old place again, Fredericksburg and exactly where we crossed before. Part of our corps are across the river but do not seem to show any signs of attacking and I think our business is to be merely to watch the rebels. We have just seen a large column of rebel troops moving up to the right over the hills opposite us. I trust Hooker will be strong enough for them.[23] I can hear nothing from the right. We have seen a great deal of smoke, heard firing and seen a balloon to-day in the rear of Fredericksburg all of which we trust are signs of Hooker's army.

I rec'd your letter last night and will give you my advice. The first question is which will be more agreeable to you keeping house or boarding. It is not probable I shall return home to stay until the war is over, and Willie, we know, will not. If you can get anybody agreeable to come and live with you, I don't mean to take boarders, but as Jim is likely to leave at any time and I don't think you ought to be alone so much. I think you might enjoy housekeeping better than boarding. On the other hand if you should decide to board you get an agreeable place with plenty of room no matter how much it costs, for your comfort should be first thought of. I have no particular objection to Burnet St. and like the house very much but as to the price I of course can give you no advice but should leave that to those at home who are capable of judging. The whole thing resolves itself to this. Do whatever you think would be the pleasantest for you and you may rest assured that your boys will be satisfied. Perhaps you may think I have not given you much advice but I will leave it to yourself which is just what I want.

I find I like the position of Adjutant in the field better even than when in camp, especially if the walking be muddy.

The boys seem to bear it very well that they are not allowed to participate in the fighting that is going on, not but what they would willingly go wherever ordered but they don't "hanker" after it so much as at first.

Frank sends regards to you all and especially to Marie

Good Bye
Your aff son
Os

Unlike his brother, Will Tracy's experience at Chancellorsville was life altering. The young officer found himself in the midst of the battle in action that would help to define his war and that of his family. For Osgood and his family, Will's heroics were cause of concern and celebration and secured his place in history. Will wrote of his experience and injury in a postwar account published in *Deeds of Valor: How Our Soldier-Heroes Won the Medal of Honor.*

23. As Hooker moved the Army of the Potomac northwest to cross the Rappahannock and Rapidan Rivers in an attempt to flank Lee's army at Fredericksburg, he left the Sixth Corps opposite Fredericksburg. See Stephen W. Sears, *Chancellorsville* (New York: Houghton Mifflin, 1996), 228.

An unidentified newspaper clipping in Mrs. Tracy's scrapbook, titled "Rebel Opinion of Mr. Tracy's Exploit," noted:

An officer who was taken prisoner by the rebels on Sunday at Chancellorsville told me a few days ago that while a prisoner several soldiers asked him if he knew what officer it was who rode through their lines the night before (Saturday). He could not tell them not knowing anything of it, but it was undoubtedly Tracy who was referred to. It seems he rode directly by A. P. Hill's headquarters, and Hill himself gave the order to fire on him. All were much surprised at his escape, and voted him a damned brave Yankee. General Hill said it was the boldest thing he ever saw done.

On May 7, in a bedside ceremony, General Slocum promoted Will to captain, then wrote the Tracy brothers' mother:

Dear Mrs. Tracy,

Your son is at Aquia Landing in hospital, well cared for. Several inches of the bone of his right arm have been removed and strong hopes are entertained that his arm will be saved.[24] I sent him with a message to General Williams', when the Eleventh Corps broke, and he got inside the enemy's lines. They ordered him to surrender, but he said "he could not see it," and put spurs to his horse. A volley was fired at him. One ball passed through his horse's ear; another into the saddle; another into his rump; and one hit Tracy in the arm. I will see that he wants nothing. He is a brave fellow. His commission as captain came today.

Yours truly,
H. W. Slocum

The next day, Osgood wrote their brother, Jim.

I received your letter of May 4th this evening. We moved to our present position, near the camp we occupied during the winter, this forenoon. It is a much pleasanter and better location. Yesterday afternoon I received a letter from General Slocum's staff saying Willie was at the corps hospital at Aquia Creek wounded in the arm. I did not get it until five o'clock and immediately asked permission to go but Colonel Shaler, expecting we were going forward again this morning, refused me. As soon as we got in camp again this afternoon I commenced again and

---

24. Though amputation is commonly associated with the Civil War battlefield, surgeons often tried to save limbs. One method was resection, which involved removing a portion of the damaged bone with the hopes that the two segments would grow back together. This surgery was performed on Will following his wounding. His experience was recorded in *The Medical and Surgical History of the War of the Rebellion:* vol. 2, part 3, *Surgical History* (Washington, DC: GPO, 1883).

have just succeeded in getting a pass from General Sedgwick and shall start early in the morning. I am afraid that I shall be too late and that Willie will have started for Washington. If so I shall go to General Slocum's Headquarters and learn all the particulars in regard to it-

I was thinking yesterday afternoon how fortunate mother had been to have both her boys pass through safe (for not having heard anything from Willie I presumed he was all right) when the orderly brought me the note, but tell mother she must feel thankful now that the wound is not in a severe place and I trust that a few weeks of her care will soon put him right again. If he has not already started for home I shall try and get him off and if possible accompany him as far as Washington. You can imagine what a "stew" I have been in all day thinking of him wounded and so near as Acquia Creek and yet unable to go to him.

I see the 149th has suffered some. I shall stop there on my way back. I was told tonight that General Hooker issued orders yesterday to lay a bridge at Port Royal and to advance but the President countermanded it. We have been unable to get any New York papers as yet since the fight and are therefore very much in the dark. It is getting late and I have some business to arrange to-night, as I shall not have time in the morning.

Good-Bye

Your aff brother

Os

After receiving news of her son's wounding, Sarah Tracy went to Washington, DC, though it was one week before she could obtain permission to join him. She remained until early June, when Will was able to go home to Syracuse. After his arm healed, Will took to the field again, rejoining General Slocum and his regiment on August 15, serving under General Sherman on his March to the Sea.

Camp 122 Reg't N.Y. Volunteers near Fairfax Station, Va.

June 17/63

Dear Mother

We have had a very hard time since we commenced changing base. We recrossed the river on Saturday night, in the midst of a severe rain-storm, without the loss as far as I have learned of a single picket. Ash Allie made his appearance that afternoon and was with me during the operation. He said you were to leave for home on Monday morning but from subsequent operations I judge you did not wait until Monday. On Sunday we marched to Stafford Court House, resting for the night. On Monday we marched to Dumfrie [Virginia] arriving there about 6 P.M., took a bath went to bed, got up about 2 A.M. and off we started arriving at this place (about a mile from Fairfax Station) yesterday afternoon pretty much used up. The "old soldiers" acknowledge that it beats anything they ever have suf-

Osgood and William Tracy, wartime, shortly after the Battle of Chancellorsville. William is holding his injured arm. (From the photo album of Osgood Tracy)

fered. Frank Lester was used up on the second day's march almost fainting away, but he is all right now. On our road here, we would often see evidences of the retreat in the shape of remnants of burned wagons ammunition, lying by the side of the road and overturned sutlers wagons. The boys seeing that Uncle Sam was destroying his own property thought the sutlers could suffer a little out of sympathy. Yesterday we halted at noon at Wolf Run Shoal where I had just time to drop you a line. We had a splendid swim in the Occoquan Creek, and it was amusing to see the crowd in swimming.

To-day they are giving us a rest but Gen'l Newton, I heard, told the doctors they must cure up all the sore feet in readiness to-morrow. Yesterday I saw a Washington paper giving an account of Lee's doings. I wish they would draft all the "Copperheads." I suppose this will "rouse the North." Is it not discouraging that after a year we are just where we were, with the prospects of another Maryland campaign before us? The boys don't like to go back there fearing they will be obliged to pay for the chickens &c stolen last Fall.

If Jim did not belong to Co. D I should rather enjoy the idea of the 51st Reg't being ordered out. I should like to see the Corps, soldiering.

The 12th Corps passed through here the day before yesterday but tell Willie that the boys with the wagon train said that the most of the Corps passed through the second day as stragglers. the 149th they said had about 100 men when they passed. I am very anxious to hear from you and Willie but we have rec'd no mail since Saturday and probably shall not for some time to come. We came up with our wagons yesterday and to-day were indulging in the luxury of a change of underclothing. Hereafter I shall carry a change with me. I found in my trunk a package from you which Smithy brought and which was sent by Birdseye[25] who gave it to Andy. I have not opened it yet but will when we next get into camp and convert it to some use.

Love to all

Your aff boy

Os

P.S. After a good trial I am convinced that I can ride just as far as the reg't can walk—

Camp 122 Reg't N.Y. Vols

June 21 1863

Dear Mother,

I received Jim's letter last evening announcing yours and Wills arrival in Syracuse. I was very much delighted as I was beginning to feel quite anxious about you. Tell Willie that I think Gen'l Slocums acceptance of his resignation would note valid in this Corps and I have by the advice of our Brigade Adj't Gen'l forwarded the official notice he sent me to Corps Hd Qrs, where Gen'l Sedgwick will probably issue an order discharging him.

We are still in the same position as when I last wrote you i.e. about a mile from Fairfax C.H. I was so busy yesterday making out reports that I did not go over, but hope to do so to-day. I see by the papers that the bulk of Lee's army is in front of the old Bull Run ground and this morning there has been and is now while I am writing, artillery firing in that direction. As Hooker has so "disposed of his force as to baffle their designs," I suppose we have nothing to fear. Night before last I received a very kind letter from Mr. Murray in which he expressed a great deal of sympathy for Will and wished me to let him know when you were to pass through so he could be of assistance to you. For the last two days it has been more or less rainy and consequently much cooler, which is very refreshing to the poor fellows who have been used up by the heavy marching and hot weather. Dr. Tefft has rejoined the reg't now. He has a little son about 10 years old with him, who is a very nice little fellow and bears the dear family name of Eddy. I of course have taken quite a fancy to him, and am cultivating an acquaintance rapidly.

---

25. Mortimer Birdseye was twenty-one years old when he enlisted in the 149th New York on September 3, 1862. He appears later in this volume as one of Osgood's friends and confidants.

I hear that George is having a flirtation with Nellie S. I trust you will see that he does not take an unfair advantage of my absence. I hope the furlough systems will be renewed soon so I can go home and investigate the matter.

I rec'd a very pleasant letter from Dudley the other day, He seems to think that Uncle does not improve any. I trust that his projected visit to the seashore may be of service to him.

Last evening Jim Hall,[26] formerly on the Binghamton Road and now a lieut. in Frank Lester's company presented me with a very handsome pair of spurs. I had been "subsisting" upon the Government previously.

Quite a squad of rebels passed here yesterday, and as the boys marched down to the road one of them sang out, "It is the first time we have seen you Yankees run." "Yes," after you, I suppose you mean" answered one of our boys.

This lieut. [William] Tracy in the Chasseurs told me a day or two ago that he had rec'd a letter from his father, to whom he had written in regard to his genealogy, saying that he was 4th cousin to Charlie Tracy so that we have concluded that we are relations after all. He is a very nice fellow and a good officer. He has a slight touch however of the constitutional infirmity of the Chasseurs—a slight fondness for whiskey. But if those Chasseur boys do drink some they are most of them gentlemen which is a redeeming feature down here.

I am very glad you have got back again as I shall not get any "regular ration" of letters, which with all due deference to my other correspondents, I have sadly missed. Please say to Willie

> Camp 122d Reg't N.Y. Vols
> near Centerville, Va.
> June 25th 1863

Dear Mother,

We marched here from Fairfax C. H. yesterday afternoon, and if there be any truth in rumors, it is probable that our Division will remain here for sometime. Abercrombie's[27] division that we relieve is going to Thoroughfare Gap. We are expecting to move this afternoon to get into a position. We are now only bivouacked upon a field, but probably shall not be more than two or three miles from here at any rate. We shall undoubtedly be on picket about half the time, but in this pleasant weather that will not be much of a hardship.

Today I am 23 years old, and wish that I could drop in on you this evening and

---

26. James Hall, thirty-five years of age, enrolled on August 9, 1862, at Fayetteville, New York, to serve three years. He was mustered in as sergeant of Company C on August 14, 1862, and later to lieutenant.

27. Brig. Gen. John Joseph Abercrombie was an 1822 West Point graduate who served in posts across the South prior to the Civil War. He was appointed brigadier general of volunteers in August 1861, though his "activities were confined mainly to garrison and administrative duties, including command of depots around Fredericksburg and White House, Virginia." Warner, *Generals in Blue,* 3.

receive your congratulations. Frank Lester presented me with a very handsome gold pen and case, which is the only present I have received. I succeeded in getting some bottled cider to-day, which did for champagne for the boys to drink my health.

I see the news from Pennsylvania to-day is very discouraging. The rebels are certainly playing a bold game.

I walked over to the town of Centerville or rather to the few houses that are left, yesterday afternoon. From an earthwork we got a most beautiful view of the Bull Run country. The first battle took place about four miles from here and I intend if possible to go out and take a look at the ground. Last evening I was blessed with the sight of your familiar writing again. I received your letter of the 21st and was delighted to hear that you and Willie reached home with so little difficulty and that the Capt is still doing so well. I shall think that it is entirely Willie's fault if he is not engaged to 3 or 4 different young ladies, for "brass buttons" always are so interesting. must be doubly more so when the Captain has been wounded.

We shall be near enough to Washington now I trust to get any little comforts. We are now able to get green peas, lettuce & c. Well, I trust that my stupidity this afternoon is not to be an index of my future birthdays, but I suppose the weather can be blamed for it.

Yours

Os-

Camp near Poolsville Md—

June 27, 63

Dear Mother,

I have just got an opportunity to send the enclosed, and have time to add a word. We marched about 20 miles yesterday, camping near Drainsville and have marched about 14 miles today. We started about 4 this A.M., and the rumor is we are to go to Frederick City to-morrow so it behooves us to get as much rest as possible.

The weather has been very cool, raining part of the time for that last two days & splendid for marching. The night of the 25th we spent on picket on the road from Centreville to Bull Run and it *did* rain, my blanket has not got dry yet.

As we were crossing the Potomac to-day at Edwards farm I met Van Brock . . . Jim's friend on the pontoon bridge. My new horse suits me much better than the old one which I now use for a part time . . .

I will write again at the next opportunity but it is impossible to tell when that will be.

Yours lovingly

Os

Camp 122d Reg't N.Y. Vols
June 30, 1863

Dear Mother,

We arrived at Manchester, Md., to-night, this being the 5th day of continued marching averaging 20 miles a day. We passed through Westminster to-day a very pretty town and the inhabitants were very kind giving the boys things to eat without charging them, and well might they be thankful for last night they had a brigade of rebel cavalry there who left upon our approach. Kilpatrick's brigade of cavalry is after them and I trust will catch them. Our boys are almost used up the continual marching but I am all right.

Yesterday I was so unfortunate to lose my pocket-book containing about $50. It is rather tough but it will teach me to be much more careful in the future.

We have had no mail since the 25th but rumor says we are to have ours tonight. It is said to-night that we are going to York, Pa. to-morrow about 25 miles. We are now but about 4 miles from the Pa. Line. I am writing this without any certain means of getting rid of it but trust I shall be able to send it off to-morrow

June 30/63 [continuation of letter above]

I have been over to Manchester to-night and took supper at a hotel and was waited upon by a beautiful young lady. Only think of it. I have just returned and find that our supper is not ready yet, so I shall have to eat two to-night. Well, good night. Our . . . needs all the sleep he can get now-a-days.

Your boy
Os

CHAPTER FIVE

"The Rebels Are Certainly Playing a Bold Game"

Gettysburg, July–October 1863

"When this cruel war is over" and we are all once more reunited, I know you will feel happiness for the sacrifices you have made in sending your boys to the war.
—Osgood Tracy, August 24, 1863

❀ Until July 1863, Osgood's personal experiences in the military were rather mundane. Though the 122nd New York was a part of the Army of the Potomac and the Sixth Corps and near the fights at Antietam, Fredericksburg, and Chancellorsville, the men sat on the sidelines watching others earn glory on the bloody fields of battle. As the larger confluence of the war and military action passed, Osgood dutifully continued to write to his mother, assuring her of his well-being and speaking to local gossip, rumors, and routine of military life. The spring of 1863 saw the Union war effort in the east falter, and stunning victories by the Army of Northern Virginia further stoked divisions among Northerners. Osgood was keenly aware of this and he wrote with some disdain to his mother about the Copperheads, antiwar Democrats, in their midst. Yet, he remained optimistic. As Lee's army turned north, and Osgood turned twenty-three years old, the young officer, his comrades, and the rest of the Army of the Potomac took up the chase.

In the wake of his victory over Hooker at Chancellorsville, Lee turned his army toward Pennsylvania. He hoped to accomplish a number of goals with this move. The Army of Northern Virginia had yet to be defeated by its Union counterparts, and Lee believed his army invincible. Moving north into Pennsylvania relieved pressure on Richmond while threatening Baltimore, Philadelphia, and Washington, DC. Lee's presence in that area would force the Union army to fall back in defense. For two years, the two armies had wreaked havoc on Northern Virginia, and Lee also hoped that moving his beleaguered men north would allow him to resupply his army while also alleviating the strain of war on that region. Finally, a victory on Northern soil could potentially tip Northern public opinion in favor of peace.[1]

Lincoln replaced Joseph Hooker with George Meade on June 28. The Sixth Corps was already on the move; it had left Bristow Station on the night of the twenty-sixth. "The darkness," recalled George T. Stevens, surgeon of the Seventy-Seventh New York, in his memoirs published soon after the war, "was intense, and a drizzling rain rendered marching disagreeable." The men of the corps were pushed to their limits in pursuit of Lee's army when they heard of Hooker's replacement. "The announcement of this unexpected change at such a time, was received with astonishment, and by many indignation," Stevens recalled. "To deprive the leader of a great army of his command just upon the eve of a great battle, when, by the most brilliant marches and masterly strategy, he had thrown his army face to face with his enemy, thwarting his designs of moving upon the capital, without some offense of a grave character, was an act unheard of before in the history of warfare."[2]

Unlike the regiment's experiences at Antietam, Fredericksburg, and Chancellorsville, the men of the 122nd New York finally faced the enemy in battle on the bloody fields of Gettysburg those hot July days in 1863 and did so, according to Osgood, heroically at Culp's Hill, where they repulsed a day of Confederate assaults on the Union line.[3] Years later, as Osgood and his comrades of the 122nd New York returned to Culp's Hill to erect a monument to their service, he recalled his experiences at Gettysburg. His words provide some context to those bloody days in July of 1863 as the young officer and his comrades lived them, and help to expand upon the feelings and emotions poured forth in Osgood's letters immediately after the battle:

> To those of us who participated, the events of the war seem so real that we forget the years that have passed. . . . In the early part of June 1863 the armies were confronting each other along the lines of the Rappahannock River when Lee decided upon the invasion of Pennsylvania. As he moved north the Army of the

1. See, for example, Stephen W. Sears, *Gettysburg* (New York: Houghton Mifflin, 2003); Allen C. Guelzo, *Gettysburg: The Last Invasion* (New York: Alfred A. Knopf, 2013); Kent Masterson Brown, *Retreat from Gettysburg: Lee, Logistics, and the Pennsylvania Campaign* (Chapel Hill: Univ. of North Carolina Press, 2005).

2. George T. Stevens, *Three Years in the Sixth Corps: A Concise Narrative of Evenings in the Army of the Potomac, from 1861 to the Close of the Rebellion, April 1865* (Albany, NY: Weed, Parsons, & Company, 1866), 236–37.

3. Culp's Hill, which is about three-quarters of a mile (1,200 meters) south of the center of Gettysburg, Pennsylvania, played a prominent role in the Battle of Gettysburg. Its two rounded peaks are separated by a narrow saddle, with its heavily wooded higher peak 630 feet (190 meters) above sea level.

Potomac moved also on an inner parallel line keeping between Lee's army and Washington. Leaving the Rappahannock river about the middle of June, 1863, we had constant severe marching until the afternoon of July 1, 1863 found us at Manchester, Md., about thirty-six miles from Gettysburg, where we enjoyed a much needed day's rest after our continuous and arduous march from Fredericksburg. But the battle had begun, and the Sixth Corps was sadly needed there. Our Division Commander, Gen'l Newton, was called to take the place of Commander Reynolds who had fallen in defense of his native state.

We left Manchester at dusk on the evening of July 1st and all through the dreary night pushed on toward Gettysburg—as morning dawned the sound of the second day's battle greeted our ears, faint at first but growing more & more distinct as we hurried forward to the assistance of our comrades of the Army of the Potomac. Halting only for the occasional five minutes rest and twice to make coffee, we struggled on through that hot July day nerved to renewed efforts as the sound of the battle grew louder and louder. We reached the banks of Rock creek, just in the rear of the battle field, at 2 o'clock that afternoon, and redeemed the promise our noble Sedgwick had made the night before: "Tell General Meade" he said to the staff officers who brought him the order, "tell General Meade, I will be at Gettysburg, with my corps, at 2 o'clock tomorrow afternoon."

Part of our corps was engaged that night marching on to the field in a double quick after their long and arduous march, and assisted in relieving the third Corps. Our brigade went into bivouac a little in rear of the front line of battle, sleeping on our arms. We men roused again before daylight and moved over to Culp's Hill, our extreme right, and for a short time were in reserve but Lee was making a desperate attempt to turn our right and a regiment in front of us having got out of ammunition, we were ordered forward to take their places. We charged across the knoll and reoccupied the breastworks which, with other regiments on our right and left, we held against their repeated charges until they abandoned their attack in despair. While behind the breastworks and in the midst of the fight, a regiment moved up and took the place of one on our immediate left, and it proved to be the 149th New York regiment, organized in this county the next month after ours, and which belonged to the 12th corps, and this was the only time during the war that we met as regiments.

During that morning's fighting we had ten men killed and thirty-four wounded, which was a large proportion to the number actually engaged, as our numbers had been considerably decreased by our long and arduous march. For an hour or two there was a lull in the battle, and then was opened that terrific artillery fire which was intended to sweep the crest of cemetery ridge of our batteries and troops, preparatory to Pickett's famous charge. But that has been so ably described by another, that I will quote his words, merely stating that our brigade was moved during the artillery fire as a support to the centre, but were not actually engaged at that point:

"In the shadow cast by the tiny farm house, which Gen'l Meade had made his headquarters, lay wearied staff officers and tired correspondence—There was not wanting to the peacefulness of the scene the singing of a bird which had a nest in a peach tree in the yard. In the midst of its warbling a shell screamed over the house instantly followed by another and another and in a moment the air was full of the most complete artillery prelude to an infantry battle that war ever exhibited. Every size and form of shell known to British and American gunnery shrieked, moaned, whirled, and whistled and wrathfully fluttered over the ground, as many as six in a second, constantly two in a second, bursting and screaming over and around the headquarters, made a very hell of fire that amazed the oldest officers. A shell tore up the little step of the headquarter's cottage, another one soon carried off one of its two pillars; soon a spherical case burst opposite the open door, another ripped through the low garret. Not an orderly not an ambulance, not a straggler was to be seen on the plain by the temptest of orchestral death thirty minutes after it commenced. Were not one hundred and eighty pieces of Lee's artillery trying to cut from the field every battery we had in position to resist the proposed infantry attack and to wipe away the slight defense behind which our infanty were waiting? Forty minutes, fifty minutes-counting the watches that ran-oh so languidly—shells through two of the lower rooms, a shell in the chimney which did not explode—shells in the yard—The air grew thicker and fuller and more deafening with the howling and whirring of their infernal missiles—and the time measured on the sluggish watch was one hour & twenty minutes. A shell exploding in the cemetery killed and wounded twenty-seven men in one regiment. Yet the troops lying under the fence, stimulated and encouraged by General Howard, who walked coolly along the line, kept their places and awaited the attack. It was 2:30 o'clock. "We will let them think they silenced us," said General Howard. The artillerists threw themselves on the ground beside their pieces.

Suddenly there is a shout "There they come!"

Every man is on the alert. The cannoneers spring to their feet. The long rebel lines emerge from the woods and move rapidly over the fields to the Emmitsburg Road.

Howard's batteries burst into flame, throwing shells with the utmost rapidity. There are gaps in the rebel ranks but onward still they come. They reach the Emmitsburg road. All of Howard's guns are at work now. Pickett turns to the right, driven in part by the fire of the 5th and 6th corps batteries. Suddenly he faces east, crosses the meadow, comes in reach of the muskets of the Vermonters. The three regiments rise from their shallow trench; there is a ripple, a roll, a deafening roar. Yet the momentum of the rebel column carries it on. It is bcoming thinner and weaker, but they still advance.

The second corps line is like a thin blue ribbon. Will it withstand the shock?

"Give them cannister! Pour it into them!" shouts Major Howard, running from battery to battery. The rebel line here reached the clump of shrub oaks. It has drifted past the Vermont boys- onward still.

"Break their thin lines—smash their support," says Howard, and Osborne and Wainwright send the fire of fifty guns into the column; each piece fired three times a minute. The cemetery is lost to view, covered with sulphurous clouds flaming and smoking like Sinai on the great day of the Lord. The front line of rebels is melting away, the second is advancing to take its place, but beyond the first and second is the third, which reels, breaks and flies to the woods from whence it came, unable to withstand the storm.

Hancock is wounded, Gibbon is in command of the second corps. "Hold your fire, boys; they are not near enough yet," shouts Gibbon as Pickett comes on. The first volley staggers, but does not stop them. The move upon the run-up to the breastwork of rails—bearing Hancock's line to the top of the ridge, so powerful is their momentum. Men fire into each others faces not five feet apart. There are bayonet thrusts, sabor strokes, pistol shots, cool, deliberate movements on the part of some, hot passionate separate efforts with others—hand to hand contests—recklessness of life—tenacity of purpose—fiery determination. Then ghastly heaps of dead men; seconds are centuries, minutes ages, but the thin line does not break. The rebels have swept past the Vermont regiments. "Take them in the flank," says General Stannard.

They swing out of the trench—turn a right angle—move forward a few steps, and pour a deadly volley into the backs of Kemper's troops. Other regiments catch the enthusiasm of the moment and close upon the foe. The rebel column has lost its power—the lines waver, the soldiers of the front rank look around for their support. They are gone, fleeing over the field—broken, shattered, thrown into confusion by the remorseless fire from the cemetery and the cannon on the ridge. The lines have disappeared like a straw in a candle's flame. The ground is thick with dead and the wounded are like the withered leaves of Autumn. Thousands of Rebels throw down their arms and give themselves up as prisoners.

How inspiring the moment! How thrilling the hour! It is the high-water mark of the rebellion, a turning point of history and human destiny.

Gettysburg was the Flying Onondagas' first true brush with the enemy and the young officer spoke eloquently of the unit's action in the battle years after the war, filling in the blanks left in letters home he penned immediately after the fight. This correspondence, likely written in haste in the chaos of the fight at Gettysburg, give us a glimpse into the thoughts of a man who had just witnessed history and, like in his earlier letters, those Osgood penned home in July took on both national and personal issues and are largely void of any grand proclamations of glory or attempts to preserve his place in the history of the war. Concerns with the growing Copperhead movement and the draft appear often during this time, as does the legacy of the Army of the Potomac in light of its escape south of the Army of Northern Virginia from those bloody Pennsylvania fields. As the war dragged into its third summer with no end in sight, Osgood's letters take on a sense of futility.

The day after the battles of Gettysburg, Osgood wrote his mother twice in one day, likely speaking to his own anxiety about her worrying about him as the 122nd Regiment participated in the battles.

> Camp 122d Reg't N.Y. Vols
> July 4, 1863
> 11. A.M.

Dear Mother,

We had a hard fight yesterday . . . we had 7 men killed, 31 wounded besides Maj Davis who had his jaw broken & Lt LaRue who was wounded in thigh. They were the only officers who were wounded. Two men—one each side of me were wounded etc. but I providentially escaped unhurt. Our regiment behaved splendidly. We were at this time attached to the 12th and were fighting side by side with the 149th behind the same wall. Was it not a remarkable coincidence that these two regiments should have met for the first time in such a place –

Maj Randall[4] of the 149th had just shaken hands with me before he was hit.

We drove the rebs away from the stone wall by which they lay by the heavy fire behind our breastworks.

The rebs were repulsed at every point and on our left their loss is very heavy, much more *so* than ours. We have taken a larger number of prisoners.

All is quiet this morning. I guess we had our celebration yesterday.

> Good Bye &
> Yours lovingly
> Os

I enclose a wild rose picked up on the field and an old execution I picked up

---

4. Charles B. Randall, late captain of Company K, Twelfth Infantry was commissioned (not mustered) major on March 17, 1863, with a rank from the same date, and mustered into the regiment as lieutenant colonel on June 8, 1863, with a rank from March 1 of the same year. He was wounded in action July 3, 1863, at Gettysburg, Pennsylvania. He was killed in action July 20, 1864, at Peach Tree Creek, near Atlanta.

Camp 122d Reg't N.Y. Vols
July 4, 1863

Dear Mother

I wrote you this morning saying I was safe knowing how great your anxiety would be but I am very thankful this time that you have had but one "chicken" to worry about.

We arrived at Manchester Md on the night of the 1st laid shelter on the 2nd until about 5 o'clock when we rec'd orders to march. We marched all night & the next day until about 4 P.M. making in all about 30 miles. During the night I was so sleepy that I had to get off my horse and had to walk to keep myself awake.

After our arrival near Gettysburg we laid quiet for about an hour and then were ordered up to the front and then remained all night. The next morning (yesterday) our brigade was detached and ordered to report to Gen Slocum. . . .

We were put in behind a large breastwork of logs. The rebels were behind a stone wall about 200 yards distant. I happened to be with the left wing when the 13th Maryland who were in front and came running in from the breastworks maintained. I supposed that they were being driven in but as soon as we learned the state of the case the 6 left companies advanced and took . . . in the breastworks in our front. I can tell you the bullets whistled some. We kept our frontline and finally drove the rebels from their position—soon after we took possession of the breastworks a regt came & relieved the regt on our left & judge of our surprise & pleasure to find it was the 149th. Was it not remarkable that the first time the two regts from Onondaga have met should be fighting behind the same breastworks. Capt Doran was wounded near me & Lt Col Randall had but left me when he was hit.

Grail Gravy under whom immediate command we were, spoke very highly of our conduct. I introduced myself to him & he pretended that he recollected us.

After this "rebs" were driven away we were exposed to quite a severe shelling & one man in the Chasseurs was killed.

About 4 o'clock we recd orders to move back to the left and in moving up to or present position the shells flew about rather promiscuously. We are still in the same position we were last night. All is quiet except a little picket firing.

In front of where we are now laying is where the rebs made some desperate charges upon a battery yesterday. Information in the aftermath . . . get horsepower on a road in the rear of us but they were . . . with terrible slaughter—Frank and myself have been out towards the front this morning & where this charge was made it looks like "Antietam." Very near to us is the hospital of the 2nd Corps. Our men have about all been brought to a hospital further in the rear but there is a larger number of rebel wounded, including many officers, who are boys have been taking care of this morning.

I saw two colonels both of whom they said were in command of brigades yesterday.

We have taken 15 strands of colors—between 5000 and 10000 prisoners.

Our loss has been heavy but not near as bad as the rebels I think.

I saw this Battle flag of the 8th Virginia which had been taken.

Of course everyone had the usual number of escapes yesterday. Lieut Hoyt of "E" Co had his blanket which was slung about his body hit by a bullet.

Frank [Wooster] had his two men killed and thirty wounded in his company. I gave a full list of killed & wounded to Mr Osborn the Herald reporter who lives at Brig Hd Qrs. You must keep a lookout for the Herald account of this affair as I understand . . . gives our regt a good deal of credit.

I have just heard from Maj Davis.[5] He is severely but not dangerously wounded. His jaw is thought to be broken. Lieut LaRue is also doing well.

Some of the rebel officers we have been taking care of are very pleasant and intelligent fellows & appear to feel very grateful for the attention shown to them.

Good Bye

Yours lovingly

Os

Camp 122 Regt N.Y. Vols

July 8th, 1863

Dear Mother,

Since my letter of the 4th, we have had some tough marching.

We left the battlefield on Sunday morning, July 5 marching on the road to Emmitsburg over the same road the rebels had retreated as soon as we got a few miles beyond the battlefield we began to see the rebel wounded every barn & house in sight had a red flag on it denoting that it was used as hospital—One that I went to had 260 & another over 300 all rebels there were one or two rebel surgeons left at each hospital, but their medical supplies were very limited and the poor fellows must have suffered terribly. We halted just beyond Emmitsburg about 1 o'clock that night [Monday]. It is quite a town and near where we . . . was an . . . busy building a Catholic Institution.

Tuesday [yesterday] morning we started again & crossed the . . . Kittodan mountains in a rain storm and just as little the darkest night I ever saw. It began to grow dark when we were about half way up and rained like blazes. We got to a little town on top of the mountain and I laid down in the rain & slept till morning.

We started again this morning & marched about six miles to our present position. There is firing in the direction of Boonsboro and I think we may have to start again tonight

5. Joshua B. Davis, enrolled at Syracuse to serve three years and was mustered in as major, August 28, 1862. He was wounded in action July 3, 1863, at Gettysburg. On January 15, 1864, he was discharged for disability caused by wounds.

I used to think that the man who as . . . Blanc was considerable of a fellow, but after last night's experience I feel fully equal to him and got off at walking.

I was too dash to ride & stumbled through the weeds & stones until I began to think that we should reach Heaven before we should get to the top of the mountains. Our particular . . . in the brigade acknowledge that it was little the worst marching they ever had and their boys have been short of rations.

Today we rec'd the news of the fall of Vicksburg which quite repaid us for our hard marching & if we only succeed in "squashing" Lee's army I will feel very well satisfied.

July 9

I did not have time to finish my letter last night & as . . . go straight in mail later. I finished on horseback—Capt Truesdall of Gen Shaler's staff went to see the 7th yesterday and found them . . . living without even shelter tents . . . and boards that have been picked up . . . Hope you are well.

Good Bye
Your loving son
Os.

Camp 122d Reg't N.Y. Vols
July 11, 1863

Dear Mother,

I was double blessed this morning in receiving two letters from you—one from July 2 and another of July 5th and very glad to notice that up to the date of your last you were not aware that the 122d had been engaged and trust that before you did find it out that you rec'd one of the letters that I wrote you on the fourth announcing my safety—after reading your letters Brower, Wooster, Cossitt and myself went down to a little house near here and had *such* a breakfast it was worth the price of breakfast to eat off such a clean table cloth and at the risk of offending you, I must say the soda biscuits were about equal to yours—At this house is the finest spring I have seen since "I went for a soldier." It boils up at the corner of the house in a basin about 8 feet square and runs off and around and under the house so they have a running stream under their kitchen floor from which they can get water without stepping out-of-doors.

In this country where they have no ice you can imagine what a cool cellar such a stream would make. I told the Colonel that a 10 inch pipe would not convey the water off. He thought we were exaggerating but upon seeing it he concluded that a 16 inch pipe would hardly do it.

But it is about time to inform you of my whereabouts. I finished it day before yesterday A.M. That day we marched to Boonsboro and halted for the night. It is a small town on the Hagerstown turnpike. Towards night quite a sharp skirmish took place between our cavalry and the rebs, our force driving the rebs toward Hagerstown.

As we passed Gen'l Pleansanton's HdQrs I saw Dr. Pease for a few minutes. He inquired with a great deal of interest after the "Captain."

Yesterday morning we advanced upon the Hagerstown pike about three miles occupying the round from which the cavalry drove the rebs from the night before. There appears to be some movement this morning and my idea is that we are to go into position and await an attack from them. For every days delay as long as they cannot cross is an advantage to us. We have possession of the Sharpstown crossing, confining them to the crossings between Williamsport and Hancock.

If Lee's army should escape, it cannot be laid to the Army of the Potomac for they have done all that men could do but rather it would be a gone case with Lee's army

Hagerstown is only about 7 miles distant. The news we get is that the bulk of Lee's army is in position extending from Hagerstown to Williamsport. I think there will be another big battle before Lee's army gets away which it did last.

Two more of our boys who were wounded just died and two more are not expected to live.

That night we crossed the mountain in the rain and darkness my darkey was in the rear of the column leading my pack horse but when morning came the darkey and horse were missing and have been since until yesterday Provost Marshall Lester found the horse in the possession of the Lt. Col. of the 4th Vermont who picked him up that night on the mountain. He of course gave him up but the "pack" is missing. I sent one of the boys back and am in hopes he will find the darkey (who probably unloaded the horse and tied him up but the horse afterwards got away) and they pack and pick up a horse and bring them along.

I had nothing very valuable on the horse except our "mess kit" which is not very expensive but very difficult to replace them. However as we have made some mess arrangements with Brower we should not suffer.

When I lost my pocket book I regret to say it contained that last supply of stamps that you sent me and has left me entirely destitute so please send me some.

I have not seen any detailed account of the fight yet but the Herald editorial of the 6th said that on the 3rd the rebs made a severe attack on the left when a "Brigade of *New York troops*" composed mostly of *Pennsylvania militia* went in and saved the day. This was Shaler's Brigade of the 6th Corps and as the 122d was the only reg't of the brigade engaged I suppose we can claim the credit of "saving the day" and I will account [missing] for, Will's benefit the reputation of the 12th Corps.

I hope Gen'l Slocum will give us proper credit . . .

I am delighted to hear of Willie's improvement and trust that he will get back by the 1st of September—You know that all the corps of the Army of the Potomac have badges now—I would like to get a little pin made of blue enamel just lined with gold somewhat this style.

The cross is a square cross. I should like it about an inch long lined with gold on the edges, the 122d N.Y.V. to be in gold letters. The cross I want to have a little pin in this style.

Don't do anything about it but merely enquire what such a thing would cost and if you can suggest any improvement do so. I intend to come on a furlough just as soon as furloughs. . . . You may imagine that we feel rather proud of our 6th Corps badge. The "rebs" have more respect for them than they do for "Stars and Crescents" and the like

Yours lovingly

Os

P.S. Ask George if he is taking a mean advantage of my absence, captivating the fair Nellie that he is ashamed to write to me.

Camp 122d Reg't New York Vols
July 21, 1863

Dear Nell,

Your description of the wedding was received this morning and I shall dream of nothing but red curtains and white lillies for a week to come. Your parlor must have looked beautifully and as to the bride, my opinion has already been too frequently expressed to need any repetition. It seems as though I was fated to miss those weddings that I most wish to attend. First, Flo and then Marie. Is it always to be so I wonder? I sometimes think that I shall not be allowed to be present at my own but be married by "Deputy."

I of course could have wished that Marie's choice might have been someone that I like better than I do the major,[6] but I presume it is much more important that she should be satisfied than that I should, and my only prayer is that she may have chosen wisely and that her wedded life may prove to be as happy as it now seems to promise. As for the major I consider him the most to be envied of any young man of my acquaintance. I rec'd a short letter from Marie written the evening before her marriage informing me of the plans and requesting me to continue the correspondence or rather to address to the care of Mrs. Hillic which I considered as a hint to that effect. Now, I have never exactly approved of corresponding with married ladies, but if both Marie and the Major see no objections I shall not deprive myself of the pleasure of receiving an occasional kind letter from the dear girl—I mean Mrs. Jenney. I also received the wedding cake and many thanks for your

---

6. When the war began, Edwin "Ned" S. Jenney (1840–1900) joined the Zoaves as second lieutenant. He then organized a company of men from Oneida County, and the two companies went out together. In October 1862 he organized yet again, this time as a captain, of what became known as Jenney's Battery, and he was soon promoted to major. When the 185th New York Regiment was organized in Syracuse and mustered in on September 22, 1864, Jenney was assigned as colonel until February 1865, when he resigned. See *Syracuse Herald*, June 29, 1900.

thoughtfulness. It is a pleasure to be reminded that one is not altogether forgotten. Frank Lester starts for home to-day with Col. Titus and Cap't Brower to bring on the conscripts for this regiment. They are ordered to Elmira, but probably will be at Syracuse a portion of the time. We are now on the road from Berlin to Warrentown the same that we travelled last fall. I trust that we shall be able to return by the way of Richmond this time, not "individually" but as an army. Indeed I have already advised Frank to make his arrangements to rejoin us at Richmond as by the time this (the) conscripts are ready I hope we shall be there.

With regards to your mother and family, renewed thanks for your kindness I remain

Your friend

Os

Camp 122d Reg't New York Vols

near Warrentown, Va.

August 7, 1863

Dear Dudley,

Yours of the 3rd is rec'd. I have been quite busy getting off back reports which accumulated rapidly when we were away from our wagons and books, but have about finished. I am quite disgusted with actions of the Common Councils at home raising money to pay the "draft exemption." If it is allowed I don't see how the Government is to get any soldiers. In my opinion the #300 clause was a great mistake. Every man who was drafted should have gone or sent a substitute. Brig. Gen'l Terry has been assigned to the command of this Division. No one has ever heard of him before. He comes, I believe from the "Investment of Suffolk." Gen'l Bartlett returns to the command of his old Brigade, Slocum's original brigade.

Good Bye

Yours &c

Os.

Camp 122d Reg't N.Y. Vols

August 21, 1863

Dear Mother,

Yesterday Connie and myself had quite a little "adventure" for we call most anything so that breaks the monotony of camp life. We took a walk yesterday morning on the Orleans road where Frank Lester's company under command of Lt. Hall is doing picket duty. When we got to the "reserve" where Hall was he told us that near his outpost a wealthy old "secesher" lived. Connie and myself thought it our duty to investigate. We found a very comfortable house and quite a pleasant old fellow who was very hospitable, and immediately invited us to stay to dinner. We declined but kept talking until dinner was ready when thinking it might be impolite to leave at last concluded to accept of his hospitality, and judge of my astonishment when taking my seat and "timidly" looking up I beheld seated opposite me a very pretty young lady with such black eyes. I was completely captivated and would add unable to do justice to the dinner, but I know you wouldn't believe that of me.

I ascertained that she was unmarried and lived at Culpepper C.H. She was very sociable. After dinner we were talking with the old gentleman I remarked that I thought we passed his house coming in to Warrenton and as I could hardly keep from laughing. As we passed his house on the march the Colonel sent me there to hurry up some stragglers and this identical old fellow came to me worrying about his potatoes that the boys were digging up, not feeling particularly amiable at the time I remember telling that I hoped they would get all his as he had no business to be a rebel and all I wanted was to get our boys along. But fortunately he did not recognize me and no wonder for if you could see me on the march after we have been away from our baggage for a week or two I doubt if you would recognize me, especially as I am so trouble with my beard growing so rapidly. The old gentleman intimated he would give anything for a little of that medicinal beverage which is said to be made in the best manner at Bourbon Co. Ky, and we intend to purchase a little from our Brigade Commissary and present it to the old gentleman and win his everlasting gratitude.

This morning Cap't Platt who has command of the pickets at Waterloo Bridge sent up a couple of our cavalrymen who came into our lines during the night claiming to be escaped prisoners. As "straggling" is one of the great crimes of the army I did not entirely believe their story and when one of them informed he was a Lieut in the 5th N.Y. Cav. He had on no straps but I was convinced from his statement and conversation that we was and accordingly had my horse saddled and rode with him to Brigade HQrs Corps Hqrs and finally to Warrenton where he got a pass to rejoin his command. Knowing my "faculty" it will needless to inform you that I got quite well acquainted with him. He had been taken prisoner 5 days ago by Mosby while on picket near Thoroughfare Gap and succeeded in getting away last night by travelling some 20 miles reached our lines. His name is Kroahn and having formerly resided in Binghamton we soon found that we had mutual friends. He also was acquainted with Harv Baldwin—having formerly been in Stahls division.

I had a very pleasant letter from George to-night who informed me that the "brave little Captain" left on the 17th. I shall look forward to seeing him soon as I am sure that he will lose no time in coming here. We have no news of any intended movement except this Lt. Kroahn said that he inferred from what he heard and saw that another cavalry raid was contemplated by Stuart.

Good night
Your boy
Os

Camp 122d Reg't N.Y. Vols.
August 24, 1863

Dear Mother

Still "suffering" as when I last wrote you. Connie and myself have just returned from a nice "swim" in the Rappahannock or at least the North Fork of it. The other evening I accompanied Cap't Walpole around the picket line and as we passed Mr. Withers house, my friend Thornton hailed to us 'to come back, get some supper—how could we refuse—and we didn't. During our supper my "young lady friend" happened to make some remark about her "husband in Culpepper." This knocked my air-castles all to pieces.

Last evening we received the papers containing the names of the conscripts in Onondaga Co. I did not see many familiar ones, but noticed that Jim's old friend Bigelow of Baldwinsville was one of the lucky ones. It was quite rich to hear the shouts of laughter from the boys when they read the names of their friends at home. Several had brothers drafted. Occasionally you would hear the exclamation, "He's secesh," I am glad of it." I am quite anxious in regard to the decision in regard to the city and although I should like to pay off some old grudges by doing a little drafting there myself. still I trust that we may have the honor of filling our quota by volunteering.

I am looking forward every day either to see or hear from Will but nothing as yet. You must miss him sadly, but I shall not wish you to have any more society at such a dear price. But, be cheerful my dear mother for "When this cruel war is over" and we are all once more reunited, I know you will feel happiness for the sacrifices you have made in sending your boys to the war.

Yours lovingly
Os

Camp 122d Reg't N.Y. Vols.
August 27, 1863

Dear Mother

This morning I rode down to Cap't Gere's station on the road to Salem, took dinner with him and then started out for a visit to his picket line. We called at the house of a Mr. Payne whom I was quite anxious to see, having heard several of the officers speak of him. He is an old bachelor aged about 50 and was at one time a member of the Black Horse Cavalry. That organization was raised by the State of Virginia at the time of the John Brown excitement and was composed of rich young fellows mostly from this county, I believe. At the time the war was broke out there remained about six months of their two years and they were turned over to the Confederate Gov't for the balance of their term, at the expiration of their time he left and has been living his fame since. This I heard before going there. The Captain and myself spent about an hour there. I felt that it was the first time

I had ever met one of the "first families." He has quite a pleasant house and large farm which he told me had been in possession of the family for 75 years. His "darkies" have pretty much all left him and his farm is of course worth nothing now but he bears his losses very cheerfully—but does not profess to be a Union man—but says his sympathies are with the "State of Virginia."

Speaking of Charlestown he said that the South Carolinians were regular cowards that when the war first broke out. Their troops were always saying, "Show us a Yankee" but when it came to fighting they did not seem so anxious to have their wish gratified. He very politely urged us to call again saying how much he regretted his inability to entertain us in a better manner and very kindly to go with me to call on a Mrs. Scott, a neighbor, whom he was anxious to have me see, as he said she was a specimen of a real "Virginia" lady. His admiration for Virginia in general and Fauquier Co. in particular is intense.

I received a letter from Willie to-night. He sent an orderly with my bundle to Warrenton Junction, but it is needless to say that said orderly did not succeed in finding me. He is very anxious that I should come down to see him and after I get my monthly reports off, about the 5th or 6th of September, I shall apply for a two days leave to go over and see him but I trust that before that time he may be over to see me.

Everything quiet and to all appearances likely to remain so.

Good night
Your boy
Os

Camp 122d Reg't N.Y.Vols.
August 29, 1863

Dear Mother,

Your letter of the 23d although a "dunning" one, was most welcome. I had been congratulating myself that I owed no debts and was owner of real estate but like other wealthy men I find that my liabilities when figured up, make an awful hole in the "assets." As I hardly like to reduce my balance at the savings bank, it being fully as small now as is suggestive of wealth. I will with your permission wait until next Pay-Day. I trust to your clemency in not commencing an "action" against me in the meantime. I don't think that there is any danger of us boys ever quarrelling over our property and I only wrote in regard to those taxes fearing that my credit might suffer from having my property sold for taxes. My tastes are not so extravagant as Capt. Lester's, and it is needless to say that I should "omit" the diamond.

The Chasseurs officers have had a cross got up by Tiffany which will cost about $18 as soon as they come I will if I like them get one. Willie is perfectly welcome to my sword though it will be much better for riding if he has a steel scabbard made for it. those leather scabbards soon wear out and a steel scabbard costs but $5. If he has not already done so I shall advise him to send to Washington and have one mad.

I was sorry to hear of Mr. Baldwins' death. He was so much of a gentleman in his manners and do you know mother that I have never learned to prize gentlemanly deportment so much as since I have been in the army. You cannot imagine how much difference it makes in intercourse with those over you to have gentlemen to order you about.

I wish you could see our adjutant General Cap't Rooney he is perfectly splendid. Our boys who sometimes are inclined to be a little sulky towards "Staff" officers always give way to him on the march with utmost readiness and because in giving an order he is always polite and pleasant.

Wooster, Marks and myself made another call on Scott Rayne again yesterday. I asked him about Ashby. The one who was killed was a very intimate friend of his and a splendid fellow, very different indeed he says from Mosby, for Ashby would always meet a man fairly and not speak about as Mosby does. Before the war broke out there were two militia companies here between whom there was quite a rivalry one (The Black Horse Cavalry) commanded by Cap't Payne, a cousin of his, and the other was commanded by Ashby. When the war first broke out they both went into the service of the government, and he says that all that are left of the Black Horse (to which he belonged) that have not been killed or wounded are still in the service either as officers or privates, and he says they are the first young men of Fauquier Co. He being over the age left home. He acknowledges that he voted for secession and talks about "our" people and "your" people and I must confess that I have twice as much respect for him and would trust him much quicker than those (whiney) fellows who are eternally telling you that they are Union men &c. I am delighted to hear of the improvement in uncle's health and trust it may prove to be permanent.

Love to all
Yours lovingly
Os

Head Qrs 122d Reg't New York Volunteers
Sept. 6, 1863

Dear Mother,

I have been very busy for the last few days, hence my neglect. I was rejoiced to see Will looking in such good health, and to see that he bears losing the use of his arm so well. By the way, Dr. Emanuel, the best surgeon in our Brigade says he thinks a splint can be made with a joint that will give him the use of his arm or rather that will enable him to bend it. But he says it is better to leave it as it is for the next few months as the muscle will grow stronger.

We rode into town to see Smithy, and took dinner with him at Division Hd Qrs and then rode over to Corps Head Qrs expecting to see a race which was to have come off, but one of the parties backed out. On Friday we were relieved on picket by the 82d Reg't and took possession of their old camp about two miles from

Warrenton. I had a very pleasant visit from him and shall endeavor to return it soon. Cap't Urquhart, a cousin of Sturdevants, is commissary for the 3d Division of the corps has agreed to go over with me.

Our boys were rather sorry to leave the picket line as they had very comfortable houses built beside the facilities afforded for getting milk, corn &c. Now we have the pleasure of attending Brigade Drills and have used up pretty much all this (Sunday) forenoon in attending a Division Inspection. On some accounts, it is pleasant having the regiment together once more as it makes it more sociable, having more officers near me.

Wooster is detailed on a Court Martial as they have their "sittings" at a house a little distance from the camp. Wooster who is slightly lazy got permission from the colonel to engage boards there and comes around now pitying poor fellows who don't have "even a feather bed to sleep on." I feel that I am living quite luxuriously now as I am using some sheets Brower left and last night after taking a bath and going to bed (I had them washed yesterday) it seemed almost like Saturday night at home. We are occasionally troubled by Guerrillas between the Infantry and Cavalry pickets. Cap't Ives of the 10th Mass. ventured out beyond the infantry line to a farm house the other day and was gobbled up while eating his dinner.

Gen'l Shaler was here a little while ago and told Co. Dwight (of whom he made inquiries in regard to some houses on our old picket-line) that he had been applied to for a guard at these houses but if the guard, or any officers who accepted of their hospitalities were taken by Guerrillas that he should destroy their houses and property. I have just heard that about 20 Rebs got through the lines at New Baltimore and made a dash at Gen'l Bartlett's Head quarters and came very taking the Gen'l but were driven off by the "Provost Guard."

I regret to say that Willie is not a very good judge of horses. He actually made fun of my valuable mares which are said only to be equalled by Browers' celebrated team and wanted to know why I kept them so poor, not seeming to understand that I purposely kept them at a "racing weight."

Regretting that I have no "Vesper Service" to attend this evening, I remain

Yours lovingly

Os

Camp 122d Reg't N.Y. Vols
Sept 8th/63

Dear Mother

We left our camp near Warrenton, Va., yesterday morning and marched to Rappahannock Station. The rebels were in force on this side of the river but our troops advanced and drove them out of the works and across the river taking 1500 prisoners, 2000 stand of arms and 4 cannon. 3 companies from our regiment. "A G" and "I" were in the front line of skirmishers and they had 7 men wounded the remainder of the regiment were in the reserve. And under a heavy fire, a shell exploded in "B" Co., instantly killing Serg't Philo Ruggles and Private Kelly and wounding Lt. Gilbert, Serg't Sherlock and privates Cooney and Brott. Sherlock has since died. Cooney used to work in the coal yard. The poor fellow had one foot blown off and part of the calf of the other leg. It is feared that he will not live. Please have Jim see Rombach and he will break the news to his wife. If possible I will go to the hospital and see him to-day but a pontoon is now being laid and I expect we shall move forward. Lt. Gilbert is not very badly wounded. Col. Dwight was only a few feet distant. Gen'l Shaler complimented our 3 companies on the excellent manner in which they advanced as skirmishers.

I enclose a list of casualties for publication. If you receive this before the news gets home, I have got a chance to send this.

Good Bye—Love to all
Your boy
Os

P.S. have a readable copy made of the enclosed list before sending it for publication.

HdQrs 122d Reg't N.Y. Vols
Sept. 9, 1863

Dear Mother,

I received your letter last evening. Poor Maria has so much trouble that I shall certainly follow your advice and not get engaged. And by the way I don't think there is any danger of my being engaged at present. All my fair friends having a disagreeable habit of marrying someone else.

I was at Brigade Hd Qrs this morning and Capt. Rooney said that there would be no difficulty in getting a pass to Bealeton Station so I shall have the pleasure of spending next Sunday with Will. But you may be relieved by the thought that if you should be very sick I could come home. Capt Rooney is very kind and in any urgent case he interests himself personally to get a furlough through. This morning Capt Platt and myself rode into Warrenton to make a few purchases and had the pleasure of seeing two or three pretty girls and even that is considered a blessing by us poor soldiers. I do wish I was acquainted with some of the fair secesh there. It would seem mighty pleasant to spend an evening in ladies society again.

I enclose a letter for Sam which I wish you would direct and forward to him as I do not know his direction.

Good Bye
Your boy
Os

HdQrs 122d Reg't N.Y. Vols
Sept. 10th 1863

Dear Mother,

A letter of yours is always welcome and doubly so when as tonight it is unexpected, as I received one only a night or two ago. I am very glad to hear of George's appointment and only hope that he may be assigned to the Army of the Potomac instead of being sent to the West and then I should look forward to seeing him every two months. I hope it will have an improving effect upon his health. I also received a letter from Marie enclosing a photograph of the "Unitarian Beauties" all of which are excellent likenesses except Nellie, but with the aid of my "imagination" I can form some idea of the young lady. Marie says that the major sees no objection to our continuing our correspondence and she certainly does not. Therefore why should I especially when I am the one particularly benefited by the arrangements?

I have sent in an application this evening for a pass for 48 hours, to go the Hd Qrs 12th Army Corps. If it comes back approved I shall start Saturday morning returning on Monday, thus having a nice visit with the "infant"

I should be delighted to avail myself of your invitation to visit you while Miss Gordon was with you but Gen'l Meade has "requested" me to say that he thinks "circumstances repugnant to the acquiesce will prevent my acceptance of the invite," but you may rest assured that I shall not waste a moment longer after the "softening" of Gen'l M's heart on the furlough question, becomes evident than is necessary, for my turn to come, for you must remember that we have officers here, and among them my friend Wooster, who have not been home since we left Syracuse a year ago.

We have heard some cannonading for the last few days that has had the tendency to make us all "sick" but as no orders for a move have been received we are rapidly recovering. It is getting late so Good Night

Your boy
Os

Dear Mother,

I received a pass for 48 hours yesterday to go to Gen'l Slocum's HdQrs and had made all my arrangements to start early this morning when we received an order late last evening to be in readiness to move at a moments notice, so I concluded it would be best to give up my visit for the present, and as my pass will be good at any time it will only be a postponement of my visit and as we are having quite a rainstorm so I shall fall back on my old maxim that it is "all for the best."

We have heard nothing more in regard to a move but a little cannonading and I think there has probably been a cavalry advance and we were held in readiness in case they should bring on a general engagement. There has been an absurd rumor afloat this morning that the enemy have fallen back from Culpepper and that the order received last evening was in consequence of the cavalry having been ordered out to "feel" of them and see if there be any truth in the rumor. I consider the whole thing however, a yarn.

As I presume Frank will be returning one of these days I wish you would send three cotton sheets or linen (if they are cheaper) now, about 1½ yards wide and 7 feet long. Since Brower has been away I have been using his and grown quite luxurious. We have learnt a good deal more how to make ourselves comfortable than we knew how last Winter and are already looking forward to what comfortable houses we shall have next Winter (Will it be at Centerville or Richmond).

I received the Gospel of Peace which George sent me and we are all very much pleased with it, thinking it quite ahead of Artemus.

I am getting to be more and more of the opinion that the Army of the Potomac is to remain quiet this Fall unless Gen'l Lee disturbs us. The Vermont Brigade which was sent from our Corps to New York to quell the riots[7] instead of being returned to us has been sent to Charlestown I am told, and they would assuredly weaken this army any more if further movements were contemplated. And I must say that I feel quite resigned to this state of affairs. We are not quite so anxious to get a sight of the "Rebs" as we were about a year ago this time as we were marching from Washington through Maryland.

You had better have those sheets marked with my name.

Your boy

Os

P.S. When I was at Berlin I sent my watch to Washington to get it cleaned by the sutler of the 37th Mass. That Reg't is now at Fort Hamilton and I will write to the sutler this evening to send it to you by express and you can send it by Lester.

Yours

Osgood

---

7. For discussion of the July 1863 New York City Draft Riots, see Iver Bernstein, *The New York City Draft Riots: Their Significance for American Society and Politics in the Age of the Civil War* (New York: Oxford Univ. Press, 1990); Ryan W. Keating, *Shades of Green: Irish Regiments, American Soldiers, and Local Communities in the Civil War Era* (New York: Fordham Univ. Press, 2017); Ryan Keating, "All That Class That Infest NY: Perspectives on Irish American Loyalty and Patriotism in the Wake of the New York City Draft Riots," in *Contested Loyalty: Debates Over Patriotism in the Civil War North,* ed. Robert Sandow (New York; Fordham Univ. Press, 2019), 239–67; William B. Kurtz, *Excommunicated from the Union: How the Civil War Created a Separate Catholic America* (New York: Fordham Univ. Press, 2016); Susannah Ural Bruce, *The Harp and the Eagle: Irish American Volunteers in the Union Army 1861–1865* (New York: New York Univ. Press, 2005); Christian Samito, *Becoming American Under Fire: Irish Americans, African Americans, and the Politics of Citizenship during the Civil War Era* (Ithaca, NY: Cornell Univ. Press, 2009).

Camp 122d Reg't N.Y. Volunteers
Sept. 18, 1863

Dear Mother,

On the afternoon of the 15th we broke camp and moved on to the Sulphur Springs road about two miles bivouacking for the night. The next morning we started early in the direction of Culpepper but turned off to the right and about ½ after five in the afternoon arrived at our present position which is near Stone House Mountain on a turnpike which I am told leads from Culpepper to Sperryville. We are about six miles N. W. of Culpepper. There was some firing yesterday and I was told that the 5th Corps had moved off towards Gordonsville. I expected that we should move this morning but it rained all last night and to-day until noon. When we arrived at Sulphur Springs the Brigade halted for about half an hour giving us a fine opportunity to inspect the famous watering place. The Principal hotel was burned by Pope during his famous campaign but most of the cottages are still standing, they were situated like this.[8]

The lawn inside the semicircle was nicely laid out with plenty of shade trees and cozy seats so suggestive of flirtations and in . . . as it is one could easily imagine how splendid it must have been its day with the accession of moonlight-music and pretty girls. The water is very pleasant for sulphur water, in fact the best of that peculiar style of beverage that I have ever tasted.

I rec'd a letter from George last evening who is comfortably settled at Washington though they have not been assigned to any duty yet. I shall write to him to-day but as we shall probably be on the move now I shall hardly expect to see him at present.

Your letter was received this morning and the report you mentioned of Grove Johnson's[9] proceedings was confirmed by the account given by the Standard. What a pity that he should have behaved so. I feel very sorry for his wife Gus and the family. Some of the boys thought he must have been pretty shrewd to have fooled such known smart shavers as Alf. Wilkinson, Charley Blair and Ira Gage Barnes, and I do not think that they felt a very large amount of sympathy for them.

I received a letter from the Colonel the other day in which he remarked that he should probably be back soon. I trust not, however, for we are getting along very nicely now.

8. Gen. John C. Pope was given command of the Army of Virginia in June 1862 and campaigned in the Shenandoah Valley that year. The officers in this army tended to be more radical than in other Union armies, and its organization and efforts reflected a true shift in the Federal government's war aims toward emancipation. See John C. Matsui, *The First Republican Army: The Army of Virginia and the Radicalization of the War* (Charlottesville: Univ. of Virginia Press, 2016).

9. In 1863, Grove L. Johnson (1841–1926), a lawyer in Syracuse, was accused of falsifying endorsements on promissory notes worth $250. In the wake of the scandal, he fled to Arizona where he became a quartermaster's clerk for the Union Army. After the war he made his home in Sacramento and became a politician. See Michael Weatherson and Hal Bochin, *Hiram Johnson: Political Revivalist* (Lanham, MD: Univ. Press of America, 1995), 1–2.

The 37th Mass. which was sent from Division to New York at the time of the riot has I understand returned, and Miller a private of "G" Co. who returned from a furlough yesterday said that trains from Alexandria to Culpepper are crowded with conscripts. I feel now that if we could only have troops enough we could give the rebels a severe if not a finishing stroke.

What a sad blow poor Annie Tracy's death will be. I don't think I ever saw a family where there appeared to be more affection among the children and I shall never forget the pleasant time I had there during the week I spent at their house.

This move of course has prevented my seeing anything more of Willie but I shall seize the first opportunity to make him a visit, and the movements may bring our corps near together.

Good Bye, with love to all

Your boy Os

Camp 122d Reg't N.Y. Volunteers

Sept. 21, 1863

Dear Mother,

We are still where I wrote from last, that is about six miles from Culpeper Court House. I had an opportunity to send a letter to Will by an officer who was going to Army Hd Qrs yesterday and to-day I made another application for a pass for 48 hours to go and see him and Capt. Roome said that he would try and get it through for me to-day so that I could start in the morning. I trust that we shall receive no marching orders this time to put a stop to my expected visit. The 12th Corps are about six miles below Culpepper but as I own such fast horses that distance will be nothing and even if I should get into the neighborhood of Guerillas I should be able to valiantly run away from them, however there is not much danger of the latter as I understand that troops line the road all the way to the 12th Hd Qrs.[10]

We have had some excitement in our regiment to-day in regard to the McClellan testimonial which it is proposed should get up by the Army of the Potomac.[11] Contributions are limited to 10 cents for corporal and privates, 25 cents for sg'ts,

10. There is much interest in guerrilla warfare in the Civil War era. See, for example, Joseph M. Beilein Jr., *Bushwhackers: Guerrilla Warfare, Manhood, and the Household in Civil War Missouri* (Kent, OH: Kent State Univ. Press, 2019); Joseph M. Beilein Jr. and Matthew C. Hulbert, eds., *The Civil War Guerrilla: Unfolding the Black Flag in History, Memory, and Myth* (Lexington: Univ. Press of Kentucky, 2015); Brian D. McKnight and Barton A Myers, eds., *The Guerrilla Hunters: Irregular Conflicts during the Civil War* (Baton Rouge: Louisiana State Univ. Press, 2017); Matthew C. Hulbert, *The Ghosts of Guerrilla Memory: How Civil War Bushwhackers Became Gunslingers in the American West* (Athens: Univ. of Georgia Press, 2016).

11. General Sedgwick began a petition among the men of the Army of the Potomac to raise $20,000 for George McClellan. See John J. Hennessy, "We Shall Make Richmond Howl: The Army of the Potomac on the Eve of Chancellorsville," in *Chancellorsville: The Battle and Its Aftermath*, ed. Gary Gallagher (Chapel Hill: Univ. of North Carolina Press, 1996), 22–23.

$1.00 for Lieuts, $1.50 for Captains etc., to $20 for a Major General. Our reg't is rather anti McClellan and the total contributions amounted to but $19.00 three companies and the Field & Staff giving nothing.

In Company "K" one of the lieutenants being a strong McClellan man copied all the names of the members of his company and paid the amount himself. We hear the captain protested against that course of procedure and got his company together and question (ed) each man as to whether he was willing to have his name used in getting up a testimonial and twenty-eight declined. I have no objection to getting up a present for Gen'l McClellan but I am "agin" giving the Copperheads any such good political capital to use in electioneering for McClellan whom I have no doubt will be their candidate for the next Presidency.

Good Bye love to all

Yours Os.

September 23/63

Camp 122d Reg't New York Vol.

Dear Mother,

I this morning wrote to Dudley enclosing a draft for $150—$50 of which I directed him to pay to you or place to your credit.

No further marching orders yet although we are expecting them daily or rather hourly. The latest report is that three corps are across the Rapidan.

I will keep this letter open until this evening trusting to get a letter from you to-night.

Evening

I received your letter of the 21st and Jim's of the 18th this evening.

Dear Anna,[12] what a jolly breakfast we should have had if I could have dropped in upon you.

I saw by a notice in the Standard that Uncle was quite ill at Salem and am very glad to hear of his improvement.

What does Jim mean in reference to employment at Oswego? I have not heard anything of it before.

We all look first thing every night in the Standard to see if Johnson is caught yet, and I must say that my wishes coincide with the gentlemen that you spoke of.

Don't ever be afraid of your letters being tedious to me for you know how much I prize them and how welcome they are.

Good bye

Yours

Os

12. This is a reference to Osgood's cousin Anna Putnam. Mrs. Tracy often read Osgood's letters to the family of her half sister Elizabeth Osgood Putnam.

P.S.

My letter was left out of the mail by accident last evening. During the night we received orders to have eight days rations in the hands of the men and to-day Cap't Roome told me that the General would not approve my application for a leave for 48 hours as he thought that there was too much probability of our moving, and to-night the report is the 2d, 11th & 12th Corps are across the Rapidan.

The news from Rosencrans[13] would indicate without a doubt that a large portion of Lee's army had gone to reinforce Bragg and I have no doubt but that we shall push on here.

Our paymaster arrived to-day but I understand says that he will stick by us until he pays us all off.

I begin to think I shall not have a chance to visit Willie until we get to Richmond. I see that his old reg't (the 10th Indiana) suffered severely. What a fortunate fellow he is, to miss the fights, but alas I forget Chancellorsville. God grant that he may pass through the rest of the war safe. It is so cold nights now that one can only really enjoy himself in bed, to which place I will betake myself and bid you good night.

Yours

Os

Camp 122d Reg't New York Vols.

September 25/63

Dear Mother,

I enclose a picture of "our mess." I thought at first that I had better not send it home as it might change the opinion some of you appear to have formed in regard to my beauty but on reflection adapted to my style of beauty. At all events please keep it for the "picture gallery" I shall have after the war is over.

Yesterday afternoon the rumors were so indicative of a move that we got things ready to start at a very short notice and expected to be off during the night or very early in the morning, but up to this time (12 o'clock) there has been no orders received. I almost wish that we would move as I dislike this uncertainty.

---

13. Ohio-born Maj. Gen. William Rosecrans graduated from West Point in 1842. At the outbreak of the Civil War, he volunteered for service and was promoted to brigadier general with rank dated to May 1861. He was transferred to the western theater and given command of the Army of the Cumberland in late 1862. In spite of victories at Iuka and a draw against forces under General Braxton Bragg at the Battle of Stones River, Rosecrans's loss at Chickamauga defined his military career. See David G. Moore, *William S. Rosecrans and the Union Victory: A Civil War Biography* (Jefferson, NC: McFarland, 2014); William B. Kurtz, "Old Rosy Reconsidered: A Look at the Flawed but Successful Civil War Career of William Starke Rosecrans," *Civil War Monitor* 9 (Summer 2019), https://www.civilwarmonitor.com/table-of-contents/i32; William B. Kurtz, "'The Perfect Model of a Christian Hero:' The Faith, Anti-Slaveryism, and Post-War Legacy of William S. Rosecrans," *U.S. Catholic Historian* 31 (Winter 2013): 73–96.

Yesterday Serg't Major Birdseye of the 149th was over here and says that he saw Will the other day and he was well. It is rather aggravating to be within ten miles of the boy and not be able to go over to see him but I am waiting patiently trusting that the "move" will bring us together again –

Yours lovingly
Os

Camp 122d Reg't New York Vols.
September 27, 1863

Dear Mother,

Yesterday morning I had some business to attend to at Culpepper and heard several different rumors in regard to the movements of the 12th Corps so to satisfy myself I pushed on to Army Head Quarters where we have a clerk from our regiment and he informed me that the 11th and 12th Corps had been ordered out of this army. He enquired for me as to the whereabout of Gen'l Slocum and was informed that he had probably gone to Chattanooga and I must confess I returned feeling slightly "Blue" at the thought of Willie leaving this army where I had an occasional sight of him and that too without an opportunity to bid him "Good Bye."

On my return I laid down and was awakened from my sleep and informed that a fellow by the name of Hunt wished to see me. Not being more than half awake I did not realize at first that it was really George, but is was sure enough and he was doubly welcome from the fact that he had taken breakfast with Willie that morning. Major Truesdall having a regiment to pay in the 6th Corps they wisely came directly to our regiment and as the Lieut. has ordered no work to be done on Sunday they have remained with us to-day. It will be of course useless to attempt to tell you anything in regard to the movement of the 12th as I presume Will has written you all about it.

The rumor says that Slocum has tendered his resignation declining to serve under Hooker and if it should be accepted I am inclined to think that the "boy" would feel called upon to resign also, but I do not anticipate any such result but trust that the matter will be so arranged as to give Slocum some other command. I am waiting very anxiously to hear from Willie as to how the affair is settled. You, of course, can imagine how I enjoy seeing George once more.

Last evening we went over to see Andy and he took me over to a "jamboree" at Corps Head Qrs which gave him an opportunity to see how Staff officers "suffer" for their country. This afternoon I mounted him on one of my "untamed steeds" and took a little ride bringing up at Division Headquarters where at Andy's invitation we remained to dinner. George appears to be quite delighted with his situation and with his experience of army life, and I only trust that Major Truesdell may be assigned to the Army of the Potomac.

The sending away of the 11th and 12th Corps would indicate that no move was to be made here and the general impression is that we shall fall back toward Washington and perhaps into the "defences." If we are not going to advance there is no earthly object in holding the country between here and Washington and on the contrary we are too far from our "base of supplies" and could cover Washington with a much smaller force thus releasing a large portion of this army for duty elsewhere. In fact one rumor is afloat that the 3d & 6th Corps are to form a "covering" army before Washington and the remainder of the army to be sent elsewhere. We are already building air castles or rather I might more appropriately say "air log huts" and making plans in reference to "garrison duty" next Winter. Now wouldn't you like to obtain a position as "cook" for our mess? If we are to move back I suppose we shall start very soon as nothing will be gained by delay.

Good Night, Love to all

Your boy

Os

Camp 122d Reg't New York Vols.

September 30, 1863

Dear Will,

Your letter of the 28th was received this evening. I heard from you by Hunty and have been anxiously watching the papers to see if anything had been decided yet and am still flattering myself with the belief that no news is good news. I have no fears but that you would be able to earn your living out of the army for you have learned to write so well that you would have no difficulty in keeping books again, but I should hate to have you leave the army because you seem to like the life so well. I entirely sympathize with you in regard to your feelings as to Gen'l Slocum's treatment and think you would be perfectly justified in resigning but I trust the government will recognize the value of his services and make some arrangement which will obviate the necessity. I cannot tell you how much of a loss it is to me having you go out of this army for, although I could not see you often I felt that you could be got at if anything here should be wanted but never mind this "cruel war" will soon be over and what a glorious reunion we shall have at Syracuse. We have been expecting to fall back for of course we are not strong enough now to assume the offensive but no news as yet. My regards to all the staff and be sure and write me as soon as the affair is decided.

Your aff brother

Os

Camp 122d Reg't N.Y. Volunteers
near Catlett Station, Va.
October 4, 1863

Dear Mother,

We were considerably surprised on the evening of the 1st just after finishing supper by the receipt of orders to be in readiness to move at 11½ o'clock. We marched all night and about daylight it commenced raining and kept up very steadily until about 2 P.M. when we halted near Bealeton Station. We had just got up our tents and got down our supper when it commenced raining again. Everyone got more or less wet and I don't know how our boys got along all of them wet and many without a woolen blanket.

Yesterday was a beautiful day and we arrived here about noon. We take the place of the 11th Corps and our Division is detached from the Corps at present. One brigade is stationed at Rappahannock Station, one at Bristows and our own at Catlett's, Division Hd Qrs are also here. We have got a beautiful place for a camp in a piece of oak woods. To-day being Sunday we have not commenced to clean up but the men are all at work at their own tents and as the 11th Corps left quite a stock of lumber in their old camps our boys are cutting up very good houses and as I sit in my tent writing it sounds like a good sized boat yard. The prospects are that we shall remain here as long as the army remains at Culpepper or has occasion to use this railroad. It seems to be the general impression however that the whole army will soon fall back and it is hinted by some that we are holding back until after the Pennsylvania election. There is a Division of cavalry, whose Hd qrs are at Bealton Station which are to do the guard duty along the railroad and our Division is to act as a reserve.

I have heard nothing from Willie since the 28th nor have I seen anything in regard to the acceptance of Slocum's resignation although Lt. Tailoff of the Chasseurs told me yesterday that he saw by the Herald of the 30th that it had been accepted. I trust however that the report may prove to be no more correct than Herald reports are apt to be. If Willie should resign on account of the Generals treatment, I think it will be the best for you, if he will only be contented at home.

I received a letter from Lester this morning. He actually has something to do once in awhile, it seems and does not seem to look forward to any definite time for returning.

If you have received my watch be sure to send it by him also my coat and the sheets. If necessary you can get a cheap valise to send them in and fill up the corners with anything "handy."

I was quite surprised to hear of the deaths of Hones and Cushing. Where is Sam? I wrote to him sometime ago sending the letter to you and have received no answer. Please ask his mother to "jog" his memory the next time she writes.

How I should enjoy a furlough home now, and what fun I should have with the Phelps. Tell them that the other evening when George was down, we were at Corps. Hd. Qrs. and some fellows sang "rally round the flag, boys." It is the first time I have heard it since they sang it for me last March, and notwithstanding it was sung very nicely. I should have much preferred to have been in their parlor. George promised to write me, as soon as he could find out anything in regard to Gen'l Slocum's affairs and I expect a letter to-night.

I see by the Syracuse papers that the drafting has fallen through again in Syracuse. How they do play on the "hopes and fears" of the "wouldn't be conscripts."

The 82nd P.V. in our brigade, received 190 conscripts the other day. This is the 2d regiment that has received them and I trust that ours will be along soon. I fear our "conscript Fathers" are not so anxious to get back as they might be.

How I should like to surprise you this evening and I don't believe any Vesper service (Anna, don't laugh) could tempt me away.

Love to all

Your boy

Os

Camp 122d Reg't New York Vols

Near Catletts Station, Va.

October 4/63

My Dear Mr. May:

I was very much pleased with Robert Dale Owens' letter to Mr. Seward published in one of the anti-slavery Standards you sent me—I feel that we may now begin to look forward as to the policy to be pursued at the close of the war.

The Battle of Chattanooga I do not consider a defeat by any means and with the aid of the reinforcements which have been sent him I trust that Rosecrans may be able to advance—The general impression here seems to be that the Army of the Potomac will soon fall back towards Washington and with the exception of enough troops to cover Washington that it will be distributed to the other armies. If we are not going to advance the country between Culpepper C.H. and Washington is not worth holding. On the night of the 1st our Division left Culpepper and arrived here yesterday taking the position held by the 11th Corps. There is a division of cavalry who do the patrol duty along the railroad and one brigade of our division is stationed at Rappahannock Station, another at Bristows and our own at this station.

We have a very pleasant camp and expect to remain as long as the army has use for the railroad. The country about here has changed possession so many times that it is completely desolate. But to return to Mr. Owen's letter—His suggestions were excellent and I most heartily agree with him in the conclusion that it would be worse than folly ever to admit the seceded states again without an efficient guarantee that slavery should be abolished. I am glad to see that President Lincoln does not recede at all from his Emancipation policy.

I regret that I shall not be at home this Fall to vote Andrew White and Dudley.[14] What a different state of affairs there would be if all our politicians were such men.

Our old Bible Class is getting somewhat scattered. Mrs. Jenny has left I believe, and I understand that you are soon to lose Mary Bassett.

Our regiment is in fine condition and I am looking forward to the arrival of the conscripts to fill up the regiment to something like its original number once more. It is quite a loss to have the 12th Corps leave this army for although I did not see Willie very often yet it was a very satisfactory feeling to think that he was somewhere near me.

I have just received a letter from George Hunt informing me that the difficulty between Genls Slocum and Hooker had been satisfactorily arranged and that the Gen'l had gone to Louisville.[15]

My regards to your family, believe me

Yours truly,

Osgood V. Tracy

Camp 122d Reg't New York Vols.

Catlett's Station, Va.

Oct. 7, 1863

Dear Mother,

Your letter of the 4th inst. was received this afternoon, much to my delight. I am astonished that you should think that any picture of mine was not handsome but perhaps you are excusable in this case. Wooster declared that it bore a strong resemblance to a "cadaverous" chap who has been in the employ of our sutler.

I received a letter from Mary Bassett and believe I wrote you in regard to getting something in the shape of a present for her. I was rather surprised to hear of Charley Snow's engagement. Well, Hattie is a very nice girl, I guess. I should not

14. Andrew D. White (1832–1918) was a US diplomat and history and English professor at the University of Michigan and cofounder and first president of Cornell University (1865–85).

15. During the Battle of Chancellorsville, Slocum's Twelfth Corps advanced down to the Plank Road to Tabernacle Church, but late in the day on May 1, Hooker, losing confidence in his position, ordered Slocum, and a number of other Union divisions to fall back, an order protested by a number of generals (Slocum included) because they felt they were in a favorable tactical position. Slocum urged Hooker to reconsider this order. Hooker refused and Slocum left deeply impressed that Hooker was not in fit condition to direct the army in the impending battle." Walter H. Herbert, *Fighting Joe Hooker* (Lincoln: University of Nebraska Press, 1999), 199–200. "From this point on," historian Brian C. Melton notes, "Slocum was Hooker's enemy," and Slocum became "one of the major forces behind this new revolt" of Union generals against their commander and begged Lincoln "for the sake of the Army and the Country, that [Hooker] should be relieved from the command of that Army." Brian C. Melton, *Sherman's Forgotten General: Henry W. Slocum* (Columbia: Univ. of Missouri Press, 2007), 110.

dare to come home on a furlough now for fear that I might become entrapped. The "disease" appears to be contagious.

I am much obliged to aunt for her selection for me but fear that I was too much frightened when we visited them. There were so many girls to have produced a favorable impression. Young ladies are not generally captivated, I believe, by bashful young men.

The report you allude to in regard to Gen'l Patrick having the command of our division probably arises from the fact that Gen'l Terry our Division Commander, was offered Gen'l Patrick's present position. He however declined to accept it preferring to hold his present position.

"Furloughs" are impossibilities as far as regimental officers are concerned but Andy surprised me by sticking his head in my tent the other morning before I was up and inquiring if I had any commands for Syracuse. He informed me that Gen'l Meade insisted upon his sticking his head in my tent the other morning before I was up and inquiring if I had any commands for Syracuse. He informed me that Gen'l Meade insisted upon his taking a rest of 15 days from his labors and he felt compelled to obey. He promised to bring back my coat so please get an old satchel as I requested and pack my coat, three sheets, and send it by him i.e. if he can bring the extra satchel as well as not. but at all events send the coat by him. Please be polite to him as Andy never neglects an opportunity to accommodate me. If you send the satchel put in a couple of pounds of good black tea.

I hope that the furlough system may be renewed during the Winter but if it is not, I shall ask you to get me up another box about Christmas time trusting that I shall not be twice unfortunate.

I received a letter from Dudley, also to-day, acknowledging the draft I sent him—I am glad to hear of uncle's improvement. Does he still continue to be troubled with the Rheumatism?

A man by the name of Bowley of "B" Co., this regiment, who deserted last year, was arrested and has been tried and sentenced to be shot on Friday next—Col. Dwight has made an appeal in his behalf on the ground that he deserted at a time when the government was very lax in regard to deserters—That he thought that the salutary effect would not be produced upon the regiment is desired from the fact that several much more aggravated cases had been tried and very light sentences imposed.

This appeal he took, approved by Gen'ls Shaler and Terry, to Gen'l Meade who although he would not approve the paper referred to the Pres't and allowed Col. Dwight to detach an officer to take it personally to Lincoln. The Col. accordingly detailed Wooster, who went to Washington early this morning. We have not heard from him yet, but I think that he will succeed. He is a lawyer and will be able to put the case in the best light and besides he is very persevering and will not give up until the last chance is gone.

All the preparations are being made for the execution, however, and orders have been issued to parade the Brigade. All officers and men, not on other duty are requested to be present. I have got a letter to write to Dudley so I must say

Good Night, Yours

Os

Rappahannock Station
Monday Oct 8/63

Dear Mother,

I was disappointed in not getting my letter off yesterday—This morning I received yours and learned the sadness of Will Holyoke's death.[16] Please tell aunt how much I feel for her.

Our brigade is still here and the remainder of our Division has gone on. We have been all over the works here this morning, The fort was taken by the gallant 6th Maine, deployed as skirmishers and when the rebs realized to what a small force they had surrendered they turned and attempted to take it, but our supports arrived just then and they gave up all such intentions. Along the rifle pits opposite to where our 3 companies who were out as skirmishers were stationed the rebs abandoned everything, Rifles, cartridges boxes, & even officers appear to have left their swords. One reason was that they had a river in their rear, and none wished to be last. Two brigades of Early's Division, Ewell's Corps, was opposed to us, and they were whipped by a much inferior force and they had the advantage of position. Indeed we took more prisoners than our attacking force consisted of.

The 6th Maine is the same regiment who first arrived at the crest of Marie's. They lost quite heavily here, about 30 killed and 100 wounded.

Cooney[17] has been sent to Washington and I have therefore been unable to see him—but the doctor does not think there is much hope for him. Don't fail to have Jim go to see John, at the coal yard. I have made another copy of the loss in our regiment, which you can send to the Standard & Journal.

Good Bye

Yours,

Os

16. Will Osgood Holyoke, Sarah Osgood Tracy's nephew and Osgood's cousin, was the son of Maria Osgood Holyoke (1802–1868), wife of Edward Augustus Turner Holyoke II (1827–1862), Sarah Osgood Tracy's half sister. Will was a member of Capt. James Liberty Fisk's 1863 expedition to the Idaho Territory. A September 17, 1863, letter from Fisk to Ellsworth Denslow and Albert Younglove notes Will's death. His last words, Fisk recounted, were "Tell my mother and sister that I tried to reach the summit [of the Rocky Mountains] but I could not quite." See William Griffing, "1863: Albert C. Younglove to George Osgood Holyoke," *Spared and Shared* (blog), June 30, 2019, https://sparedandshared19.wordpress.com/2019/06/30/1863-albert-c-younglove-to-george-osgood-holyoke/.

17. Michael Cooney, was age thirty-six years upon enlistment in Syracuse, New York, on August 4, 1862, to serve three years. He was mustered in as a private, Company B, on August 6, 1862, and wounded in action November 17, 1863, at Rappahannock Station, Virginia. He died of his wounds November 8, 1863.

P.S. I have just given Col. D. who is writing to one of the papers the list so I will not trouble you with one.

Camp 122d Reg't New York Vols
Catlett Station, Va.
October 9, 1863

Dear Mother,

Yesterday we received orders to parade at 12 Noon to-day to witness the execution of Bowley. At 12 the line was formed and as not a word had been heard from Wooster, I thought that the poor fellows chances of a pardon were very slim but as we were moving towards the ground an orderly met us with an order from the President granting him a full pardon on condition of future good behaviour.

We returned to camp and Col. Dwight made a few very appropriate remarks detailing what steps had been taken and assuring the men that this case must not be taken to mean that desertion is to be treated leniently but on the contrary he hoped that the narrow escape of this man would be taken as a warning and that they might rest assured that in the case of any future desertions there would be no appeal for mercy.

He concluded by proposing three hearty cheers for the President which were given with a right will and then three more were proposed for Col. Dwight which were given full as heartily.

To-night Wooster returned. He was unable to obtain an interview with the President until 10 o'clock this morning and as Bowley was sentenced to be shot at twelve it was rather a narrow escape.

We all felt very much relieved as a great deal of sympathy was felt for him throughout the regiment and the entire Brigade. The man himself could have had no severer punishment than his sufferings for the last few days.

This afternoon we were all invited to Flag raising at Gen'l Shalers' and had a nice time—I saw Captain Urquhart, Col. Stuarts' Sturtevant's brother-in-law, who told me that he had received a letter from the Col. saying that "Tracy had gone to Syracuse with the General." I trust for your sake that it is true and for the boys, that he is doing some more left handed "waltzing."

But I am quite anxious to learn what it means in regard to the General and whether he is still to remain in command of the 12th Corps. I hope I hear from you soon however that it is all right.

We have got our camp in nice shape and most of the officers and men have built very comfortable houses but to-night alas we received orders that 8 days rations would be again issued and that we should be held in readiness to move at a very short notice.

Is it forward or backward? The general impression still remains that we are to fall back.

My love to the boy and tell him not to leave such a very favorable impression with the young ladies that all my attempts to be fascinating, in the event of a furlough would be fruitless.

We have considerable picket duty to do here and as adjutants are exempt therefore I am enjoying myself "muchly."

With love to all and a double portion for yourself

> I remain
> Your loving son
> Os

P.S. send my coat and things that I wrote for since my last, by Andy, just the same, notwithstanding the expected move.

> Camp 122d Reg't N.Y. Vols
> October 17, 1863

Dear Jim,

Your letter was received this afternoon. I only regret I have not been at home to attend some of those weddings. We are in the position from which I wrote last viz. about 3 miles North of Centerville. There is a great dearth of news in regard to the rebels in our front. The guerrillas however are very bold and day before yesterday captured a wagon containing supplies for officers belonging to our Brigade Commissary, the clerk and several teamsters, between here and Fairfax C.H. inside of our lines. Several officers have also been gobbled within the last few days and among others Capt. Urquhart, our Division Commissary and a relation of Col. Sturtevant of Slocum's staff, also Capt. Dalton Adj't Gen'l of the 2d Brigade of our Division. if you see Andy don't forget to tell him of these two captures. To-night just at sunset. we were ordered to pack up and get under arms, but we did not move. There was quite a sharp attack it is reported on a portion of the line and as that it's favorite time for rebels to make their attack we expected a fight.

I received a long and interesting letter from Will to-night written at Murfreesboro on the 9th. He still seems to think that Gen'l Slocums affairs are in a very uncertain state. Dr. Slocum, on whom I called to-day says he has heard from his brother and I he. If the Pres't does not very soon do as he positively agreed to viz. to place him under some other commander. He shall tender his resignation again. The most gratifying intelligence from Will is, that he is gaining so much strength in his arm. It really looks as though he would be able to regain much use of it.

And what glorious news from Ohio and Pennsylvania. With such an example I trust the good people of N.Y. will not allow themselves to be beaten by Copperheads. I *only wish New York soldiers could.* You ought to be able to electioneer with a good heart now. I see that Howell is to have charge of a road from Schenectady to Catskill. Will you get a chance there?

> With much love to mother

I remain

Yours affy

Os

P.S. In regard to my watch—I sent it from Berlin by the sutler of the 37th Mass. in July last to be cleaned. Soon after that reg't was ordered to N.Y. I wrote to him in regard to it and he answered me that it was in good order. I wrote back to him to express it to you—so that Lester could bring it back but have not heard from him since. The reg't ret'd to-day and as soon as the sutlers (who have all been ordered to the rear) come up, I will see about it.

I must add another line to express my delight at the manner in which McClellan has "showed his hand." Even his best friends (and the Lord knows I am not one of them) can't stand it.

Cmp 122d Reg't New York Vols

October 21, 1863

Dear Mother,

Here we are back at Warrenton, and Connie and myself have just returned from a ride into town, which looks natural.

We have quite a campaign since we left Catletts and I think if General Stonewall Jackson was still living it might have been a more disastrous one, for it is generally conceded that we got to Centerville just in time and if Stonewall had been living I think the rebel columns would have been too much for us.

It seems quite a luxury to have our wall tents, tables and other "fixins" again, after having lived in shelter tents for a week or so.

Andy's time is up to-night but I shall hardly expect him for a day or two but I trust that he will bring my coat as my present dress coat is getting rather shabbu and Gen'l Shaler like to have his officers look well.

It is three months to-day since the "Conscript Fathers" left us and no signs of a conscript as yet, although the 147th NYV (John Butler's regiment) have received some, I have heard. I am rather inclined to think that those officers who are home are more anxious to prolong their leave than to get conscripts.

To-day I met Cap't Smith, who used to be Commissary on Slocum's staff last Winter. He is now commissary of the 5th Corps and told me that he thought we should cross the Rappahannock again. I felt rather stupid to-night as you probably perceive and the Colonel, Walpole, and Connie are all in the tent talking so I must . . .

Camp 122d Reg't N.Y. Vols.
near Warrenton, Va.
October 23/63

Dear Mother,

We moved again yesterday a short distance and are now in camp West of the town very near the ground we occupied when we first came here in July last. We have not got a very good place for our camp. The regiment lays on a side hill, the company officers tents are on the crest of the first ridge and our tents on the top of a ridge still above that so that is quite a journey from my tent down to the regiment. Wooster and Cossitt who mess with me declare that we ought to establish a mess tent halfway between us as it is asking too much of them to climb the hill three times a day. I can learn nothing, of course in regard to the probable length of our stay. Army Head Quarters are established at Warrenton. No sutlers have yet come up and on appealing to one of the citizens here Mrs. Lee, for butter were informed that she did not wish to sell it but we might take some at $1.00 per lb. This is too steep even for army prices.

To-day Sunday's mail from home arrived but for a wonder did not bring me a letter. Soon after Andy Smith made his appearance and one of the first questions I asked, "Did you see mother?"

Judge of my surprise and disappointment on learning that he had not seen you, and upon questioning him I found that from some remark Jim made about having "considerable" company &c when he suggested calling he thought Jim did not want him to come. I trust that Jim did not intend to treat him impolitely for he has always been my kindest friend here and as he told me to-day "I would not have brought that coat for anybody else but you, Trace."

If I thought it at all necessary I would have requested that he might have been treated politely but I do think but that you would have wished to have seen any-body who could give you a personal account of your boys welfare and much more one who has always done what he could to make that "young ones" army life easier and pleasanter. I should be ashamed at any time to accept—half the invitations he gives to dinner and certainly shall be now.

As the railroad is in running order only as far as Gainsville, some twenty miles distant. Andy left his trunk in Washington to be brought over by a sutler of the Division so I have not seen my coat yet. Smithy wished to know if it wasn't intended for an overcoat but I am not much alarmed that it will be any too heavy for this Winter.

I have been building "air castles" recently imagining how nice it would be to surprise you by my arrival the night before Thanksgiving but I must not expect so much pleasure but keep my Thanksgiving here and be grateful to that kind Father who still spares me, such a mother and who has preserved Willie and my own life thus far amidst the dangers and, and that we shall all be able to meet once more in that home which has always been so pleasant and where our characters were so formed that we have been able to resist many of the temptations surrounding us.

I trust that Aunt may hear some favorable news from Willie that will render her Thanksgiving a joyous one.

Captain Urquhart of our Division Staff who was captured by the guerillas was heard from at Warrenton on his way to Richmond. He and some other Union officers were allowed to call on some of their lady friends whose acquaintances they formed when here in August, and were also allowed to hire a conveyance to take them to Culpepper, and rode out of town singing, "When this cruel war is over." It seems Capt. U—had quite a presentiment he was going to be taken and when a valuable horse he has was brought up (He had to go over to Fairfax, C.H. on business) he directed the darky to put the saddle on his other horse, and bid the rest of the staff goodbye, requesting them not to "go through" his "wardrobe" for 48 hours.

I have been very busy to-day on some Ordnance Reports, which I wish to finish before we move again and although it is rather late for "camp hours" yet I thought I had better write to-night and if I get a letter to-morrow before the mail goes I will try and add a postscript. If Miss Gordon is with you give her my regards and tell her that the photograph is the most correct likeness of your loving boy.

Os

Why does Sam not write to me, ask Mrs. S—to give him a "bleeping."

Saturday evening

P.S. We have just received orders to be in readiness to move at a moment's notice—but I think it a little doubtful whether we get off to-night. At all events I should much prefer my old dressing gown, slippers and that back parlor of yours with the thought that to-morrow is Sunday, to even the idea of marching, but it is all for the Cause.

Camp 122d Reg't New York Volunteers
October 27, 1863

Dear Mother,

I hasten to congratulate aunt on the joyful intelligence published in the Syracuse papers received this morning, that Cap't Fishers party are safe. I trust that she may soon hear from Willie direct.

I received my watch all safe this afternoon after is its long journey and it appears to be in good order.

The railroad is still only open to Gainsville (18 miles distant) and as no sutlers have yet arrived it has been rather poor living, "hardtack" and "salt pork" constituting the principal luxuries and as our picket line does not extend out very far it is impossible to get anything from the citizens. It would have amused you to have seen the excitement produced to-day by the arrival of the supply train with soft bread and potatoes.

I have not been able to go out to see any of the acquaintances formed when last here. They live beyond our present picket line but only think of my disgust at hearing the other day that Scott Payne of whom I wrote you in July, and whom I think is the finest specimens of a Virginia gentleman that I have seen, is in command of a guerrilla Company. When I called upon him he acknowledged his sympathies with the rebel cause but was "down" on guerillas in general and Mosby in particular.

Last evening Wooster and myself called on Andy and met Lt. Fitzhugh of the artillery, the same officer who was on Gen'l Buell's staff with Wright. He is from Oswego you know and quite well acquainted in Syracuse as that we had a very pleasant chat about mutual friends. He is a fine looking agreeable fellow.

From what I can learn the destruction of the railroad between here and Manassas Junction has been complete. In many places they took up the ties made a large pile of them—put the rails on top and then in burning the ties the rails bent by their own weight so as to render them unfit for use. they have blown up the culverts shoveled away the road bed, filled up cuts, and in fact it would be about as easy to build a new road.

The idea here is that Lee merely made the movement on our right flank so as to compel us to fall back and then he set one whole corps at work destroying the railroad and he thus prevented our advance again for two weeks for we cannot move until that road is in condition to bring us supplies, and that he is rapidly sending his forces to oppose Burnside, trusting to get them back again by the time we are ready to advance.

If this supposition be correct Lee as usual has beat us in "strategy." What changes in the Western army. I hope that it may bring Slocum out from under Hooker. I enclose a photograph of our hospital Steward which please add to my collections. I also enclose a piece of Southern rock which Connie picked up somewhere. I think that the Rebels call the first Bull Run, the "Battle of Manassas."

I forgot to answer your inquiry in regard the exact amount to spend for Mary Bassett's present. If you have not purchased it yet, I would suggest $10 as the maximum.

All sorts of stories are afloat as to the cause of the failure of this move and it said that there was a lack of concert of action among the Corps Commanders. It is also said that the failure was partially owing to the slowness with which the 3d Corps moved.

I have just heard the reason for the orders of last night. The enemy crossed the river but have retired again to-day, and the prospect seems to be that we shall remain here for some little time.

Col. Dwight received a very kind letter from "Father Waldo" this morning acknowledging the receipt of $100. The officers of this regiment went in for a

Thanksgiving present and requesting a list of the names that he might send them each a photograph. I will send mine to you for safekeeping. I think yours and Lucy's idea of sending me a box is an excellent one and would suggest Christmas as a very suitable time. I hardly think I can be twice unfortunate. Don't send anything that will be likely to spoil ("Fruit cake and mince pies for instance")

Tell Jim I will answer his letter in a day or two.

With thanks to our Heavenly Father who has again spared my life, and with the trust that our next Thanksgiving may be passed together I remain

Your loving son

Os

P.S. I beg your pardon about that mistake in paying you. Please let me know what I owe you stamps & all.

CHAPTER SIX

"Fall Campaigns"

November–December 1863

I feel that if we could close the Fall campaign, without meeting
with any disaster, even if we should not accomplish anything decisive,
that we could go into a winter quarters with a good heart and with
the hope of closing the war next summer sure.
—Osgood Tracy, November 24, 1863

❀ As the weather turned cold, the men of the 122nd New York were no closer
to Richmond than they had been a year before; the massive campaigns of 1863
left them again stalled on the banks of the Rapidan River. The letters Osgood
wrote during this time trace his regiment's movements in and around Northern
Virginia, but he also had time to reflect on broader war news, in particular the
growing importance of the US Colored Troop (USCT) regiments to the Union
cause. Throughout his time in the service, Osgood came face to face with the
realities of slavery, an institution that his family and others from his community, among them the Sedgwicks, had so vocally denounced in the antebellum.
His opinions regarding the slavery and the slaves he encountered were positive,
though measured, his comments reflecting a lingering abolitionist sentiment that
needed little explanation to those at home who shared his attitudes.

In early December, in what may have been a response to rumors that units of
the USCT might be joining the Army of the Potomac, as well as his own views
of the service of the USCT thus far in the war, Osgood wrote frankly. "What a
different feeling there is in regards to the negro soldiers," he told his mother. "I
have not heard anyone here that was copperhead enough to exult in the fact . . .

that the brave Col. Shaw was buried with his 'niggers.'"[1] His attitude reflected that of many in the Army of the Potomac by this point in the war. Though fierce debate over emancipation occurred in the wake of the Emancipation Proclamation, by 1864 "emancipation and the use of black troops has become . . . a 'military necessity,'" and though prejudices still existed among white soldiers, the voices of dissent had quieted some.[2] As part of the broader history of the war, though, Osgood's none-too-subtle comments regarding slavery in his letters to his mother illustrate the complexity of soldiers' motivations. Men marched to war and fought for a variety of reasons, and abolition as a moral imperative was only one of many ideologies that drove men to sacrifice all for the Union. For many men, the sanctity of the Union was the primary driving force. That slavery was dealt a crushing blow as the Confederacy crumbled under the sheer weight of the Union advance across multiple fronts was a consequence that many soldiers willingly accepted.[3] Osgood, an avowed abolitionist from a family of abolitionists, must have had his sentiments only strengthened as the war progressed.

The men of the 122nd New York staggered into the Christmas season fresh off of Gen. George Meade's stalled Mine Run Campaign, during which the commanding general swung south through the Wilderness in an attempt to turn the right flank of the Army of Northern Virginia, a campaign that ultimately stalled in front of Robert E. Lee's fortified line along the Mine Run River.[4] Many soldiers in the Army of the Potomac, though, saw Meade's decision to cancel the assault on the heavily fortified Confederate line as the best possible outcome, and it is likely that Osgood and the rest of the men of the 122nd New York felt relieved that they did not have to charge across an open field into withering Confederate fire that cold December day. They had been spared at Fredericksburg and were spared once again by their commanding general's prudent decision.[5]

---

1. Tracy to Mother, Dec. 8, 1863. On the Fifty-Fourth Massachusetts, see Russell Duncan, *Where Death and Glory Meet: Colonel Robert Gould Shaw and the 54th Massachusetts Infantry* (Athens: Univ. of Georgia Press, 1999); Ira Berlin, Joseph P. Reidy, and Leslie S. Rowland, *Freedom's Soldiers: The Black Military Experience in the Civil War* (New York: Cambridge Univ. Press, 1998). USCT Regiments joined Ambrose Burnside's Ninth Corps of the Army of the Potomac in January 1864. See Noah Andre Trudeau, *Like Men of War: Black Troops in the Civil War, 1862–1865* (Boston: Back Bay Books, 1999).

2. John J. Hennessy, "I Dread the Spring: The Army of the Potomac Prepares for the Overland Campaign," in *The Wilderness Campaign*, ed. Gary Gallagher (Chapel Hill: Univ. of North Carolina Press, 2012), 77–78.

3. James McPherson, *For Cause and Comrades: Why Men Fought in the Civil War* (New York: Oxford Univ. Press, 1997); Robert Hunt, *The Good Men Who Won the War: The Army of the Cumberland Veterans and Emancipation Memory* (Tuscaloosa: Univ. of Alabama Press, 2010); Gary W. Gallagher, *The Union War* (Cambridge, MA: Harvard Univ. Press, 2011); James Oakes, *Freedom National: The Destruction of Slavery in the United States, 1861–1865* (New York: W. W. Norton, 2012); Elizabeth R. Varon, *Armies of Deliverance: A New History of the Civil War* (New York: Oxford Univ. Press, 2019).

4. Chris Mackowski, *The Great Battle Never Fought: The Mine Run Campaign, November 26–December 2, 1863* (El Dorado Hills, CA: Savas Beatie, 2018).

5. Hennessy, "I Dread the Spring," 66–68.

Camp 122d New York Vols
November 2, 1863

Dear Mother,

Your letter of the 28th of October was received this evening and I will devote the half hour before the mail closes to you.

To-day we had a review of the Division by General Sedgwick and it is the first time that I ever saw that officer dressed up. The day was a beautiful one and troops looked finely. I can assure you, that I am growing prouder every day of the "blue crop." We got back about noon and this afternoon Connie and myself have been busy making further improvements in our abode, doing what Lucy delights in and what you abominate viz: "changing furniture." It is astonishing how much room there is after all in a tent 9 × 12. We have two beds (to be sure one is a "trundle bed") two desks, a fireplace, and plenty of room to entertain friends in beside.

I expect that I shall be contented with a very small house when I get home again and trust that some young lady may be left amidst all the marrying mania, whose view will coincide with mine. Is the Col. Hollister whom Louise Ballard is about to marry, her old "flame?" How come she is to drop Ham Benedict, or did he drop her? She told me once that I looked like a friend of hers by the name of Hollister—what a handsome fellow he must be.

Tell Sam to remember that I am in the 3d Div. 1st Corps and that he must not lose any time before he comes to see me. How glad I am to hear of George Holyoke's prosperity. Those boys have had such hard luck.

I am happy to say that my fast horse has improved finely. I paid Smithy $40 for her and he offered me $60 yesterday if I would let him have her back.

We are all wishing that we might be at home to-morrow night to hear the election returns come in. I cannot feel much doubt about the result in our state and here our only discussions are as to the size of the Union majority.

I am glad that you went to Geneva and only wish that you would take more pleasure excursions. I think it must be better for you to go visiting now that you are necessarily so much alone (now don't make any sarcastic remarks about how great my devotion is when I am at home.)

Dr. Slocum was here yesterday. He had not heard from his brother very recently, but his last letter said that he was still under Hooker but there had got to be a change very soon.

To-day when on review, we heard the welcome sound of a car whistle and I understand the road is open to Warrenton. If so we shall soon be better supplied. The Army of the Potomac has been in this desolate country so long that they would not know how to restrain themselves in such a fertile country as Will represents Tennessee to be.

Near our present picket line is an old negro woman who strange to say is of secession sympathies and declines to sell anything to the Union soldiers. A day or two ago one of Company A's men was stationed near there and he had picked up a secesh uniform coat, so putting that on he got one of his comrades to take him there as a secesh prisoner under guard and the old wenches heart was immediately opened and the fellow for a good supper. Our fellows have gotten to be "old soldiers" and are up to all the tricks of the trade.

> Well, good night, and with much love
> Believe me
> Yours affectionate
> Os

> Camp 122d Reg't N. Y. Vols
> November 5th 1863

Dear Mother,

Who should make his appearance in camp to-day but Major Jimmy Hinman of the 11th New York. I did not suppose I should be so glad to see him but he has improved considerably and I had quite a pleasant visit. He took dinner with me and we rode out to see Cossitt and Wooster who were on picket. He was accompanied by Col. McDougall, of whom Jim wrote me. Jim H. had a very pretty picture of Eva Sabine and made very mysterious allusions in regard to some wedding that is to come off in Syracuse before a great while so that I was inclined to think that it might be Eva's. We had quite a talk about the Department of the gulf where he was when in the 75th N.Y., and among others he happened to speak of Marie's old lover, Will Kameth of Boston, a Cap't of the 6th Mass. Battery. He says that he is a splendid fellow and a gallant officer, and that he was married to a young lady in that part of the country. Jim seemed to think that she rather missed it in accepting Jimmy in preference to Kameth.

What glorious news from New York. We have no particulars as yet, only a telegraph from New York City that the Union ticket was elected by 50,000 majority.[6] I am anxious to hear the result in our county although I feel but little doubt as to the result.

I noticed that Dudley made no speeches during the campaign and rather wondered at it. I am quite glad that the election is over as I trust we shall get some news in the papers.

> Well, good night
> Your boy
> Os

6. Abraham Lincoln and Andrew Johnson ran together in the 1864 presidential election under the banner of the Union Party against George McClellan and George Pendleton. Osgood's note of the rumor here about Lincoln's victory in New York City may be optimistic regarding a city that appeared so vehemently against the war, especially during the summer of 1863, when the Draft Riots broke out. Election numbers published in the *New York Times* on November 9, 1864, however, show that McClellan won the city by more than thirty thousand votes.

Camp 122d Reg't N.Y. Vols.
near Brandy Station, Va.
November 18/63

Dear Jim,

What a glorious time you must have had in Syracuse on election night. How I did wish that I could have reached home just in time to vote and to participate in the rejoicing afterwards.

Cap't Platt and myself rode over to the 1st Division and were in the attack at Rappahannock Station and took 4 "reb" battle flags and about 600 hundred prisoners. They are the biggest feeling lot of fellows I have seen. Dr. said that they had all sorts of trophies. Among other things they got hold of some boxes of officers clothing that had not been opened and several of the officers got nice new black overcoats. One Cap't had several little silk secesh flags, which had evidently been worked by some of the fair ones at home each having initials worked on them.

I did not see John Down as he had gone off visiting. Every time I do run across we have a very pleasant time chatting about our Syracuse friends and I post him up on all the news. Their regiment did not suffer much more than ours and got the "reb" flags too but never mind, we shall have a chance yet.

It was not the turn of our regiment to go in, as we were the only regiment of our brigade engaged at Gettysburg, but I presume at the next fight we shall be kept in the back ground.

When we came into the brigade a year ago, I had that disagreeable feeling that we were green and untried and they could not depend upon us, but now I feel that we are just as good as any of them.

We have improved so much since Titus has been away that I dread the thought of his coming back and as he will probably have forgotten the little he did know, he will make sweet work handling the reg't.

I heard a good story in regard to Brig. Gen'l Neil of our corps. He is very eccentric in his manners and a good bit of a dandy. He is a Cap't in the regular infantry and I feel likely Mrs. Sumner knows him as "Bricky Neil."

Not long since, his brigade broke camp up to play and struck up "When this cruel war is over." This exasperated "Bricky" and he burst out, –"Go back to your quarters——you: It is not a cruel war—it is a honest and just war——you go back to your quarter—never play that tune again:——you——.

You should hear him talk once to fully appreciate the manner in which it must have been said.

I received a letter from mother last evening saying that you had gone to Oswego and expected to be employed there, I suppose you are quite delighted at the idea of getting to work again.

Tell mother I will commence numbering my letters again but I will not make any rash promises as to keeping it up correctly,

I am going out to-morrow or next day to hunt up Win Sumner. Gen'l Pleasantons head quarters are quite near us and I can there ascertain his whereabouts.

Tell mother I am very careful about getting out of sight of camps for the recent accounts of the Richmond prisons have not increased my anxiety to get there.

By the way, where is Mary Sumner now and what is her husband's rank and position in the army? She might be useful in case I was unlucky as to be gobbled.

Yours

Os

Camp Sedgwick

November 20th 1863

Dear Mother,

The "fightin sixth" has had a grand review to-day by General Sedgwick[7] and we had some British officers as spectators. Their uniforms were quite plain (blackcoats). I believe they belong to the Royal Guards.

It has been a beautiful day and the troops looked finely. After review Connie and myself rode over to the 121st N.Y.V. and took dinner with Dr. Slocum. After dinner John Down and myself started out to find Win Sumner.

We went to army Hd Qrs and then to Gen'l Pleasontons but Win we found was about a mile beyond Culpepper so it was impossible to get to him to-day. The officer, whom I saw at Gen'l Pleasontons, informed me that an orderly was soon going out to Win, and I took the opportunity to send a note telling him of the effort we had made to see him, telling him where he could find me and requesting him to make an "effort" as Mr. Raymond would say. I found out what Brigade and Division he is in, so that we can find him more readily, but as the cavalry are generally at the "front" it is not so easy to get at them. John came back and took supper with me. He desired to be remembered to you and Jim.

I received two long letters from Will this morning, one dated on the 3d and the other on the 11th. His stories illustrating the lack of discipline among the Western troops are quite rich. I am glad to see he is able to write so well with his right hand, it looks quite like his old writing.

Everett's oration at Gettysburg is published in yesterday's Chronicle. How splendid the opening is, and how masterly the argument on State Rights. I am

---

7. Gen. John Sedgwick (1813–1864) was a military officer and Union army general. Born in Cornwall, Connecticut, he was named after his grandfather, John Sedgwick (brother of Theodore Sedgwick, an American Revolutionary War general) and was first cousin to Charles Baldwin Sedgwick. He was a graduate of the US Military Academy, class of 1837, fought in the Seminole Wars and received two brevet promotions in the Mexican-American War. After returning from Mexico, he transferred to the cavalry and served in Kansas in the Utah War and in the Indian Wars. During the Civil War, he commanded the Sixth Corps and died at the beginning of the Battle of Spotsylvania Court House on May 9, 1864.

sorry to see that he makes the same error in regard to our Brigade when he says Wheaton's Brigade reinforced Geary on the morning of the 3rd. It was our brigade and when you read the speech don't forget to insert Shaler's name in place of Wheaton and to bear in mind that the 122d Reg't was the only regiment of our brigade actually engaged so that the credit given to Wheaton's Brigade really belongs to our regiment. Truly the definition given by some one of glory, "To lose one leg and have your name spelled wrong in the Gazette," is not far from right.

Frank Lester made his appearance in camp this morning much to our surprise. It was a pleasure to see someone who could say they had seen you recently and were able to assure me, from personal observation, of your good health. Frank is here now and is talking some of giving up his position on the staff and returning to the regiment but has not decided yet. Among other gratifying intelligence that Frank brought was his assurance of the Colonel's continued absence. He does think that he will return before spring. By that time Col. Dwight will have the regiment in such good shape that I think Gen'l Shaler will trust Titus with it.

I wrote Frank sometime ago in reference to having a seal made for me but he did not get the letter in time to have it made before he left and therefore wrote to him about. Please ask him to attend to it immediately. Chase, the engraver, will make it. Have it put into a little paper box and sent by mail. I will describe it again. I enclose a diagram of the thing. I would like it to be the size of the diagram. The "impression" will be this—a Corps Cross in "relief" and the letters 122d N.Y.V. in "relief" on the horizontal bar of the cross. You may think this not very tasty for a private seal but I intend it more for office use, and as everybody comes to the Adjutant's office to seal up packages it will be for general use. Have it made from brass, or sound hardwood, Chase will know about that, which will be the best. Please have it made as soon as convenient.

We are having a slow steady rain to-day which is decidedly suggestive of bad roads and no move. We have got such a pretty place for our Headquarters tents that I shall be very well content to remain here. We have also a fireplace and talk of putting a floor to-morrow, and these two constitute the luxuries of camp life, this time of year.

Please don't aggravate me with accounts of pretty girls dining with you it is enough to drive one distracted who has only quartermasters and "line" officers for companions. John Down and myself amused ourselves last evening in talking over old times, and imagining ourselves in Cobleighs waiting for the music to "strike up." What a large amount of "back" dancing to do when I do get home and I trust that I shall not lack for opportunities.

Love to all
Your boy
Os

Camp Sedgwick
Near Brandy Station, Va.
November 24, 1863

Dear Mother,

The long expected orders have come and we are ordered to be in readiness to move at an "early hour in the morning." As to our destination, rumor says everywhere from Knoxville to the Pamunkey, but by the time you receive this you will have probably heard from the army and I will not hazard my reputation as a prophet by telling you what I think.

Yesterday we received an order from the Hd Qrs of the army, saying that hereafter the soldiers would be required to carry but five days rations instead of eight and here fore. This is the best order we have had for months—after repeated trials, the "powers that be" have concluded that it is impossible for men to carry eight days rations in addition to their other loads. To-day we received about 100 express boxes for the regiment and as our cook was among the fortunate ones we have had home-made "nut cake" cookies &c in any quantity. Cap't Roome,[8] our Brigade Adjutant General, is coming over this evening to play cribbage and we are able to make quite a "spread." Dave Cossitt received a loaf of fruit cake.

Last evening I had some business at Brg HdQrs and had a very pleasant chat with Roome. He is one of the exceptions in the army of an officer who neither drinks or gambles. He has promised to make a visit to Syracuse after the war is over and you may rest assured that he will be met with a hearty welcome for the boys think that there is nobody like Cap't Roome.

To-night the news from Burnside is rather disheartening. I feel that if we could close the Fall campaign, without meeting with any disaster, even if we should not accomplish anything decisive, that we could go into a winter quarters with a good heart and with the hope of closing the war next summer sure.

Brit Lester is here and will get this letter into the mail at his Head Quarters. The mail already having left here.

Trusting that Providence may preserve me through whatever may occur I remain
Your loving boy
Os

Camp 122d Reg't New York Vols
Near Brandy Station Va
Nov. 25, 1863

Dear Mother,

The expected march did not take place. It was raining hard when we awoke

---

8. William Poe Roome was originally commissioned as second lieutenant of Company F, Sixty-Fifth New York Infantry, in June 1861. He was promoted to adjutant general on February 27, 1863.

yesterday morning. We packed up but did not strike tents. We have received orders to move to-morrow morning and Andy Smith told me that we should certainly move. I understand that the army are to cross the Rapihan but that the 6th Corps are not to be in front.

This afternoon Cap't Cossitt, Cap't Platt and myself rode over to call on John McCuir Botts. He did not find him at home much to my disappointment. He has one of the finest places I have seen in Virginia and what was to us rather a novel sight, about 300 sheep. It is unnecessary to add that he has a guard over them. I understand that he has bought several farms here paying for them in Confederate money so that when the war is over he will be a very wealthy man.

Last evening Cap't Roome came over and we passed the evening playing cribbage. During the evening, Crumb our sutler, came up and we thought from his voice, as he came up to the tent, that it was Col. Titus (The Colonel has been ordered back to the regiment) much to everyones consternation. Cossitt had some very nice fruit cake which he had received from home and of which I partook freely and the consequence was that I had a sort of night mare, dreaming that Col. T had actually returned and I was having all sorts of trouble. Crumb brought us a cook stove made of sheet iron and 25 lbs of Buckwheat flour so we shall have an improvement in our bill of fare.

Our mess is rather too large and I think when we get established in Winter quarters, if ever, that we will divide it, Connie and myself forming a mess together.

I have purchased a jacket, from the government. It is so much better to ride in than a dress coat and on the march "coat tails" are decidely in the way.

Dr. Knapp, our ass't surgeon, has just received some dentists tools and gold foil so that I shall be able to have my teeth fixed one of the fillings that Dr. Smith put in for me when I was at home in March. Dr. Tefft says he shall resign as soon as we get into winter quarters.

The mail is closing. I will write as soon again as possible.

Yours lovingly
O. V. Tracy

Camp near Ely's Ford
Dec. 2d, 1863

Dear Mother,

Our campaign, begun on Thanksgiving has ended with it probably all operations for the Army of the Potomac this winter. We left the 'front' last night about 9 o'clock, marched all night crossing the river at this point about 8 o'clock this morning. I am therefore too sleepy and tired to say anything more than to assure you of my safety and good health. Our regiment was not engaged, although exposed to some artillery fire. We had one rainy day and three or four mighty cold ones while over the river. I will not attempt to give you any account of our movements until my next. With bright visions of "Winter quarters" and with the greatest love for you all I remain

Your aff. Boy
Os

Near Brandy Station
Dec. 3/63

Dear Mother,

I add a line before the mail goes. We marched about 10 miles farther yesterday afternoon on our way to our old camps at Brandy but stopped about 3 miles from there as it got to be dark and our men were completely exhausted. We marched from 9 o'clock the night before until 8 yesterday A.M. Started again at 1 o'clock yesterday afternoon and marched till 6 P.M. making about the hardest 24 hours work we have ever done. We shall go into camp this morning.

Good Bye
Yours
Os

Camp 122d Reg't N. Y. Vols
near Brandy Station, Va.
December 8th 1863

Dear Mother,

Yesterday Connie was sent outside the lines with a train to get lumber for the General and we got a wagon load for our use. Connie expects to draw a small tent this month which we are going to put up in rear of our present tent for a bedroom and this will enable us to live very comfortably. The boys having been ordered to raise their beds from the ground, and not finding any lumber near "allied" on the barns one of our "neighbors" so that the regiment is quite well supplied. In the operation some pigs got loose and of course came to an untimely death, our cook was fortunate enough to secure a "quarter."

Everybody is engaged fixing up as if they expected to be here for sometime, if not for the Winter.

Walpole lent me the November number of the Atlantic which contains several interesting articles. One of the most interesting I think is Miss Alcott's article the "Brothers"[9] (Miss Gertrude had marked, in pencil, the name of the author of each article) –

What a different feeling there is in regards to negro soldiers. I have not heard anyone here that was copperhead enough to exult in the fact as I believe the Courier did, that the brave Col. Shaw was buried with his "niggers."

9. This was Louisa May Alcott's 1863 short story "The Brothers," *Atlantic*, Nov. 1863.

How beautifully Miss Alcott turns the intended insult into an honor

The Herald of the 5th (I believe) has an excellent map of our operations over the river. On the 30th our position (which is not named on the map), was on the left of the 2d Corps, and we could see without the aid of a glass the rebel cavalry on the side of Clark's Mountain. I notice that the Herald speaks of the probability of Meade's removal[10] but I hear nothing definite in regard to it here.

Tuesday evening

I kept this letter until our mail arrived hoping to hear from you and forgot to send it by to-nights mail. Wooster and myself just returned from a walk over to Division Hd Qrs. Wooster is Judge Advocate of a court martial now in session and had some poor prisoners to consult in regard to their trial for a Judge Advocate has to be both prosecuting attorney and prisoners' counsel, rather a novel position for a lawyer to be on both sides of a case at the same time.

On dress parade this evening I noticed that our flag given to us by the ladies of Fayetteville is getting badly worn and although I cannot say "riddled" with bullets yet it has had a few through it, I believe, at all events our grey headed color bearer says so, and I wondered if the ladies of Syracuse thought that our regiment had reflected enough honor on Old Onondaga to deserve a new flag for a "Christmas Present." Suppose you suggest it to some of your lady friends who can make an "effort" for such a good purpose.

You may send my box as soon as it is convenient for you. Please put in about half a dozen white linen handkerchiefs (I am getting "above" bandanas as well as Will) a black silk neck tie, and another tie, something fancy. Direct the box plainly to Adjutant O. V. Tracy, 122d N. Y. Vols. 1st Brigade 3d Division 6th Corps Army of the Potomac.

Don't think from the above that I intend to hasten you any, but express boxes come through more readily, and whenever you are ready I am.

Love to everybody

Yours

Os

10. Gen. George Meade and Lincoln's relationship was rocky in the wake of Lee's escape from Gettysburg, but Meade's leadership of the Army of the Potomac became increasingly confusing after Ulysses S. Grant was promoted to general in chief of Union armies in March 1864. See Tom Huntington, *Searching for George Meade: The Forgotten Victor of Gettysburg* (Mechanicsburg, PA: Stackpole, 2013), 248–51.

Camp 122d Reg't New York Volunteers
December 10th, 1863

Dear Mother,

Since we have been here and the prospects of our remaining increase the Generals have been sending all over the county after lumber and Gen'l Shaler[11] has been very kind in letting us have wagons and we are fast getting fixed up for the Winter—ie. If we are allowed to remain. Our regiment is in a very bad place for wood and water and I should be willing to break up our pleasant quarters—(our tents are in a little pine grove) for the good of the regiment.

Connie has been out three days this week with wagon trains, after lumber for the Brigade, and to-day Cossitt and Connie started out after lumber and had a pass as usual outside of the lines, and came back to-night with ten wagon loads. Connie got to a saw-mill and as the lumber was all gone he tore off the sides and took up the floor of the mill but the richest thing was the collection of furniture they brought. They found a house where the family had left taking off their "niggers" with them and when Cossitt and Connie arrived they found Gen'l Sedgwick's Head quarters team taking furniture so Connie, who was going over further after lumber, left Cossitt with part of the guard to "hold" the furniturer until his return.

When they came in to-night they brought the mattresses, half a dozen arm chairs, one rocking chair, three or four tables, a sofa—so large that we cannot get it into our tent until our bedroom is built—(A very nice hari-cloth covered one) a pair of "and irons" (just the thing for our fire-place) and other things too numerous to mention, among the rest of things Connie had a light buggy hitched behind to one of the wagons and next Sunday, Connie and myself intend to take a drive. I only wish you were here to take a ride with me.

I received a splendid long letter from Willie to-night—six pages—giving me an account of his visit to Chattanooga. Poor Holland Johnson,[12] he writes me, was killed at Lookout Mountain.

I enclose a photograph of Newton[13] and also one of Gen'l Meade. Gen'l Newton is not very good but Gen'l Meade is an excellent likeness. I have got a good

---

11. Gen. Alexander Shaler of New York was promoted to the commander of the First Brigade, Third Division, and later oversaw the Union prison at Johnson's Island, where Osgood and his comrades would spend the winter of 1863–64 on guard duty. See Ezra J. Warner, *Generals in Blue: Lives of Union Commanders* (Baton Rouge: Louisiana State University Press, 2006), 434–35.

12. Per a report of the adjunct general of the State of New York, John Holland Johnson (1838–1863), "Holland," was age twenty-three when he enlisted September 2, 1862, at Syracuse, New York to serve three years. He was mustered in as sergeant, Company H., 149th Regiment, September 17, 1862. Commissioned second lieutenant, he was killed in action November 24, 1863 at Lookout Mountain, Tennessee.

13. Virginia native and 1842 West Point graduate Gen. John Newton was a corps commander in the Army of the Potomac until 1864, when he was transferred to the western theater and fought during the Atlanta Campaign and in Florida. See Brendan Wolfe, "Newton, John (1822–1895)," *Encyclopedia Virginia*, Feb. 12, 2021, https://encyclopediavirginia.org/entries/newton-john-1822-1895/.

one of Gen'l Shaler which I will send in a day or two, as I wish to obtain his autograph on it.

We had a rumor in camp yesterday that Meade had been relieved by Pleasanton but I have heard nothing official in regard to it.

We received an order from the War Department to-night indicating that furloughs would soon be granted freely. Connie has got an application for one in now and if it is granted he will go and see you when he is in Syracuse. After he gets back I shall try and get away as soon as I can get reports and up which will probably be about the 10th of January 1864.

I feel terrible about Kitty Sedgwick's "jilting" me—as I felt sure of her. I trust that she does not have much influence in her "family."

Good night—if I have time to-morrow I will add more.

I forgot to say that Connie and Cossitt apologized for not bringing the piano, from that house, for lack of transportation.

Did you ever hear of "woolen sheets?" If there is such a thing wouldn't that be better for me than cotton? You had better put the sheets in my box.

> Camp 122d Reg't N.Y. Volunteers
> December 11th 1863

Dear Mother,

Yours of the 8th was received this morning. I received the stamps you sent me but shall not settle with you until I come home on furlough, so of course this will add to your desire to see me. Connie left yesterday morning, and promised to call upon you. He is a very nice fellow and always very kind and accommodating to me, which I know will be his best recommendation to your favor. Here the amount of transportation is limited so there is nothing like being on good terms with the quartermaster.

I send another General to add to the gallery. It is a very good picture although you never see him dressed up except on review.

I have been expecting a visit from Sam as I wrote to him where we were but I have seen nothing of him.

The cavalry are generally out to the front, beyond our infantry pickets that it is not safe to go without an escort in this country of "guerillas."

Dr. Tefft has fully decided to resign the first of next month. I shall feel very sorry to lose him. He says if he were ten or fifteen years younger nothing would tempt him to leave the service. Knapp, the asst. surgeon, will probably be made surgeon. He is from Jamesville and is quite a good surgeon and a clever fellow.

You must save some of your gaiety until my "leave of absence" but I have no fears but that you and myself can have a pleasant time together—parties or no parties. I already am enjoying my visit in anticipation, and am planning various excursions for us. I have promised Dav. Cossitt to drive out to Onondaga Hill to see his father and you must manage to have some sleighing for us to enjoy.

Connie gave me full authority to hitch up his buggy and if it is pleasant to-morrow I will certainly call for her in her new house when I am at home.

I have not heard from George Hunt in a long time. I wrote him sometime ago.

You had better get something for Lulu and Anna for Christmas, for which I will also settle when I come home.

Love to all

Your boy

Os

Camp 122d Reg't N.Y. Vols.

December 15th 1863

Dear Mother,

This afternoon Cossitt and myself rode over to spend the afternoon with Dr. Slocum but upon our arrival there found that orders had been received for a Corps review. As we had permission to be absent until after dress parade we concluded not to go back to the regiment but to take part in the review as "spectators." We had hardly got posted upon a hill in rear of the artillery, when along came Gen'l Meade and staff accompanied by the "Russians." I have often heard of "sailors on horseback" before but I never really appreciated it until today. One of them let go the reins and hung on to the saddle and his horse went charging over the field wherever he pleased. Another got thrown and profiting by his experience, declined to mount again, and went wandering around on foot. Meade's staff appeared to have their hands full chasing them round.

I am inclined to think that however an opinion the Russians may have of our army they will not entertain a very good opinion of our horses.

We have plenty of rumors about moving and the latest is that we shall move sometime this week and probably fall back as far as Fairfax.

With what regret I shall leave all my furniture however as I am "acting" Q.M. I shall endeavor to save my mattress.

I enclose a photograph of Gen'l Shaler. It is very good and I think you will agree with me in considering the most soldierly looking officer you have seen.

Good Bye

Yours Lovingly

Os

Camp 122d Reg't N.Y. Vols.

December 19th 1863

Dear Mother,

Your letters of the 13th and 15th are before me. Well I am surprised at Charley Fitch's engagement. Sarah Ballard has been so intimate with Elize during the last two years that she cannot but be aware of all of Charley's "peculiarities" and she must either have a romantic hope of reclaiming him or else her desire to be related to Elize blinds her. However Sarah is a real good girl and she may be after all the means of saving him—and Carry W too—and a Spanish "Countess" at that—upon the whole you may speak to Miss C . . .

I can assure you it is a great disappointment to me not to be able to be at home New Year's but I dislike to leave my reports to the charge of my Sergeant Major, and as it is the end of a quarter as well as a month my reports are about double and therefore feel as though I must wait, but not patiently, till about the 10th or 15th of January. As to looking hard I shall make no rash promises but will agree to look as happy as a . . . returning to such a home and such a mother—after nearly a years absence, ought to—and if happiness will make me handsome I shall not be afraid to compete with even Leon.

I was very much amused at the notice of our State flag in the Standard. In the first place it said flag was given us by the government (and not the ladies) of New York and furthermore has not to my knowledge a single bullet hole in it. I beg pardon, you saw two. The flag was not in the battle of Gettysburg but was quietly reposing in our wagon about 20 miles off. It has been so badly tattered that we have not carried it for some time. With these few corrections the account is correct. But the flag that I am anxious that you ladies replace, our national flag, has been with us always and can I believe boast of two or three bullet holes. The flags I have seen in the army have been oftener "riddled" by the wind than by bullets.

In regard to the box I think perhaps you had better not send it. I should hardly get it before I go home. You need not get anything very expensive for the girls something to remind them of their absent cousin, say $5 or so for the two

I received a letter from Connie yesterday written at the Delavan House on Sunday. He was delayed on the road and obliged to spend Sunday in Albany, much to his disgust. He was mean enough to send me a bill of fare from the Delavan, showing me what sort of "rations" he was enjoying and the rascal was impatient enough to head it.

We are having a very cold, disagreeable, windy day and you can judge of our delight a few minutes at receiving a circular saying that the usual Brigade Drill was to be omitted (two brigade drills a week are all the drilling we have now).

The government are holding out very strong inducements to the troops whose term of service expires during the coming year, to re-enlist. The total bonus now at amount to about $700 and the government promises each soldier who shall so reenlist a furlough for 30 days to be granted sometime before the expiration of his original three years and where three fourths of a regiment reenlist they are allowed to go home for the purpose of reorganizing and re-enlisting, as a regiment. The portion of the regiment which does not reenlist are to be transferred to some other regiment for the remainder of their term of service.

I think many will reenlist as adjutant of a Vermont regiment who was in to see me to-day says his regiment is reenlisting very rapidly and they hope to be in Vermont by the 1st of January. We feel quite confident that by the close of next summers campaign this rebellion will be pretty much used up and Wooster made a bet the other day that the last battle of the war would be fought before a year from the 1st of January. I think that if our army could have been as successful as Grant's, the rebellion would have been used up this Winter.

Anyone who has noticed how splendidly the 11th and 12th Corps have fought out West can think that the army has failed so often for lack of good material and hard fighting and notwithstanding our hard fighting has proven to be almost useless through the incapacity of General S yet it is the highest praise that can be given us that we have never become discouraged thanks to Miss Gerty's kindness to the "Captain." I get a glimpse of the Atlantic every month.

Have you read the article in the December No. entitled "man without a country?"[14] It is very interesting but I can hardly credit its truth. Nolan's advice to the author after that scene on board the slave-ship is splendid and Miss Gerty has been bountiful in her pencil marks on that passage.

I am very sorry that George Jenkins has no more taste for study but as to enlisting as a private soldier. I think he would be very foolish—a private's life is no easy one yet you would be surprised to see how well some our smallest boys stand it.

I have been talking to Andy about getting 15 days but he has said that he had a talk with Col. McMahon, Sedgwick's Adj't Gen'l, who told him that it was impossible to get more than 2 days except you belong to a Western or New England regiment. However 10 days will give me a week at home and that is considerable time, when I consider that my business will not occupy my time—but I forget, my real estate may need some improvements. I shall think of you on Christmas Eve and shall imagine myself at Mrs.—give her my kindest regards and give Theo. a kiss for me at the wedding and earnest hopes for her future happiness. I am sorry to hear of Dudley's continued sickness but trust that the next letter will bring better news.

Love to all

Your boy

Os.

[Undated, early December 1863]

Dear Will,

Orders of last winter in regard to furloughs are renewed and everybody of course is delighted. I shall probably go as soon after the 1st of January as I can get my accounts settled and reports off, probably about the 11th or 15th. I should like very much to be at home on New Years, as, from mothers accounts, the festival at Whiting Hall will be quite a pleasant affair. I shall make strenuous efforts to get

14. Edward Everett Hale, "The Man without a Country" *Atlantic*, Dec. 1863.

15 days but not with much hopes of success. However I shall be thankful for 10 days and have no doubt but that I shall enjoy myself at any time at home. Connie, who tents with me left yesterday morning. He got 15 days. We are all fixing up for Winter quarters though as far as our regiment is concerned we have got a miserable place quite a distance from wood and water. Connie and Cossitt went out with a train after lumber the other day and found a deserted house containing furniture of which they brought a few "samples." We have now got more furniture than we have room and next week I am going to build a bedroom, so that I can get my "sofa" into the house. We have got a mattress-rocking chair, an arm chair, and brass topped "and irons" for our fireplace and in fact about everything that serves to make camp life comfortable. I suppose our campaigning is over for this winter, at least I trust so. I feel mortified to think that the Western Army did so much better than we did but feel quite satisfied to think that we got established for the winter without meeting with any serious disaster. The day after I wrote you I saw a splendid map in the Herald of the recent operations over the river (rather better I think than my map) which I should have sent you had I not supposed you were in reach of the Herald yet. I presume a young man of your proclivities could exist with that sheet. I am acting now both as Quartermaster and Adjutant, yesterday drew clothing and issued it to the companies coming out all right,

If you see Hunty ask him why he does not write.

Good Bye
Yours
Os

[Undated]

Dear Mother,

I have been spending the afternoon very pleasantly with Andy and Frank at Division Hd. Qrs and took dinner with them. I have just returned and was gratified to receive a letter from you and I seize the few minutes before the mail closes to once more express my regret at the impossibility of my leaving before the 10th of January or thereabouts. I am very sorry to miss both the "tree" and wedding but remember, the number of "festivities" there is the more you will have me at home and, as I have before remarked, I have no fears but that I shall enjoy myself. As nearly all my old friends have either been married or gone away from Syracuse, please say to Miss Sedgwick that I beg that she will do neither until after my furlough and as George and Marie are both away I shall have no one else to devote myself to when I am away from you.

I took a "short" leave of absence in my dreams last night and saw you all at home. In fact I am already enjoying my visit in anticipation, but to return to the army, the latest rumors are that we are not to fall back at all. I wish they would decide it. I have got the "walls" of my bedroom up but am waiting for some reliable news before I put a roof on and put a door in the back of my tent. There is a Tribune correspondent tenting with Lester by the name of Hayes, quite an intelligent and pleasant fellow but "born in Boston" and prejudiced in favor of that village as only her "children" are. Everyone, that knows them, is much surprised to hear of the engagement between Charley Fitch and Sarah Ballard. Jim Hinman was here to-day and I astounded him with the announcement of it.

I am glad to hear such good news from the "Captain"—have not heard directly from him since immediately after his return from Chattanooga.

It is time for the mail to close and I will wish you a "Merry Christmas" only regretting I shall not be there to seal it with a kiss.

Lovingly yours

Os

❀ ❀ ❀

CHAPTER SEVEN

"Winter Guard Duty"

Sandusky, Ohio, January–April 1864

The rebel prisoners were well fed, clean—comfortably housed
and well treated—in great contrast to the condition and treatment
of our poor fellows confined in Southern prisons.
—Osgood Tracy, postwar recollection

❀ As the New Year dawned in 1864, the Union war effort stood at a crossroads. Though George Meade had successfully stopped Lee's invasion of Pennsylvania that July, the Gray Fox had escaped back into Virginia with his army bloodied but intact. The Confederates also brought with them a significant amount of captured supply, which would prove invaluable to the Southern war effort during the coming year.[1] Meade was unable to capitalize on the Union victory and follow-up efforts to push the Army of Northern Virginia south toward Richmond were in vain, as exemplified by the experiences of Osgood and his comrades in the late fall of 1863 during the Mine Run Campaign. From a military perspective, things looked considerably better in the West. New Orleans, the Confederacy's largest city and port, fell to Union forces in April 1862, which coincided with another important Federal victory, at Shiloh in Tennessee.

During the next year, Federal forces began to expand their hold over the cotton-growing regions of the Deep South in campaigns that ultimately culminated on the slopes of Vicksburg. The "Gibraltar of the West," sitting astride a hairpin bend in the Mississippi River, was a vital strategic position for the Confederacy. So long as they held it, Southern forces controlled a portion of the Mississippi River,

---

1. See, for example, Kent Masterson Brown, *Retreat from Gettysburg: Lee, Logistics, and the Pennsylvania Campaign* (Chapel Hill: Univ. of North Carolina Press, 2005).

securing the link between the eastern and western parts of the Confederacy and preventing the Union from freely navigating that waterway. The city fell to Union forces under the command of Ulysses S. Grant on July 4, 1863, an event that served as a springboard for broader campaigns into the heart of the Confederacy, which ultimately brought that fledgling nation to its knees.

Despite advances in the west, the nation's eyes were on events in the East, where the inactivity of the Union army in the wake of Gettysburg was undercut by larger political events, most importantly, the New York City Draft Riots, which broke out around the same time and appeared as the manifestation of growing war weariness and dissent among Northerners. This was exacerbated by the vocal emergence of the Copperhead movement, which sought an immediate cessation of hostilities. For many, the Union cause appeared to be hanging in the balance as the nation moved toward 1864 and a looming presidential election that might very well decide the fate of the grand experiment in democracy.[2] The regiment's stay in Virginia was short-lived, as they soon boarded trains west, headed for Sandusky, Ohio, and garrison duty at Johnson's Island, a Union prison on Lake Erie that housed Confederate officers. In the days before their departure, which the men were not made aware of in advance, Osgood wrote the following letter and then one explaining the train ride to Ohio.

> Camp 122d Reg't New York Vols
> near Brandy Station, Va.
> Jan. 3d, 1864

Dear Mother,

Yesterday I received your letter written on the 29th and one from Willie written on Christmas day—you two are the only regular correspondence I have now—George seems to have dropped me entirely.[3]

What can induce people to having morning weddings by gas light? I always remember what a disagreeable feeling it used to be when I attended panoramas in

2. For discussions on the importance of the Mississippi River and, especially, Vicksburg, see Michael B. Ballard, *Vicksburg: The Campaign That Opened the Mississippi* (Chapel Hill: Univ. of North Carolina Press, 2004); Donald Stoker, *The Grand Design; Strategy and the U.S. Civil War* (New York: Oxford Univ. Press, 2010), 107–14; Richard E. Beringer et al., *Why the South Lost the Civil War* (Athens: Univ. of Georgia Press, 1986), 128–31; Brian Holden Reid, *America's Civil War: The Operational Battlefield, 1861–1863* (New York: Prometheus Books, 2008), 135–36. The existence of vocal and visible dissent in the form of the politicization of the Copperhead movement in the North and resistance to authority in communities North and South are the predominant themes in Robert Sandow, *Deserter Country: Civil War Opposition in the Pennsylvania Appalachians* (New York: Fordham Univ. Press, 2009); Jennifer L. Webber, *Copperheads: The Rise and Fall of Lincoln's Opponents in the North* (New York: Oxford Univ. Press, 2006); Ryan W. Keating, *Shades of Green: Irish Regiments, American Soldiers, and Local Communities in the Civil War Era* (New York: Fordham Univ. Press, 2017).

3. In letters like this one, Osgood seemed obsessed whether George Hunt was having a "flirtation" with Nellie Sedgwick and assumes that perhaps his friend was not writing to him for this reason.

the daytime and came out in the daylight again and I think a wedding of this kind would affect me somewhat in the same way.

New Years passed off very quietly. Lester invited Wooster and myself to dine with him but Connie and myself had accepted an invitation from Col. Dwight. The Col. gave us a very nice dinner winding up with a plum pudding which would have disgraced your table (Can I give it any higher praise?).

I was very much pained to hear of Aunts sickness and Uncles continued illness. I do hope that I shall find them both better when I come home.

By the way, I cannot learn anything definite as to when leaves of absence are again to be granted but apply to Smithy for information every time he makes his appearance. I shall have about 6 hours in Washington and if you will send me Nell's address I will try and call, for your sake. I am almost tempted to swear, when I think how all my old friends have deserted me, everyone either married or gone away. Well, I shall have to cultivate some new acquaintances.

Wooster just came and said that Lester and Mr. Hayes, the Tribune correspondent, were coming to dine with and proposed inasmuch as the tent is rather small that we should join with him and we furnish the dining room and he would furnish the turkey. I shall be inclined to think that young man Wooster is seeking for popularity. This entertaining correspondents in the army is decidedly suggestive.

Lt. Armstrong of Gen'l Shalers' staff died last evening after a very short illness "malignant encipela." He was a very fine fellow indeed and very popular in the Brigade.

The night before New Year's we had quite a scare, receiving an order late in the evening to be in "readiness to move, by rail, at a moment's notice." The 3rd Brigade of our Division did pack up in a rainstorm about midnight and march to Brandy Station where they took cars for Washington. I understand that they have gone to Harpers Ferry, the rebels being reported in force at Winchester. We have received no further orders and I understand that there is now no probability of our going.

We have had very cold weather for the last day or two. Yesterday morning after our fire had been going sometime the thermometer (you see we are not entirely deprived of the "luxuries" of life) stood a few degrees below the freezing point. But we soon got warmed up and were very comfortable for the rest of the day. One of our men had his feet freeze quite badly while sleeping in his tent but as it was New Year's night I fear the poor fellow must have been drinking enough to make him stupid.

To-day is much warmer. What a jolly time Willy must have had Christmas eve at the dance at Decherd but the young rascal took away half the champaining by mentioning that they found a few "snuff sticks" on the floor after the fair ones had departed. He also writes me that his arm is steadily improving.

Sunday is always a quiet day in camp and I think I miss home more then, than at any other time. I always look back with pleasure to the hour just between daylight and darkness when we used to sit without candles and attempt to sing and only wish to-night that Willie and I could draw up our chairs on each side of you . . .

On the Balt & Ohio R.R.
near Harpers Ferry
Jany 7/64

Dear Mother,

On the afternoon of the 5th we rec'd orders to hold ourselves in readiness to move at a moment's notice by rail. We broke camp at 12 o'clock that night and marched to Brandy Sta— took the cars and arrived in Washington about 4 P.M. yesterday. We expected when we left camp to go to Harpers Ferry but at Washington our brigade rec'd orders to proceed to Johnson's Island off Sandusky, Ohio, for the purpose of guarding rebel prisoners confined there. We shall probably remain there all winter. It will be very easy work I imagine and a very pleasant place for Winter quarters. We had but two or three hours in Washington and I had no opportunity to see Mr. Davis or anyone else.

We were obliged to ride up from Brandy Sta. in box cars without fires, and as my blankets were with my horse on the next train, it was rather cold work. To-day the officers are accommodated with a passenger car. I expect we shall not reach our destination until to-morrow night but will probably be up with the things in a week or so. We are almost inclined to doubt our good luck and are afraid that our present orders may be countermanded, but we may be destined to have an easy time for once.

I will write you as soon as I arrive at a stopping place. Excuse this writing and bear in mind that it was executed riding on the rail.

Love to all
Os

Wheeling, Va, Jany 10/64

Dear Mother,

We arrived here late last evening, it being our fourth day on the road. We got the men into some halls for the night and Col. D and myself secured a room at the McLure House and I can assure you we did an immense amount of sleeping in a short space of time. We are however quite restored from the fatigue of our four days ride.

This is a very pretty place and much larger than I expected. I have but time to write a few lines, as getting in late last night our men are necessarily somewhat mixed and as they are divided between two halls I am trying to get the companies straightened out. As the men during the journey have had rather free access I regret to say that part of the brigade got exceedingly "boozy." Crossing the mountains the trains were broken up and changed so that one train got in with but few officers on board and the citizens learning that they belonged to the 6th corps were very kind to them and and the consequence was that they got very tight. I am very happy to say however that I have seen but one drunken man that belonged to our reg't and this morning's report shows that we have not lost a man by the way.

Cap't Rooney just told me that we shall probably leave here this afternoon or to-morrow morning. We are detained for want of transportation. If we remain the Colonel and myself are going to church. It is so long since we have enjoyed that privilege that it will be quite a treat. Yesterday I was in a car all day with about twenty officers representative from every reg't in the brigade and we had a very jolly time singing & c. At one place a Virginian got on and as we thought he did not seem very sociable we struck up "John Brown." All along we have understood that our stay at Johnson's Island was to be permanent, for the winter at least, but Dr. Retherbridge of the Chasseurs just said he heard we were only going up to escort rebel prisoners down to Pt. Lookout. I don't believe this last as I heard Gen'l Terry[4] say what comfortable quarters he was going to have for us this winter and therefore shall believe the first report, viz; that we are to be stationed at Johnson's Island near Sandusky to guard the "rebs" confined there.[5]

But I must go and find Col. D. If I have anymore time I will write further to-day.

Yours

Os

Wheeling

W. Va. Jany 11/64

Sunday Evening

I have just returned from the Episcopal Church where we had quite a good sermon on faith and saw a number of pretty girls. Cossitt, Hayes, the Tribune correspondent and myself have been to church three times to-day. This morning at the Presbyterian Church we had a stiff orthodox sermon, much to the disgust of myself and Hayes, who is a good Unitarian. We expect now to leave tomorrow afternoon this will bring us to Sandusky probably the next evening. If we are going up to escort rebel prisoners down to Pt. Lookout I think we may be stationed in the city during our stay.

---

4. Gen. Henry Terry. See "Island History—Civil War Era, Union Guard Garrison," *Depot of Prisoners of War on Johnson's Island, Ohio,* Johnson's Island Preservation Society, 2015, http://johnsonsisland. org/history-pows/civil-war-era/union-guard-garrison/.

5. For discussions of Civil War prisons and the POW experience, see William B. Hesseltine, *Civil War Prisons* (Kent, OH: Kent State Univ. Press, 1962); Lonnie R. Speer, *Portals to Hell: Military Prisons of the Civil War* (Lincoln: Univ. of Nebraska Press, 2005); Evan A. Kutzler, *Living by Inches: The Smells, Sounds, Tastes, and Feeling of Captivity in Civil War Prisons* (Chapel Hill: Univ. of North Carolina Press, 2019); Angela M. Zombek, *Penitentiaries, Punishment, and Military Prisons: Familiar Responses to an Extraordinary Crisis during the American Civil War* (Kent, OH: Kent State Univ. Press, 2018); Michael P. Gray, *Crossing the Deadlines: Civil War Prisons Reconsidered* (Kent, OH: Kent State Univ. Press, 2018).

I put on my "campaigning" clothes when I left Brandy Station and shall hardly be presentable in society until the baggage arrives. You can direct your letters as usual until further orders.

Yours affy

Os

Osgood's correspondence from his time in Ohio appears lost or destroyed, for he wrote on April 19, 1864: "Now that we are away from Sandusky I fear my letters will be rather dull," a statement that suggests that he not only wrote, but his experiences there were rather exciting. One is left to wonder what happened to the letters Osgood wrote home from Sandusky. Many of the regiment's men found comfort in the friendship of local women, and perhaps Osgood, who seemed a private man, did not want that information shared or read by others, perhaps even Nellie, at a later date. After the war, Osgood inserted a brief account of his time at Johnson's Island as an addendum to his otherwise extensive and frequent letters home, an interesting choice for a man who wrote home nearly every day during his time in service.

> We were stationed at Sandusky, O. for three months most of the Brigade were on Johnson's Island (in Sandusky Bay) acting as guard for the Rebel officers who were confined there and to prevent the possibility of a rescue, while the lake was frozen, by any expedition organized in Canada—The rebel prisoners were well fed, clean—comfortably housed and well treated—in great contrast to the condition and treatment of our poor fellows confined in Southern prisons—There not being room on the island for the whole brigade our regiment was left in town—the men were quartered in a block, the office boarded where they chose—We made some very pleasant acquaintances—Mother came and made me a visit—

The following letter was written from Sandusky to Osgood by a woman who appears to have been his landlady:

Sandusky, April 26th 1864

Many thanks, my dear young friend, for the redemption of your promise to me, of your photographic semblance, so perfect a representation of the original is it, that it seems right uncivil in you to sit before me as you do, and not respond to the sentiments my pen is transcribing, for you must know that the impression you have left here is that of an exceedingly courteous and agreeable young gentleman. (An old woman certainly can say this much without being accused of flattery).

The Sanduskians have contracted a life interest in the three months acquaintances, brought so unexpectedly to our doors, in obedience to the orders of Uncle Sam, whose stay with us, has opened new avenues to our thoughts and affections,

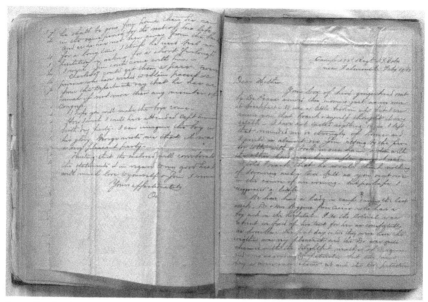

Letter book of Osgood Tracy, with letter signed "Affectionately Yours, Osgood" (From the private collection of Osgood Tracy)

marking each day of your sojourn here with pleasant memories for those quiet hours which we feel are coming apace, and then at your exit from the conscience of your new but sorrowing friends, did not the elements express full sympathy with those sad adieus supplying tears for the multitude? I had quite felicitated myself upon the idea that your Mother would come out here this summer and you would establish a little domestic circle of your own on the Island which would give occasion for those little neighborhood associations which contribute so much toward making up the sum of earthly happiness, now. I'm afraid you will never know of the benevolent design in the way of canned fruit, pickles, &c which some of your would-be neighbors were making upon you.

I regret to hear that your brother "Will" as you call him could not have been permitted to join you in the East, although it is most difficult to select a desirable locality for our loved ones in such perilous times as these. The Militia call has caused such fluttering in our community—It strikes hard on the businessmen. I'm glad the call is in earnest as I want our troops in the field to have unconquerable numbers, and all the support, moral and physical, which can in the least benefit them. I am no croaker, I anticipate nothing but victory for our righteous cause, but I want that to be speedy and lasting.

When you write your Mother tell her I still hope she will take your advice regarding her picture, and shall expect it at your hands so soon as you receive it. I am under many obligations for your letter and would be happy to repeat the acknowledgement could there anything agreeable to you come of it. With prayers for your safety, I wish to be remembered as,

Your Sincere friend, Mrs. S. W. Buth

❀ ❀ ❀

CHAPTER EIGHT

"Capture and Escape"

Battle of the Wilderness, April–June 1864

I am almost tempted to swear, when I think how all my old friends
have deserted me, everyone either married or gone away.
—Osgood Tracy, January 3, 1864

❀ As the men from New York disembarked trains from Sandusky, they shouldered their rifles and marched forward in a campaign that would ultimately take
a year and lead to the Confederacy's destruction.[1] Tracy later explained, "We returned to the army . . . to find them preparing for Grant's Richmond campaign
but our long line of 1,000 men with which we left home less than two years before, had dwindled away. We probably had less than 400 men fit for duty when
we started on that bloody campaign." The road to Richmond was seventy miles
long, blocked by the Army of Northern Virginia. Though Lee's vaunted veterans
had stalled the Army of the Potomac on the banks of the Rapidan River for more
than six months, spring found the Confederates in a dangerous position, and the
rebel commander "faced one of the gravest crises of his military career. Crip-
pling shortages in food, fodder, and men had locked him into a defensive posture
strikingly out of character with his usual aggressiveness."[2] This was compounded
by the fact that fresh troops could no longer fill the gaping holes in the ranks of

---

1. For further reading on the Overland Campaign, see Steven E. Sodergren, *The Army of the Potomac in the Overland and Petersburg Campaigns: Union Soldiers and Trench Warfare, 1865–1865* (Baton Rouge: Louisiana State Univ. Press, 2017); Gordon C. Rhea, *The Battle of the Wilderness: May
5–6, 1864* (Baton Rouge: Louisiana State Univ. Press, 1994); Gary W. Gallagher, ed., *The Wilderness
Campaign* (Chapel Hill: Univ. of North Carolina Press, 1997); Mark Grimsley, *And Keep Moving On:
The Virginia Campaign, May–June 1864* (Lincoln: Univ. of Nebraska Press, 2002).

2. Rhea, *Battle of the Wilderness*, 8–9.

the one proud army, and as Grant took the offensive, Lee received news from the Confederate Bureau of Conscription that "fresh material for the armies can no longer be estimated as an element of future calculation for their increase," meaning that "Lee would have to do his best with the soldiers he already had."[3]

Tracy, recently promoted to liuetenant and adjutant, and his comrades were cast into the fray, engaged with the enemy more often that spring than in any prior time in their service. In explaining his experience at the Battle of the Wilderness in May 1864, he wrote,

> Crossing the Rappahannock, which we had crossed before at Fredercksburg, Chancellorsville, and Mine Run, only to return defeated, we plunged into the Wilderness. This was a thickly wooded country with a few main roads traversing it and cut up by numerous wood roads. As we crossed the river going south we swung around somewhat to the west, facing Lee's army. Our corps occupied the extreme right of the army and the lines of battle stretched across the country probably for six or eight miles. General Grant pushing out the left of his army endeavoring to get around Lee's right, and thus between him and Richmond.

Tracy's service was cut short, though, when he was captured by Confederates during the battle. His experiences as a prisoner of war and his subsequent escape with a fellow officer, reprinted throughout New York, made him a military hero. The published account appears at the end of this chapter, a detailed description of the young officers' escapades behind Confederate lines as they attempted to make it back to the Union side.

Grant did what no other commanding officer of the Army of the Potomac had: he advanced and kept advancing. With more men and supplies, the Federal army had an advantage, and Grant used that fully, pushing his army forward against Lee's stiff defenses, never withdrawing to give his opponent the time to regroup. When the massive Army of the Potomac began to move from its winter camp on the Rapidan at the end of April, the Army of Northern Virginia had no option but to meet the threat, and the two armies clashed on May 5 in the densely forested Wilderness, close to Chancellorsville, where they had collided just a year before.

The 122nd New York was cast into the thick of things, on the far right of the Union flank, where the men "encountered the hardest fighting" of their war, losing 119 men and countless others injured.[4] Osgood was one of the captured. On May 6 he and a number of other men, including his comrade James Gere and brigade commander Gen. Alexander Shaler, were captured when Confederates turned the

---

3. Rhea, *Battle of the Wilderness*, 9–10.

4. "122nd Infantry Regiment," *New York State Military Museum and Veterans Research Center*, Division of Military and Naval Affairs, accessed Oct. 8, 2021, https://museum.dmna.ny.gov/unit-history/infantry-2/122nd-infantry-regiment.

Union right flank. While privates were sent to Libby Prison in Richmond, officers and generals were sent south to Lynchburg, to the Warwick House, where Osgood spent only a brief time in captivity before he and a comrade escaped and, in a harrowing two-hundred-mile trek made it back, unscathed, to Union lines.

Camp 122d Reg't New York Volunteers
near Brandy Station, Va.
April 19th 1864

Dear Mother,

Here we are back into our old camps or rather upon the same ground where our old camp was for scarcely a vestige remains. Individually however I am more fortunate for my tent, fire place and all, remains standing, in just as good condition as when I left, it having been occupied during our absence by one of the men left here. Yesterday afternoon when we arrived it really seemed a little like home.

Connie will act as Brigade quartermaster for the present (Cap't Ford having been left at Sandusky), and will remain at Gen'l Shalers Headquarters. Poole is acting as regimental quartermaster and will tent with me. Last night we had a tent full, as the line officers had not got their tents up, we took them in with us.

We are very fortunate in having pleasant weather in which to pitch camp again. It is a little cool however, just enough so to make my fireplace very attractive. Indeed I am getting to be a very popular fellow for the time being.

The Corps was reviewed by General Grant yesterday but we got here too late to participate. There are rumors of a speedy move but nothing definite in regard to the time. Lt. Col. Reed formerly of Gen'l Terry's staff who was ordered on here from Sandusky about a month ago, called on us this morning and we had a very pleasant chat over Sandusky and its people. Indeed he is so well pleased with it that he intends to go into business there, at the expiration of his term of service, about seven weeks now.

I am very anxious to hear from Will. Dillingham told me that he had heard that Slocum was to command Vicksburg. I fear it will be a little while before our letters get around straight again. I enclose a couple of photographs to be deposited in my chest. I read Grant's report of the battles of Chickamauga & c published in the Tribune. Have you seen it? It is very plainly written without any glorification of himself. He gives a great deal of credit to "Baldy" Smith[5] as he is called.

It seems rather queer to come down to camp life again but I imagine it will be a good thing for me as my dissipation in Sandusky rather wore on me, but this summer I trust that I shall get a little more fleshy and perhaps again that "bloated" appearance which some of my friends noticed when home a year ago.

---

5. William "Baldy" Smith (1824–1903) was a Union general who served in the Sixth, Ninth, and Eighteenth Corps.

Kate Smith (Andy's wife) heard from home a confirmation of the report you wrote me that Alf. Colvin was engaged to Julia Hovey and furthermore that they were to have been married immediately after "Lent." I cannot believe it, for there is no one in Syracuse but what knows what a character Alf was. We are expecting Wooster and Walpole back every day. It is rumored that Wooster is to go on Shalers staff as Brigade Inspector. The Colonel is going to send forward a request I believe that Capt's Smith and Lester be returned to their regiments but even if it is granted and Smithy returned he has so many friends in the corps and at Gen'l Sedgwick's Headquarters that he will soon have another appointment.

I suppose you are by this time settled at Lucy's. I know it will be pleasant for you and it is much better I think than for you to be alone so much. Tell the children to write to me, the next time you write.

Now that we are away from Sandusky I fear my letters will be rather dull, for this camp life will be quite a change, but you may rest assured that I shall write often for the next best thing for me to receive a letter from home, is to write one. It always seems to me when writing to you as though I was sitting down and talking with you.

I enclose $5 which I wish you would ask Dudley to invest in a box of cigars for Jim and send them to him by express—I feel as though I wished to make a peace offering for not visiting him when home.

Don't imagine that I have commenced using "mourning" paper merely because we were compelled to leave Sandusky but a bottle of ink broke in our stationery box on the way down and just tinted the edge of the paper. Well I must write to Jim so good bye

Your boy
Os

Camp 122d Reg't N. Y. Vols.
April 30, 1864

Dear Mother,

As I wrote you yesterday I have hardly materials for an interesting letter tonight but I thought I would not let your birthday pass without writing you. Tonight it is storming a little and if it continues will probably delay the move but if it amounts to nothing I think we shall start sometime next week. A column of infantry has been moving towards the "front" past Brandy Station to-day. It is said to be Burnsides Corps. Several of our men left on duty in Sandusky arrived last evening. They say that the 23d Reg't got over into town after we left and created a great deal of disturbance.

I believe I spoke to you in a former letter of some verses to the tune of the "Virginia Lowlands" written by Col. Hamblin on the way back from Sandusky. The following will serve as a sample—

"Those who cherish beauty
Will love thy maids divine
Will drink thy native wine
The "Veterans" round their fire by night
Fond tales of thee will tell
Oh scene of such short lives delight
Sandusky, fare thee well
For the old Virginia lowlands & c"

The tune is a very pretty one, but you probably would have been amused if you had been in my tent to-day and heard a party of which I was one of the principal performers trying to sing it.

I trust that we may be able to celebrate your next birthday—all reunited once more. Trusting that your life may be spared still longer and that you may yet be able to indulge and pet "grandchildren," I remain with much love—

Your affectionate boy
Os

Sunday Evening

Platt, Wooster, Connie and myself went over to the 121st N.Y. this afternoon and took tea with Dr. Slocum—John Douw[6] was the senior Captain present—the field officers being absent, and received the dress parade which was very fine. The manual of arms was executed better than I have ever seen it. We did not get back until after six o'clock so this letter missed the afternoon mail. On my return I found a letter from Mrs. Buth which I enclose[7]—I trust that you will have your photograph taken now and send it to her for she certainly deserves it. I shall write again later at some better time. Did you notice Col. D——'s [Dwight's] letter in the Syracuse Journal? I thought it was very good—Dr. Slocum seemed to think that we should move to-morrow or next day certainly. Well you will probably hear of it as soon as it happens. If there should be a battle try and not feel too anxious and rest assured that I will write at the first opportunity.

Good Night
Yours Os

The next correspondence in Osgood's letter collection is to his mother, from Colonel Dwight, announcing her son's capture.

---

6. John Douw was twenty-five when he enlisted, on July 18, 1862, at Mohawk, New York, to serve three years. He was commissioned first lieutenant on September 10, 1862, and was promoted to captain of Company K on April 24, 1863. He was wounded at Cedar Creek, Virginia, on October 19, 1864, and died of his wounds on November 11.

7. This is the final letter in Chapter 7.

Bivouac 122d in the field
May 7th 1864
Mrs. James G. Tracy
Syracuse, N.Y.

Dear Madam

I am obliged to discharge the painful duty of informing you that your son Osgood is without doubt prisoner of war, taken at the same time as Gen. Alex. Shaler yesterday. He distinguished himself throughout the fray and gallantry—and was taken after . . . to Aide-de-Camp. I do not think there is any doubt he is taken, as he was last seen close to a line of the enemy who held a road where many of our men including the General tried to retreat and were taken. Our loss was heavy as you are sure to see in the papers. I commiserate you on this misfortune and hope he may soon be restored to you and us.

Very Truly Yours
H. W. Dwight
Liet. Col. Comdg

Osgood's mother wrote the next letter to him, with no address or salutation. Osgood noted at the top, after the war: "When this letter was written I had been prisoner two days having been taken prisoner May 6—though of course mother was not aware of it."

My dear darling boy you can well imagine the overwhelming anxiety which is torturing me today, and although I received your kind letter last evening, noticing my birthday and exhorting me to "try not to feel anxious" I have not succeeded but feel as if I can hardly bear the state of suspense to which I am doomed, Sunday you know precludes our getting the Telegraph dispatches. The news we have thus far received is meager but fills me with alarm as we learn there has been severe fighting and that 4,000 on our side have been wounded including several officers of high command Cap't Cossitt called last evening on his way to Washington he thought the 6th Corps had not been seriously engaged but I saw they had crossed immediately after the 5th much to my surprise I saw Frank Lester at church he will take this letter and has faithfully promised to take care of you if you have been wounded and give me the earliest information. Major Jenney and Marie were at church I was not aware they had arrived, the Major desired to be particularly remembered to you.

I have not received a line from Willie since he arrived at Vicksburg but yesterday morning saw in the papers a telegram from Cairo that an attack on Vicksburg was momentarily expected. This is a drop in my cup I had not anticipated. I felt as if Willie was entirely removed from any danger from fighting my only anxiety for him as the unhealthiness of the climate.

The gentlemen here treat the rumor of Vicksburgh being attacked as absurd, I hope it may be so but I must confess it does not look improbable to me that the Rebels knowing there is not a large force there may attack it on their land side. Dudley and Lucy left last Thursday for New York they both need the change especially Dudley whose labors are very arduous. I shall be glad to have them return however we miss them so much.

I see by the papers that Gen. Grant has forbidden any communications between the army and Washington. I presume it has reference only to private letters. Of course he is in correspondence with the government there. I cannot account for the delaying of your last letter reaching me it was dated the 30th and I did not receive it till last evening. What a pleasant letter Miss Butler wrote you and if she had daughters to dispose of I should think the good lady flattered. I take that last sentence back nothing can be said too good of my darling.

And now my dear boy it is a consolation to your mother to know that whatever trials you are called to bear you will look up with faith and confidence to your Heavenly Father to sustain you and that you may be kept safe in the midst of danger prays your loving mother.

While a prisoner at Gordonsville, Virginia, Osgood wrote the following letter to his mother, but she did not receive it until after his escape and return. On the reverse side of the envelope was written: "Adjutant Tracy not yet heard from—reason to believe that he is alive a prisoner."

Gordonsville, Va.
May 9, 1864

Dear Mother,

Was taken prisoner on the 6th. I am safe and well. Cap't Gere of our reg't is here also Gen'l Shaler (I am in good company). Write to Mrs. Miller at Oswego that her husband Col. F. C. Miller 147th N.Y.V. is a prisoner wounded in the side—not dangerously—Don't worry about me I shall get along well enough.

Love to all
Yours
Os

Have been treated well—and *had enough to eat* so far. Gen'l S—— talks of putting me on his staff—I have plenty of money.

With Osgood's whereabouts unknown, worry abounded on the homefront. Letters were written on his behalf in attempts to locate him. The next, undated and with a message for Mrs. Tracy, was written by Colonel Titus's daughter, Mary Titus, in response to Dudley Post Phelps.

Mr. Phelps, Sir.

The following is the substance of a brief note I've received from Father last evening relative to the sad fate of our friend Lieut Tracy. "I wish you to go and see Mrs. Tracy, try and comfort her, I sincerely hope he is only a prisoner; but she must be prepared for the worst. Lieut. Tracy was one of the best officers of my Regiment. I hope he may be spared to comfort that Mother he loved so well. If alive he is a prisoner and probably wounded, still he may not be, it was so dark it was impossible to tell more. Remember me kindly to Mrs. Tracy, tell her I hope for the best. I will give her the first intelligence possible.

Respectfully
Mary E. Titus

Mrs. Tracy wrote her own letters of inquiry and received the following in return.

Washington
May 12th

My dear Mrs. Tracy,

In Mrs. Davis absence I immediately attempted to find some explicit answer to your telegram. I dispatched a reply to that effect and within a few moments Cap't Frank Lester called and gave the information contained in my second telegram. In the present extreme uncertainty it seemed almost impossible to learn the truth of any thing regarding these terrible battles. The city is filled with wildest rumors. Messengers are hourly arriving from the front, telegraphic dispatches flying through the air, and wounded men are brought in by the thousands to the merciful care of that blessed Sanitary Commission. Only official intelligence, of course, can be relied upon. I fear I can add nothing to the tidings in regard to your son conveyed in my telegram that three wounded officers from the same regiment are confident he was taken prisoner, but have no reason to suppose he was wounded. Cap't Lester is going on tonight to the Sixth Corps with his regiment. Of course he will do all he can to ascertain more definitely, after he reached the front. I am told that the Sanitary Commission can learn about the missing more quickly than any one else can and have set to them the necessary directions for enquiry. I sympathize with your anxiety most deeply my dear Mrs. Tracy, and will make every effort to send you tidings of your loved one.

Ever truly yours
S. M. Davis

Washington May 16, 64

My Dear Mrs. Tracy

I reached here last night and devoted what time I could to day to inquire news about Osgood. I greatly hope that he will be found unwounded and a prisoner, or with the 500 re-captured by Sheridan. He was not wounded up to the time of the night attack on Friday and he was with Shaler and his men who in the darkness went into the movement on the enemy's left most of whom have not been heard from since as being captured in a body. Gen. Shaler was taken with them and was two days since at Gen'l Lee's Headquarters. Horace Walpole and Col. Dwight of the same Reg't started out with the same body of men but when they found themselves surrounded managed to secret themselves in the woods and remained there the rest (of the) night when they got back to our lines. I hope for the best about Osgood and I shall not fail to make every possible inquiry about him and advise you. He is a gallant boy and I loved him for his self and his parents sake.

Very Sincerely Yours
Theo. T. Davis

Rumor says to night that Lee is utterly routed and his army flying panic stricken before our brave and enduring soldiers. The world has never seen such battles before. I pray our country may never witness such again.

Battlefield of Spotsylvania
Court House Va 17th May

My Dear Mrs Tracy:

I am informed that a Col Dwight has already written you concerning the disappearance of Osgood. At the time he wrote you I was on picket and was not aware that a mail was going out. He may have written you all the particulars but I *may* be able to add some as I think I was the last person in our Regt who saw him.

On the day he was last seen we were on the extreme right of our line of battle in occupation of rifle pits, our right flank was turned by the enemy thus compelling us to evacuate our works and the enemy appearing a little to our rear at the same time created some confusion, the men becoming panic stricken, going towards the center of our line about 500 yards from our original position. I found Genl Shaler Genl Seymour and other officers making great efforts to stop the men in their flight and force them in a line of battle running perpendicular to our line of earth works in order to stay the progress of the enemy who were all the time steadily advancing and pouring into us a heavy fire of musketry and also using some light artillery. While doing what I could to assist in rallying the men I met Osgood similarly employed—his features glowing with patriotic excitement—we instinctively grasped each other by the hand and bidding each other God-speed, parted about five minutes after that I observed the enemy (whose line of battle over lapped ours) swinging around our right, to our rear, and communicating that fact to those in the vicinity we fell back, then near the centre of our line near Genl Shaler (where I have no doubt Osgood was) were captured by the enemy, 2 men of my co saw Genl Shaler captured and were themselves taken prisoners escaped. They saw nothing of Osgood but say that the fire in front closed for a short time prior to Genl Shalers capture as the enemy could not fire in that direction without hitting their own men whom they knew were getting to our rear. Thus you see that if O was injured it would have been in an interval of 5 minutes which, though possible, is not probable.

If, as I have no doubt he is a prisoner, I have cause to congratulate you than to sympathize with you, as we have since were, and for the next few weeks are likely to be, subjected to so much hardship and danger that a slight wound or being taken prisoner is regarded as a fortunate incident which may well excite envy. If on the contrary he has met with a more serious disaster my own feelings are such as to convince you that it would be more than useless for me to attempt to console you. I shall have lost my most valued friend, the cause of liberty and justice one of its most gallant brave and devoted defenders, and you more than all a talented and affectionate son.

Capt Cossitt did not arrive until after Osgood disappearance and as we are both destitute of postage stamps the . . . your letter enclosed some to Osgood we took the liberty of opening it and taking them out and destroying the letter which we hope you will, under the circumstances, pardon. We enclose $1.00 of the stamps.

Hoping that my letter may make you feel as confident of Osgoods safety as I myself do I remain

Very Respectfully Yours
F. M. Wooster

In an effort to determine Osgood's fate, Mrs. Tracy's nephew George Bridges[8] wrote this next letter to General Shaler's wife:

New York, May 28/64
Mrs. Gen'l Shaler

Madam,

A serious misfortune is my excuse for addressing you, to whom I am a perfect stranger. My Aunt has a son as Adjutant in the 122d Reg't N.Y. Volunteers in Gen'l Shalers brigade who has not been heard from since the battle although seen just before the capture was made. My Aunt desires me to ask if you are in correspondence with the General and if so if you would be so kind as to inquire if Osgood V. Tracy, Adjutant of 122d Reg't of N.Y. Volunteers, 1st Division, 6th Corps is a prisoner in Richmond or if he can give any information in regard to him. I am aware it is a forlorn hope and may seem almost useless among the hundreds that

---

8. George Osgood Bridges (?–1868), the son of Sarah Osgood Tracy's half sister Rebecca Osgood, died in New York City in 1868. His younger brother, Charles Moody Bridges, died in 1864 while in military service in Mississippi, of acute dysentery. Another brother, Isaac Osgood, died in 1862, in Andover, Massachusetts.

were taken, to ask the General if he can account for *one,* but the deep anxiety of a widowed mother must be my apology. If you can give any information that may lead to ascertain the fate of my cousin you will confer a great obligation on an afflicted mother and a host of sympathizing friends.

Yours Respectfully, Geo. O. Bridges, 86 Market St. New York

On the following letter, which Will wrote to Osgood, there is a printed location, "Headquarters 12th Army Corps," and Osgood penciled a postwar note: "This letter was sent through the lines to me at Vicksburg to Gen'l Shaler's camp. He received it after I had escaped and forwarded it to me."

District of Vicksburg
Vicksburg, June 5th, 1864

Dear Os,

We are all well being only anxious to hear from you. I received a letter from mother dated the 22nd. She was not certain whether you were a prisoner or not but had strong hopes you were alive. Please write and let me know if this letter is opened. I will seal it with wax. If not opened I will be able to send you money in this way. It takes about 11 days for a letter to reach home from this place. Everything is progressing favorably on our side of Mason and Dixon line. T. B. Fitch[9] and Duell[10] have gone as delegates to the Baltimore convention. They are for Lincoln who will of course be nominated for the presidency.

The 149th have not lost much so far. Gen'l Knipe[11] was severely wounded in the fight at Resaca and all his staff killed or wounded. The loss in the 122d is reported as 108 wounded, 3 killed and 42 missing some of whom I suppose are with you. Everything is quiet along the Mississippi barring a boat being fired into occasionally by guerillas. Very little damage is done but citizens aboard are generally pretty badly scared.

9. The 1864 Baltimore Convention in 1864 renominated President Lincoln for the presidency. According to the August 27, 1879, *Syracuse Daily Journal,* during the Civil War, Thomas Brockway Fitch, Esq. (1810–1879) had devoted time and influence to the Union army. Fitch was a prominent Syracuse businessman. Among many accomplishments, he was one of the founders and trustee of the Syracuse Savings Bank, where Osgood Tracy would later work.

10. This was likely Abner Duell (1799–1884), the postmaster of Manlius, New York, and owner of a store there.

11. Gen. Joseph Farmer Knipe had enlisted as a private in the US Army in 1842 and fought in the war with Mexico before returning to civilian life in 1848. When the Civil War broke out, he was commissioned colonel of the Forty-Sixth Pennsylvania, was wounded at the Battle of Cedar Mountain, and fought with the Twelfth Corps as Sherman's army advanced toward Atlanta and in command of the First Division, Twentieth Corps. There is no record of his wounding at Resaca. See Ezra J. Warner, *Generals in Blue: Lives of Union Commanders* (Baton Rouge: Louisiana State Univ. Press, 2006), 272–73.

Mary Longs' husbands name is Armistead L. Long.[12] He is a Brig. Gen'l and Chf of Artillery on Gen Lee's staff. I hope you will not get any thinner on prison fare as you have so little flesh that you would certainly miss every least particle. I do not know whether you are in Richmond or not. I suppose of course you are with Gen'l Shaler and Gen. Seymour and the last accounts represent them as being at Charlottesville. Gen. Seymour is making a speech. Don't get downhearted. There are so many prisoners now that they will exchange them before long. I think. If there is anything you want let me know and I will do my best to send it to you. We have an officer with us now who spent 8 months in the interior of the Confederacy. He didn't like the situation.

Yours truly
Wm. G. Tracy

While his family and friends frantically awaited news, Osgood sat in a Confederate prison, planning his next moves. His experiences during that time, later published in the *Syracuse Herald,* appear below.

CAPTURED

As we advanced through the thick woods on the morning of the 6th of May 1864, we had quite a sharp skirmish, but finally gained a little crest, where we established our line, throwing up a breastwork of logs. The rebels were in line a short distance in our front, also behind breastworks. Our pickets, who were posted in our front, reported during the day that the rebels appeared to be moving troops to our right, and word was sent to General Shaler, who commanded our brigade, but he was assured that there was a cavalry force on our flank that connected with the Ninth corps, which was in the rear in reserve; but he felt very anxious, and has since told me that he sent word repeatedly to the corps' headquarters that we were "out in the air," and our flank much exposed, and to correct it in a measure he put a strong picket-line on our flank.

With the light of later information I have thought that General Grant, endeavoring to get around their right with his left, did not much care how far they went to his right, as that was where he wanted them. But just before dusk, as I and several of my messmates were eating our supper, a sharp firing began on the picket-line which had been established on our flank. The picket-line fell back, followed by a charging, yelling line of rebels. A flank attack is always demoralizing, and the men fell back from the breastworks in front, forming a line at

---

12. Armistead L. Long (1825–1891) was aide-de-camp for Gen. Edwin Vose Sumner but later became a Confederate brigadier general and close friend of General Lee. Long married Sumner's daughter, Mary Heron Sumner. Their son born in 1864 was named Edwin Vose.

right angles to their former position, to meet the new attack. At the same time the rebel line in our old front commenced to advance, firing, and all was confusion. We were driven back to one of the narrow roads I spoke of, where I found General Shaler, our brigade commander, and Generals Sedgwick, and Wright, our corps and division commanders, busily engaged in rallying a line of men.

A line was soon formed, consisting of officers and men of various regiments, the separate regimental organizations having been largely broken up in the confusion. We advanced some 200 or 300 yards into the roads again towards our old right flank, which had now become our front, driving back their rebel line; but they soon brought up fresh troops, and the balls began to come from three directions—our old right flank, which had now become our front, our old front, the latter probably from some of our own troops, and our old left flank, now became our rear who did not know we were there. At this moment I met for an instant, as we passed engaged in our respective duties, my best friend, Lieut. Frank Wooster. We instinctively grasped each others hand, and it proved to be our last farewell, for in a few moments I was a prisoner, and the very day I reached our lines poor Wooster was killed at Cold Harbor. With a premonition of coming events he wrote to my mother: immediately after my capture, "If your son is alive and a prisoner I feel I can congratulate you rather than console with you, as we have since been, and for the next few weeks are likely to be subject to so much hardship, or danger, that a slight wound being rather prisoner is regarded as a fortunate incident which may well excite envy." You must remember he was trying to relieve a mother's apprehension, for the regiment had no braver soldier than he.

The line under fire from so many directions rapidly broke up, and finding none of my regiment in my vicinity I started through the woods, when I met Capt. James M. Gere of the One Hundred and Twenty-second. We concluded our best move would be to go to our old rear, and thus work around in hopes of finding more of our regiment.

It was rapidly growing dark and we had gone but a short distance when we were surrounded by about twenty rebels and ordered to "throw down our arms," which consisted of our swords. They did not search us or treat us unkindly, and one of them informed me they had just captured a Brigadier General, and from their description I knew it must be our commander, General Shaler, and I asked them to take us where he was. I found there also General Seymour, the commander of another brigade in our corps, and a number of officers and soldiers of our brigade, and eight or ten members of our regiment—all companions in misfortune, but much more fortunate than many a poor fellow who was left wounded on the field.

Among those of our regiment who were taken prisoners that night and who still live here are Comrades Ostrander, Hubbs, Manzer and Austin. The three former were wounded and both Ostrander and Hubbs had amputations of the leg and foot performed by rebel surgeons. Repeated efforts were made by their brigade commanders to change front and check over advances, but the approaching darkness and the attack from this unexpected quarter made great confusion and prevented organized resistance. The enemy's killed, according to the account kept by the pioneer officer, amounted to nearly 400—among them one brigade commander. Several hundred prisoners were captured, among them two brigade commanders, General Shaler and General Seymour. Besides them many hundreds were passed to the rear and made their escape in the darkness. I must be permitted to add that had the movement been made at an earlier hour and properly supported, each brigade being brought into action as its front was cleared, it would have resulted in a decided disaster to the whole right wing of Grant's army.

COLONEL MILLER WOUNDED

We were taken back a short distance and a line of guards placed about us, and kept until morning. In the morning the word was sent that a wounded officer would like to see some of us to take a message for him, and I went and found Colonel Miller of Oswego quite seriously wounded, and he begged me to avail myself of the first opportunity to convey news to his wife, and my telegram, when I reached our lines, conveyed the joyful intelligence to one who had already put on the widow's garb, so certain had been the news of his death. Colonel Miller lived to return home.

General Shaler had taken the road where the line I spoke of was rallied. Our line having gone forward, he saw some soldiers further down the road, and supposing them to be our men, he rode rapidly down to order them up. Here the officers and men were separated—the men were taken to a camp in the outskirts of the town, and eventually to Andersonville, and you can never realize the horrors of that place until you hear a survivor tell some of his experience. As my friend Oscar Austin says, "You may know what it is to be hungry for a day or two, but you cannot imagine until you have tried it, what it is to be hungry for three or four months at a time." While the rebel authorities were, perhaps, at times unable to supply sufficient quantities of food for their own soldiers, yet a great deal of suffering at Andersonville was, I understand, from lack of room and water, and all of which might have been supplied. At one time 15,000 men were compelled to live on about eight acres of ground.

At Lynchburg the officers were quartered in the second story of a block on the principal street. There was one stairway leading from the street to a square hallway in the center of the building; from this hallway a door led to some rooms in the rear, where most of us were quartered. The room I was in was a small one, and when we were disposed for the night we covered the floor—

no mattresses being furnished. Leading from this same hall to the front of the building were two rooms—one occupied by the rebel provost marshal, who had charge of the prisoners, and the other by General Shaler, General Seymour and some of the officers of higher rank who had given their promise not to attempt to escape. We were allowed, one or two at a time, to cross the hall to the General's room—there being a guard stationed at the head of the stairs leading to the street, which was near the door to our room.

PLANNING THE ESCAPE

We had in the back yard to which we were allowed access, a sort of kitchen where our daily rations were served, provided only with a negro cook. Feeling sure of his fidelity I went to the cook; I told him I would give him $10 of Confederate money if he would bring me a rebel jacket the next night, which he did, bringing me a coat which was apparently equal in value to the Confederate money I gave him, but which was worth its weight in gold to me.

We were now about ready to start, but waited a day or two to learn, if possible, more about the town. Lynchburg is situated on the south side of the James river, being connected with the northern shore by a long, covered bridge, which we could see from our window. We learned from cautious inquiries that there were no guards up on the bridge. Meanwhile our daily rations consisted of a loaf of rye bread about four six inch cube, and a small piece of fat boiled bacon. I must confess I was not hungry enough to eat the bacon. We were allowed to buy vegetables, and one day our room all exchanged their rations, and we bought additions and had a "stew" which was quite palatable.

THE START

But we were getting impatient, and the 14th of May (Saturday night) we decided to start. I was anxious to get a more disreputable hat than the soldier's hat I had, and noticing one of the officer's, Major H. H. Lyman of Oswego, whom some rebel had convinced him to exchange hats with him, I told him I was going to attempt an escape that night, and told him to exchange hats with me. He kindly consented.

Birdseye had succeeded in getting a war map of Virginia, and at dusk that evening, getting permission to go to the General's room for a moment, we slipped off our coats, put on our rebel jackets and cloth hats and coming on as though from upstairs, boldly walked past the guard (whom Captain Gere, by previous arrangement, was busily engaging in conversation) rapidly down the stairs into the street. We had gone but a few steps when we met the sergeant of the guard, whom we saw daily in the prison, but realizing that his face was more familiar to us than ours would be to him, we walked coolly past him. We walked to the bridge and found that we had been correctly informed, that there was no guard, and soon we were on the north side of the river, but a long distance from our lines. Our idea had been, in starting, that we might get through some passes of the Blue Ridge Mountains and find loyal forces, who at the time we were captured were up the Shenandoah valley, but we found as we got farther up, they had been driven back, and we finally had to go to Harpers Ferry (about 200 miles) before we struck our sentinels—but I am anticipating.

After fairly getting over the river and away from the bridge, we secreted ourselves until late at night, when we pushed on north by the main road until daylight on Sunday morning. We then secreted ourselves in a swamp until about dark, when we returned to the negro quarters on William Rucker's plantation in search of food. Five dollars in Confederate script secured a good meal of fried bacon and hoe cake.

Leaving the Rucker plantation, which is twelve miles north of Lynchburg, we walked all night on the road and you can judge of our disgust on Monday morning to learn that we were still only twelve miles from Lynchburg. The night was dark and cloudy so we could not see the stars, and we had made a detour to the east instead of pushing on north. After this first night's experience in traveling we decided to lay off and save our strength whenever the north star was hidden, for we were not certain of our course. Having determined to take the traveled road and pass ourselves off as rebel soldiers and claim to be going back to the army, the first thing necessary to do was to decide to what regiment we would belong, so we concluded to enlist in the Second North Carolina cavalry, though I doubt if our names will be found on the muster roll of that regiment. We went to detached houses as much as possible, and had no special adventures for the first day or two. One day we took supper at a doctor's who refused to take any money from us, as he never took money from soldiers, and to whom his pretty daughters expressed a wish, while we were at supper with them, that all the Yankees were dead—a wish in which we were heartily obliged to join, in spite of our secret amusement at the thought of what would have been their feeling if they had known they were breaking bread with two Yankee officers.

HELP OF NEGROES

We had been out only a few days when Birdseye's shoes began to give out, and with the long tramp before us we were in despair; but that night, just at dark, we met in the road a negro with a string of shoes hanging down his back, and we found he was a plantation cobbler. He begged us to take him with us, but we did not wish to add to the dangers of our situation by having a runaway slave with us, who would be sure to be followed. We told this cobbler our trouble, and he took us to his cabin, and as he was short of leather I sacrificed the tops of a pair of riding boots I had on, converting them into laced shoes and using the tops for the repair of Birdseye's.

After we had been out for five or six days we struck the railroad running from Stanton to Charlottesville, near a place called Meachum's station. At this point was a detached house, occupied by the overseer of the plantation where we went to inquire for breakfast. They kindly gave us some, and inquiring if there were any soldiers about, the woman informed us that there was a squad of eight or ten encamped upon the plantation pasturing horses. When the rebel cavalry horses got run down they would send eight or ten men with 100 horses to some plantation to recruit. Before we had finished breakfast we saw one of them coming across the fields towards the house, and when we had finished breakfast we found him on the piazza. He questioned us pretty closely—asked us to what brigade our regiment belonged, and when we told him Rosser's, replied he guessed not—he belonged to Rosser's brigade, and there was no Second North Carolina in it. We gave an evasive reply, and Birdseye asked him if he had not been in any of the recent fighting. He said he had been in the provost guard, and had charge of the prisoners in the first day's cavalry fight.

A CLOSE CALL

I noticed Birdseye seemed anxious to cut short our conversation with the "Johnny," and get away from the house, which we soon did, remarking that we must hurry to Meachum's Station and get the train. As soon as we were out of sight of the house we made for the wood and secreted ourselves all day. Having got fairly away from the house and Rebel soldiers Birdseye told me that this man was one of the sixteen rebels that had marched him from Todd's tavern to Orange Court House the day of his capture, and that he first recognized the man from a badge of three laurel leaves he wore on his hat, the same being the badge of Rosser's Laurel brigade. After this close shave we decided to travel as little as possible day times on the road, but push on north at night. As morning came we would select some house at which to apply for food—approach it from the north and leave it going south, as we always claimed to be going back to the army. One morning Birdseye was entrusted by a girl where we breakfasted with a letter to her lover in the army, which we were to mail when we reached Washington Court House. Birdseye afterwards sent it through the lines, and I trust it finally reached its destination.

For three nights in succession we had rain, and it was so dark we had great difficulty in finding the road, and I remember that, wet, tired and hungry, we crawled into a barn overnight and buried ourselves in the hay, and it seemed to me I was just getting warm and comfortable when daylight came, and we had to get out of our snug quarters and hide ourselves in the woods. . . . turning a bend in the road, we met three rebel cavalrymen. Fortunately, according to the plan we had opted to travel south, we were able, consistently, to tell them we had been North a ways, and were now on our way back to the army. They asked us for news, so Birdseye told them that we had heard there was a squad of Yankee cavalry up in Loudoun County. After no further questions they left us, much to our delight, but our fears turned when, after going a short distance, they turned their horses and, tracing their steps, soon overtook us, we asked them what they were going to look for, and one of them said his horse had lost a shoe and he wanted to go back to a blacksmith shop. We walked slowly, and were glad to see them disappear around the corner, when we disappeared into the woods as quickly as possible.

Soon after this, and when we were within a day or two march of our destination, we had probably our narrowest escape. At night, just as we were getting out for our usual nightly run, we found a house some distance up the road, and I waited at the woods while Birdseye went up prospecting. After waiting some time and hearing nothing from him, I concluded he had found a supper, and decided that I would join him. I was sauntering leisurely up the lane when Birdseye came down on a run exclaiming, "Come on." It is unnecessary perhaps, to add that "I came." We ran down the road some distance hopping over the fence, and secreted ourselves in a wheat field before I had an opportunity to ask an explanation. It seems when Birdseye got to the house he found two men there—an old man and a young one, Birdseye told them he had a squad of six men (he thought he would outnumber them, anyway) down at the gate, and he wished to get some hoe-cakes baked for them.

The old man suggested that he should go and get his squad and bring them up to supper, but he made an excuse that they were tired and anxious to get on, and he would like a few hoe-cakes cooked and get started as soon as possible. While the hoe-cakes were baking, and Birdseye said he never saw hoe-cakes bake so slowly, the men asked him a great many questions, and he finally turned to the young man and said, "Why are you not in the army?" and he replied, "I am in the army; I belong to Mosby's company." While the reluctant hoe-cakes were still baking the young man went out, and Birdseye feared he would find me at the gate and discover that his squad of six men had melted into one, who might tell a very different story, and then they would make short work of us. But if the "Johnny's" suspicions were aroused he probably went off to get help before attempting to capture the six—thus we escaped.

TAKEN FOR YANKEES ONLY ONCE

We were taken for Yankees but once on the whole trip, and that was by a woman near Snickerville, the morning before we reached Harpers Ferry. Retracing our steps from the north a short distance, we had stopped at a house for food just after daylight. A white woman came to the door, and after Birdseye inquired the road to Upperville and Snicker's Gap, we asked for something to eat. While the woman was preparing breakfast Birdseye asked if there were any of our soldiers about. The woman replied, "Yes, the Fifteenth New York cavalry come down from Harpers Ferry every few days on a patrol. Ain't you a Yank? You talk like one." All Birdseye could say was that he had scouted so much in the Yankee's lines and practiced their way of talking until it became natural for him to talk like them. Birdseye at once began to fire at the woman Virginia phrases, such as, "I reckon," 'right smart," "dog-gone," "you all," "we uns," "whar do you live at," "over you," etc., and the woman soon allowed he was a Southerner, sure.

But we were nearing the end of our journey, and on the night of the 31st of May—our eighteenth night out—we started on our home stretch, as from the map and Birdseye's knowledge of Loudoun county, we should strike our pickets before morning. We summoned up all the energy we had left, and marched very rapidly for about fourteen miles. Looking at the map and Birdseye's knowledge of Loudoun County, we thought that we should strike pickets before morning. We summoned up all the energy we had left, and after marching very rapidly for about fourteen miles, in the early dawn we were greeted with the welcome "halt," and knew we were safe at last.

Not having had much experience in coming upon a picket front at night, and perhaps with the thought in my mind that they were our own men, instead of dropping down in the road where I stood, for I was very tired, I moved forward a few feet to a large stone after I was halted and we afterwards learned from the sentinel that hearing someone moving he came very near firing at Birdseye, whom he could see, as there had been trouble with guerrillas creeping up and shooting at the sentry, which would have been a sad ending to our journey. We encountered our picket lines on the road leading from Loudoun Heights down to Harpers Ferry, about one mile from the suspension bridge that crosses the Shenandoah river into Harpers Ferry. We had been seventeen days and eighteen nights on the tramp and had walked the entire distance from Lynchburg, Va.; passing through the counties of Amherst, Nelson, Albemarie, Greene, Madison, Culpepper, Rappahannock, Fauquier and Loudoun.

GERMAN PICKETS

The men on picket were of a German regiment, and we experienced some difficulty in making them understand and believe we were a couple of Federal officers escaped from a rebel prison, as they were inclined to think we were either guerrillas or deserters from the rebel army. After parleying awhile with the sergeant of the outpost, we were sent back to the main reserve, and there had to wait until the picket was relieved—about 7 o'clock. They gave us a cup of coffee and some hard-tack. While waiting at the reserve we endeavored to learn something of the movements of our army since our capture. Their knowledge was meager, but I managed to understand, with deep sorrow, of the death at Spotsylvania a few days after my capture of General John Sedgwick, the beloved commander of the Sixth Army Corps.

To guard against a rebel dash into town it was the custom to remove a part of the plank on the bridge over the Shenandoah and carry it to the Harpers Ferry side. When these planks had been laid, and about 7 o'clock, the picket-relief made its appearance, and we were taken into Harper's Ferry to the headquarters of the officer in command. As he was not yet up we persuaded the guard to take us to the telegraph office, where I sent a dispatch announcing my safety, and which was the first news my mother had heard from me since I was reported as missing—on the 6th of May. From there we went to breakfast, which we invited the guard to take with us, and I can assure you that after a diet of hoe-cakes for three weeks, we did full justice.

Upon reporting to General Max Webber, commanding the post, we easily convinced him we were what we represented ourselves to be, and, equipping ourselves in the army blue once more, we were sent to Washington, where we received a leave of absence for twenty days. At the expiration of my leave I rejoined my regiment in front of Petersburg, to find it sadly depleted in numbers, to miss my friend Wooster's cordial greeting, and to find that the same day Wooster was killed Poole had lost his arm.[13]

Sam Sumner rejoiced in his cousin Osgood's safe return.

U.S. Mustering Office
Waltoon, Ill.
June 12th 1864

My dear Cousin

Allow me to add my congratulations with the rest on your successful escape from Dixie. I know of no better way Os of expressing my self than by saying that few if any of your many friends thought of you often during the three weeks of uncertainty. Often, very often, during that time I picked up my album and turning to your picture I would sit and think over the very pleasant times we have had together and wonder whether you are really gone. Nan wrote me a note enclosing a newspaper account. She spoke of having been up to see you and gave me something

---

13. For further reading and detail, from Birdseye's perspective, see "Escape of Two Onondaga Union Prisoners From Lynchburg, Virginia," *Syracuse Herald,* Mar. 29, 1914 (clipping in Tracy scrapbook) and at https://sarahtracyburrows.com/historical-documents/.

of a description of the "Syracuse Lion." We are a lucky family Os few have sent more out to the war and lost less in battle and we have all been in pretty tight places.

I have been in this little one horse Western town over a month but day-light begins to dawn once more for I mustered the last regiment in yesterday and shall

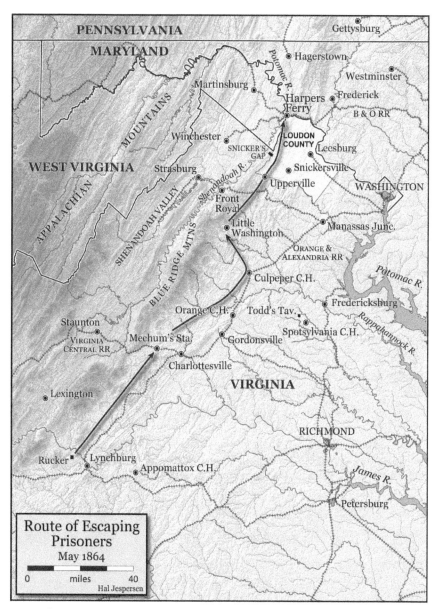

Route of Escaping Prisoners (Map by Hal Jeperson)

probably return to Springfield in a few days. I have had command here until a day or two since, and I assure you to have charge of 1600 men all recruits with officers perfectly ignorant is no small task. Please congratulate your mother for me on your safe return, and with hopes that we will all meet again soon, believe me as ever

Your affect cousin

Sam

The following is an undated presentation speech accompanying engraved swords and belts that Osgood and Birdseye were given.

To Lt. O. V. Tracy Adjutant 122d Reg't N. Y. S. Vs. and

Lt. M. P. Birdseye 2d N. Y. Cavalry

Gents:

A few of your friends have united in procuring for each of you a sword and belt, upon which are appropriate inscriptions, to present to you, as you are about returning to your positions in the Army. You left your homes at the call of the country, and entered the ranks as citizen soldiers to aid in the Suppression of Treason. By your meritorious service, you have each been promoted to command in your respective regiments. Participating as you have done in the remarkable campaign now progressing in Virginia under the leadership of Gen'l Grant you were made prisoners and taken to Lynchburg on your way to a Rebel Dungeon, a fate worse almost than death—The sagacity, courage and resolution which you exhibited in your remarkable escape is a complete vindication of the confidence . . . in you. We tender to each of you this sword and belt as appropriate to your present position and while we fervently hope that Peace may soon enable you to return to your homes, we believe that you will worthily bear your part in this most gigantic struggle, to maintain the Government and Constitution of our Country, and the liberties of ourselves and our posterity.

Your Friends

Syracuse, June 18th 1864

Charles Andrews [Mayor]; Geo. N. Kennedy; J. T. Wilkinson; E. R. Judson; Karl White; Willard V. Hanley; O. Ballard; Price & Wheeler; George Barnes; Allen Munroe; D. M. McCarthy; H. B. Wilber; D. P. Phelps

In return, Osgood wrote a thank-you letter.

Syracuse, N.Y.

June 20th 1864

Messrs Charles Andrews, Hamil White, J. F. Wilkinson & others

Gentlemen

I tender you my most sincere thanks for your elegant present and kind expressions of regard, doubly valuable coming as they do, from citizens of my native place. Unfortunately taken prison so early in the campaign I have been debarred the honor of participating with the regiment in the severe trials through which they have passed but, thanks to the plans and skill of my friend Birdseye, I am once more enabled to rejoin them and trust that nothing in my future conduct will cause my friends to regret the confidence they have reposed in me.

I am gentlemen very respectfully

Your obedient servant

O. V. Tracy

CHAPTER NINE

Back on the Campaign Trail

July–December 1864

The wet and tired fisherman who at Camp Sumner calls
As going up or down Cold Brook; he passes by the falls,
Will please remember it was built to shelter loyal man
And is for vagabonds no place, for "Copperheads" no den.
Sile Allen built it in three hours, and none as well as he
Knows how to tree, or trap a bear, or what a camp should be,
We give it brave old Sumner's name and curse the rascal scamp—
Who scouts the flag he fought for and then lodges in this camp.
—Dudley Post Phelps, Camp Sumner, Cold Brook Falls, June 1864

❀ Having escaped from captivity and spent a furlough at home in Syracuse, Osgood rejoined the 122nd just as the Confederacy was collapsing under the weight of renewed Union military offensives across the south and the crumbling of the fledgling nation's infrastructure. As summer drew to a close, the Army of the Potomac stood outside the gates of Richmond, blocked by the rapidly shrinking Army of Northern Virginia.[1] As Osgood made his way back to Union lines and after a thirty-day furlough at home, he rejoined his comrades during their regiment's most active time in the war. Attached to the Ninth Corps, the men from

1. On the Overland Campaign and the end of the war, see Joseph Glatthaar, *General Lee's Army: From Victory to Defeat* (New York: Free Press, 2008); J. Tracy Power, *Lee's Miserables: Life in the Army of Northern Virginia from the Wilderness to Appomattox* (Chapel Hill: Univ. of North Carolina Press, 1998); Gary W. Gallagher and Caroline E. Janney, eds., *Cold Harbor to the Crater: The End of the Overland Campaign* (Chapel Hill: Univ. of North Carolina Press, 2015); Steven E. Sodergren, *The Army of the Potomac in the Overland and Petersburg Campaigns: Union Soldiers and Trench Warfare, 1864–1865* (Baton Rouge: Louisiana State Univ. Press, 2017).

Syracuse fought hard during the Overland Campaign, May 4–June 24, 1864, and were bloodied at Cold Harbor, where Osgood's best friend, Frank Wooster, was killed, a death Osgood felt for the rest of his life. During this time, Gen. John Sedgwick was also killed by Confederate artillery at Spotsylvania Court House. The well known, popular, general was mourned by the army, Sedgwick family, and friends.[2] As the summer drew to a close, the regiment was transferred back to Washington, where they pushed back Jubal Early's attempt to capture Washington that summer. When Osgood arrived, the 122nd moved to the Shenandoah Valley as part of Gen. Philip Sheridan's successful campaign, which ultimately gave the Union control of that vital supply point for the Army of Northern Virginia.[3]

Camp 122d Reg't New York Volunteers
August 8th 1864

Dear Will,

I received your letter of the 16th day before yesterday. After chasing around Maryland for the last week or two we are now encamped near Halltown about four miles from Harpers Ferry, The appearances indicate that something is going to be done in this Department and I would respectfully suggest that it was about time. Yesterday we rec'd an order from Gen'l Hunter assigning Gen'l Sheridan to the immediate command of the forces in this Dept. but Smithy told me last evening that Gen'l Sheridan is assigned by the War Dept. on account of the safety of Washington. Grant has come up here himself to ascertain what force the "rebs" have here and then clean them out and take us back to Petersburg. As you seemed so anxious to have a little active service I suppose these late expeditions were very acceptable but I presume you find no difficulty in returning to the comfort of civilized life once more. This army has had rather an extensive campaign. It is

---

2. For further reading, Gen. Thomas Webster Hyde's letter to Nellie Sedgwick about Sedgwick's death Hyde (1841–1899), of the Seventh Maine, was beside Sedgwick when he was shot and died. The letter is available at https://sarahtracyburrows.com/historical-documents/; and Hyde's book, *Following the Greek Cross; or, Memoirs of the Sixth Army Corps* (Boston: Houghton Mifflin, 1894). Hyde (1841–1899) was awarded a Congressional Medal of Honor for his actions at the Battle of Antietam.

3. In early September, Gen. Philip Sheridan's Union army moved against Jubal Early's at Winchester, forcing the Confederates to withdraw up the valley to a position at Fisher's Hill. It was, according to Early, "the only place where a stand could be made." Early, with approximately eighty-five hundred men, faced Sheridan's advancing force of nearly thirty-five hundred. A Union victory, the battle of Fisher's Hill was "key to the Confederate collapse in the Valley." Early counterattacked in October at Cedar Creek, gaining initial success before Sheridan arrived with the rest of his army, counterattacked, and pushed the Confederates back in retreat. Robert E. L. Krick, "A Stampede of Stampedes: The Confederate Disaster at Fisher's Hill," in *The Shenandoah Valley Campaign of 1864*, ed. Gary Gallagher (Chapel Hill: Univ. of North Carolina Press, 2009) 162, 167; and Jack H. Lepa, *The Shenandoah Valley Campaign of 1864* (Jefferson, NC: McFarland, 2003); George E. Pond, *The Shenandoah Valley in 1864*, vol. 11 of *Campaigns in the Civil War*, 16 vols. total (New York: Scribner, 1884); Scott C. Patchan, *The Last Battle of Winchester: Phil Sheridan, Jubal Early and the Shenandoah Valley Campaign, August 7–September 19, 1864* (El Dorado Hills, CA: Savas Beatie, 2021).

over three months since we left Brandy Station and they have had no rest to speak of since. Cap't Dwight rejoined us a day or two ago. He is not fit for field service as the cords of his leg have been cut so that he cannot "work" his foot, but the surgeon ordered him back from the Annapolis Hospital. He says after a fair trial if he cannot get along he shall resign.

I had a letter from Dave Cossitt written by a "Christian Commission" man, a few days ago. He is improving and expects to be able to go home in a few days, but the surgeons say that he will not be fit for duty again in less than six months. I don't suppose that he will ever come back to the regiment again. Dave was the last of the old "clique" "Smithy Lester & c" and now I feel quite alone. Last evening Smith called on me. He says that if Dwight would consent to let me go he could get me a position on Gen'l Rickett's staff. Gen'l Rickett commands the 3d Div. And Andy is, at present, acting . . . but after thinking the matter over I told him I thought I ought not to leave the regiment at present. We have now only seven line officers for duty, including Cap't Dwight, but when I get to be a Captain, there are only two that rank me now. I think I would go if I could get the place. Don't say anything to mother about this or she would be in a "stew" to have me get it. I suppose you hear all the news from home, what a place of resort Glen Haven[4] is getting to be—Georges return &c.

There is another thing I wish to speak to you about and I wish you to write the boy a "*strong*" letter against it. I had a letter from Jim the other day saying that if there should be a draft in the 4th Ward he would not take the chances but would enlist in the reg't. I wrote immediately advising him to do no such thing and I wish you would do likewise. Be very careful and don't mention it to anyone.

Regards to everyone I know

Yours affectionately

Os

Hd qrs 3d Division 6th Corps

August 31/64

Dear Will,

I know you will be pleased to learn that I have received an appointment as Inspector Gen'l of the 3d Div. of our Corps which at present is commanded by Gen'l Rickett. Andy Smith is (Cmm'y) of musters for the Div. and during Cap't Kings absence is acting as adjutant Gen'l which makes it very pleasant for me. I was in some doubts about taking the position fearing that I might not be able to perform the duties but Andy convinced me that if I had not a good opinion of my own abilities, I should never get along and accordingly I determined to try it. I like the Gen'l very much and the other officers on the staff are very pleasant fellows.

---

4. Osgood likely meant the hamlet of Glen Haven near Skaneateles, New York, known for its scenic valley.

We are now near Charlestown in the same position where we had the skirmish a week ago Sunday. After that skirmish we fell back and took a position near Hall-town and entrenched ourselves. We remained there about a week, and then advanced again to this position. Day before yesterday Merritts division were engaged out towards Smithfield about four miles from here and were being driven back but our Division was ordered out to support them and the "Rebs" immediately fell back to the other side of the town without any attempt to make any stand. The report to-day is that the entire army that they have here in the valley are concentrating at Bunker Hill which is about ten miles distant I believe and where I am told they have a fine position. Our Division is still two miles out though we have not moved our Head quarters. This morning I rode out to our cavalry picket line which is just this side of Smithfield. Nothing can be seen of the Rebs except a few cavalry videttes. I suppose you have learned that a new regiment is to be raised in Onondaga Co. and that there is some prospect that Ned Jenney[5] will command it.

Cap't Dwight of our regiment who was wounded in the Wilderness and incapacitated for duty in the line is going to make an attempt to get the Majority and I trust that he will succeed. He is a good fellow and a brave and efficient officer. I am at present messing with the General and Smith. Mrs. Rickett has been here for the last week. It is refreshing to have a lady about and particularly such a pleasant and agreeable one as Mrs. R. I have as yet seen no notice of the General assuming command of the 20th Corps but as "Col. S" says he is daily expected I will direct you there. Hereafter please direct to the "Hd qrs 3d Division 6th Corps" Washington, D.C.

My regards to Morely and believe me

Yours affectionately

Os

Hdqrs 3d Div. 6th Corps

September 21, 1864

Dear Lucy,

We had a hard fight near Winchester day before yesterday and though at one position of the day affairs looked gloomy yet the final result was a glorious victory. Thanks to the protection of a kind Providence I escaped unharmed, although occasionally the shells and bullets came a little closer than was agreeable. The Army all feel in the best of spirits and we have this morning received congratulatory dispatches from both the S'cy of War and Gen'l Grant. Gen'l Russell, who was killed, used to be stationed in Syracuse a good many years ago recruiting. I think Dudley knew him. He was a splendid officer and is a great loss. We are now near

---

5. Ned Jenney, who led the 185th New York as colonel, married Nellie Sedgwick's friend Emma Saul in 1863.

Strasburg with the "rebs" in a very strong position in front of us, but we feel this morning that we can whip them anywhere.

Love to all

Yours affectionately

Os

Hd.qrs. 3rd Div. 6th Corps

Strasburg

Oct 8/64

Dear Dudley,

I enclose a draft on the U.S. Treas for $100, which please place to my credit. We left Harrisburg day before yesterday and as we fall back are burning all grain. This would seem to indicate that we were going to leave the valley. Indeed, we begin to see Petersburg as our destination, very plainly. We proceed over Fishers Hill, the scene of our 2nd victory, this morning and are now encamped within a mile of it. It is much stronger than I had even supposed.

Regard to all the loved ones at home

Yours aff

Os

From New Brunswick, New Jersey, David Murray wrote on November 20:

My dear Osgood,

Your letter came to hand in my good season having been only two days on the way. I can tell you, I was very glad indeed to hear from you, and to know that you are yet well and safe. Since then you have had some marching and counter-marching, but not very much fighting, I believe, as out-siders can form but little idea of what is to take place, and what the plans for the future are. And yet we perhaps know just about as much as thee—racious correspondents of the Herald and other papers. The great point of interest now is Sherman's great Seaward Campaign. Nobody knows where he is bound, but things seem to point chiefly towards Mobile. We shall know before long. I am delighted at your notion of stopping at New Brunswick on your way home. I don't want to take your time from your visit home; but I *should* be *very* glad if you could stay a day with me. At any rate telegraph to me and I will visit you at the cars. Direct the telegram *City Hotel,* New Brunswick. New York City is hoping to send 40,000 turkeys down to the army for Thanksgiving and I hope you will get a good decent joint and a piece of breast and as much more as you want. What a dreadful time it is for turkeys.

Well, father Abraham rules yet another four years. The election passed off very quietly, thanks to the presence of Gen. Butler in the North. There were a great many apprehensions, but they were mostly allayed by the terse foresight, and ample provisions made for any difficulty that might arise. On my pleasant nature of this election is the ready and cheerful acquiescence that was the result of almost all the democrats. The truth is a great many of them did not want McClellan elected very much and were rather glad than otherwise that Lincoln was chosen, although they did not go so far as to vote for him. It was a narrower miss in New York than it ought to have been. But New York City swarms with Southern Refugees, 60,000 they say, and the influence and votes of these men got an intercourse vote for McClellan there. Do you see, the gallant little states of New Jersey are plucky enough to stand out, and shake their little fists in Father Abraham's face and flourish their little tin swords. Three cheers for N.J.

Let me hear from you again before Christmas. I suppose you will have to go into winter quarters before too long; and military operations must cease for a while. I do not see why you may not get quite a long furlough, especially as your general is still unable to assume duties.

Good bye, my Dear fellow, and take good care of yourself and remember me ever as

Your Very Sincere Friend
David Murray

P. S. I add you as Captain. Please tell me whether you have the two bars or not

On stationery embossed with "Headquarters Third Division, Sixth Army Corps," Osgood wrote Nellie:

December 28th 1864

Dear Nell,

I enclose a copy of a Sixth Corps song which is very popular here now and I trust that your partiality for the corps will enable you to overlook the poetry for the sake of the *truth* contained therein. We are very pleasantly situated here and as there is no immediate prospect of a move—very well contented. The other armies are so successful that I hope it will not be thought best to attack the works here. I was very sorry to miss Col. Jenney. He left the day before I arrived. All your acquaintances at Corps Hd qrs inquired after your welfare. I had a very pleasant call on Col. Hyde day before yesterday. He had elegant quarters –

A Merry Christmas and "Happy New Year" to you

Your friend
Os

Hd qrs 3d Div'n 6th Corps
N'r Petersburg December 29/64

Dear Will,

I am much disappointed in not yet having heard from you since your arrival at

General Thomas W. Hyde (From
the private photograph collection
of Osgood Tracy)

the coast. We have all been very much interested in the accounts of your wonderful march across the country and hope soon to receive a full account from you. Since you left Atlanta our corps has been transferred from the "Valley" to this army before Petersburg. Our corps is near Warren Station on the old Weldon road and very near the extreme left of our line. Grant's famous military R.D. runs from City Pt to the left of the line just a short distance in rear of the breastworks, though this means the army is well supplied. We get our mails and papers regularly, have good comfortable quarters and in fact are very happy considering the dread with which he looked forward to coming back. The Division is now commanded by Gen'l Seymour, who we like pretty well. Gen'l Slocum can tell you all about him as they were in the same regiment in the "old army." Col. Keifer (now B'vt Brig. Gen'l) who commanded our Division at the battle of Cedar Creek has made his report of that engagement in which he speaks very handsomely of the several members of the staff. Cap'ts Smith and Dawson and myself have been recommended for Brevets for our services that day.

I got a leave for fifteen days just before we left the valley and had a very pleasant visit at home. It was quite gay while there the "hard tack" parties being the principal attraction. I trust that you will soon be able to get home and enjoy some of them yourself. I had quite a little flirtation with your friend of the Irish "persuasion" (Mike Murphy). I assure it was only to look after your interests. While at home I received a very handsome letter from Jenney offering me the Majority of that regiment. I declined it then but since I have returned I have been over to the regiment had a long talk with Lt. Col. Sniper[6] on the subject and have concluded to take it if the vacancy has not been filled. I therefore telegraphed my decision to Jenney, who is now at Syracuse, and I expect to get it. I am also informed that Jenney does not intend to remain in the service so that I get my majority and do well in it, the Lt. Colonelcy will be likely to follow.

But please say nothing about this letter and indeed I hope that it will not occur until I may have some experience as Major. Mother did not wish me to accept it for she imagines that it is so much safer on staff but the most general rule in the army appears to be never to refuse promotion. I was very much pleased with the appearance of the regiment. Their camp was in excellent condition and that is always an excellent indication of the discipline of the regiment. The term of service of the regiment expires next September only a month later than the 122d.

I rec'd the check for $25 you sent from Atlanta for a Christmas present for mother and upon Lucy's advice got a cloak for, but upon arriving in New York I found it would be difficult to get a cloak ready made that would suit her and so at Ophelia's suggestion I bought the cloth necessary for a cloak and sent it to her. It was very handsome and cost $43.50 so I owe you a little of the $25. I will leave this letter unsealed unto to-days mail arrival in hopes, my dear boy, I shall hear from you.

Yours affectionately

Os

December 29/64

No letter yet I hope to hear from you soon. A happy New Year to you and I do hope that on the 1st of Jan'y 1866 we may all be united at home once more.

Good night

Yours

Os

---

6. Gustavus Sniper (1836–1894) was twenty-nine years of age when he enrolled in the 185th New York State Regiment at Syracuse, to serve one year. He was mustered in as lieutenant colonel on September 23, 1864, and as colonel on March 10, 1865.

❀ ❀ ❀

CHAPTER TEN

The War Draws to a Close

January–May 1865

I don't believe there will be any desire to attempt another Rebellion
until the memory of this shall have perished which will at least
insure peace and happiness to my great-grandchildren.
—Osgood Vose Tracy, May 11, 1865

❀ As the new year dawned, Osgood settled into the trenches around Petersburg, Virginia. Osgood and Nellie began to correspond more often, perhaps an indication that they had rekindled their relationship. Osgood yearned to see Nellie, inviting her to visit the regiment when she was in Washington with her father. As winter turned to spring, the end of the war loomed, and Osgood's correspondence provides readers with a personal look into the closing months of the war and the hope that men and women had for the future, despite President Lincoln's assassination.

Head Quarters 3d Div'n 6th Corps
Jan'y 2d 1865

Dear Will,

I rec'd yours of the 22d of Dec last evening. This is the first intelligence I have had of your arrival and relieved my anxiety. That must have been a rich scene when you voted Georgia back into the Union. How disgusted must any of the citizens have been who were present. Have you got acquainted with Hayes of the Tribune. If not do so at once. He is quite a nice fellow.

Yesterday we had a very jolly time here for Sunday. We kept "open houses" and had callers from all the corps in the Army of the Potomac. We had various kinds of drinks and some of our visitors got rather "swipy" but I am happy to say that the "staff" all kept sober except our Provost marshall (a very quiet fellow ordinarily) over whom we had a great deal of fun. I occasionally run across some of your acquaintances. Cap't Smith who was your Commissary for a time is now Commissary of the 5th Corps and whenever I meet him he always inquires after you. Dr. Elwig of a Pennsylvania reg't in our Division was also formerly in your corps and remembered you very well. I called on McNulty the other day (He is now Medical Director of the 2d Corps) but he had gone home on leave. I have heard nothing from Jenney yet since telegraphing him that I would accept the Majority. I think probably I am too late as when he got home and heard that I declined he probably recommended some one else. Lt. Col. Snifer called here yesterday. He seems to be very anxious that I should get it for he expects that Jenney will resign and then he will be Colonel and if any of the Captains who are all inexperienced are promoted he could not depend upon them. Of course I should like it but as long as I can retain my present position I shall not be at all dissatisfied.

It has been very quiet here since my return except a couple of mornings ago when we were routed out just before daylight. A party of about 100 rebs came up under cover of some woods and made a dash on our picket line killing two and capturing 2 from our Division and about 16 from the 1st Div'n. They were immediately driven back and the line re established. A deserter who came in soon after said that all the party came after was overcoats and rations. We have about one or two deserters come in daily. There is a Div'n in our front composed principally of North Carolina troops and the deserters represent that they are all heartily sick of the war and if they were not afraid to trust one another would desert in large squads. I agree with you in regard to this indiscriminate pillaging and one of the worst features of it is the demoralization it makes among our own troops. It is awful when these individual cases are brought to your notice and yet when I look at the subject *generally* I feel that it is but a judgement on them for commencing this war. We are having quite cold weather not at all suggestive of the Southern climate. Well old boy, I trust your next campaign will be as successful as your last and that you may pass through as safely.

Good Bye

Yours

Os

Head quarters 3d Division 6th Corps
in front of Petersburg, Va. Jan'y 14 65

Dear Nell,

Many thanks for your congratulations but I am not entitled to them. When I decided to accept the Majority of the 185th, it had already been given to a Cap't Bush of that regiment. I suppose you have seen the list of brevets. Smith and myself are both Majors, about the whole of the Sixth Corps have been remembered. They have been given so indiscriminately (to be sure we might not have got *ours*, if it had been otherwise) that we cannot feel very proud of it. However I am consoling myself with the reflection that I may pass myself off as a *real* Major when I go home next Spring. Andrew leaves on Tuesday for Phila where he expects to meet his wife. Andy has built a very fine house and I imagine Kate will enjoy a taste of army life, exceedingly. I also look forward to her visit with a great deal of pleasure. I like her very much.

I wrote to Julia to ask her to send me the rules of bizigne. We are rather crazy at present on "cribbage" and generally play an hour or two every evening and I think a new game would be a pleasant change. I have met George Dana several times since my return and like him very much. Col B speaks in the highest terms of him. I called on Ned Jenney on Wednesday and had a very pleasant chat with him. He is expecting to resign soon. I believe if I were thrown constantly into his society he would counsel me to like him in spite of myself, so Marie may expect that in time her wish may be gratified.

I have been hoping that when you go to Washington your father would get up a party to come "to the front." We should be delighted to place our horses at your disposal.

I had a very pleasant call on Col. Kent to-day. He and Cap't Franklin have a very large house, large enough for dancing, but I fear we shall not be able to enjoy the society of many ladies as Gen'l Meade sternly refuses all applications (Mrs. Smith has a pass only to City Pt) for all officers wives. George writes me that the next "Hard tack" is to be given at Mrs. Longstreets' and the rules are to be deviated from and it is to be a full dress party. He fears that they will not be able to return to their informal rules again. My regards to Marie when you write her

Your friend

Os

P.S. Direct to Cap't Tracy as I have not turned the *bars* into *leaves* yet.

Hd qrs 3d Div. 6th Corps

January 29th 1865

Dear Mother,

I am ashamed to say that I got so interested in "bazigne" that I neglected your letter last evening. Steve, Andy and myself went out calling in the morning and had quite a pleasant time although it was rather cool riding. We stopped at Corps Hd qrs and also at George Barnards's.

George's "latest" is the following—Some Swedish naval officers were visiting the army and George was showing one of the counts (with an unpronounceable name) around and at one of the Brig. Hd qrs were a squad of men who were being inspected to decide who should have the furlough for twenty five days which by a recent order Gen'l Meade gives to the most soldierly man in each brigade. The squad was composed of the best men (one from each regiment) in the brigade. "What is dat" asks the Count and George replied, "Oh these are men who are sent up to be punished for not keeping clean and for being unsoldierly in their appearance." The Count must have rec'd a very exalted opinion of the army if these were the dirty men.

Steve and Andy went to City Pt. yesterday afternoon. Andy will be back to-morrow morning and will probably bring Mrs. Mickles with him but Steve thought he should start for home to-morrow. He promised to call on Dudley and impress upon him his duty in regard to making me a visit. I shall go down to City Pt. Some time during the coming week, probably. Daniels wishes to make a call on the bride and Mrs. Smith and I will go with him.

To-day I went over to see Dr. Slocum who is now in charge of the 1st Div'n hospital which is quite near us. We had a very pleasant chat. I was quite amused at one piece of information he gave me. He said that Col. Russell—the General's nephew—asked him if he knew a lady and her daughter of Syracuse who came to the General's funeral. Russell could not at first remember the name but finally said he believed it was a Mrs. Sabine. As the Dr. understood it she said at some relatives of the Russell family. Don't mention this.

I enclose a very pretty little thing I found in the last Harper's Weekly which seemed appropriate to the dear boy's letters. Don't you think it worthy of a place in your scrapbook?

We are all very much disgusted with the account of the battle of Middletown (Cedar Creek) in the February No. of Harper's Magazine. It is written by an officer of Gen'l Emory's staff and and he tries to make out that the 19th took an honorable part in the action as indeed he leads one to think—the principal part—whereas in the words of the Sixth Corps song.

At Cedar Runs fierce battlefield
The Eighth Corps ran away
The Nineteenth broke and left the Sixth
To bear the brunt that day

And the rascal falsifies the report of the Corps. He puts the 6th at 1300 whereas it was over 1800, and now for all their gallantry & c they are rewarded being sent to garrison Savannah. There is a report that two corps are coming from Gen'l Thomas' army, under Gen'l Schofield, to join in the operations against Lee's army. It is suggested that they are going to attempt to move up to Lynchburg but I don't believe it possible for the lines of communication are too long to ration an army there. That was the only thing that I could see that prevented us going to Lynchburg last Fall when we were under Sheridan. We are not getting any papers lately the last we had were of the 24th inst.

Evening

No mail, but we got a paper of the 27th which contains Porters' answer to Butler. Seems to me Benj F is rather a used up man. By the way I was somewhat amused by the General saying the other morning that he had received several letters the evening before, all of which began, "What a —— fool you have made of yourself." In reference to his letter, as you might not have seen it at the time, I enclose a copy now.

Will you please ask Dudley if he did not receive a check from me about two weeks or so ago for $102, which I directed to be credited to Dr. Slocum to whose orders it was payable? Dr. S. has been spending the evening with us.

Good night
Yours affy
Os

Head quarters 3 Div'n 6th Corps
February 14 1865

Dear Mother,

I know of no young lady who is as much entitled to a "valentine" from me as you are. Would that I could write some pretty little verse appropriate to the day but alas I am not gifted and therefore must content myself with prose and even then I fear it would be impossible to express my love and affection for you. How I should like to transport myself to Syracuse this evening. I assure you that there are no young ladies in Syracuse, or indeed anywhere else, to entice me out, but on the contrary my old dressing gown, a pair of slippers and the prospect of spending the whole evening with you is about my highest idea of pleasure now. The following I happened to find in a copy of Willis this evening is very pretty.

> Mother: dear mother the feelings worst
> As I hung at thy bosom, clung round thee first.
> T'was the earliest link in lives warm chain—
> Tis the only one that will long remain
> And as year by year, and day by day,
> Some friend still trusted drops away,
> Mother: dear mother: oh don't thou see
> How the shortened chain brings me nearer thee!

I received your letter of the 9th last evening just as I had sealed my letter to you. I suppose ere this your mind is fully satisfied that the 3d Div'n were neither engaged or "demoralized."

I trust that aunts sickness may not prove too serious and also that the little baby's life may be spared. It seems hardly possible that you have so much snow North when we have not a bit of it, although we have had some weather lately which to say the very least was decidedly suggestive of Winter.

I went over to the reg't to-day and had a little chat with Col. Dwight. The Col. seemed to be quite "cooled" down and did not even get excited over Clapps' promotion although he (expressed) disapproval of it. Andy has gone down to the Pt. again this evening and Kate come up to-morrow. Dr. Slocum called in this evening and we had a very pleasant chat. We are getting to be very good friends. Gen'l Crawford of the 3rd Corps (whose men ran away the other day) dined with us to-day. He was formerly a surgeon in the regular army and is not of very large calibre. Mrs. Sumner probably knew him. Gen'l Miles of the 2d Corps whose troops we relieve the other day has taken off everything and so much so that Gen'l Seymour said this evening that he thought of sending an officer to him to ascertain if he proposed to dig up the ground he had occupied and take off the fire with him. Our men are beginning to get very comfortable quarters but for two or three days they suffered considerably.

On next Valentines day I trust I shall be able to deliver mine to you in person.

Your loving boy

Os

Hd qrs 3d Div. 6th Corps

February 15th 1865

Dear Will,

Our Div'n did not take part in the late movement towards Hatchers Run, although one of the papers reported we were there and "demoralized. " Our only "demoralization" was at the prospect of being ordered out. The movement appears to be considered to have accomplished all that was intended. It lengthens our lines some three or four miles but does not as I understand it bring us any nearer the Southside R.R., that much desired object. I have not been out on the new line yet. This extension of our lines has necessitated some movements of troops, and we have had to change the position of one brigade of our Div'n at one time we feared that the whole Div'n and consequently our Hd qrs would have to move which was rather annoying to us as we have just got nicely fixed up, good comfortable houses built.

Lt. Col. Dwight has just got back to our regiment. His hand is considerably swollen yet he never will recover the full use of it. He seems a little more *subdued* than he used to appear. Jenney has resigned and gone home. He had command of the Brigade in this last move at Hatchers Run. If I had got that Majority I should be Lt. Col. now. Well I shall be perfectly contented if I can remain where I am until my term of service expires which is only "six months and a few" now, and perhaps after all it is better to be a decent Cap't than to "fizzle" out as a Lt. Colonel. Andy goes to City Point at every opportunity. He spends his Sundays there and runs down occasionally during the week. Gen'l Meade will not allow any ladies to remain permanently at the front but will only grant passes for the day. Kate has been up twice. Quite a number of Syracusans have been down and I am hoping and expecting to have a visit from Dudley. Steve Estes was with us for a few days. I like him very much.

Tom Wilkinson said when I was home that as soon as you got near enough to us so that he could visit us both in the same trip he was coming down. We are all feeling anxious about your campaign knowing that our movements will depend very much on your success. I trust, my dear boy, that you may be spared and that we shall all be permitted to assemble at home once more and drink *that* bottle of wine in honor of the close of the war and *free* America—

Yours affectionately
Os

Hd Qrs 3d Div'n 6th Corps
February 25, 1865

Dear Mother,

The mail came in this morning bringing me your letter of the 20th, and also one from Jim. The only deserters the enemy got from us are those really "bounty jumpers" that the brave and valiant people of the North send down here to do their fighting for them. You should hear the general hold forth on this subject. Nothing delights him more than to have an opportunity to pitch in to a citizen on the question of substitutes &c. I expect if Dudley comes he will have such an effect on him that he will be inclined to go home and raise a company (N. B. perhaps you had not better mention this to Lucy or she will not allow him to come). We got three more "Johnnies" during the night, making a total of fourteen on our Div'n picket line for yesterday. I have not heard the whole number in the Corps.

And now in regard to coming home. If everything is quiet and likely to continue so, the latter part of next month I shall endeavor to persuade the Gen'l to let me go, but if the movements of Sherman are as successful as they have been lately I shall imagine that we shall be on the go before that and although, my dear mother, you know how anxious I am to see you, yet after being in this army for nearly three years and although I don't exactly "hanker" after fighting, yet I should hate very much to be away at the grand finale and fall of Richmond—which must come soon. And then try to bear in mind that in six short months I shall be with you to remain, and may we not hope that our Heavenly Father who has thus spared the lives of myself and Will will continue his mercy to us and care over us but if he should deem it best for it be otherwise, it will be a consolation to you to feel that we tried to do our duty and did not belong to the "Home Guards."

But this is no time for dismal thoughts when everything looks bright, and the troops are improving in spirits everyday and will start on the next campaign with much greater confidence than they did last Spring even. The deserters say that at the last fight the old Stonewall brigade (Jacksons' old brigade) behaved very badly and would not rally although "Old Bob" (Gen'l Lee who the reb soldiers really love) did his best to stop them, offering to lead them in himself and besought them with tears in his eyes not to disgrace themselves but without avail. We have such a poor opinion of Crooks'[1] troops that it was with a sort of satisfaction that we heard that he was gobbled, although I don't know but what he himself, is a good officer. His men though can run faster and further—away from the enemy—than any troops I ever saw, except, of course Earlys'.

I wrote to Will last evening. The boy urged me to write often as he says it is very pleasant to get a whole batch of letters when the mail does come, all of which I know by experience.

I am surprised that Gerty Hillis should not have been married at home. It may have been owing to the fact that the Episcopalians hardly consider a marriage legal which takes place outside of the church, but let me assure you that you shall be consulted about mine notwithstanding what the future Mrs. Tracy shall desire.

I wrote Forman Wilkinson last evening to hurry up or he would not be in time to see the end and I thought by the time he got here that Slocums' Corps might be in visiting distance. Do make Dudley come. I shall never forgive him if he does not come. [The rest of this letter is missing.]

Head Quarters 3 Div. 6th Corps
Febry 28th, 1865

Dear Will,

I supposed you had rather have short letters occasionally than long ones at greater intervals.

The Corps staff set the example of wearing strap and acc . . . the little of their Brevet rank and we have followed their example, the senate having confirmed our appointments, but after all their single breasted majors (we are not allowed but one now of buttons) are rather plenty.

To-day we have received the news of the capture of Wilmington but have heard nothing of your movements since the . . . and are anxiously looking for some intelligence.

No news of importance here. Yesterday morning we expected an attack on our lines and got all ready for them but they did not come.

---

1. For a brief biography of Gen. George Crook of Ohio, Ezra J. Warner, *Generals in Blue: Lives of Union Commanders* (Baton Rouge: Louisiana State Univ. Press, 2006), 102–3.

Desertions from the enemy are increasing daily. 67 came in on our corps picket line during the last 24 hours, and they are generally a very good class [?] of men— old soldiers. They all agree in representing their army as very much demoralized and rapidly going to pieces but of course they give the worst picture of it. I imagine we shall one or two sharp fights before this thing is over but if this last call for 80000 men is filled this summers campaign ought to be the closing one.

Theodore Poole is in the 2nd Div Hosp, near our HdQrs. He was wounded in the arm at Cold Harbor and came back expecting to be able to do duty. His arm troubled him so much that he decided to have an operation performed but the bone was found to be badly diseased that they were obliged to amputate the arm at the shoulder, dislocate it as it is called. He is getting along nicely and hopes to be able to remain until next August acting as quartermaster of the reg't. Fortunately it is his left arm.

Jerome Hickox, formerly of Syracuse now in Col Bradley's office at City Pt, has been spending a couple of days with us and we have had a very jolly time.

Frank Shafer came over to see us the other day. He is now Adjutant of the 10th N. Y. Cav (Avery's regiment). Hank Stevens, who lived on James St, is Lt and regt Commissary. Shafer inquired particularly after you and desired to be remembered. He did not seem to remember Johnny Butler with kindly feelings.

A sergt and eight "Johnnies" just came in. The Sergt was a very intelligent fellow and seems to think they are preparing to evacuate Richmond and Petersburg.

He belonged to Finnigans Brigade and he and the General fought over the battle of Olustee again—

Well old boy good night

Ever Yours

Os

Head quarters 3d Div'n 6th Corps

February 28th 1865

Dear Nell,

Learning that you are expected home about the 1st of March I trust that this letter may find you at Syracuse. I have not written before imagining you would not care to be bothered with letter writing while you could employ your time so much pleasantly visiting. I received a letter from Dudley Phelps on Sunday evening containing the said intelligence of Mary Wilkinson's death. I deeply sympathize with Johnny in this affliction and when I think of my last visit to them in their pleasant home, just started on a life which seemed to promise nothing but happiness I cannot realize the sad change.

There have been one or two changes at Corps Hd qrs. Maj. Whittier has gone to the 2d Corps as A. A. Gen'l for Gen'l Humphries with the rank of Lt. Col. I understand that Cap't McClellan will be made senior-aid with the rank of Major in Whittier's place. Col. Kent, Farrar and Franklin are still there. Col. Hyde remains in command of the brigade to which our regiment is attached. The boys in the regiment express themselves very highly pleased with him. I understand you have been at Newport and suppose of course that you had a "jolly" time with the Navy.

And so Marie is to live next door to you. Isn't that a greater degree of happiness than you ever expected. I quite envy those fellows who are at home but we are on our last six months now and all feel confident that we shall see the end of the war by next August. 10 P.M.

Three "Rebs" have just come in who tell the same old story. One fellow said, "What are we going to do with Grant in front and Sherman coming up in rear when we can't whip either of them alone!" I wish they would of them see their cause in this light—like this fellow give it up. One day last week, sixty-seven were received on the picket line of our Corps. Last night a 2d Lieut. and ten men came in on our Div'n line. What do you think must be the condition of any army when even its officers desert to the enemy?

Good Night
Your friend
Os

Osgood's friend David Murray wrote on March 9:

My Dear Osgood

I received your kind letter and welcome note in answer to mine sent through Col. Jamesway. I was very glad to hear from you I assure you; and if you enjoyed receiving as much as I did in sending the ring I am sure you enjoyed it. Somebody says "Happy is that nation that has no history." Perhaps it is so with individuals. The winter has been quite gay here for us. All eyes are concentrated on the vicinity of Richmond, and every body holds their breath to see what is going to be done next. Every body feels that the Rebellion is to be finished up this Spring, without fail. One fear is that there must still be some fighting done before the end comes. For although the Rebel army is dwindling away and hope is gone from many hearts, yet there is still some desperate stuff in them, that will not yield without a struggle.

I am ashamed to tell you that my adopted state has arrayed itself against constitutional amendment, and does what little it could to oppose the tendency of the age. It is too bad. It is the more shameful thing it has ever done, ten thousand times worse than casting its vote for McClellan. But no matter, the very outrages committed against humanity and decency will arouse a spirit which will overturn the party in power and bring about a better state of things.

What are you going to do when the war is over and you have a chance to come home again? Have you had enough of it, or do you want to join the army permanently? There must be a great menace to the regular army when the war ends, and growing officers may find positions. But I think I would rather see you at home again, in some occupation, peaceful and industrious, rather than warlike and un-productive. Won't it be a joyful time when we see our brave fellows coming back after all this dreadful fight is over: What a beautiful joy will spread through every heart, and what a grateful thanksgiving will go up to God.

I enclose herewith a note of introduction to Gen. Patrick.[2] If I mistake not he will receive you very kindly; he is at heart a thoroughly kind, and noble hearted man. If you are in trouble and want advice from a cool head and a good heart, I think Gen. Patrick will give it. It is too bad he has not been promoted to Major General. He ought to have been long ago. But I think he has not been entirely on the best terms with the authorities at Washington. He was a strong McClellan man for a long time, and I suppose this has estranged him. And I think it is only because of his usefulness in his position that has kept him where he is. I think Cap't Prentice is on his staff who is a son of E. P. Prentice who lives at Mt. Hope below Albany.

Write to me again soon. I suppose there is not hope of seeing you this Spring before the campaign. I repeat to you what I said before, that if anything happens to you and I can be of service to you, I wish you to my word. And may God protect you from any danger, and bring you back to us in safety.

Ever truly Sincerely
Your friend
David Murray

As Murray promised, he enclosed copy of the letter he had written to General Patrick on Osgood's behalf:

Dear General,

I beg the special privilege of making known to you my particular friend Cap't O. V. Tracy. He is on staff duty at the Hd qrs of the 3d Div'n, 6th Corps. He was with the Corps in its brilliant campaign in the Shenandoah Valley and was breveted Major for gallantry at the battle of Cedar Creek (ahem:) These young fellows ought, and I know my young friend will, feel most grateful for the friendship and counsel of an old campaigner like yourself, and I have told him that if he ever needs the advise of a cool head and a good heart, Gen'l Patrick is the man to give it. In the hot and bloody campaign that is likely to open in the Spring, you may find ways to be of service to him. If so you could not place me under greater obligation.

With grateful remembrances of all your kindness, I am yours &c
David Murray

We see your old friend Sheridan is after Early again. Poor old Early, his troubles never to have an end.

2. This is likely a reference to Marsena Rudolph Patrick (1811–1888), a Union brigadier general who was appointed provost marshal for the Army of the Potomac in October 1862. See Warner, *Generals in Blue*, 361–62.

Head quarters 3d Div'n 6th Corps
March 11th 1865

Dear Will,

Not a word from you since your letter dated "Sisters Ferry Feby 3d" and indeed we have had nothing direct from Shermans' army since. We only get our news through the "reb" papers and they seem disposed to say very little about your movements which convinces us that so far you are all right. We are having quite a number of visitors in the army now, quite a party of Syracusans. I feel very sorry for poor Mrs. Jenkins. George[3] was her idol and his death has nearly broken her heart. She came down with this party with the expectation of going to Newbern to get George's remains and also she desired to see those who were with George in his last sickness, but before she got here Win had his remains sent home.

The day they were here Andy took charge persuading the gentlemen to exchange their "stovepipes" for felt hats and you have no idea what a fancy little military man T. B. made. I have a horse that trots very fast and I must say somewhat hard which I was anxious Dominic Caufield should ride thinking it would shake some of the old "foggy" ideas out of him but Andy would not let him take said horse inasmuch as he was going to ride with them. We took them all around our portion of the lines, where they could see the Johnnies very distinctly. They also saw a review and a Brigade Dress Parade. Andy felt quite elated over his success in getting T. B. and Dr. C to take a drink of whiskey together (don't mention it). Dr. C: "wouldn't take it only that his surgeon had often recommended it." Andy wished some of the Presbyterian blue lights of Syracuse had dropped in on them as they stood with their glasses in their hands. As we sat at dinner with those familiar Syracuse faces around me, it seemed quite aggravating to think that Mother was not with the party, and all the more so as I have given up all hopes of going before next August. I had expected to be able to make a visit this Spring but we are not liable to move at any time and after being in this army for nearly three years I should dislike very much to be away when we take Petersburg.

Bv't Gen'l Hamblin, who you remember was instructor to our reg't when we first came out, then a Major—now commander of a brigade in our Corps—the other day I was quite gratified at a request from him for me to take the Adj't Gen's position of his brigade with the promise that I should have his influence to get a regiment went home I should have received said appointment, if it were a possible thing, I should have a fifteen days leave of absence. Notwithstanding I felt highly complimented at his offer yet as I do not desire to remain in the service after next August I decided to decline it.

I received a long letter from Jenney last night in regard to the Lt. Colonelcy of

---

3. This was Pvt. George Sumner Jenkins (1846–1864), of the New York State Volunteer Rifles, who died of yellow fever. His maternal grandfather was Maj. Gen. Edwin Vose Sumner.

the 185th. The understanding was that Sniper was to be made Col. and myself Lt. Col. but I told Jenney I should not make any noise about it at home but if he could arrange it quietly I would take it. I enclose Jenney's letter which I wish you to not to show anyone and which I desire you to destroy. Since receiving that I am very glad that I did not get it. You heard enough so some experiences in the 12th as to the unpleasant position of an "outsider" to know what my position there would have been. I was highly amused at the tone of Jenney's letter as to what *he* would have done and that his officers would not have *dared* to have done different &c. Please destroy it at once.

Good Bye

Yours

Os

P.S. I am still expecting a visit from Dudley. Hereafter you may direct to *Major* Tracy—for we are "on" our brevets now and as I am holding a position consistent with my brevet rank I think it all right,

Head Quarters 3d Div'n 6th Corps

March 12th 1865

Dear Mother,

It has been a beautiful day. I took a very pleasant ride this morning with Rob Moser and then inspected one of our regiments. They looked very finely. The brigade to which it belongs has been turned out for parade, one or twice lately for the benefit of Gen'l Meades' visitors, as they are encamped near a portion of the line which is a particular point of interest for strangers but the men take it as a great compliment and are fixing up greatly. This afternoon I accompanied the General to church in the chapel of the 50th Engineers. He pronounced the sermon decidely slow but it is so long since I have been at church that it really seemed good to hear anything like a sermon. I regret to say that the attendance of neighbor officers or men was as large as at the negro concert that I attended there last night.

I rode over to call on General Hamblin to-day to tell him, that although feeling highly complimented at his offer to make me his Adj't Gen'l yet I had decided to decline it. I did not however find him at home.

I received a very pleasant letter from Murray this evening which I enclose. I trust that you stow all his letters away in my chest for I wish to preserve them.

Petersburg, VA

March 15, 1865

Dear Nell,

We were quite excited last evening over orders to be in readiness to move. The sick were sent away and all sutlers ordered to City Pt. and it really did begin to be suggestive of a campaign, but the indications to-night are that we shall not move for the present. I am very sorry for Emma Saul, such engagements are very unfortunate. I agree with you that one ought to be very sure they love a person before they think of becoming engaged, and in regard to saying "No," you certainly "practice what you preach."

Perhaps my judgement in regard to Walpole may be influenced by prejudice. Although Walpole has been made Lt. Col. of the 122d yet it the regiment is not filled up he will not be able to be mustered but will have to remain a Captain. I suppose you know that [Edwin Sherman] Jenney exerted himself to secure me the commission of Lt. Colonel in the 185th made vacant by his resignation and the promotion of Lt. [Col.] Sniper, but was unsuccessful. I have been quite surprised and very much gratified by interest Jenney has taken in my behalf, for I know him but very little, but now I shall try to become acquainted with him and learn to like him, for Marie's sake if for no other reason, and, Nell, I do really believe he must be a *good* fellow or he would not have won Marie's love.

Col. Kent has left our corps and been assigned duty as Insp. Gen'l for Gen'l Augur[4] at Washington We are all very sorry to lose him and I shall particularly feel his loss for, an Inspector, I was more immediately connected with him. Col. Hyde is working very hard with his brigade. The officers and men of our regiment speak in very high terms of him. Cap't McClellan has been made senior aide-de-camp to Gen'l Wright (in Whittier's place) with the rank of Major (N. B. a *real* Major and not one of *those* "brevets").

There are a great many visitors, both ladies and gentlemen, to the army now. The principal business of Gen'l Meade's staff seems to be entertaining company. I regret to say that they monopolize the young ladies and we poor *Division* staff officers gaze at them (the young ladies in silent admiration) and try to be thankful that we are even allowed to look at them. How I should delight to have a visit from Marie and you and some of the "old set." We are feeling very jubilant over the intelligence from Sherman, meagre as it is, and I am looking forward with great anxiety for the first mail from his army. And glorious "little Phil" has been successful also, you may have no idea of the enthusiasm our men feel for him. Gen'l Meade does not seem to be the kind of a man to inspire that feeling and while we all have a high opinion of his ability yet there is none of that *love* we felt for Sheridan when we were under his command. I imagine the army used to feel somewhat so about McClellan but we did not join the army until just before his removal, and never participated in that feeling.

The subscription for the bronze statue of Gen'l Sedgwick to be erected at West Point has been made and the regiments sum ($10,000) has been raised. The readiness with which this sum was raised shows how he is remembered in this corps.

Do you hear anything of Frank Lester? Mother spoke in a recent letter of his

---

4. On Christopher Columbus Augur, see Warner, *Generals in Blue*, 12.

having been seen down in the oil region and understood he had been successful. I understand that Sherman Canfield has made a considerable money in that business. Andy Smith sends his kindest regards to your mother, to which add mine and believe me

Very Truly, your friend

Os

Head Quarters 3d Div'n 6th Corps

March 31, 1865

Dear Will,

I was considerably startled last evening by the following paragraph in the Herald, viz: "Cap't William Tracy (Gen'l Slocum's staff) slightly wounded. God grant that for once the papers may be reliable and that it is *only* slight, yet I cannot help feeling very anxious until I hear from you.

We expected to have had a hard fight this morning. The 2d and 5th Corps—Sheridan's cavalry moved out to the left day before yesterday. Three divisions (two white and one colored) are holding the line to Hatcher's Run formerly held by those two corps. We have not heard yet what they have accomplished although there is a rumor that Sheridan has got the Southside R.R. but yesterday afternoon orders were received for our corps to assault the rebel works in our front at daylight this morning. All the Div'n and Brigade commanders in the corps went out and looked the ground over and I went to bed about ten with a delightful feeling of uncertainty as to whether I should be able to do the same thing and wishing that I was sure of only a slight wound which might bring us home together, but during the night the order for the assault was countermanded. Yesterday it rained nearly all day and this morning it has commenced again making it very unfavorable for the movements now taking place. I am delighted to see that Gen'l Slocum did so well in the recent engagement. One paper says he deserves the thanks of the nation.

You can imagine how much surprised we were when we heard that Sherman was at City Pt. I should not have been much more so if you had dropped in on me yourself. There was a consultation at Gen'l Grants' Hd Qrs at which were present Grant, Sherman and Sheridan, Meade—Ord and Admiral Porter—quite a "consultation." We all feel that everything was so arranged that there will be a full understanding and hearty cooperation.

Dr. Slocum rushed over last night as soon as the papers came he learned that you were wounded, but I was away and did not see me. I am very sorry to notice that Col. Morse is wounded. Moreley and Gurndon I presume came through all right. Before the mail closes something else may turn up so I will leave this letter open

Yours affectionately

Os

Hd Qrs 3d Div'n 6th Corps
March 31, 1865

Dear Will,

I never expect to pass through such an exciting 8 days again. A week ago on Sunday morning we laid in front of the rebel works on the Petersburg line, which were considered impregnable. Today we are near Appomattox C.H. and Lee's "army of Northern Virginia" surrendered to us. Do you know we all feel particularly delighted to think the old and much abused "Army of the Potomac" did it without Shermans help. I passed through all safe, although I got my coat torn and my *back* (don't feel ashamed of me) was slightly bruised by a bullet. Andy got hit at Sailor Creek on the 7th the ball passing between the bones of the lower leg without injuring either. The General says it is a "beautiful" wound.

We are all pleased to learn that Gen'l Ewell sent a note to Gen'l Wright saying that he *surrendered himself and command to the 6th Corps* but the cavalry as usual rushed in and gobbled them before we got them. The scene yesterday when the news of Lee's surrender was announced is entirely beyond my powers of description. Artillery music and cheers were all blended in one anthem of praise. It was glorious. The general impression is that the whole thing is given up by the "Johnnies." Davis has left for parts unknown but part of the rebel cabinet are said to be with Lee, so we all believe the war is over and are looking forward to getting home. It is supposed that Johnson's army will surrender to Sherman so my dear boy, before you receive this I trust that you also will be celebrating the coming peace—

Yours affectionately
Os

Head Quarters 3d Div'n 6th Corps
March 31, 1865

Dear Mother,

Do you know that I write you with a decided feeling of satisfaction this morning. Last night we were under orders to assault the rebel works at daylight this morning and although we felt very confident that we could take them yet we knew that there must be considerable loss of life and that it was not probable that all of the staff would pull through. Indeed I felt that I should be happy if I could only be assured of a slight wound just enough to take a fellow home for two or three months and be able to accompany you to the sea-shore and perhaps Will's wound would be slight enough to bring him home too. I was going to write you, feeling the uncertainty but Gen'l Hamblin was in and said "Don't you do it. I always write after the battle and not before it." But about midnight the order was countermanded and now it will not be made.

The rain which was so unfavorable for operations yesterday continues to-day. There was some very severe fighting on the left towards night, but we have not yet heard the result. This morning there is considerable artillery firing that direction and some musketry. It is now half past ten A.M.—the rain has stopped and it looks as though it would clear up. The ground was so very dry that I do not believe the rain can do us any very great harm if we don't get anymore. If Sheridan has got the Southern R. R. and can hold it perhaps it will compel the evacuation of Petersburg, without any hard fighting. Gen'l Ord is on our left with three Div'ns from the army of the James. I understand Win Sumner is now on his staff. I shall try to see him as soon as possible. Charley Fitzhugh of Oswego, from whom we used to have such pleasant visits in the Valley and of whom I have often written to you, is now Colonel of cavalry and commands a brigade. The General has just sent for me to ride out with him. Good Bye for the present.

Yours affectionately
Os

Head-quarters 3d Div'n 6th Corps
April 17th, 1865

My Dear Mother,

The Sixth Corps are jubilant—their services have been acknowledged—Gen'l Meade says that they struck the decisive blow of the last great and glorious campaign—Hip—Hip—Hurrah!

This morning the flags captured by the corps in the recent campaign were sent to Army Hd qrs (each rebel flag being borne by its captor) with a guard of honor of three regiments, one from each Division. Upon arriving at Army Hd qrs, the regiments were formed in line and as Gen'l Meade made his appearance the troops presented arms and the bearers of the flags (19 in all) advanced toward him. Upon arriving within a few paces they halted and Major Farrar of Gen'l Wright's staff in a very neat little speech presented the flags. Gen'l Meade responded handsomely, and in the course of his remarks, said, "That while he wished to make no insidious comparisons between the different corps and while he wished to do full justice to the part taken in this campaign by other corps and other armies yet he must say, that in his opinion the decisive blow of the campaign (which compelled the evacuation of Petersburg and Richmond and the final surrender of Lee's army) was struck when the 6th Corps broke through the rebel works in their front." These are as near his words as I can remember them but Hannum took down his speech in "short hand" and you will see it in the Herald.

We all feel so delighted that justice has been done us at last, for we have got rather a poor stick of a correspondent with us and the other corps having a great advantage of us in that respect. We have thought that the papers have hardly noticed the important part taken by our corps.

Col. Hyde, Nell's friend, had command of the escort—three regiments—this morning and did his part finely. He offered me a position on his staff, that of

Inspector, but I am so much more pleasantly situated here that I declined it of course. Indeed he said he did not expect I would be willing to come down to a brigade, but was kind enough to be very complimentary in regard to the subscriber and wished that I was with my regiment now so he could see me.

We expect a mail this evening so I will have this letter unfinished hoping to have one from you to answer. I have not heard since the 7th.

Yours affectionately

Os

Monday evening

The mail has come and "nary letter" for Os. We got the papers of the 14th but unaccountably Hannum's account of the "sailer creek"[5] fight has not yet appeared, and as that was exclusively the fight of our corps and the cavalry probably no other account of the fight will appear. It makes me mad to see that the other corps had so much chance for show &c at the surrender and the officers of the 6th Corps—the corps that struck the decisive blow—so Gen'l Meade says—had so little chance for a splurge—but Gen'l Meades speech of to-day will set us right before the country.

Good night

Your boy

Os

Head quarters 3d Division 6th Corps

Burkesville, Va. April 18/1865

My dear Will,

I intended to have answered your long letter before. I suppose that ere this you will have understood that *when* the Army of the Potomac changes its quarters, although it may grumble a little at the prospect, it does it to some purpose. And yesterday in receiving the rebel flags Gen'l Meade said that while doing justice to the other corps and other armies yet in his opinion the decisive blow of the campaign (which compelled the evacuation of Richmond and Petersburg and the final destruction of the army of Northern Virginia) was struck—When the Sixth Corps broke through the rebel lines near Petersburg.

I had already heard through mother, much to my delight, that your wound was a very slight one. And now a word in regard to the principal topic of your letter. I don't think we need worry. We are all three young men and without conceit I may say of sufficient energy to get a living. Jim it is true has been unfortunate but I believe his talents will be eventually appreciated and he will get a situation in accordance with them. My intention is to get a place, of some kind, as soon as possible after getting

---

5. After Lee's evacuation of Petersburg, Union cavalry under command of Philip Sheridan cut off nearly one quarter of Lee's Army at Sailor's Creek forcing their surrender. See Derek Smith, *Lee's Last Stand: Sailor's Creek, Virginia, 1865* (Shippensburg, Pa: White Mane Books, 2004).

home, for if I am able, I feel that I shall be discontented and keep at work at said something until I can find some business that suits me. And then my acquaintances formed in the regiment which comes from all parts of the county will be of considerable service to me going into business in Syracuse. I should on many accounts like to go West and go into business but have about decided, as long as mothers life is spared to us, to remain in Syracuse for I don't think she would be happy anywhere else. Salaries are much better now and although the number of young men returning from the war may rather "overstock" the market, yet I don't think Syracuse has furnished a large enough number to the war, as to make their return affect the number of situations to any extent. Every time I have been home I have had an opportunity to go into the coal office and of course I should not take the situation without a decided increase of salary. As for you, my dear boy, I have no doubt but that you will get some good situation but first let us finish up here feeling satisfied that we have been doing our duty here, and trusting that the kind Providence who has spared our lives during the dangers &c we have passed through will still continue to care for us, and remembering that in this country no young man of good habits, a passable education, and a little energy of character can fail to get along.

I hear good news from Andy Smith, he having left City Point for home several days ago, doing nicely. We are all cast down the sad news of the assassination of the President. Isn't it horrible? We are as yet without any particulars but I hope it has not been the work of Southern leaders.

My kindest regards to all

Yours affectionately

Os

Brinkersville, Virginia April 22, 1865

My dear Mother,

We had quite a long ride to-day, some twenty miles in all, but there was quite a large party of us, and we had a very pleasant time. We fought the battle over again (N.B., it was decidedly an improvement not to have bullets whistling around us while making our observations). We stopped at the spot where Andy was wounded and indulged in a few complimentary remarks in regard to the young man. I picked up one or two relics in the shape of a spur &c, one of them I will send Murray, as coming from the last battlefield of the war,

On our way out this morning we stopped at a house to get a drink of water, where there was quite an intelligent old colored woman. There were some six or eight of us in the yard and Damon told her that Col. Foster[6] of the 4th Vt. was Gen'l

---

6. George P. Foster (1835–1879), was a schoolteacher, colonel, brigadier general, and a US Marshal (nominated by President Grant in 1870, appointed January 24, and served until his death). He was in the First Vermont Brigade and Fourth Vermont Infantry between 1861 and 1865. See G.G. Benedict, *Vermont in the Civil War: A History of the Part Taken by the Vermont Soldiers and Sailors in the War for the Union 1861-5* (Burlington: Free Press Association, 1888), 162–68.

Grant (Foster is a splendid looking fellow and considered by some the handsomest man in the 6th Corps). "Lord bless me, I hears tell so much of that man, do let me get a look at him." It was hardly right to fool the old darkey, but we all kept a sober face and she will always believe that she has seen Gen'l Grant. I enclose a letter which I picked up there today which is quite above the average of "reb" letters.[7] I had a very nice letter from Jim, this morning.

We get the Richmond Whig (a Union paper now) (although it is edited by the same man) daily. I will send you a copy.

A report comes to us through the 24th Corps that "Extra Billy" Smith attempted to make a speech to the citizens of Lynchburg recently urging them not to despair that the war was not yet over and they drove him out of town.

There has been a little change in this department. Gen'l Grants' Hd rs are now in Washington. The Department of Virginia including the Army of the Potomac and much parts of the North Carolina as are not occupied by Shermans' forces are formed into one Department styled the "Military Division of the James" and commanded by Maj. Gen'l Halleck, whose Headquarters will be in Richmond, don't see that the change affects us at all and only hope that Halleck will be a good man to settle with these repentant "Rebs."

I enclose $5 which please credit on my a/c. As you may imagine I feel rather tired after my ride so "good night."

Yours
Os

Orders have just come to move towards Danville at daylight to-morow morning. I don't know what the move is, but nothing probably but a desire to see the country and give the people a realizing sense of this Yankee nation.

Ever your affectionate son
Os

Danville, Va., May 11th

My dear Mother,

It does seem as though the "powers that be" did not know their own minds for this afternoon the Gen'l and Mrs. Ricketts were at Corps Hd qrs and learned from Gen'l Wright that he had received orders to delay moving for the present so it is very uncertain when we shall get away. But if we are here when the review is about to take place I shall certainly go to Washington if it is possible to obtain a leave of absence.

I received your letter of the 7th inst. this P.M. (Do mine go through to you as quickly?). What a vast difference from a year ago. This time and especially in my

---

7. This was a letter from a teacher to her student; see https://sarahtracyburrows.com/historical-documents/.

own case. Then I was a prisoner with the prospect of a long captivity before me and with the greatest anxiety in regard to you fearing I had been reported killed. Truly we have much to be thankful for when we reflect that our Heavenly Father has spared us through that terrible campaign and permitted us to see the closing year and thank God, the triumphant close of this war

I called on some fair young ladies last evening and did my best to persuade one, the prettiest one of course, to take a horseback ride with me. The young lady I fancy might be tempted to overcome her hatred for the "Yanks" sufficiently to enjoy a ride but "Papa" is rather secesh, so she told me she would see if it were possible. We induced one of the young ladies last evening to sing the Northern version of "When this cruel war is over."

I have been very unfortunate in my attempts to see Win Sumner. I do hope, if Sam comes back to his regiment we may get a sight of one another.

While I was in the Generals tent this morning with the papers, to be acted on, Gen'l Seymour made a call. He and Mrs. R were describing what would become of all the Generals when the army was reduced. It will be rather hard for them to go back to commanding companies. Gen'l Rickett fortunately is a Major of artillery so he will get a post anyway. I don't doubt but that we shall have a much larger army——a much larger standing army than we have ever had—some think 100,000 men and if so I do hope Gen'l R may be retained as one of the general officers. Gen'l Cooper, the Adj't Gen'l of the Rebel Gov't, is to visit at a house just across the Dan River. Gen'l Wright went over to call on him but the Gen'l and Mrs. R think he is too much of a traitor. Mrs. R told me that he did not leave Wash'n, he was Adj't Gen'l of the U.S.A. until May 1861, and of course I was able not only to injure us by deserting so important a post at that time but carried valuable information to the rebels. Knowing as he did everything about the strength and position of all our forces, but in spite of treachery in the highest places we have whipped them at last, and I don't believe there will be any desire to attempt another rebellion until the recollection of this shall have perished which will at least insure peace and happiness to my great grand children.

I am not ambitious and feel willing to yield all claims to a house from the admiring citizens of my native city, provided they will give us that Headquarters flag. I have sent the dimensions to Mrs. Andy and wish we could get it in time for the grand review, provided there should be one. It will be a very handsome thing to present to Mrs. Ricketts when the Div'n is broken up. I shall write Kate to order it and if you citizens of Syracuse do not raise enough the "staff" will subscribe the balance.

Well, good night to you, and may you dream of the "good times coming" when we shall all be together once more.

Yours affectionately

Os

CHAPTER ELEVEN

Postwar

June 1865–1909

You must go home now and comfort your mother, who has spared
you so long, only because your country needed you—You have
enough already of "hair breadth scapes" to entertain your children and
grandchildren with, as long as you have a voice to tell them.
—David Murray, Spring 1865

❀ Mustering out of the army with his regiment in Washington, DC, on June
23, 1865, Osgood returned home triumphant. He was honorably discharged in
July. Having served his state and nation with distinction, Osgood would similarly
serve his community. He accepted a job with C. C. Loomis & Company, wholesale coffee and spice dealers. Within two years, he had become a partner in the
firm. In 1870, 122nd New York State Volunteer veteran Charles Ostrander joined
the company, and its name changed to Ostrander, Loomis & Company. By 1886,
Osgood was sole proprietor of what became O. V. Tracy & Company.

On June 19, 1867, Osgood and Nellie were married, just shy of five years after he
had first asked for her hand. They celebrated at a reception at the Sedgwick home.
In 1869, the couple had a son, Charles Sedgwick Tracy. In 1871, the family wel-
comed a daughter, Sarah, "Sally," and on Christmas Eve 1873, James Grant Tracy.
In 1875, Sally died from diphtheria, at three years seven months of age. Family
members recollected that Sally's death was heartbreaking for Nellie, who never
allowed her daughter's room to be changed. That same year, just nine months after
Sally's death, Lyndon Sanford joined the family, then, in 1879, Frank Sedgwick
Tracy. All four sons graduated from Cornell University between 1891 and 1898.

In 1893 Osgood admitted as partners in O. V. Tracy & Company his son Charles,
who later became an authority on contract bridgework, and John Hurst; both had

been special partners since 1885.[1] Osgood also served as an officer in the Solvay Process Co., beginning with its organization in 1881 and was a trustee of the Onondaga County Savings Bank and director and secretary of the First National Bank. He was a member of the Loyal Legion and Root Post Grand Army of the Republic and one of the original directors of the Onondaga Historical Association.[2] When the state legislature created the Intercepting Sewer Board in 1907, Mayor Alan C. Fobes appointed Osgood as chairman to form that body.[3] Later, Osgood and Nellie's son James Grant Tracy, now a lawyer, was named director of O. V. Tracy & Company and president of the Syracuse Land Company.[4] (Osgood's father had been president of the latter until his death in 1850.) After Charles Sedgwick and his wife died, James supervised the subdivisions of Sedgwick Farm, managed other properties and land, and donated a hundred-acre tract to the New York State Agricultural Society Agricultural Society for the New York State Fair usage.

Nellie also kept busy in Syracuse's growth. She became an active organizer, supporter, and trustee of the Syracuse Memorial Hospital. She was also one of the founders of the Syracuse Employment Agency and a trustee of the Society for the Prevention of Cruelty to Children. Osgood and Nellie were also active in regiment reunions. Osgood remained lifelong friends with 122nd veterans and fellow Syracuse residents Charles Ostrander, Alexander Hubbs, and Hubbard Manzer, all officers of the reunion regiment.[5]

The following short stories, taken from postwar interviews, were published in *Thrilling War Experiences*. Each relates to letters Osgood wrote during his service and indicates that twenty-five years later loose ends were still being tied up.

LOVE LETTER DELIVERED   1890

The letter that Lieutenant Birdseye was entrusted with by the young Southern lover, Annie, to her man in the army, was discovered in his mother's attic, unopened, at her death in 1890. Birdseye, upon opening it, read the "Dear Tom" note, which bore the woman's love for the man. Birdseye, who had promised to

---

1. John Hurst (1810–1880) was an Irish-born immigrant whose brother Samuel Hurst (1814–1903) operated the New York State Fair in Syracuse.

2. Dwight Hall Bruce, ed., *Onondaga Centennial: Gleaning of a Century*, vol. 2 of 2 (Boston: Boston History Company, 1896).

3. Charles Elliott Fitch, LHD, "Osgood Vose Tracy," *Encyclopedia of Biography of New York, A Life Record of Men and Women of the Past, Whose Sterling Character and Energy and Industry Have Made Them Preeminent in Their Own and Many Other States* (New York: American Historical Society, New 1916), 75–77.

4. The transition may have been made after Charles died unexpectedly, on May 31, 1928, age fifty-eight, of a gunshot wound, either accidental or self-inflicted. Charles's wife, Ruth Pickering, had died at thirty years of age, after a lengthy illness, in 1911, two years after marrying. The couple had no children.

5. Osgood Vose Tracy obituary, *Syracuse Herald*, Feb. 1, 1909.

mail the letter on his trek back north but never did, "as I did not care to hunt a post office," felt guilty. He wondered whether he might have ruined this love's chances. In an interview upon their return home, Lieutenant Tracy stated, "One morning Birdseye was entrusted by a girl where we breakfasted with a letter to her lover in the army, which we were to mail when we reached Washington Court House. Birdseye afterwards sent it through the lines, and I trust it reached its destination." After many inquiries, Mortimer Birdseye tracked down Annie and discovered her and "Tom" did, in fact, fall in love and marry. Annie and Tom Vigis of Sperryville, Virginia wrote Birdseye back, thanking him for his "timeliness" in delivering the wartime letter, which now hung on their wall. They invited the Birdseye's and Tracy's to visit, which they did as well as numerous times after. In return, Tracy and Birdseye invited them to the 25th Gettysburg reunion where they entertained them by their northern friends. Just as the surgeon working in the tent after the Battle of the Wilderness told Tracy, "Twenty-five years after this war ends, North and South will be friends, mark my word."

AN OLD HAT   MID-1890S

Some thirty years after the Civil War ended, on a snowy Christmas morning, Mrs. Emily Lyman opened the door of her home, in a small town outside Syracuse, to discover a package. She closed the door and turned back to the living room. There, she remarked with sarcasm to her husband, Lieutenant Henry H. Lyman,[6] a veteran of the 147th New York Volunteer Regiment, "Well, I guess, Henry, you've *got* a nice Christmas present after all." When Lyman opened the package he found a slouch butternut hat, the same one, in fact, that he had lent Colonel Tracy to help him escape from Rebel prison. Tracy had included a letter, stating that the old hat had weighed heavily on his conscience for thirty years. Lyman thought back to that day, thirty years earlier, when Lieutenant Tracy had a rebel uniform but no Confederate hat. He had traded his old hat that he had found on a battlefield for Tracy's nicer one. And now all those years later, he had his old hat back in his possession.

MISS JENNIE LINCOLN   MID-1890'S

In a different city a few weeks later, Major James Potter, veteran 122nd New York, of Syracuse, who happened to be in town on business, knocked on the

---

6. Henry H. Lyman, adjutant of the 147th New York State Volunteer Regiment was twenty-two years of age upon enrollment, on August 21, 1862, at Richmond, to serve three years. He was mustered in as first sergeant, Company C, on September 22, 1862, then as second lieutenant, February 20, 1863, and first lieutenant and adjutant, January 17, 1864. Lyman was captured in action at the Wilderness on May 5, 1864, and exchanged on March 1, 1865. He was discharged May 12, 1865.

door of an old comrade. Captain Lucius Dillingham answered the knock and Major Potter found his face too familiar to forget. Yes, his old friend's hair was gray and his face older, but he was the same man. The two sat in an easy chair as they discussed their old army life and the romantic winter season at Sandusky. Just as Major Potter asked Captain Dillingham if he had ever caught up with Miss Jennie Lincoln again, a young woman appearing to be in her mid-twenties, walked into the living room, lighting up the room, and he had his answer.[7]

In speeches they gave these later years, Osgood and his brother William recalled their regiment's participation in the war's greatest battles as well as expressed their concerns now as veterans. At Long Branch Park in Syracuse, Will delivered a reunion speech. His speech and one that followed by Osgood were printed in a news article titled "A Soldiers Picnic, The 122nd Regiment Celebrates An Anniversary."[8] During his speech, the younger Tracy urged that veterans be appropriately honored and, if needed, taken care of financially, and funds be raised for monuments to be erected in Syracuse and at Gettysburg, reminiscing eloquently:

> We meet today, the veteran survivors of this regiment, in this pleasant grove, and upon this fair mount of our county, to commemorate the most notable events of our lives; the noblest acts of our career; to recount the dangers that we have passed; to relate our former triumphs won, and to mourn for our heroes fallen. We have all borne our part in the heat and burden of the day of strife. We have all endured the long and weary, dusty march, under Southern skies; we have dropped to earth almost too tired to rise again; we have shivered through the night in the cold and wet bivouac, and frequently suffered the real pangs of hunger and thirst. To us all the sharp ring of a rebel bullet has been a familiar sound, as well as the dull and sickening thud that announced the bullet had reached its mark; the very earth has sometimes trembled under our feet from the discharges of musketry and artillery; we have known the despair of defeat and felt the blood pounding through our veins as we joined in the surging wave of victory. Once more, sometimes as a strain of martial music strikes the ear, or a discharge of cannon is heard, a vision arises before us of other summers, of fields of yellow grain and tangled forests; once more we see the serried lines of gray and blue, we hear the shriek of the shell and the yell of the rebel charging column, and once again the tragedy of violent and immediate death of well-beloved comrades is enacted before our eyes. By these, our re-celebrations of

7. "An Old Hat," 1894 news article from Mrs. Tracy's scrapbook.
8. A Soldiers' Picnic. The 122nd Regiment Celebrates An Anniversary. Bennett's Grove, Near Fairmount, invaded by Troops Last Saturday—Address by W.G. Tracy, and Other Features of the Day, undated news article in Sarah Tracy's scrapbook.

dangerous defeats passed, of sacrifices made, of triumphs won, of noble aims and their complete and entire fulfillment, the body of veteran soldiers throughout the land is knit and welded together.

Over twenty-five years have passed since I myself buckled on my knapsack, shouldered my musket and started for the front. In fact, I am an older veteran than the regiment, and feel as if I could speak in some sort as a father of his children. Of course we are proud of our war record, and whenever we meet we have to talk about it. It has always pleased me to think that I enlisted in the first company that left Syracuse for the war, and the older I get the prouder I am of it. And it seems to me that this feeling is entirely natural and proper. We have never done anything before or since, for which we are so much entitled to respect and admiration from the public, as for our service during the rebellion; and if we have a right to boast about anything we have ever accomplished, we have certainly a right to boast about that.

We have all of us reached middle age, and some of us, with frosty locks, are quite beyond that period. In looking back over our lives we can not but remember deeds that we regret, time misspent and opportunities wasted; but it will always remain a matter of congratulation to us that the one supreme opportunity that came to us, the course of our existence, we did not fail to grasp; that there was at least one time and one occasion when we were equal to the hour and the demand upon our manhood, and that we cheerfully responded to it. We shall never cease to feel a thrill of pride so long as we continue to breathe, that in the morning of our lives, when everything was at its brightest and its best, when the dew was on the flower and the night was on the wave, when life was still "the roses hope while yet unknown," that we were willing to sacrifice it all for the love of our common country. That we were willing to give up the full pleasures of this world which we had just begun to experience as men, to throw down our work, to destroy the careers we had marked out for ourselves, and all for no other purpose than to preserve intact the nation that gave us birth. Our lives were as sweet, our happiness as dear to us then as life and happiness are now to the men who walk our streets to-day, yet were we willing to surrender all, without hesitation and without scruple.

While the sentiment of the people of the county of Onondaga, from time of the rescue of Jerry, was strongly anti-slavery, and undoubtedly that sentiment was particularly pronounced in this regiment, the feeling that generally animated us was, that this country, just as it was then, was worth living for, worth fighting for, and worth dying for; and we went forth to preserve and defend the union of the States, and in that faith we fought and conquered. We built better and stronger than we knew; and the work so begun also resulted in the enfranchisement of a race. We saved our Union, and at the same time created a nation of free men from a race of slaves. Without criticism of those who felt that duty to themselves or to their country required them to remain at home, we can at least cheerfully thank God that it was vouched to us to see our duty in other lights, and to act courageously according to our convictions. For the foes of our government, who met us with arms in their hands, and face to face in the field, we can certainly feel respect; for when great masses of men are willing to fight and die for a cause that they have chosen in accordance with the dictates of conscience, although such belief will not justify their cause, the sacrifices that they make will so far ennoble their lives. For our foes in the North whom we left behind us, and who continually endeavored to obstruct the progress of the war, we can only feel disgust and contempt, and it is a satisfaction to think that the name of "Copperhead" will remain a brand of disgrace to them through successive generations.

The 122nd New York was recruited from the yeomanry of this county, from the hill tops and the valleys, more than any other organization that left it. It was a regiment largely composed of farmers' boys, and formed from the best material the county could furnish; its officers were men of intellect and character, well fitted to perform the duties assigned to them. The regiment, from its first entry into the army until the close of the war, was always in active service, and participated in every campaign of the Army of the Potomac, and we all know what that means. It formed a part of a leading division in the Sixth Corps, one of the leading corps of the finest army of the North, of course you thought it was the best and Shaler's brigade was a well-known and reliable body of troops in that army, who could always be depended upon in any emergency.

The members of this regiment have experienced all the different casualties and vicissitudes incident to active service. The remains of some lie buried in the Wilderness of Virginia; others sleep their last sleep about Cold Harbor and Petersburg, and some be nearer home in the soil of our sister state Pennsylvania. Some were wounded and captured, and in addition to the horrors of rebel imprisonment, sustained the pain and suffering of wounds improperly cared for. Some succumbed and died in captivity; some men fortunately escaped and made their way to safety to our lines, over a long stretch of hostile territory occupied by the rebels. The record of this regiment is without a . . . and it can be truthfully said of the members that they have proved an honor to their race and their country.

But passing from the past to the present, there are duties resting in part upon us veteran soldiers. One is to see that proper memorials are erected to our fallen comrades; the other that living survivors are properly cared for. Last Fourth of July with other members of this regiment it was my good fortune to visit the battlefield of Gettysburg. We approached that place through picturesque scenery, waving fields of grain and a rich and prosperous country, surpassing the finest farms of our county. Large and splendid barns marked the fatness of the land, and it seemed an agriculture paradise of the Pennsylvania Dutchman. Similar fields of rich grain undoubtedly gladdened the eyes of Lee's army as they tramped by them twenty-three years ago, flushed with their success at Chancellorsville, and marching about they believed to a certain victory at Gettysburg. But it was not to be; they counted without their host; and then and there was fought one of the bloodiest engagements of any time, and one of the most momentous battles of the war. The tide of rebel victory then turned and never rose again, and for the last time an invading army then marched upon the soil of a Northern State. Their reception at that time did not encourage them to come again. It was my first visit to Gettysburg, and it was gratifying to find that this battlefield, at least, is to be fitly commemorated. I was astonished at the work that has been done there, and it is a place where your children and their descendants through successive generations will in the long years to come visit again and again with pleasure and with pride.

The Gettysburg Association, formed from the veterans of the army, have purchased the land upon which our line of battle rested and they have preserved the line intact and the places of batteries, are being thoroughly and actively marked; large part of the rifle pits upon Culp's Hill where the 122nd and 149th fought side by side are preserved. To anyone who has seen service, the line of battle and the movements of the respective armies can be understood at a glance. This valuable work when completed will present a picture not elsewhere to be found in the realized world; for it will represent with absolute precision the lines and movements of one of the heaviest battles of any time. The most decisive in its general results, perhaps, of any engagement during our war. The position of every regiment in that battle will eventually be marked by a handsome and stately monument. The inquiry of course arises, by whom has this been done? Different States, whose troops fought upon that field, have contributed large funds to the Association to enable them to purchase the land; and anyone may become a life member of the Association upon payment of ten dollars. But this is not all that has been done. Many of the regiments have erected beautiful monuments upon the places occupied by them in the field. The first regiment to do so was the Second Massachusetts, a crack regiment of the Twelfth Corps, who participated with this regiment in the engagement on Culp's Hill. The State of Massachusetts in this as in many other matters relating to the war, has led the way. In addition to the $5,000 given the Association, it has donated to the veteran organization of every regiment from that State who took part in that battle, the sum of $500, to be expended in the erection of a monument upon the very spot where the regiment was stationed. Frequently the regimental organizations have raised additional sums, and these monuments, as well as many others, are being rapidly placed in position, and are very handsome structures. Five hundred dollars is sufficient to erect a proper and sufficient structure. Shall the great State of New York, whose broad fields and populous cities were saved from invasion and destruction by those bloody days in July, do less for its heroes who perished there than the far-off State of Massachusetts has done for her children? It is time that this State moved in the matter and as I am informed, our Legislature will be asked at its next session to pass such a bill; and suggest that the members of the Legislature from this country be requested by proper resolutions passed at the meeting of veteran organizations to unite with other members in procuring the passage of such an act.

. . . One other sacred duty remains for us to perform, and that is to aid and assist our surviving comrades and families all we are able. Some of us have succeeded and some of us have failed in the subsequent battle of life. Success in every pursuit depends upon favorable circumstances, and upon the rigorous observance of certain conditions necessary to secure it. Providence fights on the side of the strongest battalion, and however industrious a man may be, however moral and upright, errors of judgment will necessarily produce as great disasters as bad habits or crime. And when without evil conduct on his part we find a comrade unable to earn a decent and respectable living, we should see that he has it. In my judgment he is fairly entitled to it for his services during the war; they were given ungrudgingly, without stint, and he should be rewarded in the same way.

Let us resolve, then, to be worthy of our past and when we depart from this life our friends and family will faithfully say of us: In his youth he took up arms for the defense of his country; in his middle and old age he fulfilled the glorious promises of his youth.

On June 13, 1888, the State of New York dedicated a monument to the 122nd Regiment on Culp's Hill. Osgood attended the dedication, and spoke of the regiment's experience in words that give us some insight to the memory of those bloody days as the young officer and his comrades lived them and as they resonated with him later in life.[9]

> Comrades of the 122d N.Y. Vols. of Shaler's Brigade I take the place of one of our survivors today, to whom had most appropriately been assigned the duty of making the address on this occasion, Major J. B. Davis who, doing his duty, bravely behind these very breastworks received a severe wound that incapacitated him for further service with the regiment.[10] He had fully intended to have come from his distant home in Nebraska to meet his old comrades but a telegram received the latter part of last week advised us that a sudden severe illness would prevent his attendance and I regret it on your account as you miss the excellent address he would have made.

9. The speech was published in *New York at Gettysburg,* vol. 1 of 3 (Albany, NY: J. B. Lyon Company, Printers, 1900), 2:846–49. *New York Monument Commission of Battle of Gettysburg and Chattanooga Final Report.*

10. Davis's jaw was broken.

The 122d N.Y. was enlisted entirely in the County of Onondaga in the fair garden of Central New York and mustered into service at Syracuse, N.Y. August 28—1862. We left Syracuse August 31—1862 a thousand strong under command of Col. Silas Titus who is with us here today. A. S. Dwight, Lt. Col.; J. R. Davis, Major: S. J. Smith, Adjutant; Frank Lester, Quartermaster; N. R. Tefft, Surgeon; J. O. Slocum & E. H. Knapp, Assistant and Lt. W. Dickerson, Chaplain. Col. Titus remained in command of the regiment until after the Battle of Gettysburg

Osgood Tracy, 25th 122nd NYSV Reunion Address speech at Gettysburg, later published in New York at Gettysburg 1-2-3 Vol. 1 (From the private collection of Osgood Tracy)

when compelled to leave on account of ill health. Col. Dwight assumed command, which he retained until killed in action before Petersburg, Va., in March 1865. Maj. Brower, who succeeded Maj. Davis, having been killed at the Battle of Cedar Creek, Oct. 19, 1864. Maj. Clapp, one of the best and bravest officers we had, upon Col. Dwight's death, took command and was succeeded by Capt. Walpole who had been promoted to Colonel and who brought the regiment home at the close of the war which came soon after.

Our corps, during our three years service men killed in action, 5 officers 59 enlisted men. Died of wounds 1 officer and 29 men Died of disease 3 officers, 68 men accidentally killed 2 men drowned 1 man died in rebel prisons 14 men a total of 179 deaths. The number of wounded reached to nearly 500 making the total casualties of the regiment more than half of the original number.

While time forbids that a fitting tribute should be paid to many a gallant comrade who fell, I must pause for a moment to speak of two, Col. A. W. Dwight, to whom the efficiency of the regiment was so largely due. Serving under him as Adjutant I can bear testimony to the good discipline he maintained. His courage, his faithfulness even unto death, which came just as we were to reap the fruits of our three years of trials and sufferings in the closing victory of the war. The other, Liet. Frank Wooster, a brave and capable officer for whom no march was long enough to stop the flow of his spirits, who always was disposed to see the humorous side of even the trials of our army life. Never shall I forget my last sight of him, his face aglow with the ardor of battle as we involuntarily clasped hands as we passed each other in that hastily formed line in the Battle of the Wilderness repelling the flank attack. In a few moments I was a prisoner and the very day I succeeded in regaining our lines at Harper's Ferry poor Wooster was killed at Cold Harbor. With a premonition of coming events he wrote May 14, 1864, to my mother after my capture, "If your son is alive and a prisoner as I believe him to be, I think of what we have been through for the last ten weeks and what we are likely to go through in the next few weeks to come, I feel I have to congratulate you rather than console with you."

Upon our arrival at Washington we went into camp for a few days when we were ordered to join the Army of the Potomac. Fortunately for us we were assigned to Cochrane's, soon to become Shaler's Brigade, composed of the 23rd, 61st and 82nd Pa., and 65th and 67th, N.Y. I don't think any of us will forget the day when we joined the Brigade at Orfut's Cross Roads. The old regiments were to recover in numbers by the Peninsula Campaign that we were not surprised as our long line filed past to be greeted with the shout, "Hello, what Brigade is that?" We were kindly received in the Brigade and if they did take a little advantage of our greenness and credibility, told us big stories of the Peninsula Campaign and the Seven Days fight we soon learned to be "old soldiers" ourselves and held our own with them and after Gettysburg and the Wilderness we never heard quite so much of the Seven Days fight.

Soon after joining the Brigade Maj. Hamblin of the Chasseurs was assigned to our regiment for a short time and I think I but express the unanimous voice of the regiment when I say how much we are indebted to him for his instruction and advice and how he won all our hearts by his courtesy and good humor. Would that he might have been spared to be with us here today. General Cochrane left us before we had hardly time to know him and was succeeded by that thorough and gallant soldier, Gen'l Alexander Shaler. If at first we thought he was rather strict in his discipline and even in his drills, after having been in battle under his command we appreciated the value of it all and know that whenever he sent us he was near us himself caring for us and always ready, if necessary, to lead us. Gen'l Shaler commanded the Brigade until the disastrous flank attack in the Wilderness when in the confusion while attempting to repel the rebel advance, was in the confusion taken prisoner and I, following my general as I had been taught, found myself a prisoner with him.

Upon my escape from Lynchburg and return to the regiment I found it brigaded with other troops, Shaler's Brigade having been broken up. But, before leaving the Brigade I must not forget to mention the staff. Capt. Truesdell, the sharp-eyed inspector who looked so closely after our camps, Lt. Johnson, the handsome aid and that gallant soldier and courteous gentleman Captain Roomes who had such a pleasant way of delivering even a disagreeable order that we hastened to obey it. I will not attempt in the short time allotted me to follow the regiment through its three years service in the 6th Corps and if those efficient commanders, Sedgwick and Wright, participating as it did in every battle of the Army of the Potomac from Antietam to the Appomattox finds us serving under the gallant Sherman in the brilliant campaign in the Shenandoah Valley, but will only speak briefly of the part it took in the Battle of Gettysburg. The afternoon of July 1, 1863 found us at Manchester 36 miles from Gettysburg where we enjoyed a much needed days rest after our continuous march from Fredericksburg. But, the battle had begun and the 6th Corps was sorely needed there. Our Division Commander, Gen'l Newton, was called to take the place of the Commander Reynolds who had fallen in defense of his native state. With the monuments . . . the spots where the different regiments were engaged one can obtain a wonderful idea of the extent of a battle-field and how a battle is fought by reading a description of the battle & then visiting that memorable field.

On that pleasant July morning twenty-five years ago these peaceful woods were filled with the angry sounds of war. When might have been heard the whistle of the minie balls (bullets), or the shnick of the vindictive shell as Lee made his last desperate attempt to turn right of our enemy. In yonder ravine lay Shaler's Brigade when in the midst of the strife a regiment of the 12th Corps were compelled to fall back from these breastworks, their ammunition exhausted. Under orders from Gen'l Shaler the 122nd sprang forward with a cheer to take their places. Charging across yon knoll we re-occupied these breastworks and, assisted by other regiments, notably the 149th N.Y., who were on our immediate left, a regiment from our own county of Onondaga, friends and neighbors fighting side by side, we held this portion of the line against the repeated charges of the enemy until they abandoned their attack in despair. In the gallant charge across yon knoll in the subsequent defense of these breastworks we lost ten of our commanders killed or mortally wounded and thirty-four more, more or less severely wounded, a very larger proportion of the number actually engaged and ½ in number killed and ⅙ in wounded of the loss that day sustained by our Corps.

Through the liberality of the Empire State we today dedicate this monument, surrounded the Corps we fought under, to the memory of our comrades: Stephen Blake, Co. B.; Hiram G. Hilts and Patrick Fanning of Co. C; James Wickham of Co. E; D. Carey and John Travers of Co. G; George Parker of Co. H; and John Cain, Dennis McCarthy and William Whitworth of Co. K who gave their lives up freely in the service of their country and whose graves in yonder beautiful cemetery bear mute witness for them. Of those other comrades some of whom have died and others that have and still suffer from wounds received that day and still further in commemoration of the gallant services of our regiment in the Sixth Army Corps. A tribute to those that are gone as well as to the survivors who (as) are good citizens maintain the reputation they won in the field. As we gather year by year at our annual reunions we find our fraternal bonds strengthen as our ranks decrease and when we shall all have been mustered into that grand army above may we find that the services we rendered our country in her hour of need on this and other memorable fields will not be found to have been in vain.

Sarah Osgood Tracy, who Osgood wrote so often during his time in the service, lived until Christmas Eve morning 1901. She was one of the oldest residents of Syracuse at the time of her death, at home, in Syracuse. Her obituary describes her as

> a woman of much culture and a most delightful and hospitable hostess. . . . She was very active and fond of young people's society and, as one by one the friends of her own age dropped away, she took up the pursuits of the younger generation, where her sprightly conversation made her ever a favorite. She was fond of outdoor life and was an excellent horsewoman. Within six weeks of her death she drove her favorite pair of horses some distance herself. . . . She was a lifelong member of the Unitarian Church and an honorary member of the D.A.R. She took a deep interest in all and liberally aided in their support.[11]

On February 4, 1902, some two months after Sarah died, Confederate general John Gordon, who had held Osgood prisoner thirty-eight years before, and his

11. *Syracuse Post-Standard*, Dec. 25, 1901.

24th Reunion of the 122nd New York State Volunteers, August 28, 1886 (Courtesy of Leo Titus)

wife made a visit to the Tracys' home. This February 4, 1902, *Syracuse Herald*, story, for which both men were interviewed, suggests reconciliation but also that Osgood's imprisonment was perhaps not as harmonious for Osgood as it was for the general.

NORTH AND SOUTH: NO DIFFERENCES NOW, SAYS JOHN B. GORDON
The distinguished Confederate General the Guest of O. V. Tracy, Once His Prisoner of War, Speaks of the Days of Civil War, of Reconstruction and of Reunion.

General Gordon drove to the house of Col. O. V. Tracy, who hosted him until noon. Among the Confederacy Gordon ranked only second to General Lee. "It is an interesting subject to recall the events of that day," Gordon said. "The conditions under which we fought were indescribable. It was in the woods, the route marked by narrow paths. It seemed to be my fortune to meet the Sixth Corps more than any other port of this Northern army. It gave me some severe knocks and I guess I gave it some. In that Sixth corps were many of Colonel Tracy's crowd, some of whom stayed with us for a time. "The fight in the Wilderness was beyond description," said Colonel Tracy. "We lost from twenty to thirty prisoners, besides a number who were killed. Among those captured on that day were General Shaler, Col. James M. Gere. Former Sheriff P. A. Austin, George Casler, now of Chicago, and Charles Ostrander. The latter lost a leg in that engagement, as did Alexander H. Hubbs. After the latter had had his leg amputated and before he was able to walk on crutches he used to drag or hitch himself from cot to cot and cheer his comrades. Finally we were rescued by a detachment sent down from Washington."

"It was after this fight," continued General Gordon, "that I bought General Shaler's bay horse. It was a fine animal, which I rode until the close of the war. At Appomattox I sold it to a Union officer for twice what I paid for it." "Yes, and I well remember how Shaler kicked at having to walk after the fight," interrupted Colonel Tracy. "His horse had been taken from him, and it was interesting to see him walking at the head of the procession."

RECONSTRUCTION

"When the smoke had cleared away at Appomattox," continued the General, "I determined to consecrate the balance of my days to the reconstruction of the brotherhood of the nation and have refrained in my utterances from saying anything that would jeopardize that vow, or that would be distasteful to my hearers. I rejoice that to-day there is a better spirit prevailing between the North and the South. It is better than it was before the war. We are closer together than we ever were. Each side has learned to respect the other. We had a difference, and we fought it out. We to-day possess an element of strength which we could have secured in no other way. It is almost impossible to conceive of the spirit of recuperation which has come over the South. The close of the war found us without money, with our homes gone and all labor disorganized. . . . Now we are forging to the front, notable in cotton spinning and iron making, the two great elements to our industrial growth. . . .

GUEST OF COLONEL TRACY

When General Gordon was seen by a Herald reporter at the home of Col. O. V. Tracy in James Street this morning, he said, "It is a pleasure to meet Colonel Tracy. It is a rare treat to meet those whom you have entertained in other ways and in other days. It was my fortune at the Battle of the Wilderness, on the second day of the fight, to get the best of some of the men from this section. Some of them had to accept Southern hospitality, and now they are paying me back. Only there is this difference, they were anxious to get away, while I am certainly in no hurry to get away from Syracuse, or them. The question of slavery was the bone of contention. That no longer exists, and we are one.

NEGRO IS IMPROVING

"The condition of the negro in the South is one of gradual but slow improvement. It is my own individual opinion that if all white influence were removed they would drift into barbarism. But under white influence, I have great hopes that they will develop into a higher type of citizenship. They are peaceful, quiet, unoffending and extremely emotional in the characteristics. When fairly treated and their confidence gained there is no difficulty getting along with them. Their progress was shown in the Atlanta exposition. It was shown in the way which, when they become landowner that they accumulate and become the money getters. The reports of outrages etc are isolated. During the war, every white man had to fight. All of the women and the children were left on the plantations. There is not a single recorded instance where a white woman was outraged or even insulted by the negroes. At times they were left with several hundred blacks on the farms, who were thoroughly conversant with what was going on, but they never took advantage. There is a great era before the South. Northern capital and Northern enterprise are finding a wide field, and we welcome it. Sectional hatred is a thing of the past, and it gives a man pleasure to be able to live under such conditions."[12]

The arrival of Gordon in Syracuse must have been a spectacle, and the reporting and comments certainly underscore the broader move toward reconciliation in the wake of the war. Gordon's words underscore the lost cause narrative that cast the Civil War as a momentary schism soon mended with the nation emerging stronger than it had ever been before. Tracy left no private record of this visit. Certainly, accounts made this visit appear amicable, but as the reader can see from Osgood's letters and the postwar speeches he and his brother gave, the Tracys were staunchly in favor of memorializing the war and their role in it and saw their actions as vital to the preservation of the nation and the destruction of the institution of slavery. One wonders, then, how receptive Osgood was to Gordon's version of events, the condition of former slaves in the south, and whether "sectional hatred" was, truly, "a thing of the past."

In October 1905, Osgood and Nell invited Colonel Birdseye and his wife to join them on a trip to Lynchburg, Virginia. On this trip, Birdseye explained in a 1914 news article, they took "a three seated rig and a driver and drove for seven days over the route Tracy and I had tramped in making our escape, using the war map heretofore mentioned as our guide. On this trip we spent a couple days with the Vigis family, who gave us most hospitable entertainment." Visiting Lynchburg, Osgood was

12. We must wonder what Tracy thought of Gordon's remarks on the postwar conditions of African Americans in the South.

disappointed to find that the Warwick House, had been taken down, just months before. It would be the last time he ventured south. Generations later in 2021, Col. Mortimer Birdseye's great grandson Walter Mortimer Birdseye, explained to editor Burrows that a relative of the Confederate guard whom his great grandfather "liberated" a pistol from for use in his and Osgood's escape and trek north, wrote asking for the weapon back. Walt Birdseye's father, Mortimer Buell Birdseye Jr., in posssesion of the pistol at the time, declined, as they were "the spoils of war."

On January 31, 1909, More than forty years after he mustered out of the service of the US Army, Osgood Vose Tracy died in Syracuse, New York. He was sixty-nine years of age. The Tracy family had deep roots in Onondaga County, and when he died, his city mourned the veteran's life. "This community feels the loss of one of its strong men. His career as a public benefactor, as a sterling business man, as a progressive citizen has seldom been equaled and never surpassed in the city of Syracuse," noted the First National Bank in its statement on Tracy's death. In its obituary, the Board of the Onondaga Savings Bank recalled him as "a broad, enlightened, honest man . . . modest and rather retiring than aggressive in his bearing, his temperament was always cheerful and hopeful. His manner was genial and friendly. He gave faithful and intelligent service to the bank and was prompt and efficient in discharge of duties as a trustee." According to Osgood Vose Tracy's published biography, "Not all men order their lives to their liking; nor yet are all men true to their own selves in living as nearly to their ideals as possible, and attaining to such heights as their opportunities and talents render readily accessible. Colonel Osgood V. Tracy did not lead a pretentious or exalted life, but one which was true to itself and its possibilities. A man of strong intellectual force and mature judgement, his character found its deeper values in the wellsprings of absolute integrity and most exalted motives." Osgood "led life to itself and . . . as a citizen he was widely known and for many years prominent in several large and successful businesses and municipal enterprises which contributed to the prosperity and high character of our city. He was deeply interested in every practical movement relative to the city's welfare. He assisted many with advice, was always interested and sympathetic. He regulated his attitude toward fellow men by the golden rule—a wholesome, gracious, and considerate self-respecting man."[13]

Nellie Sedgwick Tracy outlived her husband by fifteen years. At the time of her death, on July 28, 1924, she was eighty-three years old. The following day, the *Syracuse Herald* remembered her:

A Syracuse woman whose benevolent, social, and domestic interests were very long linked with what was best in our community life was Mrs. Osgood Vose Tracy, whose death was recorded in our local columns on Monday. . . . Many

13. Fitch, "Osgood Vose Tracy," 175–77.

years before the beginning of the present generation she was a fine figure and influence in the social life of the then budding city: and this prominence and sway she retained unabated to the advent of her venerable age. . . . It is proper to specify her deep, practical and uninterrupted interest in the Syracuse Memorial Hospital and its predecessor. As one of the original trustees of the institution and through long years . . . she was a staunch, ardent and never-failing friend and supporter. This was only a single illustration of her eagerness to serve and help good causes. She was a member of May Memorial Church.

James Grant Tracy, whose brothers had urged him not to volunteer his service in the war, became a well-known civil engineer and surveyor. A graduate of Troy Polytechnic Institute, he worked for the railroad in Syracuse and had an office in the building of the Sedgwick, Andrews & Kennedy law firm. He specialized in making plans, inspections, surveys, and maps for legal cases and became well known in legal and club circles. He was one of the Syracuse Savings Bank's organizers and was one of its trustees for many years. He spent a lot of time in the South, following his interest in steam railroads. According to the *Syracuse Post-Standard* of September 14, 1903, he never married and was survived by Osgood and William when he died on September 13, 1903, after a brief illness. He died at William's home, where he boarded.

James Grant Tracy, eldest Tracy brother (From the private photograph album of Osgood Tracy)

According to his *Syracuse Daily Journal* obituary, pasted, undated, in Sarah Tracy's scrapbook, William Gardner Tracy fulfilled his obligation to himself, dutifully serving and participating in the Battle of Durham Station, on April 25, 1865, which resulted in the surrender of the insurgent Gen. Joseph E. Johnson. Will was brevetted major, and on the conclusion of hostilities, he rode at the head of his troops in the Grand Review in Washington, DC, on May 23 and was mustered out of service on October 12. After the war, he worked in a bank then studied law, graduating from Albany Law School in 1867. He practiced law in Syracuse for many years, including in a firm with Osgood and Nellie's son, James Grant Tracy. He was also vice president and director of the Merchants National Bank and a member of several clubs and organizations.

In 1875, the severity of Will's bone shattering injury sustained May 2, 1863 at the Battle of Chancellorsville was displayed in a photograph submitted to the US Pension Board examining surgeon. The Surgeon General's office deemed the nature of

William Gardner Tracy, in his elder years (From the private collection of Osgood Tracy)

the wound, the procedures the surgeons followed, along with Captain Tracy's subsequent recovery in the use of his arm were of major medical significance and warranted that the report to be included in the Army medical records. The office stated it "reflected the medical interest and innovative procedures this pioneering surgery involved, a revolutionary rejection of the so-called 'hacksaw' amputation procedures prevalent up to and through the early years of the Civil War." Tracy's excised bone specimen, housed in the Army Medical Museum file until at least 1988, was used for study by young army surgeons as a classic example of the dedication of Civil War army surgeons. It was also displayed at the Smithsonian Institute in Washington, DC. In an April 2, 1885, letter, Will wrote: "I returned to the army August 15th [1863], the wound being perfectly healed, the bones remaining disunited, and I continued to serve on the staff of General Slocum until the close of the war. My arm has become about three inches shorter. The muscles have never withered away, and sensation is perfect in the limb. I can write as well as ever but experience some difficulty in raising my arm."[14]

On January 10, 1894, from Brooklyn, New York, Maj. Gen. Henry Slocum wrote Secretary of War D. S. Lamont, requesting Will be awarded a Medal of Honor, for "distinguished gallantry at the Battle of Chancellorsville": "I make this application without the knowledge of Major Tracy who, although disabled while under my command, has asked no favor from me or from the government since the close of the war, believing it to have been an act of distinguished gallantry, as contemplated by Congress when it authorized the bestowal of Medals of Honors." On April 14 that year, Slocum died, but his request was posthumously granted on May 2, 1895. President Grover Cleveland ordered that the medal be conferred.

In 1903, Will married for the first time; his bride was Marion Gott.[15] The couple had no children. Will died December 8, 1924, age eighty-two, in their home at 776 James Street, then a senior member of Tracy, Chapman & Tracy. His obituary in the *Syracuse Standard* stated:

14. Letter received through the courtesy of Surgeon General James E. Pomfret of New York.

15. Marion Gott (1861–1949) was the granddaughter of New York representative Daniel Gott, whose youngest son, of same name, was Charles Sedgwick's half brother. Their mother, Anna Baldwin, married Gott after her first husband, Charles's father, Stephen Sedgwick (the tenth child of Gen. John Sedgwick and Abigail Andrews [1845–1811] and the brother of Henry Sedgwick [1767–1811]) died in 1830. In 1846, Gott was elected to the US House of Representatives as a Whig and served two terms (1847–51). In 1848 he offered a resolution condemning the slave trade, which passed in Washington, DC. This act, which historians have viewed as a precursor to the Civil War because it caused proslavery Whigs from the South to leave the party, led to the founding of the antislavery Republican party in the 1850s.

His integrity was unquestioned, his mind was alert, orderly, and capacious, hard work was a joy to him. He was modest. He was a cheerful companion, beloved of his friends. The old soldiers all knew him. For while his conversation and his public appearances did not tell the record he made, no man who went forth from Syracuse to the Civil War had a more brilliant record than he. That he received the highest honor his country bestows for bravery in warfare testifies his service. William G. Tracy is one of those pioneers of Syracuse whose name should always be held in grateful remembrance.

Of Will, Stephen A. Rogers, then publisher of the *Syracuse Post-Standard,* printed on May 21, 1961:

Tracy was no coward. His life, both private and military, is dotted with moments of bravery. He was offered a commission when he enlisted with Butler's Zouaves, but turned it down until he said, "I have done something to deserve one." If Tracy wasn't the most surprised by his narrow escape, then it was the Southern officers who let him get by. General Hill claimed later that it was the boldest thing he ever saw. And all the Southern officers voted him a "damned brave Yankee."

The nearly fifty-year journey has brought alive my great-great grandfather Osgood Vose Tracy, his brothers, their mother, friends, and loved ones. I am grateful the Tracy letters were preserved and are now published, for which I thank Kent State University Press.

Though I was first drawn to the letters out of wonderment and curiosity, I grew to believe it my *duty* to see them published. I was not the first person in my family interested in them, for my grandfather, great grandmother, and others certainly were and it has been touching to me to find their notes within the scrapbooks.

As I conversed about the letters with my parents, husband, children, extended family, and friends, it dawned on me that I was taking on my grandfather's storyteller role. Today, I am just ten years younger than he was when he shared the story with me, and that realization has made me consider the circle of life. Over these years I began to suspect that if I did not keep the story alive it might die along with my ancestors and me.

Fifty years after my grandfather first shared our ancestors' history with me, the Civil War still resonates the same way. These letters teach us about those who wrote them, their loved ones, their hardships, and the state of the country when they

Osgood Vose Tracy in his elder years (From the private collection of Osgood Tracy)

were written. History helps enlighten us not only to our past but our present and future, enabling us to make informed decisions for ourselves, communities and country.

I am so pleased to have fulfilled my dream of publishing Osgood's letters. Most of all, I am extremely proud of my ancestors, their brave comrades, and their families who volunteered to help create a nation of free men and women.

Index